OXFORD STUDIES IN EUROPEAN LAW

Series Editors

PAUL CRAIG

Professor of English Law at St John's College, Oxford

GRÁINNE DE BÚRCA

Professor of Law at New York University School of Law

The Coherence of EU Free Movement Law

Constitutional Responsibility and the Court of Justice

OXFORD STUDIES IN EUROPEAN LAW

Series Editors: Paul Craig, Professor of English Law at St John's College Oxford and Gráinne de Búrca, Professor of Law at New York University School of Law

The aim of this series is to publish important and original research on EU law. The focus is on scholarly monographs, with a particular emphasis on those which are interdisciplinary in nature. Edited collections of essays will also be included where they are appropriate. The series is wide in scope and aims to cover studies of particular areas of substantive and of institutional law, historical works, theoretical studies, and analyses of current debates, as well as questions of perennial interest such as the relationship between national and EU law and the novel forms of governance emerging in and beyond Europe. The fact that many of the works are interdisciplinary will make the series of interest to all those concerned with the governance and operation of the EU.

OTHER TITLES IN THIS SERIES

European Law and New Health Technologies
Edited by Mark L Flear, Anne-Maree Farrell, Tamara K Hervey, and Thérèse Murphy

The Legal Effect of EU Agreements
Mario Mendez

The Enforcement of EU Law
The Role of the European Commission
Stine Andersen

European Agencies
Law and Practices of Accountability
Madalina Busuioc

The Foundations of European Union Competition Law
The Objective and Principles of Article 102
Renato Nazzini

The Emergence of EU Contract Law
Exploring Europeanization
Lucinda Miller

Participation in EU Rule-making
A Rights-Based Approach
Joana Mendes

Regulating Cartels in Europe
Second Edition
Christopher Harding, Julian Joshua

Religion and the Public Order of the European Union
Ronan McCrea

Governing Social Inclusion
Europeanization through Policy Coordination
Kenneth A Armstrong

Judicial Control in the European Union
Reforming Jurisdiction in the Intergovernmental Pillars
Alicia Hinarejos

EU Counter-Terrorist Policies and Fundamental Rights
The Case of Individual Sanctions
Christina Eckes

From Dual to Cooperative Federalism
The Changing Structure of European Law
Robert Schütze

Conflicts of Rights in the European Union
A Theory of Supranational Adjudication
Aida Torres Pérez

Judicial Deliberations
A Comparative Analysis of Transparency and Legitimacy
Mitchel de S-O-l'E Lasser

Racism and Equality in the European Union
Mark Bell

Constitutional Principles of EU External Relations
Geert De Baere

Civil Procedure and EU Law
A Policy Area Uncovered
Eva Storskrubb

The Coherence of EU Free Movement Law

Constitutional Responsibility and the Court of Justice

NIAMH NIC SHUIBHNE
Professor of European Union Law,
University of Edinburgh

OXFORD
UNIVERSITY PRESS

OXFORD
UNIVERSITY PRESS

Great Clarendon Street, Oxford, OX2 6DP,
United Kingdom

Oxford University Press is a department of the University of Oxford.
It furthers the University's objective of excellence in research, scholarship,
and education by publishing worldwide. Oxford is a registered trade mark of
Oxford University Press in the UK and in certain other countries

First Edition published in 2013

Published in the United States of America by Oxford University Press
198 Madison Avenue, New York, NY 10016, United States of America

British Library Cataloguing in Publication Data
Data available

Library of Congress Control Number: 2013937976

ISBN 978-0-19-959295-1

Series Editors' Preface

Niamh Nic Shuibhne has tackled an important issue that arises frequently within discourse concerning free movement law, which is the coherence of the complex case law developed by the ECJ since the inception of the EEC.

The study is grounded on the assumption that the ECJ operates in the mode of a constitutional court and has the responsibilities associated with such judicial organs. Coherence is not felt to demand that different sectors must be treated in exactly the same legal manner, but rather that differences are justified by principled distinctions as between the application of free movement principles in different areas. Niamh Nic Shuibhne contends that four main factors have distorted the meaning of free movement case law, and led to fragmentation of the case law, irrespective of whether these factors reflect good impulses or not. They are the protection of fundamental rights, the proliferation of principles, the contested purpose of the internal market and free movement, and the structure of the Court and its decision-making processes. These problems are felt to be exacerbated by the Court's reluctance to engage with or reverse its previous decisions, even where it seems to be departing from them.

The discussion is organised thematically, focusing on the principles that drive the developing case law. It is framed so as to consider in turn the negative and positive scope of free movement law. The former connotes the principles that are applied in free movement law to exclude something/someone from the scope of the Treaty, thereby rendering recourse to issues of justification and proportionality redundant. This includes issues such as the horizontal reach of free movement provisions, and the status of the rule that wholly internal situations are not covered by free movement law. The latter, the positive scope of free movement law, is concerned with the principles that determine the outer reach of the legal rules in this area. The coverage focuses on the utility of the division between directly and indirectly discriminatory restrictions, and also the much discussed issue concerning the extent to which EU law should cover non-discriminatory measures.

The valuable discussion in this monograph also sheds important light on other facets of free movement law, which shape its application by the EU courts. Niamh Nic Shuibhne reveals the tensions that play out in the law in this area. Thus, on the one hand, the Treaty expresses justification arguments as derogations from primary rights, with the consequence that exceptions to those rights must be narrowly construed. On the other hand, it is clear that the arena within which justification arguments are aired has in reality become highly significant in its own right, more especially as the scope application of free movement has expanded. This leads, as the author rightly notes, to a situation in which justification is in reality about balancing and weighing, not derogating.

This book will be of interest to all those concerned with free movement in EU law. It has moreover broader significance for the way in which we conceptualize coherence and the role of courts in achieving this within the EU.

Paul Craig and Gráinne de Búrca

Preface

My research interest in the purpose, functions, and outputs of courts has two main dimensions. First, I would point to the legacy of John Mitchell, the pioneer of EU studies at Edinburgh University and indeed well beyond, who developed a still-compelling rationale for the role of courts in democratic societies in his inaugural lecture for the Salvesen Chair of European Institutions, delivered in November 1968. Professor Mitchell wrote that '[g]overnments and governmental bodies have as many reasons for conniving among themselves as they have for opposing each other and, in the evolution of government, it is important that, within acceptable limits, individuals should be able to participate through the neutral mechanisms of courts not merely maintaining the framework of rules, but also advancing its construction'. He also observed that 'there is a problem of discipline in government', and argued that in what he called a 'process of rethinking... there is a place for Universities, no matter what difficulties the tinge of politics may produce'. Central to that issue, he wrote, is the place of law and courts in society.

The second dimension is a more personal response, which has three main elements: the value of fairness, the importance of process, and both the merits and challenges of interpretation. There is also a more subjective degree of faith and idealism, captured by the words of Atticus Finch in *To Kill a Mockingbird*: '[t]here is one human institution that makes pauper the equal of Rockefeller, the stupid man the equal of an Einstein and the ignorant man the equal of any college president. That institution... is a court. Our courts have their faults, as does any human institution, but... our courts are the great levelers, and in our courts all men are created equal. I'm no idealist to believe firmly in the integrity of our courts.... That is no ideal to me. It is a living, working reality'. Courts do not always get it right; and whether a judgment is 'right' or not and on what basis are deeply contested questions anyway. But observing the way in which politics are actually practised, and regretting in particular the apparently diminishing value of statesmanship, my faith in courts as institutions that have the potential to deliver a deeper degree of fairness has become, if anything, reinforced. Of course, we also tend to question the institutions in which we have faith—but not from existential suspicion; instead, from the hope that they can simply be stronger and do even better.

In her introduction to *The Canon: A Whirligig Tour of the Beautiful Basics of Science* (Houghton Mifflin Harcourt, 2007), Natalie Angier drew from an interview with Professor Susan Hockfield, the current President of MIT, on the painful process of writing. '"It's worse than squaring a circle", she said. "It's squaring a sphere".' That description is difficult to better and books are the result of a particularly long process. It is in many respects a lonely one but in the best respects it is not. I had the opportunity to deliver my own inaugural lecture at Edinburgh

University on 9 November 2012 and to acknowledge there my appreciation of, first, my colleagues, from both within and beyond Edinburgh. I am grateful, in particular, for the valued insights and comments received on various drafts of these chapters from Tony Arnull, Thomas Horsley, Panos Koutrakos, Marsela Maci, Síofra O'Leary, Eleanor Sharpston, Jukka Snell, Isabelle van Damme, and Steve Weatherill; and for ongoing discussion of the main themes, I am grateful to David Edward. Thanks to my Edinburgh colleagues Alan Boyle and James Harrison for discussion of the International Law Commission; to Miroslava Hulvanová for her careful assistance in finalizing the manuscript; to the team at OUP, especially to Alex Flach, Natasha Flemming, and Cheryl Prophett; and to Graeme Laurie. Second, I was also able to acknowledge at the lecture the support I have received in many ways over many years from friends scattered all over the place. Finally, I thanked the family I come from; but also, two other families that I am lucky enough to have, especially as someone who left where she came from: the family members who became my friends, and the friends who became my family.

NNS
28 February 2013

Contents

Table of Cases

COURT OF JUSTICE

INTERNATIONAL COURTS

EFTA Court

NATIONAL COURTS

Czech Courts

UK Courts

US Courts

Table of Legislation

EUROPEAN UNION

Regulations

Directives

Other documents

COUNCIL OF EUROPE

NATIONAL LEGISLATION

United Kingdom

Ireland

List of Abbreviations

AG	Advocate General
Art	Article
CJEU	Court of Justice of the European Union
CLJ	*Cambridge Law Journal*
CMLRev	*Common Market Law Review*
COM	Communication
CSIH	Court of Session Inner House
CSOH	Court of Session Outer House
Colum. J. Eur. Law	*Columbia Journal of European Law*
CUP	Cambridge University Press
CYELS	*Cambridge Yearbook of European Legal Studies*
EC	European Community
ECHR	Convention for the Protection of Human Rights and Fundamental Freedoms (European Convention on Human Rights)
ECJ	European Court of Justice
ECL Review	*European Constitutional Law Review*
ECR	European Court Reports
ECtHR	European Court of Human Rights
Edn	Edition
Eds.	Editors
EEC	European Economic Community
EFTA	European Free Trade Association
EJCL	*Electronic Journal of Comparative Law*
EJIL	*European Journal of International Law*
EJML	*European Journal of Migration and Law*
ELJ	*European Law Journal*
ELRev	*European Law Review*
EP	European Parliament
EU	European Union
Eu. L.R	European Law Reports
EuCLR	*European Criminal Law Review*
EUI	European University Institute
EWCA Civ	Court of Appeal (Civil Division)
Fordham Int'l L.J.	*Fordham International Law Journal*
ICJ	International Court of Justice
ICLQ	*International and Comparative Law Quarterly*
IIC	*International Review of Intellectual Property and Competition Law*
IJCL	*International Journal of Constitutional Law*
ILC	International Law Commission
JBL	*Journal of Business Law*
JCMS	*Journal of Common Market Studies*
LIEI	*Legal Issues of Economic Integration*
LQR	*Law Quarterly Review*

LSE	London School of Economics and Political Science
MJ	*Maastricht Journal of European and Comparative Law*
MLR	*Modern Law Review*
OJ	Official Journal of the European Union
OJLS	*Oxford Journal of Legal Studies*
OUP	Oxford University Press
TEU	Treaty on European Union
TFEU	Treaty on the Functioning of the European Union
UEFA	Union of European Football Associations
UK	United Kingdom of Great Britain and Northern Ireland
US	United States of America
UN	United Nations
VAT	Value Added Tax
Yale LJ	*Yale Law Journal*
YEL	*Yearbook of European Law*

1

Introduction: The Court of Justice, Constitutional Responsibility, and the Scope of EU Free Movement Law

1. Introduction

This book examines the judicial development of Treaty provisions that regulate the scope of EU free movement law from the perspective that sustaining case law coherence is a vital constitutional responsibility of the Court of Justice. It aims to measure case law coherence by applying a threshold lower than indicators of legal *certainty* that still takes seriously the Court's obligations as a high-level judicial institution bound by the rule of law. According to Article 19(1) of the Treaty on European Union (TEU), '[t]he Court of Justice of the European Union shall include the Court of Justice, the General Court and specialised courts'. The Court of Justice—often referred to as the European Court of Justice or ECJ, and not the composite Court of Justice *of the European Union* (CJEU)—is the institution at the heart of this study. But two basic presumptions about the nature of the Court and what it does should be stated at the outset. First, the Court of Justice is an activist court. Second, when it interprets EU law, it often makes (new) law. The implications of these statements are widely debated and contested,[1] but they can be taken as a starting point for the arguments developed here.

[1] Extensive scholarship questions the scale or propriety of judicial activism by the Court of Justice, sometimes linking the concern to court/legislature debates more generally but also raising EU-specific issues e.g. the consequential erosion of national regulatory competence. See generally: E Stein, 'Lawyers, judges and the making of a transnational constitution' (1981) 75 *American Journal of International Law* 1; H Rasmussen, *On Law and Policy in the European Court of Justice* (Martinus Nijhoff, 1986); M Cappelletti, 'Is the European Court of Justice "running wild"?' (1987) 12:1 ELRev 3; G Davies, 'Activism relocated. The self-restraint of the European Court of Justice in its national context' (2012) 19:1 JEPP 76; JHH Weiler, 'The transformation of Europe' (1991) 100 *Yale Law Journal* 2403; T Tridimas, 'The Court of Justice and judicial activism' (1996) 21:3 ELRev 199; T Hartley, 'The European Court, judicial objectivity and the constitution of the European Union' (1996) 112 LQR 95; A Arnull, 'The European Court and judicial objectivity: A reply to Professor Hartley' (1996) 112 LQR 411; A Stone Sweet, *The Judicial Construction of Europe* (OUP, 2004); M Everson and J Eisner, *The Making of a European Constitution: Judges and Law Beyond Constitutive Power* (Routledge, 2007); K Alter, *The European Court's Political Power: Selected Essays* (OUP, 2009); J Shaw and J Hunt, 'Fairy tale of Luxembourg? Reflections on law and legal scholarship in European integration' in D Phinnemore and A Warleigh (eds.), *Reflections on European Integration: 50 Years of the Treaty of Rome* (Palgrave, 2009) 93; P Syrpis (ed.), *The Judiciary, the Legislature and the EU Internal*

The Court of Justice, as a constituent court of the CJEU, is conferred with the authority to interpret the meaning and boundaries of EU law.[2] But when the Court is 'ensuring that the law is observed', it is also empowered to determine what that law actually is. In that context, Article 19 points the Court beyond the words of the Treaty where necessary. The English language has only the word 'law' but French, Italian, German, and Dutch (the original Treaty languages) have two words: *Loi*, *Legge*, *Gesetz*, or *Wet* for enacted law (constitution, code, statute, etc.) and *Droit*, *Diritto*, or *Recht* (German and Dutch) for law generally. When the Treaty asks that 'the law is observed', the French, Italian, German, and Dutch versions all use the latter word, meaning any relevant rule of law, from whatever source, that is applicable in the circumstances i.e. including general principles of law, international law, and so on. The development of the general principles *of EU law* in this way is a good example of how the Court made significant 'new' EU law to develop its application and interpretation of the Treaties.

Legislation provides much of the substance of free movement law, but the Court of Justice has always been a significant lawmaker in the same field. The relevant provisions of the Treaty on the Functioning of the European Union (TFEU) are typically concise and not very detailed. If we want to understand the scope of free movement law, we have to engage with a complex overlay of case law—whether there is relevant legislation on the particular issue or not. First, even definitions created by the legislature will require further refining and interpretation. Second, since the Treaty marks the boundaries within which the EU legislator can act in the first place, and again relying on Article 19 TEU, only the Court has the authority to interpret those broader limits too. Increasingly, EU legislation on free movement aims to consolidate and bring order to a patchwork of definitions and applicable principles sourced from years of incremental case law.[3] At one level, the Court has thus made a substantive contribution to law-making in a functional sense, providing definitions for core Treaty concepts such as 'worker' or 'capital movement' that are then codified in regulations and directives. Additionally, however, these definitions are required to be applied uniformly in all of the Member States when an issue connected to EU law arises, displacing the national definitions that would

Market (CUP, 2012); F Wasserfallen, 'The judiciary as legislator? How the European Court of Justice shapes policy-making in the European Union' (2010) 17:8 *Journal of European Public Policy* 1128; A Arnull, 'Judicial activism and the Court of Justice: How should academics respond?' (2012) Maastricht Faculty of Law Working Paper No 2012-3, available at <http://ssrn.com/abstract=1986817>; M Adams, J Meeusen, G Straetmans, and H de Waele (eds.), *Judging Europe's Judges: The Legitimacy of the Case Law of the European Court of Justice Examined* (Hart Publishing, forthcoming 2013).

[2] The second sentence of Article 19(1) TEU provides that '[the Court of Justice of the European Union] shall ensure that in the interpretation and application of the Treaties the law is observed'. Before the Lisbon amendments, Article 220 EC had stated that '[t]he Court of Justice and the Court of First Instance, *each within its jurisdiction*, shall ensure that in the interpretation and application of this Treaty the law is observed' (emphasis added). Judicial panels (now 'specialised courts') were then 'attached' to the Court of First Instance (now the General Court).

[3] E.g. Directive 2011/24/EU on the application of patients' rights in cross-border healthcare, 2011 OJ L88/45; Directive 2005/36/EC on the recognition of professional qualifications, 2005 OJ L255/22.

otherwise be relevant. This is another important way in which the Court 'makes' law—and, more clearly in this instance, higher law.[4]

Accepting the premise that the Court contributes to free movement law through law-*making*, it is suggested here that, on the whole, it performs this function well. Most of the case law is neither problematic nor controversial, in terms of either substantive content or how decisions fit with previous case law on the same or similar (or even different) questions. But then again, much of the Court's free movement case law is relatively formulaic, in a good way: it is often applying clear or technical legislative rules, and/or it reaches predictable outcomes that have been (or at least, can be) clearly extrapolated from established rules and principles. Its case law is subject to critique in two main forms, however, sometimes scathing. First, individual decisions can generate extensive comment and debate on their own. This might be because the case raised a genuinely novel question of EU law and the choices made by the Court on the direction of legal travel ignite controversy; or because of the significance of the outcome for the relevant area of law, or for the complex structures and balances that make up the EU polity more generally.

Second, case law also needs to be evaluated in a more composite or systemic sense, something that is inevitably done from different thematic priorities and perspectives. In this study, the responsibilities attaching to constitutional courts mark the starting point. It will be argued that ensuring case law coherence is a key element of that responsibility, based on the fundamental value of fairness. The constitutional role of the Court extends, of course, far beyond the confines of free movement law. However, the Court's determination of the *scope* of EU free movement law is the substantive area of law reviewed here, in order to test the extent to which the Court's case law is being developed coherently. This judicial work exemplifies the constitutional functions of the Court in several respects—but perhaps most importantly, because the scope or reach of EU free movement law is delimited by the Court through a series of framework principles i.e. concepts and tests developed and applied by the Court when it interprets and applies the foundational Treaty provisions. In free movement law, these principles include, for example, non-discrimination, market access, abuse of rights, and remoteness.

The shaping of scope through principles in this way is a remarkable source of judicial power and influence. But Avbelj rightly reminds us to reflect on why we are 'using constitutional language in the first place'.[5] To take an example, legislation introduced by the Scottish Parliament to establish a minimum pricing scheme for alcohol, with the purpose of tackling public health concerns, has recently been challenged in the Scottish courts.[6] The Commission, within the framework of the obligation on Member States to notify it of draft technical regulations affecting products before they are adopted in national law, is also

[4] On the degree to which national legal cultures can accommodate that assertion, see A Arnull, *The European Union and its Court of Justice*, 2nd edn (OUP, 2006) 625–7.

[5] M Avbelj, 'Questioning EU constitutionalisms' (2008) 9 *German Law Journal* 1 at 25.

[6] *Scotch Whisky Association and others*, petition for Judicial Review of the Alcohol (Minimum Pricing) (Scotland) Act 2012 and of related decisions, [2013] CSOH 70 (judgment of 3 May 2013).

investigating the measure.[7] Whether directly—through a Commission enforcement action against the UK under Article 258 TFEU—or indirectly—through a reference under the Article 267 TFEU preliminary rulings procedure should the case continue on appeal in the domestic courts, as is expected at the time of writing—it is the Court of Justice, and not the Scottish, British, or European Parliaments, or the Commission,[8] that will decide ultimately whether the Scottish legislation can remain in place or must be abandoned as a restriction on the free movement of goods.[9] That decision will also mark the outer boundaries of alcohol pricing policy for any other Member States who have adopted or are contemplating adopting analogous measures. Similar assumptions are being made about the Court of Justice's role in eventually resolving the legal questions about EU membership that might arise in the instance of Scottish independence.[10] These examples underscore the fact that the Court is not some sort of alien or distant tribunal; its decisions have a legal effect that cannot be filtered away through national parliamentary action. It is an influential constitutional court, with the implication in turn that its performance should therefore be evaluated in those terms.

It is not, in other words, the fact of the Court's contribution to constitutional law-making that is being questioned here. Instead, whether the Court is performing its role fittingly (and how we can assess that) sets the analytical starting point. However, the methodological limitations of research focusing on the Court and its case law should also be acknowledged. First, case law is simply not 'the law'. It is just one of EU law's constituent elements and its analysis can only ever present a partial picture of legal evolution.[11] Second, case law research tends to ignore even most of the case law: mainly because, as noted above, most of the case law is neither legally problematic nor analytically significant—to put it another way, it is not particularly interesting for many beyond the parties directly involved. It is important to keep a sense of perspective in mind for this reason; to remember that the greatest volume of comment and analysis will often be generated by very few decisions in a much bigger and more stable bank of law, viewed more holistically.

[7] Directive 98/34/EC of the European Parliament and of the Council laying down a procedure for the provision of information in the field of technical standards and regulations, 1998 OJ 204/37; see further, including the text of the Commission's opinion, <www.eurocare.org./library/updates/european_commission_asks_uk_to_abstain_from_introducing_minimum_pricing>.

[8] In a different context, AG Lenz observed in *Bosman* that '[m]erely for the sake of completeness, I observe that the fact that the current rules on foreign players may possibly have been worked out with, and perhaps even approved by, the Commission has no legal significance. The Commission is neither entitled nor in a position to amend the scope or meaning of the provisions of the [TFEU] by its actions. It is for the Court of Justice alone to give binding interpretations of those provisions' (Case C-415/93 *Union royale belge des sociétés de football association ASBL v Bosman* [1995] ECR I-4921, para. 148 of the Opinion).

[9] Other arguments on EU law submitted in the case related to competition law and the Common Agricultural Policy.

[10] See e.g. <http://eutopialaw.com/2012/12/14/scotland-independence-and-the-eu-the-sturgeon-response/>.

[11] E.g. JHH Weiler, 'The constitution of the common market place: Text and context in the evolution of the free movement of goods' in P Craig and G de Búrca (eds.), *The Evolution of EU Law*, 1st edn (OUP, 1999) 349 at 351.

Third, it could be argued that research focused on case law delivers an unduly narrow or inward-looking perspective only. At one level, this is obviously true. The centre of gravity here is indisputably legal and the principal method is doctrinal. As a result, observations about the role of case law (or of the Court) from a more consciously external (e.g. socio-legal) perspective are necessarily incidental. But that is not the same thing as undertaking legal research in a way that is completely devoid of context. It is imperative that research on EU law and on the Court of Justice is both comprehensive and multifaceted.[12] Both the Court as an institution and its case law have been examined from, for example, political science perspectives.[13] There is also important scholarship that brings different disciplinary perspectives together.[14] But it does not follow that every academic output can attempt to cover all relevant disciplinary bases. Research approaches can and should be pooled, comprising complementary pieces of a bigger and richer whole. There is a very basic point to emphasize here too: if basic elements of the law are broken, then we should at least start with the law to try and improve them.

Finally, Bernard has highlighted another important limitation of research based on case law: '[t]he downside of such narratives is that they are written, necessarily, with the benefit of hindsight and may unconsciously read cases in the light of later developments and, in so doing, invest judgments with a meaning and significance that they did not necessarily possess or were meant to possess, when were first handed down'.[15] Bernard's observation reflects an argument that judges themselves have raised against charges of pursuing *une certaine idée de l'Europe*. For present purposes, it is important to distinguish between two different types of research question in that context. First, there is the intriguing but often futile quest to uncover *intent* i.e. to discern the motivations that guided the judges in reaching a particular decision or shaping a specific line of case law. But it is far from clear how or even whether judicial intent can be extracted given the single collegiate judgment delivered by the Court of Justice. This format masks the variety of views expressed in deliberations, the level of disagreement about those views, and the possibility of attributing particular stances to individual judges.[16] It is also seriously debatable whether an institution of the size of the Court of Justice at present,

[12] See generally, A Arnull, 'The Americanization of EU legal scholarship' in A Arnull, P Eeckhout, and T Tridimas (eds.), *Continuity and Change in EU Law: Essays in Honour of Sir Francis Jacobs* (OUP, 2008) 415.

[13] See e.g. Alter, n1 and A Stone Sweet, *The Judicial Construction of Europe* (OUP, 2004).

[14] See e.g. (2012) 19:1 *Journal of European Public Policy* (Special Issue: 'Perpetual momentum? Reconsidering the power of the European Court of Justice').

[15] N Bernard, 'On the art of not mixing one's drinks: *Dassonville* and *Cassis de Dijon* revisited' in M Poiares Maduro and L Azoulai (eds.), *The Past and Future of EU Law: The Classics of EU Law Revisited on the 50th Anniversary of the Rome Treaty* (Hart Publishing, 2010) 457. Similarly, Weatherill, distinguishes between 'micro' and 'macro' case law analysis (S Weatherill, 'The Court's case law on the internal market: "A circumloquacious statement of the result, rather than a reason for arriving at it"?' in Adams, Meeusen, Straetmans, and de Waele (eds.), n1, forthcoming).

[16] Woods describes the Court's 'group form of judgment' as 'an expression of the form of the agreement rather than necessarily a record of logical argument' (L Woods, 'Consistency in the chambers of the ECJ: A case study on the free movement of goods' (2012) 31:3 *Civil Justice Quarterly* 340 at 345).

operating on a system of multiple judicial chambers, could have a sufficiently *singular* sense of purpose, goal, or intent anyway;[17] or be shown to be pushing an agreed philosophy.[18]

Trying to decipher judicial motivation in a personal sense is not, therefore, the intended focus here.[19] Instead, a second type of research approach is applied i.e. free movement case law will be examined at a more systemic level against objectively defined criteria: primarily, the value of legal coherence (as fleshed out in Chapter 2). Conclusions about broader trends that the case law suggests can of course be derived from that analysis, but such views have to be treated with the qualifier of speculation. More concretely, as successive judgments broaden and deepen the construct of free movement law, a composite framework emerges. Returning to Bernard's concern, whether the resulting shape of that mainframe—*not* each individual judgment within it—was deliberately intended is the material point. The International Law Commission has put it in this way: '[l]egal interpretation, and thus legal reasoning, builds systemic relationships between rules and principles by envisaging them as parts of some human effort or purpose. Far from being merely an "academic" aspect of the legal craft, systemic thinking penetrates all legal reasoning, including the practice of law-application by judges and administrators'.[20]

[17] See further, S Wernicke, 'Au nom de qui? The European Court of Justice between Member States, civil society and Union citizens' (2007) 13:3 ELJ 380 at 381: 'judges do not seem to talk of their ideas of Europe, their mandate, of their role or the way ahead, let alone act according to some or other common aim. But they do something far more important: they decide individual cases—and by doing so they add another piece to a framework for which there is no overall design, but which is nevertheless constitutive of a union of law'. Relevant structural constraints stemming from the Court's organization are discussed in Chapter 2.

[18] G Davies, 'The Court's jurisprudence on free movement of goods: Pragmatic presumptions, not philosophical principles' (2012) 2 *European Journal of Consumer Law* 25 at 26–7: 'it is in general a mistake to understand the Court's decisions as choices between fundamental principles. To do so suggests that when it formulates the law it is seeking to state the econo-philosophical essence of trade freedom, and apply this essence in a direct and unmediated way. On the contrary . . . the Court has shown a consistent and entirely appropriate indifference to the grand philosophical scheme of things, about which there is not that much for a lawyer to say: [a] combination of textual, political, economic and constitutional factors means that there is very little realistic wiggle room for the Court on this issue'. The extent to which a *coherent* philosophy can be said to underpin the EU internal market in constitutional terms is discussed further in Chapter 2.

[19] See relatedly, recent empirical studies exploring the extent to which patterns can be discerned in the outputs of the Court's chambers: M Malecki, 'Do ECJ judges all speak with the same voice? Evidence of divergent preferences from the judgments of chambers' (2012) 19:1 *Journal of European Public Policy* 59; and Woods, n16.

[20] Report of the Study Group of the International Law Commission, *Fragmentation of International Law: Difficulties arising from the Diversification and Expansion of International Law*, finalized by M Koskenniemi, UN General Assembly International Law Commission, A/CN.4/L.682, 13 April 2006, para. 35. Exemplifying the potential for academic/practitioner synergy, the ILC also flags the work of Neil MacCormick in this context; see esp. para. 36, referring to *Legal Reasoning and Legal Theory* (Clarendon Press, 1978) and, in particular, his 'techniques of "second order justification" that enable the solution of hard cases (i.e. cases where no "automatic" decisions are possible) and that look either to the consequences of one's decision or to the systemic coherence and consistency of the decision with the legal system (seen as a purposive system)' (ILC Report, p. 25, n35). As a related point, the way in which the opinions of the Court's Advocates General are treated in this book should also be noted here: while the judgments of the Court are being evaluated against systemic coherence

Judges can properly be expected—and obliged—to be aware of the existing corpus of law and to add judgments to that framework in full consciousness of the public legal resource being unpacked, expanded, and sometimes profoundly changed in consequence. Added to that, the application of appropriate practices of engaging with *existing* authority is how the judges then show us their work. Part of the complementary function of academic research is precisely to step back from the individual decisions and to identify patterns in the overall shape of the Court's jurisprudence. We need to stop seeing that work purely as a negative form of judicial critique. It is also, more positively, a significant judicial resource.

In addition to general findings about the Court as a constitutional institution, it will be shown in the chapters that follow that four main drivers are distorting the coherence of free movement case law at present. These drivers are varied in both form and nature. They reflect 'good' impulses (*the protection of fundamental rights*); avoidable (*the proliferation of principles*) but also inherent (*the unsettled purpose(s) of the internal market and free movement*) ambiguities; and broader systemic conditions (*the structure of the Court and its decision-making processes*). It will be argued that these dynamics are causing problematic instances of case law *fragmentation* where the logic or even propriety of the Court's contribution to free movement law-making has broken down—which has substantive (for citizens, businesses, and States) as well as reputational (for the Court and for the EU more generally) consequences, and thus political, social, and economic as well as legal implications. The evaluative dichotomy of coherence and fragmentation is proposed as a paradigm that balances rigour and expectations in an appropriate but realistic way. Additionally, the combining of conceptual and practical drivers reveals as much about the Court as an institution as it does about case law trajectories: it will be argued that debates about the legitimacy of the Court go too far in this context; but that discourse on, for example, case law 'convergence' does not go far enough since it conveys a dissociated or organic momentum that fails to capture the Court's own indisputable responsibilities in the search for greater legal coherence.

Constitutions are necessarily open-textured. The application of interpretative imagination by constitutional courts is not just enabled but required, because of the ambiguity of the relevant provisions. What, for example, does a right to privacy actually mean? When does it apply and when can the State legitimately limit it? The parameters of the right to privacy are worked out in large part through consideration of the facts and circumstances that drive the disputes that lead to case law. The EU Treaties are no different—and this is certainly the case in the area of free movement law. The Court may not be able to control the constitutional text with which it is presented—but it can certainly take responsibility for its interpretation of it. A particular problem that will be highlighted, drawing examples from across the different sectors of free movement law, is the Court's tendency not to engage with or, where appropriate, reverse its own previous decisions when it seems to

criteria, the body of opinions that now exists is not being pushed through the same analytical filter. A duty of constitutional responsibility attaches to the Court as a whole, but it is the binding judgments that have to be absorbed by its constitutional subjects, as will be explained further below.

depart from them. Instead, the Court often presents significantly different legal reasoning in a very detached or isolated way—it leaves conflicting lines of case law in play without any attempt to reconcile them with the changed or new approach now articulated instead. This responsibility to construct a coherent framework of authority rather than a focus on 'precedent' more narrowly is picked up again below.[21]

In this chapter, a blueprint for the idea of constitutional responsibility will first be outlined in Section 2. It will also be shown how and why the Court of Justice is a constitutional court that is subject to this standard of responsibility. In Section 3, the study's focus on and approach to the scope of free movement law will be explained in more detail. The meaning—and limits—of the central concept of case law coherence will then be addressed in more detail in Chapter 2.

2. The Court of Justice and constitutional responsibility

To set down preliminary points of reference, the characteristics of 'constitutional responsibility' as it applies to constitutional courts will first be outlined in subsection (a). In subsection (b), that framework will be applied to the Court of Justice, leading to a more contextualized understanding of its institutional responsibilities as, it is claimed here, the constitutional court of the European Union.

(a) The responsibilities of constitutional courts

The special position that constitutional courts occupy is a vast research field in itself. The intention here is simply to outline a workable template of constitutional responsibility that can be applied to the Court of Justice, so that the duty to ensure and sustain case law coherence is more broadly framed. Towards that objective, it is submitted that the responsibilities associated with constitutional courts can be summarized as having three distinct strands. First, a constitutional court has a responsibility to protect and to further the objectives and values enshrined in 'its' *constitution*—essentially, to ensure that the rights and protection that a constitution promises are realized, but also to respect the checks and limits built into it. Second, it has a responsibility to discharge these tasks on behalf and for the benefit of the *constitutional subjects*—fundamentally, what we understand as constitutional citizens—'we the people'—but it is important to emphasize that the political, judicial, and other institutions created and profiled by the constitution are included here too. The third strand of responsibility—and one that is not necessarily placed on or within the control of the court itself—is that a constitutional court must be *structured and organized* in a way that enables it actually to discharge these functions in an appropriate and effective way.

21 See generally, J Komárek, 'Reasoning with previous decisions: Beyond the doctrine of precedent', LSE Law, Society and Economy Working Papers 8/2012, available at <http://www.lse.ac.uk/collections/law/wps/WPS2012-08_Komarek.pdf>.

It is also important to acknowledge that essential, interlinked principles will influence how we evaluate the realization of constitutional responsibility. The foundational principle reflected in this study is that constitutional courts have a responsibility to animate constitutional values, rights, and limits *fairly*. However we express or describe the value of fairness—as the achievement of justice, for example, or striving for equal treatment—it is the pulse of the rule of law, on the basis of respect for which Article 2 TEU confirms that the Union is founded. A constitutional court should also reflect the value of *integrity*. It should play its institutional part in bringing about systemic integrity—it can do this through its application and development of the law in a substantive sense, but it should also reflect the value of integrity through the quality of its judgments, something that can be achieved in large part by the articulation and insightfulness of its reasoning.[22]

Constitutional courts should also have due space for the application of *imagination*. Expressing this as a value may be more controversial than appeals to fairness and integrity; but constitutional courts are not ordinary courts. Their judgments should inspire us. Constitutional responsibility is not about constitutional stagnation. Looking at this value more pragmatically than idealistically, constitutional courts are simply more likely to be operating at the fringes of existing law. They have to be imaginative to make new law. Recognizing this as a value reflects the reality of the judicial function at the constitutional level. It also raises particular questions—and concerns—around the application of judicial *intuition*. The notion of a 'lawless science of law'[23] captures part of the essence of court-made law very well, especially (though not only) when speaking about court-made constitutional law i.e. when determining the meaning of the law, courts are not resolving legal questions only. For example, when applying a proportionality test, courts do not just establish a legal framework within which the necessity of a public act can be tested—they also take a substantive position on its *actual* necessity (or otherwise). To ensure that law made in this way is indeed more 'science' than art, the tenets of constitutional responsibility and the values that they reflect should be considered and respected collectively—for example, intuition and imagination cannot be determinative to the extent that clear markers in the constitutional text are irresponsibly displaced.

The value of case law coherence used here, which is developed further in Chapter 2, brings together the three main elements of constitutional responsibility outlined above as well as the values of fairness, integrity, and imagination.

22 These points are picked up again in Chapter 2; but see generally, G Beck, *The Legal Reasoning of the Court of Justice of the EU* (Hart Publishing, 2013); G Conway, *The Limits of Legal Reasoning and the European Court of Justice* (CUP, 2012); J Bengoetxea, N MacCormick, and L Moral Soriano, 'Integration and integrity in the legal reasoning of the European Court of Justice' in G de Búrca and J Weiler (eds.), *The European Court of Justice* (OUP, 2001) 44; and J Bengoetxea, *The Legal Reasoning of the European Court of Justice: Towards a European Jurisprudence* (Clarendon Press, 1993).

23 The 'lawless science of law' comes from Tennyson's *Aylmer's Field* ('Mastering the lawless science of our law,—That codeless myriad of precedent, That wilderness of single instances'). See further, D Edward, 'What are judges for?', 2010 Macfadyen Lecture, Scottish Council of Law Reporting, available at <http://www.scottishlawreports.org.uk/publications/macfadyen-2010.html>.

It is based on respect for the principle of legal certainty, but it is suggested that 'certainty' is not the most helpful term to apply in the context of case law. Coherence is not about striving for an unrealistic degree of perfection or rigidity. It allows for the recognition and management of necessary differences, and also for the extent to which court-made law is inherently messy to some degree at least. What coherence does demand is that differences must be explained and rationalized—and that requirement is connected to the manifestation of fairness and integrity. It is also important to emphasize that achieving coherent case law is, in broader terms, necessary but not sufficient—in other words, case law can be consistently problematic. For example, decisions can fit very well together, meeting a narrow or technical understanding of coherence, while consistently trampling across the EU/Member State competence boundaries established at a constitutional level by the Treaties. Or case law can consistently ignore or fail to adapt to more persuasive alternatives or critiques. For these reasons, instances of problematic coherence—when measured against broader Treaty objectives, for example—will be flagged where relevant. Relatedly, coherence can generate internal conflict: this occurs when case law is coherent when measured against one constitutional value (e.g. advancing the protection of fundamental rights), but fragmentary when judged against another (e.g. the centrality of a requirement to move across a Member State border). The value of fairness becomes important again here; as does the Court's position as a constitutional court—which inclines in favour of achieving systemic rather than individual fairness where choices have to be made.

Spaventa rightly cautions that 'when the cases are closely scrutinised one might be excused for feeling a slight sense of desperation as to the chaotic picture arising from the Court's jurisprudence'.[24] Reflecting further on '[t]he number of variables influencing the outcome of a case . . . one should accept that it will never be possible to provide an umbrella under which *all* cases can sit comfortably'.[25] In other words, case law is an uneven method of law-making. First, it is necessarily responsive, in that courts can only address the disputes that come before them. Courts cannot contrive to inspire the 'right' questions i.e. questions the answers to which might clarify or progress the law more fluidly. The dynamics of free movement disputes reflect the reactive character of legal evolution through case law very acutely: mainly through the happenstance of the questions that arrive at the Court (and when they arrive) through the preliminary rulings procedure, but thinking also of the discretion retained by the Commission for the initiation of enforcement proceedings against the Member States. But the uneven articulation of clear rules because of sporadic opportunities for refinement through case law channels is one thing; persistently shifting or unsettled principles, expressed in variable ways and departing from the case law mainframe without rationalized explanations, is something else.

[24] E Spaventa, 'The outer limits of the Treaty free movement provisions: Some reflections on the significance of *Keck*, remoteness and *Deliège*' in C Barnard and O Odudu (eds.), *The Outer Limits of European Union Law* (Hart Publishing, 2009) 245.

[25] Spaventa, n24, 245 (emphasis in original).

Second, the case law of the Court of Justice must be applied in all courts and tribunals across 28 Member States. This means that its decisions must (1) provide appropriate specificity for the effective resolution of the dispute in front of it; and (2) articulate workable principles for massively widespread subsequent application. Especially in preliminary rulings, this dual function reveals an important paradox about the unusual jurisdiction of the Court of Justice: it acts as *both* a dispute resolution tribunal and a supreme or constitutional court—at the same time. Some of the problems that result from this duality are discussed further in Chapter 2. For now, the challenge of presenting widely transposable principles through staggered case law steps is highlighted as a consideration to take into account when framing realistic expectations of coherent case law.

Building on the points above, a final factor to consider in respect of the responsibilities of constitutional courts in general is that they are not only lawmakers; they are also policymakers.[26] When constitutional courts resolve questions that political institutions either have not yet addressed or simply will not touch, they signal a suggested policy direction. The relevant constitutional subjects may decide to alter the steer given by the court, in accordance with the different mechanisms and procedures that their legal orders establish (for example, the decision of the court may be changed through the adoption of legislation; or the constitution may require the holding of a referendum for that purpose). But most constitutional court decisions are not challenged or reversed; and even if they are, that fact still does not detract from the contribution that the court has already made to the wider policy debate.

The function of constitutional courts as policymakers is again linked to the critical importance of adequate reasoning. Exploration of the reasoning of the Court in the chapters that follow is driven in particular by a requirement that constitutional courts should explain how new judgments either fit with existing case law or are deliberately intended to signal a departure from it—and why. As noted briefly above, this requirement is related to but just one aspect of broader debates about whether or not the Court of Justice operates a system of precedent, or the different civil law and common law understandings of such a system in the first place.[27] In the context of free movement law specifically, an empirical study by Woods, reviewing the outputs of different chambers of the Court of Justice in case law on Articles 34–36 TFEU (free movement of goods), confirms the fragmentary effect of the *variable* use of legal authority in particular. Moreover, she positions the significance of this finding in the 'role of precedent in maintaining the *coherence and integrity* of the development of the law'.[28] Looking at the Court's treatment of its own judgments—but from its different formations—her study established that the '[s]tatus of the formation generally seems not to be a relevant factor in terms

[26] See e.g. M Dougan, 'Judicial activism or constitutional interaction? Policymaking by the ECJ in the field of Union citizenship' in H Micklitz and B de Witte (eds.), *The European Court of Justice and the Autonomy of the Member States* (Intersentia, 2012) 113.

[27] For an overview of these issues and related literature, see Komárek, n21.

[28] Woods, n16, 351 (emphasis added).

of choice of authority'.[29] In her conclusions, Woods highlights the '*unprincipled* way in which the ECJ refers to its own decisions' and 'the failure to recognise any difference between the respective values of different judgments'—the dominant factor seemed, in fact, to be recentness: which is neither here nor there in a substantive legal sense.[30]

Policymakers who act through legislation have to reveal their thinking and their positions through legislative proposals and they have to respond to multi-faceted debates on those proposals. Constitutional courts can instead seem to be concealing or suppressing, or at least toning down, the policy-making dimension of their judgments. Writing about the German Federal Constitutional Court, Kumm has observed that 'the decisions themselves explicitly omitted all the information that would help to ground the case and its resolution in a specific political context... Concurring and dissenting opinions exist, but are relatively rare. For the most part the court presents itself as a monolithic whole—a corporate entity speaking in the name of the law as an objective force'.[31] For present purposes, acknowledgement of the policy-making function of constitutional courts, whether or not it is articulated in their judgments per se, adds a further layer to their responsibility to act coherently.

(b) Constitutional responsibility and the Court of Justice

The Court of Justice is not a conventional or textbook constitutional court, which is something that we usually associate with a state. It is a transnational court, serving all of the EU Member States as well as multiple EU institutions, bodies, and agencies. And it must have the capacity to work through, at present, 24 languages.[32] In accordance with Article 19(2) TEU, the Court is composed of 28 judges, with one judge from each Member State. The judges thus bring invaluable insight into their own legal systems and legal traditions. But the way in which cases are assigned at the Court does not, in contrast to procedures at the European Court of Human Rights (ECtHR),[33] operate on the basis that a judge will be involved in cases concerning his or her own Member State. Relatedly, Woods identifies some of the challenges that the Court's 'multinational nature' generates as a result of the 'variety of legal systems represented' since '[e]ach such system may incorporate different expectations as to the role of the judge, the value

[29] Woods, n16, 365. [30] Woods, n16, 366 (emphasis added).

[31] M Kumm, 'On the past and future of European constitutional scholarship' (2009) 7:3 *International Journal of Constitutional Law* 401 at 414.

[32] The 24 EU Treaty languages are listed in Article 55 TEU. See also, Article 342 TFEU and, for the language rules applicable to the Court of Justice more specifically, Article 64 of the Statute of the Court of Justice (available at <http://curia.europa.eu/jcms/upload/docs/application/pdf/2012-10/staut_cons_en.pdf>) and Articles 36–42, 57, 85, 98, 204, and 210 of the Rules of Procedure of the Court of Justice (2012 OJ L265/1).

[33] See e.g. Rules 24(2)(b) and 26(1)(a) of the ECtHR Rules of Court, available at: <www.echr.coe.int/NR/rdonlyres/D1EB31A8-4194-436E-987E-65AC8864BE4F/0/RulesOfCourt.pdf>.

of precedent and the extent to which judgments are explanatory or declaratory in form and nature'.[34]

The multiplicity of courts involved in applying and interpreting EU law and the non-linear relationships between them in certain respects present another set of challenges to consider here. For example, the Court does have a formal relationship of appellate priority with respect to the General Court (and thus indirectly with the specialised courts too).[35] At a more conceptual level, Article 19 TEU suggests that all of the courts that make up the CJEU have apparently equal authority to ensure that 'the law is observed' when applying and interpreting the EU Treaties. Additionally, most case law in the field of free movement comes to Luxembourg through the Article 267 TFEU preliminary rulings procedure—where the final decision in all cases lies with the referring national court or tribunal, which may be a court or tribunal at *any* level in the context of domestic judicial architecture—rather than through standard (for constitutional courts) appeal or special/reserved jurisdiction pathways. Nevertheless, for present purposes, the Court of Justice *is* considered to be the constitutional court of the European Union. That assessment could be rooted in three different senses of EU constitutionalism: (1) the nature of the EU legal order; (2) different normative perspectives on EU constitutionalism; and (3) recognition and impact of the Court's case law in functional terms. The persuasiveness of each of these three premises will now be examined in turn; it will be seen, however, that it is the dynamic that connects them that proves ultimately decisive.

(i) The nature of the EU legal order

As a starting point, the Court of Justice has itself repeatedly asserted that the EU legal order is constitutional in nature. Its decisions in *van Gend en Loos* and *Costa* first articulated the distinctiveness of the European Economic Community (EEC) as a polity and the related special nature of its law.[36] Since the internal market was 'of direct concern to interested parties in the Community', the Court stated in *van Gend en Loos* that the EEC Treaty was 'more than an agreement which merely creates mutual obligations between the contracting states', a view supported by (1) the reference to 'peoples' as well as 'governments' in the Treaty's preamble; (2) the 'establishment of institutions endowed with sovereign rights'; (3) channels of cooperation created by the European Parliament and the Economic and Social Committee; and (4) the indication, through the creation of the preliminary rulings mechanism, that 'the states have acknowledged that Community law has an authority which can be invoked by their nationals before those courts and tribunals'.[37] The Court thus concluded that 'the Community constitutes a new legal

[34] Woods, n16, 341. [35] See Articles 256(1) and 257 TFEU.

[36] Case 26/62 *NV Algemene Transport- en Expeditie Onderneming van Gend en Loos v Administratie der Belastingen* [1963] ECR 1; Case 6/64 *Costa v ENEL* [1964] ECR 585. These cases are discussed in several of the contributions to Poiares Maduro and Azoulai (eds.), n15.

[37] *Van Gend en Loos*, 12.

order of international law for the benefit of which the states have limited their sovereign rights, albeit within limited fields, and the subjects of which comprise not only Member States but also their nationals'.[38]

In *Costa*, the Court went further, stating that '[t]he transfer by the States from their domestic legal system to the Community legal system of the rights and obligations arising under the Treaty carries with it a *permanent* limitation of their sovereign rights, against which *a subsequent unilateral act* incompatible with the concept of the Community cannot prevail'.[39] It continued that Treaty law was an 'independent source of law' with a 'special and original nature', which could not 'be overridden by domestic legal provisions, however framed, without being deprived of its character as Community law and without the legal basis of the Community itself being called into question'.[40] This is the classic constitutional language of hierarchy among sources of applicable law. That angle was later expressed explicitly in *Les Verts*, where the Court held that '[t]he Community is based on the rule of law, inasmuch as neither its Member States nor its institutions can avoid review of the conformity of their acts with the *basic constitutional charter*, the EC Treaty, which established a complete system of legal remedies and procedures designed to enable the Court of Justice to review the legality of acts of the institutions'.[41] In *Kadi*, the Court controversially mapped the implications of the distinctive and constitutional character of EU law vis-à-vis assessing obligations entered into by the EU institutions in accordance with international law. The higher EU standards applied in that case related to the protection of fundamental rights—the development of which was itself a significant step in the modelling of EU constitutional law.[42]

This synopsis of the way in which the Court rationalized the constitutional nature of the EU and its legal order is necessarily brief. It outlines some of the pivotal case law steps in a much broader and more complex process, but what can be noted is that the Court has pulled a firm thread of reasoning from the decisions in *van Gend en Loos* and *Costa* through to the contemporary cases. The narrative outlined does not, however, address the widely debated questions that the actions of the Court have generated.[43] Moreover, alongside the Court's constitutional vision, we have to acknowledge the failure of the political effort to implant the language of constitutionalism overtly through ratification of the Constitutional Treaty.[44] Acceptance of the Court's constitutional understanding of the EU legal order needs a more solid base than the Court's own say-so.

[38] *Van Gend en Loos*, 12. [39] *Costa*, 594 (emphasis added). [40] *Costa*, 594.

[41] Case 294/83 *Les Verts v Parliament* [1986] ECR 1339, para. 23 (emphasis added).

[42] Joined Cases C-402/05 P and C-415/02 P *Kadi and Al Barakaat International Foundation v Council and Commission* [2008] ECR I-6351, paras 281–285.

[43] See generally, the contributions in G de Búrca and JHH Weiler (eds.), *The Worlds of European Constitutionalism* (CUP, 2012).

[44] Treaty establishing a Constitution for Europe, OJ 2003 C169/1.

(ii) Normative perspectives

A normative claim to EU constitutionalism must overcome political and popular disagreement about the basic nature and purposes of that polity; it must source adequate polity legitimacy in the Union's atypical and multilayered institutional structure; and it must manage a permanent existential crisis that seems impossible to shake off, whether or not the future of the EU is directly in question—can a polity whose very foundations seem doomed to reside in quicksand be conceptualized as genuinely 'constitutional'? There is another, and prior, concern in this context too i.e. disagreement about the nature of transnational constitutionalism per se. Discourse on the meaning and features of constitutionalism beyond the state, or on the degree to which those markers are exhibited by the EU, marks another huge and contested field of scholarship.[45] The definition of a 'constitution' adopted here, reflecting the case study's emphasis on the scope of relevant primary law, is from MacCormick's *Questioning Sovereignty*, building on his view that:

> Law has positivity. We look to law for answers to questions about *what is obligatory or not, permissible or not*, within some determinate and institutional sphere of decision-making. Inside that sphere of decision-making, the *given rules and principles indicate what ought to be done*, indeed what has to be done to satisfy the institutionalised system. The norms of a system of law lay down what is obligatory or permissible in the perspective of the system, not what from some ideal point of view ought to be obligatory or permissible.[46]

He then states that '[c]onstitutions can best be defined in terms of the establishment and empowerment of the agencies ("institutions" in one sense) that perform the roles of enunciating, executing, administering or judging about the norms whose institutional character is established by the very exercise of those powers'.[47]

It may seem odd to revert to the classical apparatus of legal hierarchy in light of the prevalence in current scholarship of the paradigm of constitutional pluralism—work that, ironically, developed in many respects from MacCormick's ground-breaking ideas about constitutionalism beyond the state.[48] But what is needed for present purposes is a working definition of a constitution to set a baseline or threshold boundary for the *feasible* use of that term—especially because the nature of EU constitutionalism is so unsettled from all angles. The extent to which you can or perhaps might prefer not to go along a spectrum of thicker constitutional

[45] For a comprehensive overview of related debates and scholarship, see C Mac Amhlaigh 'The European Union's constitutional mosaic: Big "c" or small "c", is that the question?' in N Walker, J Shaw, S Tierney (eds.), *Europe's Constitutional Mosaic* (Hart Publishing, 2011) 21; Avbelj, n5; and P Craig, 'Constitutions, constitutionalism and the European Union' (2001) 7:2 ELJ 125. See also, O Gerstenberg, 'Expanding the constitution beyond the Court: The case of Euro-constitutionalism' (2002) 8:1 ELJ 175.

[46] N MacCormick, *Questioning Sovereignty: Law, State and Practical Reason* (OUP, 2002) 13 (emphasis added).

[47] MacCormick, n46, 102. On constitutional *legal* orders specifically, see also F Amtenbrink, 'The European Court of Justice's approach to primacy and European constitutionalism' in Micklitz and de Witte (eds.), n26, 35 at 39.

[48] For an overview of current thinking, see e.g. the essays in M Avbelj and J Komárek (eds.), *Constitutional Pluralism in the European Union and Beyond* (Hart Publishing, 2012).

meaning than the definition adopted here raises legitimate but separate questions. Moreover, irrespective of specific debates about which institution has the 'final say' in determining legal disputes, the ideas associated with constitutional pluralism offer broader perspectives on how courts operating in multilevel legal spaces derive their legal responses—perspectives that are still relevant even in a more traditional construct of the hierarchy of legal sources.

Here, it is simply asserted that the EU Treaties *do* fulfil the criteria set out in MacCormick's definition in an empirical sense; that the Union can therefore be *credibly* presented as a polity that has a constitution; and that the Court of Justice is, in consequence, that polity's constitutional court. In EU free movement law, in other words, the Court of Justice does have the final say (bar Treaty amendment) on the scope of the relevant Treaty provisions. But this approach will only hold weight if it can also be shown that the EU actually functions as a constitutional legal order and that due recognition is given by the relevant constitutional subjects to the Court's role at the apex of free movement law in practice.

(iii) Functional constitutionalism

Building on the definition of a constitution adopted above, the extent to which the case law of the Court is acknowledged to be constitutional through *practice* will now be considered, adding functional ballast to the declaratory and normative dimensions already assessed—indeed, as noted at the outset, it is the combined force of the three dimensions that strengthens the feasibility of describing the Treaty bases of free movement law, and the Court's espousal of their scope, as genuinely constitutional law. The idea of functional constitutionalism is used here as an empirical yardstick:[49] do the Court's functions and practices align with the functions and practices that we associate with constitutional courts? It would be naïve to gloss over the fact of academic, political, and judicial resistance, expressed to greater or lesser extents at different times, to conceiving of the Court of Justice as the Union's supreme court or to respecting the degree of legal authority that comes with it.[50] Nevertheless, it is also a fact that the basic constitutional authority attributed to the Court's foundational judgments has persisted for five decades now: something that brings different shading to the 'because the Court says so' problem indicated above. We also saw that while, under Article 19 TEU, all of the courts that comprise the CJEU have authority to interpret and apply EU law, the Court of Justice is the final link in the appellate chain organizing those three (at present) institutions in hierarchical terms. The Court has also established that, owing to the objective of ensuring the uniform application of Union law in all of

[49] Functional constitutionalism has also been explored from normative perspectives e.g. M Dani, 'Constitutionalism and dissonances: Has Europe paid off its debt to functionalism?' (2009) 15:3 ELJ 324.

[50] For discussion of the qualifiers to the primacy of EU law attached by national constitutional courts, see Amtenbrink, n47, 42–52; tracing responses to one judgment in particular, see e.g. S Garben, 'Sky-high controversy and high-flying claims? The *Sturgeon* case law in light of judicial activism, euroscepticism and eurolegalism' (2013) 50:1 CMLRev 15.

the Member States, its judgments in individual cases have *erga omnes* effect.[51] A stamp of hierarchy is further imposed on that finding by the fact that the Commission's enforcement powers can, and did,[52] encompass failures by national courts to manage the obligations that stem from EU law.

It is also extremely difficult for any institution but the Court of Justice itself to recalibrate or reverse its decisions—and this is, again, something that the Member States have felt comfortable enough to live with since the Court's establishment in 1952. The so-called *Barber* protocol attached to the Maastricht Treaty comes closest to political reversal of a judicial decision, but that measure altered the temporal scope of the *Barber* judgment only and not its legal substance.[53] Moreover, while the Court was kept at arm's length from both the second and third pillars of the EU structure created at Maastricht, the changes effected by the Lisbon Treaty open up the Court's role—and, crucially, the standard operation of the preliminary rulings procedure[54]—in the Area of Freedom, Security and Justice i.e. the former third pillar at least.

The Court of Justice has empowered national courts and tribunals to give effect to the primacy of EU law established in *Costa*—irrespective of their constitutional functions (or, more typically, their constitutional impotence) in their national judicial systems.[55] In other words, while the majority of national courts and tribunals have no power to disapply relevant national law in the general exercise of their jurisdiction, they obtain precisely that power in order to give effect to the primacy of EU law in situations of legal source conflict. The Court underscored the extent of that autonomy through the creation[56] and development[57] of the doctrine of interpretative obligation. In these ways, the Court bypassed established routes of national systemic hierarchy and created its own constitutional web of judicial authority—placing itself firmly at the apex. Importantly, for example, it retains sole jurisdiction to pronounce on the validity of Union legal acts.[58] Also, from the perspective of functional constitutionalism, the existence and workings of the Article 267 procedure exemplify the significance of hierarchy—not least in the requirement that questions of both validity and interpretation of EU law

[51] Case 66/80 *SpA International Chemical Corporation (ICI) v Amministrazione delle finanze dello Stato* [1981] ECR 1191, para. 13.

[52] Case C-129/00 *Commission v Italy* [2003] ECR I-14637.

[53] Case C-262/88 *Barber v Guardian Royal Exchange Assurance Group* [1990] ECR I-1189; the text of the Protocol states that '[f]or the purposes of [Article 157 TFEU], benefits under occupational social security schemes shall not be considered as remuneration if and in so far as they are attributable to periods of employment prior to 17 May 1990, except in the case of workers or those claiming under them who have before that date initiated legal proceedings or introduced an equivalent claim under the applicable national law'.

[54] See esp. Article 10 of the Protocol on Transitional Provisions, 2007 OJ C306/159.

[55] Case 106/77 *Amministrazione delle Finanze dello Stato v Simmenthal* [1978] ECR 629. Additionally, in *CILFIT*, the Court outlined the extent and limits of national court discretion under the Article 267 mechanism (Case 283/81 *Srl CILFIT and Lanificio di Gavardo SpA v Minestero della Sanità* [1982] ECR 3415).

[56] Case 14/83 *Von Colson and Kamann v Land Nordrhein-Westfalen* [1984] ECR 1891.

[57] E.g. Case C-555/07 *Kücükdeveci v Swedex GmbH & Co. KG* [2010] ECR I-365.

[58] Case 314/85 *Foto-Frost v Hauptzollamt Lübeck-Ost* [1987] ECR 4199, paras 15–16.

must be referred to the Court of Justice where 'a case [is] pending before a court or tribunal of a Member State against whose decisions there is no judicial remedy under national law'. As argued by Komárek, '[the] preliminary ruling procedure, reflects an understanding of the ECJ as a superior authority on the interpretation of EU law that is distinct from national courts—despite all talk of "judicial cooperation and dialogue"'.[59]

The relationship between the Court of Justice and national courts is particularly critical in the context of responsibilities owed to constitutional subjects, since these are the forums in which EU free movement law happens in reality—after all, the vast majority of relevant cases will never make it anywhere near the Court of Justice.[60] As provided for in Article 267, a reference need only be sent from most national courts and tribunals when it is 'necessary' to enable that court to give its judgment—and that determination is itself part of the national court's responsibility. The input of the Court of Justice will normally be 'necessary' when a legal question arising in national proceedings cannot be resolved on the basis of existing EU law because, for example, the relevant area of EU law is unclear or because a genuinely new question about the interpretation or application of EU law has arisen. As Weatherill has emphasized, 'the Court of Justice must ensure the persuasive quality of its judgments for . . . the legitimacy of the Court is in part to be assessed with reference to the reaction of national courts who are by no means simply unthinking agents of the Court of Justice'.[61]

But a cautionary note must also be raised: there is a difference between a national judge *knowing* the requirements imposed by EU law, including its primacy over conflicting national law, and *feeling* them. A national court may seem to accept its obligations under EU law in a formal sense; but, for example, the elasticity of the proportionality test may enable a deeper-seated reluctance to displace the validity of national measures (especially legislative measures) and the political choices that underpin them to prevail.[62] A judge who does not encounter EU law very often—i.e. most national judges—will understandably find it difficult to act in ways that are simply anathema to national judicial limits more generally.

The practice and development of EU law in national courts and tribunals is one of the biggest empirical research gaps in the discipline. Even where a preliminary reference *has* been sent to Luxembourg, the final decision lies, as noted earlier, with

[59] Komárek, n21, 16.

[60] The stringent limits on standing before the Court for direct judicial review actions under Article 263 TFEU are relevant here too (e.g. Case C-50/00 P *Unión de Pequeños Agricultores v Council* [2002] ECR I-6677); moreover, the amendments to Article 263 effected by the Lisbon Treaty appear to be more marginal than was initially thought: see the Opinion of AG Kokott in Case C-583/11 P *Inuit Tapiriit Kanatami and Others v Parliament and Council*, pending (Opinion delivered on 17 January 2013).

[61] Weatherill, n15.

[62] E.g. compare the different discussions of proportionality in both of the majority judgments as well as the dissent in *The Queen on the Application of Sinclair Collis Limited v The Secretary of State for Health*, High Court of Justice Court of Appeal (Civil Division) [2011] EWCA Civ 437; it is particularly interesting to observe how the judges' framing and assessment of the applicable proportionality test keeps coming back to national constructs.

the referring national court—and there is no centralized follow-up or supervisory mechanism to find out and report on what actually happened. The scale of application of EU law in a Union of the current size, considering the volume of national courts and tribunals potentially called upon to consider disputes with Treaty relevance, also presents a significant challenge to one of the values constantly reaffirmed by the Court and referred to above i.e. ensuring uniform application of EU law in all of the Member States. The quantitative challenge in that respect is compounded by the fact that national courts are 'understanding the rulings of the ECJ from the perspective of their respective legal cultures and systems'.[63]

When delivering its preliminary rulings, the Court of Justice tends to answer the referring court in three different ways: first, the judgment appears to decide the case concretely, notwithstanding the jurisdictional boundaries built into the preliminary rulings system; second, the Court does not prescribe the outcome of the case but does provide clear guidance on the legal issues raised; third, the Court neither decides the case nor provides particularly clear or helpful guidance for the referring court. On the first type of response—where the Court effectively applies as well as interprets EU law to resolve the national dispute—scholars disagree about whether such a prescriptive judgment properly assists or unhelpfully emasculates national courts.[64] It is also important to acknowledge that since preliminary references can come from any national court or tribunal, including at first instance, the Court often has no judgment from the national proceedings to examine—the legal issues and the facts thus remain bundled together since no prior judicial analysis has already distinguished them. But the concern highlighted here is a practical one: in such cases, a constitutional court, whose task is to provide guidance on the law, is making determinations of fact as if it were the first instance tribunal—when it has worked on a second-hand presentation and review of the *evidence* submitted to the national court.[65] A prescriptive approach also leads to further references from national courts that are not necessarily distinguishable from each other on any points other than different facts: distorting the purpose of the Court of Justice as a constitutional court and reducing national courts—who should be able to interpret and apply EU law for the most part by themselves (for how else could a 28 State legal order possibly work?)—to acting like Court of Justice registries.

[63] Woods, n16, 341.

[64] Reaffirming the existence of the spirit of cooperation on which the preliminary rulings procedure is premised, see e.g. X Groussot, 'Spirit, are you there? Reinforced judicial dialogue and the preliminary ruling procedure', Eric Stein Working Papers No 4/2008, available at <http://www.ericsteinpapers.eu/images/doc/eswp-2008-04-groussot.pdf>. Arguing for greater leeway for national courts, see e.g. G Davies, 'Abstractness and concreteness in the preliminary reference procedure' in N Nic Shuibhne (ed.), *Regulating the Internal Market* (Edward Elgar Publishing, 2006) 210. See also, J Komárek, '"In the Court(s) we trust?" On the need for hierarchy and differentiation in the preliminary ruling procedure' (2007) 32:4 ELRev 467; and O Pollicino, 'The new relationship between national and the European Courts after the enlargement of Europe: Towards a unitary theory of jurisprudential supranational law?' (2010) 29:1 YEL 65.

[65] See further, N Nic Shuibhne and M Maci, 'Proving public interest: The growing impact of evidence in EU free movement case law' (2013) 50:4 CMLRev, forthcoming.

Under option three, the Court of Justice noticeably holds back, sometimes even at the level of explaining the applicable legal principles and for reasons we can only guess. Here, it leaves considerably more discretion to the referring court—but this is not necessarily an appropriate discharge of constitutional responsibility if the judgment issued is so vague or cryptic as to be essentially useless to the national court that requested it. Unsurprisingly, then, the second option is the Goldilocks outcome in terms of constitutional responsibility. In *Genc*, the Court outlined its own role and responsibilities, and those of referring courts, under Article 267 as follows:

> Article [267] establishes a relationship of close cooperation between the national courts and the Court of Justice, based on the assignment to each of *different functions*, and constitutes an instrument by means of which the Court provides the national court with the criteria for the interpretation of [EU] law which they require in order to dispose of disputes which they are called upon to resolve . . . It is one of the essential characteristics of the system of judicial cooperation established under Article [267] that the Court replies in rather *abstract and general terms* to a question on the interpretation of [EU] law referred to it, while it is for the referring court to give a ruling in the dispute before it, taking into account the Court's reply . . . The national court *alone* has *direct knowledge of the facts* giving rise to the dispute and is, consequently, *best placed* to make the necessary determinations.[66]

In subsequent chapters, fragmentary consequences that can result when this 'ideal' division of functions has in some way broken down will be flagged. As a final point in the present discussion, however, the argument in Section 2(a) that case law coherence must not be conflated with case law perfection should be restated. As Koutrakos has argued, 'a degree of uncertainty is inherent in the preliminary reference procedure. In fact, it is the direct corollary of the central position which national courts enjoy in the constitutional architecture of the Union's legal order in general and the decentralised system of enforcement set out in Article 267 TFEU'.[67] This may not fit with more rigid understandings of the uniformity of law; but more rigid understandings of the uniformity of EU law simply do not fit with the reality of adjudication as a process. The criterion of coherence helps us to establish a gauge that is properly legally meaningful but also achievable in practice.

The fusion of declaratory, normative, and functional perspectives on EU constitutionalism produces a sum of persuasiveness greater than the individual parts. Moreover, all three sources continue to persist and to develop, and through that process they harden. Joerges cautions that '[t]his tenacity of the European polity is reassuring, but no more than that. It does not, after all, guarantee that the incremental searching and learning process whereby Europe has "constituted" itself can successfully continue'.[68] To some degree, the fact that all constitutional

[66] Case C-14/09 *Genc v Land Berlin* [2010] ECR I-931, paras 29–32 (emphasis added).

[67] P Koutrakos, 'The *Emsland-Stärke* abuse of law test in the law of agriculture and free movement of goods' in R de la Feria and S Vogenauer (eds.), *Prohibition of Abuse of Law: A New General Principle of EU Law?* (Hart Publishing, 2011) 203 at 215.

[68] C Joerges, 'The law in the process of constitutionalizing Europe', EUI Working Paper, Law, No. 2002/4, available at <http://cadmus.eui.eu/dspace/handle/1814/182>, 34.

polities, including states, can be unmade places the fragility of the EU in broader perspective. But the *extent* of polity challenge levelled at the EU, depicted above in the language of existential crisis, brings sharper edges to the scythe in the transnational context. This is the challenging environment in which the Court of Justice must resolve constitutional disputes; whether related traces of defiance or timidity can be detected in free movement case law is something that can be borne in mind when reflecting on the substantive discussions in subsequent chapters; as can the relative propriety of either response.

3. The significance and scope of free movement law

Three particular aspects of free movement law will be briefly outlined in this final section: first, its significance within EU law more generally; second, the three stages of analysis—restriction, justification, and proportionality—applied by the Court in free movement case law; and, third, an overview of this project's approach to the first of those stages i.e. determining the question of scope.

(a) Significance: why free movement law?

Article 3(3) TEU provides that the EU 'shall establish an internal market'. Article 4 (2) TFEU confirms that the competence to regulate it is shared between the EU and the Member States. The internal market is then defined in Article 26(2) TFEU as 'an area without internal frontiers in which the free movement of goods, persons, services and capital is ensured in accordance with the provisions of the Treaties'. The threshold conditions for triggering EU competence to adopt measures 'for the approximation of the provisions laid down by law, regulation or administrative action in Member States which have as their object the establishment and functioning of the internal market' are set out in Articles 114 and 115 TFEU. From the perspective of 'negative' market integration, however, free movement rights are conferred by Articles 28–37 (goods), 45–48 (workers), 49–55 (establishment), 56–62 (services) and 63–66 (capital) TFEU. For natural persons holding the nationality of an EU Member State, the 'right to move and reside freely within the territory of the Member States' is protected autonomously as an element of EU citizenship (Articles 20(2) and 21 TFEU) and by Article 45(1) of the Charter of Fundamental Rights. Finally, related Treaty provisions set out the permitted derogations from (almost all of) the Treaty-based free movement rights.[69]

[69] The exception is Article 30 TFEU, which prohibits customs duties (and charges having equivalent effect) on imports and exports between Member States and from which there are no Treaty-based derogations. More generally, for quantitative restrictions on the free movement of goods, see Article 36 TFEU; for the free movement of workers, Article 45(3) TFEU; for restrictions on freedom of establishment, Articles 51 and 52 TFEU; for services, Article 62 TFEU; and for capital, Article 65 TFEU. For citizenship rights, see the general statement in Article 21 TFEU that '[t]hese rights shall be exercised in accordance with the conditions and limits defined by the Treaties and by the measures adopted thereunder'.

Through its interpretation of these rights-establishing *and* rights-limiting provisions of the TFEU, the Court of Justice fixes the legal parameters of the internal market. These are the boundaries that frame the regulatory space within which both the EU legislature and the Member States can act, and that is why determination of the scope of free movement law is one of the key ways in which the Court executes a significant constitutional function. The foundational Treaty statements on free movement rights and permitted derogations have remained largely unchanged since the original Treaty of Rome: the key exceptions being, through amendments introduced by the Maastricht Treaty, the creation of EU citizenship rights and the recasting of the provisions on capital movements. Notwithstanding the stability of that Treaty basis, however, free movement law still begets a surprising volume of unsettled questions about its reach or scope. The EEC common market was established in the 1950s; it was a compact regional trading space, in terms of geographical size and frontier range. The contemporary market is a radically different place in terms of scale—both literally (comparing a Community of six States with a Union of 28) and operationally, highlighting the impact of developments such as the Internet and affordable air travel on transforming our capacity for transnational market activity. Some market sectors and market actors are considerably more mobile than others. For example, it is much easier to participate in the virtual market (e.g. to provide or receive cross-border services or make a capital transfer online) than to uproot and move more permanently to another Member State as a worker. But the fact that cross-border activity *can* be transacted without any of the parties involved actually leaving their own State does mean that more companies and persons than ever are internal market actors.[70] Questions about the law underpinning the exercise of free movement rights thus continue to be asked of the Court of Justice. For example, annual statistics from the Court confirm that such questions still constitute a significant proportion of all preliminary references sent by national courts and tribunals (and preliminary rulings account in turn for more than half of the Court's entire caseload).[71]

As the European Parliament has emphasized, 'the quantitative aspect alone of cross-border movements cannot justify the attention paid to the phenomenon,

[70] The Commission has summarized key benefits of the EU internal market at <http://ec.europa.eu/internal_market/benefits_en.htm>.

[71] For example, it can be seen from the 2011 Annual Report of the Court of Justice (available at <http://curia.europa.eu/jcms/upload/docs/application/pdf/2012-06/ra2011_statistiques_cour_en.pdf>) that 423 of the 688 cases (i.e. just under 62 per cent) lodged at the Court in that year were references for a preliminary ruling. On a (very) conservative reading of the 'nature of the subject matter' statistics for preliminary rulings (i.e. including EU citizenship and social security for migrant workers, but excluding e.g. consumer protection, taxation, and other sectoral policy headings), 16 per cent of those references related to free movement law—however, a considerable majority of the cases classed separately under the sectoral headings actually related to the operation of the free movement rules too. The 2010 Annual Report confirms similarly that 385 (of 631) new cases in that year were references for a preliminary ruling, with 18 per cent of those references relating directly to free movement law, using the same narrow parameters applied above (the 2010 Report is available at <http://curia.europa.eu/jcms/upload/docs/application/pdf/2011-05/ra2010_stat_cour_final_en.pdf>).

which is more significant in terms of indicating the progress and limitations of European integration'.[72] However, while the internal market pushes on in real terms, the fundamental rationale for European integration—political *and* economic—is challenged, contested, and re-imagined. The intimate link between realizing a market without internal frontiers and wider ambitions of Union integration has been reinforced extensively, in both institutional[73] and academic[74] contexts. At the time of writing, however, the ongoing resolution of the Eurozone crisis and the ramifications of the prospect of an in/out EU membership referendum in the United Kingdom in the relatively near future have tinged that presumption with existential uncertainty even more strongly than usual—and with respect to the market as well as the EU itself.[75] Neither the purposes nor the benefits of the market are proving to be mechanically determinative as a response: for States, for businesses, or for consumers.[76] And neither the consensus nor the verve of the 1992 single market programme has since been recaptured at the level of policy- or agenda-making. By contrast, current political as well as economic instability heightens instead the lingering vulnerability of the EU market to resurgences of national protectionism. It has also been pointed out that there is now a greater awareness of controversies within free movement law, especially since widely reported decisions of the Court have presented acute challenges to prized national economic and social models.[77] All of these complexities contribute additional impetus to a palpably growing interest in evaluating both the Court's performance as an influential institution in this field and the substantive law it is developing through its judgments.[78]

[72] *Frontier Workers in the European Union*, Directorate General for Research Working Paper, Social Affairs Series, W 16A, section 2.2, available at <www.europarl.europa.eu/workingpapers/soci/w16/summary_en.htm>.

[73] See e.g. M Monti, *A New Strategy for the Single Market: At the Service of Europe's Economy and Society*, 9 May 2010, prepared at the request of the European Commission President, available at <http://ec.europa.eu/bepa/pdf/monti_report_final_10_05_2010_en.pdf>.

[74] See e.g. D Chalmers, 'The single market: From prima donna to journeyman' in J Shaw and G More (eds.), *New Legal Dynamics of European Union* (Clarendon Press, 1995) 55 at 60; N Reich, 'A European constitution for citizens: Reflections on the rethinking of Union and Community law' (1997) 3:1 ELJ 131 at 142; M Poiares Maduro, *We, The Court: The European Court of Justice and the European Economic Constitution* (Oxford: Hart Publishing, 1998) 8; and Weiler, n11, 350.

[75] The debate has attracted editorial comment in prominent academic journals; see e.g. P Koutrakos, 'To look without understanding was their lot' (2011) 36:5 ELRev 613; and JHH Weiler, 'Integration through fear' (2012) 23:1 EJIL 1.

[76] The Executive Summary of the 2011 Report on Special Eurobarometer Survey 363, *Internal Market: Awareness, Perceptions and Impacts*, makes for stark reading in this context; the Report is available at <http://ec.europa.eu/public_opinion/archives/ebs/ebs_363_en.pdf>.

[77] See J Snell, 'The legitimacy of free movement case law: process and substance' in Adams, Meeusen, Straetmans, and de Waele (eds.), n1, forthcoming. See also, M Everson, 'Is the European Court of Justice a legal or political institution now?', *The Guardian*, 10 August 2010, at <http://www.guardian.co.uk/law/2010/aug/10/european-court-justice-legal-political>.

[78] See e.g. D Chalmers, 'The European Court of Justice is now little more than a rubber stamp for the EU. It should be replaced with better alternative arrangements for central judicial guidance', 8 March 2012, at <http://blogs.lse.ac.uk/europpblog/>.

(b) Stages: restriction, justification, and proportionality

To resolve disputes engaging the Treaty's free movement provisions, the Court of Justice follows an established template consisting of three distinct questions:

1. Does the challenged measure or action constitute a *restriction* on free movement rights conferred by the Treaty?
2. If it does, can the measure or action be *justified*?
3. If it can, is the measure or action nevertheless *proportionate*?

This three-step methodology is one of the most predictable and formulaic features of free movement case law. That does not mean that it is uncontroversial. For example, in the context of the right to take collective action, academics have questioned whether that fundamental social right can ever be conceived as having the capacity to displace free movement rights given that '[t]he moment collective action is found to be a "restriction"... the "social" interests are on the back-foot, having to defend themselves from the economic'.[79] The extent to which national courts follow the logic of the Court's template is also questionable. For example, in a case about the banning of cigarette vending machines, both the first instance and appeal courts in Scotland proceeded to focus on proportionality even though both judgments recorded explicit doubts about whether Article 34 TFEU prohibited the measure in the first place.[80] In other words, the courts proceeded to resolve stages two and three without first determining stage one. Is such an approach unwise, a bit like being unsure about whether the elements of a criminal offence are present but going on to consider the evidential questions anyway, since if the accused can be exonerated on that basis, whether or not they committed a crime in the first place won't matter? Or is it simply an expedient way for national courts to determine whether or not, ultimately, a preliminary ruling is truly 'necessary' to enable them to resolve the case? This example, which is part of a wider trend also being tracked in other Member States,[81] underscores the need for EU lawyers to engage further with the empirical research gap on national court practice highlighted in Section 2 and raises broader questions about the frailty of functional constitutionalism at the level of *form* at least.

In any event, the first stage of the Court's methodology reflects the way in which the *scope* of free movement law is understood and explored here, returned to in Section 3(c). As a general point, it can be noted for now that restrictions on free movement rights can be (1) directly discriminatory on grounds of nationality

[79] C Barnard 'Social dumping or dumping socialism' (2008) 67 CLJ 262 at 264. This point is picked up again in Chapter 2, in the discussion on protecting fundamental rights.

[80] *Sinclair Collis Ltd v Lord Advocate*, Court of Session (Outer House) [2012] Eu. L.R. 23, para. 23; and, on appeal, *Sinclair Collis Ltd v Lord Advocate*, Court of Session (Inner House, Extra Division) [2012] CSIH 80, para. 53.

[81] See H van Harten, 'National judicial autonomy: The example of national European law precedents in the Dutch case-law on the free movement of services and the freedom of establishment' (2009) 2:2 *Review of European Administrative Law* 135.

(i.e. discriminatory in law); (2) indirectly discriminatory (i.e. not discriminatory in law, but discriminatory in result or effect); or (3) non-discriminatory (i.e. not discriminatory in law or in effect, but still restrictive of Treaty free movement rights).

An important challenge for the Court is to achieve effective internal market integration while still allowing for more localized regulatory diversity in keeping with the constitutional mandate of shared EU/Member State competence. This objective is captured by the fact that the Treaty's market-opening rights are accompanied by express exceptions enabling Member States to restrict those rights legitimately, in order to protect their public interest priorities in certain circumstances.[82] If it is established that the measure being challenged amounts to a restriction of free movement rights, the arguments submitted to establish that the measure is nonetheless justifiable will then be considered i.e. the Court moves on to stage two. Free movement rights can never be conceptualized as absolute, therefore, because the Treaty framework has always acknowledged that even a blatantly discriminatory restriction of free movement can be permitted if there is a good—i.e. within the limits of EU law—reason for it. The potential for justification is thus an inherent feature of the construct of EU internal market rules.

While there is some variation across the freedoms,[83] the Treaty-permitted grounds for derogation from free movement rights essentially coalesce around objectives in the interests of protecting public health and public security, and the potentially more pliable (though tightly drawn by the Court[84]) category of 'public policy' exceptions. Priorities within established derogation grounds will shift over time; the contemporary focus on alcohol, sugar, and tobacco in public health policy, for example, was hardly predictable in the 1950s. But the grounds expressly articulated in the Treaty have long been supplemented by a much more expansive approach in the case law. The basic rule is that directly discriminatory restrictions of free movement can be evaluated only by recourse to the grounds provided for in the Treaty. For indirectly discriminatory and non-discriminatory restrictions, however, States can raise virtually any policy argument that they wish, without being confined to the policy objectives predetermined in the derogation provisions.[85] In this way, the Court has accommodated policy concerns that were not relevant or prominent when the Treaty of Rome was drafted, such as the protection of the

[82] The extent to which the internal market must reflect or take account of a whole series of other EU and/or Member State objectives is discussed separately in Chapter 2.

[83] 'Public morality, public policy or public security; the protection of health and life of humans, animals or plants; the protection of national treasures possessing artistic, historic or archaeological value; or the protection of industrial and commercial property' (Article 36 TFEU for quantitative restrictions on the free movement of goods); 'public policy, public security or public health' (Articles 45(3), 52, and 62 TFEU for workers, establishment and services). For restrictions on the free movement of capital, see the specific limits set out in Article 65 TFEU.

[84] See e.g. AG Verloren van Themaat in Case 231/83 *Cullet v Centre Leclerc* [1985] ECR 305 at 312–14.

[85] Although hints of the Court's openness to justification arguments beyond the grounds expressed in the Treaty can be found in earlier case law, the decision in *Cassis de Dijon* is generally accepted as the more developed 'first' authority for this proposition (Case 120/78 *Rewe-Zentrale AG v Bundesmonopolverwaltung für Branntwein (Cassis de Dijon)* [1979] ECR 649).

environment or of consumers, without the need for Treaty amendment or the definitive resolution of broader debates about the relative value of either an updated but fixed list of permissible public interest grounds or codification of a more open-ended approach across the board. The Court's ingenuity also enables relatively specific or esoteric but nonetheless valid public interest arguments to be accepted without the need to shoehorn them artificially into the grounds available in the Treaty.[86] It creates, in other words, a genuinely merits-based system. It is also, of course, a striking example of the Court's law-making *and* policy-making powers in the field of free movement law: the Court has blatantly added significantly more public interest arguments to the public interest arguments specified in the Treaty. On the other hand, the Member States have never stepped in to regain constitutional ownership of the issue post-*Cassis*, and so the development is also a good example of functional constitutionalism taking root through practice—garnering implicit but, critically, legitimizing political acceptance in the process.

Recalling the point about achieving integration while enabling a concurrent degree of localized regulatory diversity, the Court's management of the justification framework can be pared down to the search for the elusive optimal point of balance in the scales of the internal market: which rules need to be the same in all of the Member States, and which rules can happily be different? In *Commission v Germany*, AG Bot confirmed the legal approach to justification as a facet of shared competence: '[t]he rules surrounding the exercise of [a Member State's] reserved powers mean that if its legislation causes a restriction of one of the fundamental freedoms of movement it must be in a position to provide a legitimate reason, given in the Treaty or recognised as an overriding reason of public interest, to justify this'.[87] But there is a searing tension at the heart of how we conceptualize justification in free movement law. On the one hand, as shown above, the Treaty expresses justification arguments as derogations from primary rights. And so, in keeping with standard interpretative canons, those rights *must* be interpreted widely and the exceptions to them must be defined as narrowly as possible. On the other hand, however, the justification framework has evolved over time to become the prime space within which public interest arguments are aired. It is where the multifaceted construction of the internal market, considered in more detail in Chapter 2, is explored and contested. It is where we pitch the market 'against' other values. Justification is, in this way, transformed to being more of a policy-engineering tool; the language is about balancing and weighing, not derogating.

We are trying, in other words, to make the justification framework operate for us in a way that its legal construction in the Treaty cannot achieve. The development

[86] The Court has accepted the possibility that free movement restrictions could be justified in principle by e.g. 'the need to guarantee the stability and security of the assets administered by an undertaking for collective investment created by a severance fund' (Case C-39/11 *VBV—Vorsorgekasse AG v Finanzmarktaufsichtsbehörde (FMA)*, judgment of 7 June 2012, para. 31).

[87] AG Bot in Case C-141/07 *Commission v Germany (Pharmacies)* [2008] ECR I-6935, para. 83 of the Opinion. An additional prerequisite is that 'there are no Community harmonising measures providing for measures necessary to ensure the protection of those interests' (Case C-112/05 *Commission v Germany* [2007] ECR I-8995, para. 72).

of justification arguments outside the Treaty derogation framework might thus be conceived as a pressure release valve. But even if that development can be thought about, and excused, as law reflecting reality, the breakdown of the relevance of discrimination for the distinction between derogation and justification shifts the discussion to another plane. Public interest arguments not specified in the Treaty are now sometimes considered in the context of justifying even directly discriminatory measures. On some occasions, the Court at least tries, if not always convincingly, to make a case for the existence of discrimination; but, in other cases, it omits that discussion altogether and speaks of restrictions in neutral terms.[88] This development produces a deeper degree of judicial creativity altogether, providing an example of the fact that rules that *converge* do not necessarily result in a coherent legal framework from the perspective of adjudicatory constitutional responsibility.

It is also important to remember, and it has been shown empirically, that even where justification arguments are accepted in principle, national measures are very often defeated by the requirements of proportionality:[89] the third step in the Court's free movement methodology. It is generally accepted that the proportionality standard applied in EU free movement law involves two tests: first, assessing the *suitability* (or *appropriateness*) of the contested measure for achieving the stated policy objectives; and, second, evaluating its *necessity* for that purpose.[90] Assessing the proportionality of a national measure in the latter sense will also involve consideration of whether alternative measures could be *equally* effective in terms of achieving the public interest objective accepted in principle, but *less* restrictive having regard to their effect on intra-EU trade.[91]

Proportionality is a significant policy tool for any court, but its assessment carries strong potential for constitutional overreach on the part of the Court of Justice: here, the view of the Court on the suitability and necessity of national regulatory choices will possibly supplant that of national legislatures. In cases being considered

[88] For an overview of this issue and relevant case law, see AG Trstenjak in Case C-28/09 *Commission v Austria (Air Quality)*, judgment of 21 December 2011, paras 79–91 of the Opinion; cf. the silence of the Court on the nature of the restriction in that case (paras 113–117). This issue is discussed further in Chapter 6; see generally, S Weatherill, 'Free movement of goods' (2012) 61:2 ICLQ 541 at 544 (who describes the approach of the Court in *Commission v Austria* as 'extend[ing] its narrative of evasion').

[89] C Barnard, 'Derogations, justifications and the four freedoms: Is State interest really protected?' in C Barnard and O Odudu (eds.), *The Outer Limits of European Union Law* (Hart Publishing, 2009) 273.

[90] It is more debated whether the concept of proportionality *stricto sensu* (i.e. the greater the impact on free movement, the greater the importance attached to satisfying the public interest objective on which the Member State relies) is a distinct third test or absorbed by the test of necessity. In either event, a Member State 'must demonstrate that the level of protection it decides to afford to its legitimate interests is commensurate with the degree of interference this causes in intra [Union] trade' (AG Poiares Maduro in Case C-434/04 *Criminal proceedings against Ahokainen and Leppik* [2006] ECR I-9171, para. 26 of the Opinion).

[91] See e.g. Case C-205/07 *Gysbrechts and Santurel Inter BVBA* [2008] ECR I-9947, para. 53 (on the proportionality of export restrictions under Article 35 TFEU, discussed further in Chapter 6). See also e.g. AG Trstenjak in Case C-10/10 *Commission v Austria* [2011] ECR I-5389, paras 67–68 of the Opinion, who conceptualizes the less restrictive measure limb as a test of 'reasonableness' (addressing the free movement of capital).

under the preliminary rulings procedure, the facts-based assessment involved in making such determinations adds, as argued in Section 2, an additionally acute layer of concern. In the context of human rights law, Kumm has suggested that 'there is nothing specifically law-like about the proportionality test', arguing as follows:

> The test provides little more than a structure for reasoned policy-assessment . . . Proportionality has become the lawyers' framework to engage in policy analysis in a way that is neither directly guided or constrained by legal authority. Courts engaged in this type of rights reasoning are no longer enforcers of a political will that has previously created and defined a set of legal rights. Such a court has transformed itself into a veto-holding junior-partner in the joint legal-political enterprise of developing and enforcing rational policies that reflect equal respect and concern for each individual.[92]

It is true that there is 'nothing specifically law-like' about proportionality, since it queries, as we have seen, the suitability and necessity of policy choices. But 'developing' and especially 'enforcing rational policies that reflect equal respect and concern for each individual' are tasks that do fall properly within the remit of a constitutional court. It also goes too far to suggest that the application of proportionality cannot be 'directly guided or constrained by legal authority'. Recalling the point made earlier the proper division of functions between the Court of Justice and national courts, it is precisely the responsibility of the Court of Justice to provide and reinforce a coherent guiding structure for the application of proportionality for cases with an EU legal dimension. It was emphasized that the actual application of that structure to concrete facts-sets should be part of the task of the referring court in Article 267 cases—since that is the body closest to the dispute itself, to the detail and discussion of the evidence submitted, and to the gradations of the public interest conceptions at stake. Woods expresses the point as follows: '[t]he assessment of proportionality is heavily fact dependent in terms of outcome in the case but the questions the ECJ should ask itself in dealing with those facts are not'.[93] National courts also have responsibilities in this regard: in their judgments, they must demonstrate through clear reasoning and engagement with authority that they have reached their conclusions on proportionality in accordance with the guidance established by the Court of Justice, which they are legally obliged to follow, even if different tests are applicable under national law.

The justification and proportionality stages of free movement case law raise numerous questions that challenge the coherence of the Court's jurisprudence. Despite the rule (of the Court's own making) that justification of directly discriminatory restrictions is confined to the public interest grounds stipulated in the Treaty, there are clear instances of such restrictions being evaluated on the basis of arguments outwith those boundaries—for example, as noted above, directly discriminatory restrictions have been considered against arguments about protection

92 M Kumm, '*Internationale Handelsgesellschaft*, *Nold* and the new human rights paradigm' in Poiares Maduro and Azoulai (eds.), n15, 106 at 110.

93 Woods, n16, 360. See similarly, AG Poiares Maduro in *Criminal proceedings against Ahokainen and Leppik*, para. 32 of the Opinion.

of the environment. Similarly, how does the Court's stretching of the scope of Treaty obligations to catch private actors as well as States in certain circumstances, discussed in Chapter 3, fit with the way in which the justification grounds are articulated in the majority of relevant Treaty provisions i.e. clearly directed at those who have responsibility for the shaping of the *public* interest? It has been emphasized that, primarily for reasons of scale, this book examines the scope of *restrictions* and the principles that the Court has developed in that context; but coherence questions raised by their justification and/or proportionality will be flagged where relevant in the chapters that follow.

(c) Scope: general approach and chapter map

The chapters in this book are organized thematically rather than freedom-by-freedom. The focus on understanding the underpinning framework principles drives this structure; for example, questions about the exclusion of a *de minimis* threshold from free movement law emerge in recent case law on both citizenship rights and the free movement of goods. The analysis does not purport to deliver *even* coverage across all of the different sectors of free movement law. First, as will be argued in Chapter 2, the standard of coherence does not require that different sectors need to be treated in the same way in law: free movement rights will be presented as establishing a mixed legal framework, in which certain rules and principles work well across all of the freedoms but others do not. For example, the regulation of situations involving natural and legal persons might be best developed similarly in some circumstances but distinctively in others, bearing in mind that only the former hold EU citizenship rights. Second, the Treaty rules on some free movement sectors are themselves differently configured when compared to the others, and these constitutional instructions should be respected. Finally, the balance of coverage across different freedoms will also vary because the extent to which the relevant questions have arisen or been pursued or become especially acute in different areas of law necessarily varies too. For example, the complexities of situations that are wholly internal to one Member State are more apparent in the case law on free movement of persons and so that context dominates the discussion in Chapter 4, even though the basic rule requiring the presence of a cross-border connection is found in the rest of the Treaty free movement provisions too.

The way in which the scope of free movement law is understood here is based on the first question in the free movement case law template—does the contested measure or action constitute a restriction of free movement rights? Analysis of this question is divided into two parts over the chapters that follow: negative scope and positive scope. *Negative scope* covers the principles that are applied in free movement law to exclude something (or someone) from the scope of the Treaty—i.e. there is no Treaty-relevant restriction on free movement rights at all and, in such cases, any examination of justification and proportionality becomes redundant. In Chapter 3, the principles examined relate to 'who' is involved and include discussion of the extent to which the Treaty freedoms are addressed to private as well as State actors. Chapter 4 then focuses on a crucial 'what' question in the context of restrictions: the shape-shifting nature of the wholly internal rule. In Chapter 5, the principles of remoteness and *de minimis* are introduced, and argued to sit at present somewhere between what-based exclusions (negative scope) and the elements that do make up a Treaty-relevant restriction (positive scope). Some shared characteristics link the principles considered in these three chapters: first, their contribution is often negatively decisive, thus constricting the scope of free movement law when invoked; second, they emerge in cases concerning all of the Treaty freedoms, but they are not always expressed through the same phrasing; and, third, while they do impose limitations of scope, this is not happening consistently, leading to damaging suspicions of convenience rather than suggesting a properly worked out, coherent framework.

The *positive scope* of free movement law is then addressed in Chapters 6 and 7. We tend to take the meaning and scope of discriminatory restrictions for granted, but definitional questions at the edges of discrimination are explored in Chapter 6—questioning, for example, the continuing value of its division into directly and indirectly discriminatory restrictions given the breakdown of that distinction at the stage of justification alluded to above. The central purpose of Chapter 7 is to explore why and the extent to which *non*-discriminatory measures have the potential to infringe EU free movement rights. In the preceding chapters, it will have become clear that the Court's use of tests such as deterrence and disadvantage as the basis for Treaty-caught restrictions has been problematic in many respects, since such concepts both expand the scope of the Treaty yet arguably lack sufficient normative weight to defend the related displacement of State regulatory competence. In Chapter 7, it will be argued that free movement rights can be reconceptualized around stronger principles of law. A principle that is based not, in line with the dominant emphasis in current case law, on access to the market, but *access to the exercise of free movement rights* will be developed. But limits that should be placed on the scope of that principle will also be articulated.

Overall, it will be argued that the complex and poorly explained framework being applied to determine the scope of free movement law at present is masking challenging fault-lines and fragmentary ruptures in judicial reasoning—especially in the use of and engagement with relevant authority—that must be resolved by the Court of Justice in order to (re-)generate a stronger degree of case law coherence: a duty that the Court owes to its constitutional subjects, especially in light of its responsibility to guide the courts and tribunals of the Member States towards their own resolution of questions on the scope of free movement law. It will be asserted that improving the quality of its judgments is necessary for a renewal of confidence in the Court as an effective constitutional institution. However, it will also be argued that the Member States need to take ultimate responsibility for ensuring that the Court is an effective institution that can actually deliver those functions.

Before the substantive analysis of free movement law is presented, the reasons behind the choice of coherence as the criterion of assessment, the way in which coherence is understood and applied for that purpose, and a preliminary sketch of the most significant fragmentation problems in the free movement case law will first be explained in more detail in Chapter 2.

2

Coherence, Fragmentation, and the Free Movement Case Law

1. Introduction

In Chapter 1, it was argued that an obligation to sustain case law coherence stems from the constitutional responsibilities of the Court of Justice. The nature and extent of that obligation will now be examined in more detail. The standard of coherence applied will be outlined in Section 2. As indicated in Chapter 1, case law coherence does not equate to case law certainty, and it is not about the pursuit of neatness or perfection for its own sake. Following a brief overview of ways in which the system of free movement law can be assessed (e.g. through the model of convergence), the work of the International Law Commission (ILC) on legal coherence will then be used, first, to explore whether that debate has any resonance for a study on EU free movement law and, second, to explain how the opposing dynamic of fragmentation captures the consequences that arise when case law coherence breaks down. In Section 3, the four fragmentation drivers introduced in Chapter 1—proliferation of principles; unsettled objectives of the market and free movement; protection of fundamental rights; and the structure of the Court—will be discussed in more detail. These challenges involve a mix of understandable impulses, framing ambiguities, unfortunate habits, and operational constraints; but their net effect has the consequence of distorting the coherence of the free movement case law and undermining its constitutional quality.

2. Coherence and fragmentation

The objective of case law coherence was connected in Chapter 1 to the values of fairness and integrity, and located in the wider domain of the rule of law and the avoidance of arbitrary decision-making. Attaching a note of *self*-responsibility to the Court, and writing specifically on its development of internal market law, Weatherill argues that '[t]his is not the common law, but the Court of Justice has itself chosen to lay down important statements of principle in its case law, and it is therefore obliged to "fit" its judgments within the pattern of previous decisions'.[1] This obligation reflects the essence of case law coherence. Fundamentally, when the Court makes interpretative choices, it should explain and rationalize those choices—especially when it departs from the law established in its previous decisions. The converse idea of fragmentation conveys the breakdown of legal coherence. It also captures the related ruptures that occur: not only in the case law substantively but also in the underpinning values and in institutional confidence, which can in turn lead to a breakdown of institutional trust. Importantly, fragmentation is not about difference per se. Instead, it gives us a mechanism to establish when and why difference is not *justifiable*. Applying that distinction to free movement law, coherence allows appropriate judicial latitude for the accommodation of material differences either within or across the Treaty freedoms. These points will now be developed further in the context of, first, related scholarship that focuses on EU law and, second, coherence questions in the field of public international law.

(a) From convergence to coherence

As a starting point, it is useful to think about fragmentation, divergence, convergence, coherence, and legitimacy as points along the same continuum. The ordering of that sequence reflects a momentum (1) *away* from the case law fragmentation caused by arbitrary decision-making; (2) *towards* a coherent jurisprudence that maximizes the potential for realizing fairness (or equality) under the rule of law—fundamental principles to which the EU is constitutionally committed by Article 2 TEU; and (3) *in turn* contributing to both institutional and polity legitimacy.

The concepts of convergence and divergence are essentially descriptive. They expose consistency and discordance in the case law; but they do not in and of themselves suggest standards that can be used to evaluate whether similarities and differences are justifiable or not. The basic premise of case law convergence is that the Court is consciously steering free movement law towards conceptual and definitional consistency irrespective of the Treaty provisions or free movement rights engaged. The articulation of a freedom-neutral definition for restrictions in *Gebhard* is a classic example of case law convergence understood in this way.[2] There are well-established meanings for the distinctive elements of the Treaty

[1] S Weatherill, 'The Court's case law on the internal market: "A circumloquacious statement of the result, rather than a reason for arriving at it"?' in M Adams, J Meeusen, G Straetmans, and H de Waele (eds.), *Judging Europe's Judges: The Legitimacy of the Case Law of the European Court of Justice Examined* (Hart Publishing, forthcoming 2013).

[2] Case C-55/94 *Gebhard v Consiglio dell'Ordine degli Avvocati e Procuratori di Milano* [1995] ECR I-4165, para. 37: 'national measures liable to hinder or make less attractive the exercise of fundamental freedoms guaranteed by the Treaty must fulfil four conditions: they must be applied in a non-discriminatory manner; they must be justified by imperative requirements in the general interest; they must be suitable for securing the attainment of the objective which they pursue; and they must not go beyond what is necessary in order to attain it'.

freedoms—i.e. for the basic definitions of goods,[3] work (and workers),[4] establishment,[5] services,[6] and capital.[7] Furthermore, in Article 57 TFEU, the Treaty characterizes services as a residual freedom i.e. to be used only when the other Treaty freedoms have been ruled out. The Court has developed principles to distinguish between potentially applicable freedoms;[8] although it does seem to depart from that framework in some cases.[9] In other cases, it has indicated—in a convergence-enhancing spirit—that whichever Treaty freedom is applied is not a material legal issue.[10] The extent to which the decision in *Keck* distorts an otherwise unified application of the principle of market access across the Treaty freedoms, discussed in Chapter 7, is a pivotal example of the counter-tension of case law divergence.[11]

[3] Case 7/68 *Commission v Italy (Art Treasures)* [1968] ECR 424 at 428: 'products which can be valued in money and which are capable, as such, of forming the subject of commercial transactions'.

[4] Case 66/85 *Lawrie-Blum v Land Baden-Württemberg* [1986] ECR 1741, para. 17: '[t]he essential feature of an employment relationship . . . is that for a certain period of time a person performs services for and under the direction of another person in return for which he receives remuneration'. Work involves 'the pursuit of effective and genuine activities, to the exclusion of activities on such a small scale as to be regarded as purely marginal and ancillary' (Case 53/81 *Levin v Staatssecretaris van Justitie* [1982] ECR 1035, para. 17).

[5] Case C-221/89 *R v Secretary of State for Transport* ex parte *Factortame Ltd and others* [1991] ECR I-3905, para. 20: establishment 'involves the actual pursuit of an economic activity through a fixed establishment in another Member State for an indefinite period'.

[6] Article 57 TFEU provides a basic outline of services that fall within the scope of EU law; in Joined Cases 286/82 and 26/83 *Luisi and Carbone v Ministero del Tesoro* [1984] ECR 377, the Court confirmed that 'the freedom to provide services includes the freedom, *for the recipients of services*, to go to another Member State in order to receive a service there, without being obstructed by restrictions' (para. 16, emphasis added).

[7] The Court has not provided a uniformly applied definition of capital in the same way; instead, it has addressed what the concept does and does not cover across several judgments; see T Horsley, 'The concept of an obstacle to intra-EU capital movement in EU law' in N Nic Shuibhne and L Gormley (eds.), *From Single Market to Economic Union: Essays in Memory of John A Usher* (OUP, 2012) 155; and J Snell, 'Free movement of capital: Evolution as a non-linear process' in P Craig and G de Búrca (eds.), *The Evolution of EU Law*, 2nd edn (OUP, 2011) 547.

[8] E.g. in *Gebhard*, the Court provided guidance on how to distinguish establishment and services (see esp. paras 23–27). More generally, the Court focuses on which freedom 'prevails' and which is 'secondary' (e.g. Case C-20/03 *Criminal Proceedings against Burmanjer, van der Linden and De Jong* [2005] ECR I-4133, para. 34; and Case C-452/04 *Fidium Finanz AG v Bundesanstalt für Finanzdienstleistungsaufsicht* [2006] ECR I-9521, para. 34).

[9] For example, the Court has created hybrid citizen-worker rights that have a distinctive legal meaning; see e.g. the case law on access to benefits for job-seekers (Joined Cases C-22/08 and C-23/08 *Vatsouras and Koupatantze v Arbeitsgemeinschaft (ARGE) Nürnberg 900* [2009] ECR I-4585; Case C-138/02 *Collins v Secretary of State for Work and Pensions* [2004] ECR I-2703), discussed in Chapter 3.

[10] E.g. Case C-390/99 *Canal Satélite Digital* [2002] ECR I-607, para. 31: '[w]here a national measure restricts both the free movement of goods and the freedom to provide services, the Court will in principle examine it in relation to one only of those two fundamental freedoms where it is shown that, in the circumstances of the case, one of them is entirely secondary in relation to the other *and may be considered together with it*' (emphasis added). This phrasing is repeated in e.g. Case C-137/09 *Josemans v Burgemeester van Maastricht* [2010] ECR I-13019, para. 50.

[11] Joined Cases C-267/91 and C-268/91 *Criminal Proceedings against Keck and Mithouard* [1993] ECR I-6097. See S Weatherill, 'After *Keck*: Some thoughts on how to clarify the clarification' (1996) 33:5 CMLRev 885 at 891–4; and C Barnard, 'Fitting the remaining pieces into the goods and persons jigsaw?' (2001) 26:1 ELRev 35. The 2009 case law on rules affecting the use of goods, also discussed in Chapter 7, has been widely perceived as an important turning point in this context, bringing the scope

Academic work on free movement case law takes the concepts beyond the descriptive, however, by assessing both the fact and the *value* of convergence.[12] A critical line of scholarship focuses on the heightened convergence momentum generated by the status of EU citizenship in particular. The argument is that free movement rights should be infused by the rights associated with citizenship irrespective of the purpose of movement i.e. merging the legal value of citizenship with the exercise of economic activity. This is not convergence for its own sake, but 'the re-conceptualisation of the market freedoms as economic rights to which all Union citizens are entitled'.[13] Moreover, a blending of citizenship rights and market access in this way is supported by statements in the Court's case law[14] and, more extensively, by the Court's Advocates General.[15] Convergence-through-

of Article 34 TFEU more in line with case law on persons, services and establishment (see esp. Case C-110/05 *Commission v Italy (Trailers)* [2009] ECR I-519 and Case C-142/05 *Åklagaren v Mickelsson and Roos* [2009] ECR I-4273).

[12] E.g. A Tryfonidou, 'Further steps on the road to convergence among the market freedoms' (2010) 35:1 ELRev 36; C Barnard, *The Substantive Law of the EU: The Four Freedoms*, 3rd edn (OUP, 2010) 25; P Oliver, 'Of trailers and jet skis: Is the case law on Article 34 TFEU hurtling in a new direction?' (2009) 33 Fordham Int'l L.J. 1423 at 1425–7; S Enchelmaier, 'The ECJ's recent case law on the free movement of goods: Movement in all sorts of direction' (2007) 26 YEL 115 at 149–56; HD Jarass, 'A unified approach to the fundamental freedoms' in M Andenas and W-H Roth (eds.), *Services and Free Movement in EU Law* (OUP, 2001) 141; and M Poiares Maduro, 'Harmony and dissonance in free movement' in Andenas and Roth (eds.), 41.

[13] Tryfonidou, n12, 37; she continues: 'although the market freedoms continue to have as their sole aim the construction and maintenance of an internal market, when read in the light of Union citizenship they are also considered to be *fundamental rights in the economic sphere to which all Union citizens are entitled* by virtue of their holding the nationality of one of the Member States' (41, emphasis added).

[14] E.g. Case C-345/05 *Commission v Portugal* [2006] ECR I-10633, para. 15: '[t]he provisions of the [TFEU] on freedom of movement for persons are intended to facilitate the pursuit by [Union] citizens of occupational activities of all kinds throughout the [Union], and preclude measures which might place [Union] citizens at a disadvantage when they wish to pursue an economic activity in the territory of another Member State'. See also, Case C-464/02 *Commission v Denmark* [2005] ECR I-7929, para. 34 (and the case law cited there).

[15] E.g. AG Trstenjak in Case C-445/06 *Danske Slagterier v Bundesrepublik Deutschland* [2009] ECR I-2119, para. 83 of the Opinion: 'a precise examination must be undertaken as to whether infringement of those procedural rules also results in an infringement of *the individual right of citizens of the Union to market access established by Article [34 TFEU]*' (emphasis added); AG Bot in *Commission v Italy (Trailers)*, para. 83 of the Opinion: 'the view taken of restrictions on [the] various freedoms displays the common feature that it is based on a single criterion, that of access to the market. However, to adopt a different approach in the area of free movement of goods is not, in my view, consistent with the requirements inherent in the construction of a single European market *and the emergence of citizenship of the Union*' (emphasis added); AG Poiares Maduro in Joined Cases C-158/04 and C-159/04 *Alfa Vita Vassilopoulos AE and Carrefour Marinopoulos AE v Elliniko Dimosio and Nomarchiaki Aftodioikisi Ioanninon* [2006] ECR I-8135, paras 40 and 51 of the Opinion: 'it would be neither satisfactory nor true to the development of the case-law to reduce freedom of movement to a mere standard of promotion of trade between Member States. It is *important that the freedoms of movement fit into the broader framework of the objectives of the internal market and European citizenship*. At present, the freedoms of movement must be understood to be one of the essential elements of the "fundamental status of nationals of the Member States". They represent the cross-border dimension of the economic and social status conferred on European citizens. However, the protection of such a status requires going beyond guaranteeing that there will be no discrimination based on nationality. It means Member States taking into account the effect of the measures they adopt on the position of all European Union citizens wishing to assert their rights to freedom of movement . . . such a *harmonisation of the systems of free movement seems to me to be essential in the light of the requirements of genuine Union citizenship*. It

citizenship also puts a different constitutional slant on some of the criticisms of the Court's approach to free movement law summarized in Chapter 1, especially concerning the balance between EU and national regulatory competence on internal market issues.[16]

But neither shaping nor realizing 'citizen-market' rights is a straightforward objective. First, the Treaty itself constructs different rules for the different freedoms in some respects. For example, the nationality of an importer or exporter of goods is irrelevant, but holding the nationality of a Member State is a required threshold condition for coming within the scope of work, services, and establishment.[17] Second, in what ways should the rights of EU citizens differ under Article 34 TFEU? What added value—precisely—does citizenship actually bring to the context of commercial activity? And why is this a desirable development when measured against the objectives of the internal market—also constitutional norms—more generally? Third, and more fundamentally, people and products are simply different. Although proponents of convergence theory argue that the imprint of EU citizenship should be felt across all of the freedoms in all cross-border situations, the more convincing argument is that citizenship in fact exposes a legally relevant personal/trade dichotomy all the more sharply.[18]

The need to take different considerations into account in personal and trade contexts sits uneasily with the idea of convergence; but it does reflect an ambition that can be accommodated by coherence. Oliver supports a similar position by arguing that we need to strike a balance between arbitrary divergence, bearing in mind the underlying goal of market integration that spans all of the free movement provisions, and giving proper attention to 'certain differences between the freedoms [that] are inherent in life and in the treaty... [N]atural persons are not mere economic units and must be treated with dignity and proper regard for their families and feelings'.[19] There is also a problem of cause-and-effect. For example, analysing the 2009 case law on the use of goods, Tryfonidou posits the Court's

would be desirable for the same system to be applied to all the citizens of the Union wishing to use their freedom of movement or freedom to move services, goods or capital as well as their freedom to reside or to set up the seat of their activities in the Community' (emphasis added).

[16] See e.g. E Spaventa, 'Leaving *Keck* behind? The free movement of goods after the rulings in *Commission v Italy* and *Mickelsson and Roos*' (2009) 35:6 ELRev 914 at 926: 'the free movement of goods provisions, *much as is happening with the citizenship and free movement of persons provisions*, become also a tool to impose a Community view of good governance, so that the way in which legislation is adopted or implemented, the finer details, will become increasingly important in determining the compatibility of national rules of the Treaty... This might not be a bad thing, leading as it can to increased economic efficiency; and yet it is also problematic, in that it further directs (and constrains) the discretion of the national regulator' (emphasis added).

[17] Confirmed in e.g. Case C-290/04 *FKP Scorpio Konzertproduktionen GmbH v Finanzamt Hamburg-Eimsbüttel* [2006] ECR I-9461, paras 62–68.

[18] See e.g. J Snell, 'And then there were two: Products and citizens in Community law' in T Tridimas and P Nebbia (eds.), *European Union Law for the Twenty-First Century: Volume II* (Hart Publishing, 2004) 49; E Spaventa, 'Seeing the wood despite the trees? On the scope of Union citizenship and its constitutional effects' (2008) 45:1 CMLRev 13 and 'From *Gebhard* to *Carpenter*: Towards a (non-)economic European constitution' (2004) 41:3 CMLRev 743; and RCA White, 'Free movement, equal treatment, and citizenship of the Union' (2005) 54 ICLQ 885.

[19] Oliver, n12, 1426.

market access approach as 'fuelled by the fact that the logic of applying a different, more restrictive, test when delimiting the scope of [Article 34] does not seem to wash in a Citizens' Europe where . . . internal market freedoms are viewed as part of the package of rights that are bestowed on the Union citizen'.[20] But this reasoning becomes problematic when the consequence is a general 'right to do business everywhere in the Union'[21]—a deeply contested position that reflects enduring controversies about the extent to which the Treaty supports, beyond the liberalization of intra-State trade, a deregulatory agenda grounded ultimately in the 'unhindered pursuit of commerce'.[22]

There is an obvious substantive overlap when case law is pushed through either a convergence or coherence filter. The fact of case law convergence across the different Treaty freedoms creates an empirical waterline above which judgments that do not fit within the dominant approach become easily identifiable. But by focusing on coherence rather than convergence, this books seeks, first, to induce a more instrumental appreciation of the Court's *own* responsibilities in resolving contested questions, for which neither 'neutral' convergence nor convergence-through-citizenship provides a sufficient basis on its own. Second, as argued in Chapter 1, that responsibility generates distinct obligations around the articulation of reasoning and appropriate engagement with existing case law authority. Finally, it is important to remember that the convergence debate focuses on harmony *across* the freedoms only; the broader test of coherence also catches fragmentation *within* them.[23]

(b) The meaning—and limits—of coherence and fragmentation

Analysis of free movement law tends not to be *framed* around concerns about coherence (or fragmentation)[24]—although there are numerous brief or passing references to case law coherence as a positive outcome or objective. In EU legal scholarship, the concepts tend to be drawn from more substantial work on the evolution of European private law,[25] on the enhanced cooperation frame-

[20] Tryfonidou, n12, 49.

[21] Tryfonidou, n12, 46 (also expressed as e.g. 'a general right for Union citizens to pursue an economic activity in a cross-border context' at 41).

[22] AG Tesauro in Case C-292/92 *Hünermund and others v Landesapothekerkammer Baden-Württemberg* [1993] ECR I-6787, para. 1 of the Opinion.

[23] See e.g. AG Mengozzi in Case C-211/08 *Commission v Spain (Hospital Care)* [2010] ECR I-5267, paras 80–89 of the Opinion, adopting a different approach to potential/hypothetical restrictions on services for receipt and provision respectively; or the differential analysis of *de minimis* within the free movement of goods, for Articles 34 and 110 TFEU, by AG Jacobs in Case C-383/01 *De Danske Bilimportører v Skatteministeriet, Told- og Skattestyrelsen* [2003] ECR I-6065, paras 55–62 of the Opinion. Other examples of fragmentation within the freedoms will be discussed where relevant in subsequent chapters.

[24] An important exception is L Woods, 'Consistency in the chambers of the ECJ: A case study on the free movement of goods' (2012) 31:3 *Civil Justice Quarterly* 340; in a different context, see also G Mathisen, 'Consistency and coherence as conditions for justification of Member State measures restricting free movement' (2010) 47:4 CMLRev 1021.

[25] E.g. S Santier, 'The interpretation of Directives to suit commercial needs: A further threat to coherence' (2012) 2 JBL 128; JM Smits, 'The complexity of transnational law: Coherence and

work,[26] and on structural or procedural aspects of EU judicial protection.[27] Neither do the terms surface regularly in judgments of the Court or in the views of its Advocates General. There are sporadic practical or factual references to fragmentation of the common market or the common agricultural market, or fragmentation of jurisdiction over EU legal disputes.[28] But there are hardly any references to fragmentation in the context of related discussions on e.g. the principle of legal certainty.[29]

By contrast, the diametric of coherence and fragmentation is a dominant theme in discourse on the framework of public international law. The main debate there considers the need to develop and assess tools that facilitate coherence, in order to avoid the fragmentation and, ultimately, the breakdown of the international legal order. Its objectives are framed largely by the final report of a 2006 Study Group convened by the ILC.[30] The international legal order is a multilevel cosmos of rules and institutions. Achieving workable coherence across essentially parallel constellations of authoritative rule-making, which are not immune to a degree of institutional law-making competition, is the challenge at the heart of the 2006 Report. States are the primary actors in the international legal order. But they frequently operate through distinct, interest-shaped regimes—each with its own institutional framework governing the making, interpreting, and enforcing of specialized law within that regime. Whilst having different areas of operation, the subject matter

fragmentation of private law' (2010) 14:3 EJCL (online journal); and H Eidenmuller et al, 'The common frame of reference for European private law: Policy choices and codification problems' (2008) 28:4 OJLS 659.

[26] E.g. M Lamping, 'Enhanced cooperation: A proper approach to market integration in the field of unitary patent protection?' (2011) 42:8 IIC 879; and S Peers, 'Divorce, European style: The first authorization of enhanced cooperation' (2010) 6:3 ECL Review 339.

[27] E.g. M Dani, 'Intersectional litigation and the structuring of a European interpretive community' (2011) 9:3/4 IJCL 714; 'S Prechal and B van Roermund (eds.), *The Coherence of EU Law: The Search for Unity in Divergent Concepts* (OUP, 2008); AM Arnull, 'Me and my shadow: The European Court of Justice and the disintegration of EU law' (2008) 31 Fordham Int'l L.J. 1174; and J Komárek, 'Federal elements in the Community judicial system: Building coherence in the Community legal order' (2005) 42:1 CMLRev 9.

[28] E.g. AG Cruz Villalón in Joined Cases C-509/09 and C-161/10 *eDate Advertising GmbH v X; Martinez and Martinez v MGN Limited*, judgment of 25 October 2011, para. 51 of the Opinion ('[t]he excessive fragmentation of jurisdictions and, possibly, of applicable laws, is difficult to reconcile with the sound administration of justice').

[29] Limited exceptions include AG Stix-Hackl in Case C-443/03 *Leffler v Berlin Chemie AG* [2005] ECR I-9611, para. 62 of the Opinion ('[t]his objective alone requires approximation as far as possible of the legal consequences of rights arising out of the Regulation, since divergent interpretation of the legal consequences would lead to unacceptable legal uncertainty and fragmentation in the area of civil procedure in particular, which is sensitive in terms of fundamental rights'); and AG Reischl in Joined Cases 66, 127 and 128/79 *Amministrazione delle Finanze v Salumi* [1980] ECR 1237 at 1270 ('[i]f the interpretation given by the Court of Justice were not to be applied to factual situations occurring prior to the delivery of the judgment, then . . . that would amount to depriving a provision of any effect, or of giving it another meaning, as regards the past and thus to the fragmentation of Community law in terms of time, and so to a failure to observe the precept of legal certainty').

[30] Report of the Study Group of the International Law Commission, *Fragmentation of International Law: Difficulties arising from the Diversification and Expansion of International Law*, finalized by M Koskenniemi, UN General Assembly International Law Commission, A/CN.4/L.682, 13 April 2006.

being regulated by different regimes nonetheless overlaps and the rules created by them will intersect. But international law does not have a clearly defined understanding of relative determinative competence: specifically, there is no established hierarchy that cuts through questions of regime overlap in all relevant situations.

The fragmentation generated by this complexity can be understood in broadly two ways. First, different rules from different sources or different regimes can apply to the same situation, producing a classic conflict of laws. As a working definition, the ILC Report characterizes conflict as 'a situation where two rules or principles suggest different ways of dealing with a problem'.[31] The idea of conflict can be understood as potentially referring to the subjects of legal rules and/or their substantive content. Conflict can stem from the relationship between two or more treaties, engaging the Vienna Convention on the Law of Treaties. But it can also arise because of a conflict between customary and treaty law, a much more complex scenario in terms of resolving questions of competence and hierarchy. The second form of fragmentation is regime-oriented i.e. it results from the fact that a single rule can fall to be interpreted or applied by different dispute-settlement bodies.

The ILC Report asserted an intensification of both legal and regime fragmentation, driven by the splintering of specialized legal systems away from so-called 'general' international law. The phenomenon of fragmentation persists because there is no centripetal court or conflict norm in the structure of international law (one of its key distinguishing features compared to EU law). It has occurred primarily through the emergence of 'technically specialized cooperation networks with a global scope' and is underpinned by a more general 'fragmentation of the international social world'.[32] In this way, the ILC Report sites the international law fragmentation debate in broader socio-political trends, from which States are not immune either. In other words, the ILC suggests that the issue of fragmentation is not solely a concern for international or transnational legal systems.[33]

The Report stresses that the counter-value of coherence is an ordering principle that has strong normative roots, but it also cautions that coherence is not a sufficient end in itself:

> Coherence is valued positively owing to the connection it has with predictability and legal security. Moreover, only a coherent legal system treats legal subjects *equally*. Coherence is, however, a formal and abstract virtue. For a legal system that is regarded in some respects as unjust or unworkable, no added value is brought by the fact of its being coherently so.[34]

[31] ILC Report, n30, para. 25.

[32] ILC Report, n30, paras 481 and 8, the latter citing trade law, human rights law, and also 'European law' as examples. Paragraph 8 continues: 'The problem, as lawyers have seen it, is that such specialized law-making and institution-building tends to take place with relative ignorance of legislative and institutional activities in the adjoining fields and of the general principles and practices of international law. The result is conflicts between rules or rule-systems, deviating institutional practices and, possibly, the loss of an overall perspective on the law'.

[33] ILC Report, n30, para. 493, where the ILC observes that even national constitutional systems are being undermined by 'the deepening complexity of late modern societies, tolerance and encouragement of conflicting traditions and social objectives within national societies, and the needs of technical specialization'.

[34] ILC Report, n30, para. 491 (emphasis added).

This approach mirrors the gradated, systemic understanding of coherence sketched in Chapter 1, on the basis of constitutional responsibilities that should also reflect the values of fairness and integrity—in other words, going beyond a call for neatness for the sake of neatness. As the ILC suggests, '[m]uch legal interpretation is geared to linking an unclear rule to a purpose and thus, *by showing its position within some system*, to providing a justification for applying it in one way rather than in another'.[35]

Can the concepts of coherence and fragmentation as they relate to public international law be usefully applied to EU free movement law? In many fundamental respects, the international law paradigm does not translate easily across the divide. First, it was argued in Chapter 1 that there is sufficient functional acceptance of the primacy of EU law—and also of the authority of the Court of Justice to interpret EU law, including exclusive authority to evaluate the validity of EU legislative measures—to enable the EU legal order to operate as a centralized and ordered constitutional legal system.[36] Notwithstanding this critical difference, however, the broad understanding of fragmentation used in international law is clearly apparent in free movement case law too i.e. either different rules seem to apply to the same situation, or the 'same' rule seems to be interpreted or applied in different ways for no obvious reason. Second, the multiplicity of legal regimes and dispute-settlement institutions as well as profoundly competing views on legal hierarchy that shape the international domain raise distinct complexities and challenges: but that just makes instances of fragmentation all the more difficult to rationalize or excuse within the comparatively singular, constitutionalized structure of the EU legal order. In other words, fragmentation of international law is construed as a problem that is somehow *understandable* (but that should nonetheless be addressed).[37] Again, however, there is no comparable *systemic* explanation of fragmentation that could justify problematic instances of breakdown in Court of Justice case law—it has a sufficiently final say on the interpretation of free movement law and does not share that jurisdiction with any other dispute-settlement regime.

Third, in the international legal system, bearing in mind the absence of a 'Court of Justice' in comparable institutional and constitutional terms, the obligation to ensure legal coherence is considered to attach primarily to the Treaty-making realm of politics and diplomacy.[38] In the EU system, the Member States have delegated the exercise of this obligation to the Court: they retain only the delimiting and, realistically, exceptional power to alter the outer boundaries of free movement law by amending the EU Treaties (or drafting completely new ones, such as the Treaty

[35] ILC Report, n30, para. 34 (emphasis added).

[36] See J Dickson, 'Towards a theory of European Union legal systems' in J Dickson and P Eleftheriadis (eds.), *Philosophical Foundations of EU Law* (OUP, 2012) 25. Perhaps the only primacy-comparable example in international law is the norm hierarchy established by the core of *jus cogens*: see ILC Report, n30, paras 19 and 361–379.

[37] The ILC notes that scholars and practitioners of international law are divided on whether fragmentation is a normative as well as technical problem: ILC Report, n30, para. 9.

[38] ILC Report, n30, esp. paras 37–39.

on Stability, Coordination and Governance[39]). This act of delegation, effected formally through Article 19 TEU, recalls the basic need for some acknowledged hierarchy of legal sources discussed in Chapter 1—as the ILC observed, 'when a party raises a point about conflict and about the precedence of one obligation over another, then a stand must be taken'.[40] The Court frequently takes these stands in the EU legal order: because it is *asked* as well as empowered to do so.

Finally, can any lessons be drawn about how fragmentation should be tackled? Many scholars and practitioners consider that the fragmentation of international law is overstated. The main arguments are that international courts do tend to follow each other's decisions in practice; there is no extensive evidence of conflicting case law; decisions of the International Court of Justice are almost always followed; most states comply with the rules most of the time—after all, they negotiated and agreed to them; and the real problem is not the enforcement of existing rules but getting states to sign up to new treaties or agree on new rules of customary law.[41] The ILC Report also acknowledges what it describes as 'natural' differences in the system (e.g. that 'international law was always relatively "fragmented" due to the diversity of national legal systems that participated in it'[42]). At the level of problem solving even for situations considered as amounting to fragmentation-proper, therefore, the ILC took a distinctly pragmatic approach:

> On the one hand, fragmentation does create the danger of conflicting and incompatible rules, principles, rule-systems and institutional practices. On the other hand, it reflects the rapid expansion of international legal activity into various new fields and the diversification of its objects and techniques. The title [of the Report] seems to suggest that although there are 'problems', they are neither altogether new nor of such nature that they could not be dealt with through techniques international lawyers have used to deal with the normative conflicts that may have arisen in the past.[43]

[39] This Treaty was signed on 2 March 2012 by all of the Member States except the Czech Republic and the UK; the text of the Treaty is available at <http://european-council.europa.eu/media/639235/st00tscg26_en12.pdf>.

[40] ILC Report, n30, para. 43.

[41] See e.g. B Simma 'Universality of international law from the perspective of a practitioner' (2009) 20:2 EJIL 265 at 276 onwards.

[42] ILC Report, n30, para. 16. Former ICJ Judge Simma expresses it more colourfully: '[Fragmentation's] connotations are clearly negative: something is splitting up, falling apart, or worse: bombs or ammunition can be designed to fragment and thus become even more destructive' (Simma, n41, 270). Nevertheless, he acknowledges the Report as being 'of immense value as a piece of work which attempts to assemble the totality of international law's devices available to counter the negative aspects of fragmentation' (at 272).

[43] ILC Report, n30, para. 14. The 'tool box' of solutions proposed by the ILC has been subject to considerable debate, engaging prominent judicial actors as well as academics. For example, two former ICJ Presidents have published diverging views on the general issues underpinning the debate. In 1995, Gilbert Guillaume cautioned against allowing the disunity of international law to intensify further ('The future of international judicial institutions' (1995) 44 ICLQ 848 at 861–2). However, after the publication of the ILC Report, Rosalyn Higgins was 'sceptical' that the solutions proposed could work and suggested more pragmatically that '[w]e judges are going to have to learn how to live in this new, complex world, and to regard it as an opportunity rather than a problem. We must read each other's judgments. We must have respect for each other's judicial work. We must try to preserve unity among us unless context really prevents this' ('A Babel of judicial voices? Ruminations from the bench' (2006)

Arguments detailed in Section 3 will similarly emphasize 'techniques' that can be applied to ensure a more coherent body of case law. Primarily, and echoing the arguments introduced in Chapter 1, 'it is *the task of reasoning* to make the unfamiliar familiar by *integrating* it into received patterns of thought or by *amending* those patterns so that the new phenomenon can be accommodated'.[44] The ILC Report also provides a useful, no-frills definition of legal reasoning: 'the pragmatic process through which lawyers go about interpreting and applying formal law'.[45] Reflecting the pragmatic understanding of case law fragmentation developed by the ILC, it is not the purpose of this book to uncover or list every anomaly in EU free movement case law, even if it was possible to do that anyway.[46] It is important not to overinflate the meaning or significance of each interpretative twist and turn in every judgment that the Court delivers. Instead, we must step back and ascertain the general health of the case law in more systemic terms. The specific criteria against which that assessment will be made in subsequent chapters will now be presented.

3. Key drivers of fragmentation in EU free movement case law

Drawing from the case law and from how academic commentary responds to it, it was suggested in Chapter 1 that there are four particularly strong causes or drivers of free movement case law breakdown at present: (1) a proliferation of potentially applicable principles and tests; (2) the unsettled (constitutional) purposes of the internal market and of free movement; (3) accommodating the protection of fundamental rights; and (4) practical aspects of the judicial function per se, with emphasis on the structure of the Court and the organization of its decision-making processes. The issues raised by each of these concerns will now be explained to frame the examples considered in more detail in subsequent chapters—which will, in turn, go on to illustrate the *consequences* as well as the causes of case law fragmentation.

(a) Proliferation

The Treaty provisions on free movement are not intended to establish a detailed rulebook, and so it is not surprising that the Court has had to develop framework principles—a series of underpinning concepts and tests—to apply and interpret them. Where a unified approach to the definition or understanding of these

55 ICLQ 791 at 804). See also, M Koskenniemi, 'The fate of public international law: Between technique and politics' (2007) 70:1 MLR 1.

[44] ILC Report, n30, para. 20 (emphasis added).

[45] ILC Report, n30, para. 27.

[46] E.g. Snell has identified numerous discrepancies in the case law on service provision alone: J Snell, 'The legitimacy of free movement case law: process and substance' in M Adams, J Meeusen, G Straetmans, and H de Waele (eds.), *Judging Europe's Judges: The Legitimacy of the Case Law of the European Court of Justice Examined* (Hart Publishing, forthcoming 2013).

principles *can* be used, it should be. But, as discussed in Section 2 in relation to the idea of case law convergence, fragmentation is not the same thing as difference. The proliferation of applicable concepts, principles, and tests is not, in other words, *inherently* damaging; but in the context of free movement law, the phenomenon will be shown to be problematic in four key ways: (1) where it leads to unresolved conceptual *ambiguity*;[47] (2) because of the 'heavy constitutional weight'[48] conferred on *adjectives*; (3) through the use of different *phrases or formulas* without making it clear whether they are intended to express the same or different principles or tests; and (4) when it results in conceptual *spillage* i.e. where the purposes or concerns underlying different principles or tests bleed into each other.[49]

It is important to site this problem within the themes feeding into a realistic conception of coherence, as outlined in Chapter 1 and in Section 2 of this chapter—e.g. balancing reasonable expectations of courts against the need for judges to rationalize their decisions properly; or, specifically for the Court of Justice, aiming to provide structural rather than outcome-prescriptive guidance for national courts. Viewing the four proliferation problems outlined above in that light rightly steers us away from fixating on every single or literal difference of expression that can be detected in the Court's case law.[50] The specific challenges generated by a translation environment that processes 24 languages will not be focused on either.[51] Malleable concepts can and do work: moreover, they *have* to work for case law that comes from a transnational and/or constitutional judicial institution, given the volume of courts (and other bodies or actors) that have to apply its decisions afterwards in an indeterminate range of circumstances. But playing about with the expression of critical principles and concepts takes a starting point of uncertainty—a 'natural' starting point, to draw from the ILC Report—and adds *avoidable* layers of further uncertainty on top of it. The resulting case law ends up being confusing and/or illogical, making it harder for the constitutional subjects—especially in the present context, for national courts—to extract and

[47] E.g. this idea is well captured in the title of J Snell, 'The notion of market access: A concept or a slogan?' (2010) 47:2 CMLRev 437.

[48] Weatherill, n1.

[49] E.g. the different concerns addressed by the tests of remoteness and *de minimis* are sometimes merged, as discussed in Chapter 5.

[50] At the level of checking the formal drafting, six lawyers at the Court (who are part of the chambers of the President of the Court and have the employment status of *référendaires*) act as *lecteurs d'arrêts* i.e. ensuring that the Court's judgments are presented (e.g. in their use of citations) and drafted in a uniform manner.

[51] See e.g. K McAuliffe, 'Language and law in the European Union: The multilingual jurisprudence of the ECJ' in L Solan and P Tiersma (eds.), *The Oxford Handbook of Language and Law* (OUP, 2012) 200 and 'Hybrid texts and uniform law? The multilingual case law of the Court of Justice of the European Union' (2011) 24:1 *International Journal for the Semiotics of Law* 97; and L Mulders, 'Translation at the European Court of Justice' in Prechal and van Roermund (eds.), n27, 45. It is useful to remember that the challenges inherent in the Court's multilingual environment go beyond literal translation concerns (for example, the need for one working language (French) may 'skew discussion at an individual level'); and the fact that 'language and reasoning are interconnected so that, in the legal context, differences may be substantive, or analytical in terms of approach to reasoning and use of authority' (Woods, n24, 346–7).

apply its legal essence, and leading eventually to accusations of arbitrary judicial decision-making.

It matters little whether this practice comes down to basic human carelessness or can be explained by translation or structural issues e.g. the fact that more than one chamber of the Court is active simultaneously on the same legal question, as discussed further in Section 3(d). Different approaches to the expression of concepts gain traction. They are picked up and re-used in subsequent judgments. The fact that substantive considerations do not necessarily govern how previous authorities are cited compounds the risk:[52] this is how different but equally valid streams of case law develop on the same questions in parallel with no citation crossover; also enabling selective citation of one strand only in some of the case law thereafter. In general, it will be shown in the chapters that follow that there is (and where there is) ample scope for refining the definition, volume, and application of the principles and tests that operate to pin down the scope of free movement law.

(b) The multiple—and unsettled—objectives of the internal market

We saw in Chapter 1 that the centrality of the internal market to both historic and prospective purposes of the European Union is consistently asserted. But what kind of market is the Union trying to establish, and why? Article 26(2) TFEU visualizes the internal market very simply as 'an area without frontiers in which the free movement of goods, persons, services and capital is ensured in accordance with the provisions of the Treaties' and, according to Article 4(2), competence to achieve this objective is shared between the EU and the Member States. Additionally, the 'proper functioning of the internal market' drives the complementary rules of EU competition law; and a whole series of Treaty provisions sets that threshold as a benchmark against which other conduct should be measured or pursued.[53]

Writing about case law on the free movement of goods but with much broader resonance, Davies argues as follows:

> The rules and principles stated by Court are far better understood as embodying a series of compromises, perceptions of fact, and pragmatic approximations which aim to deal with the problems of evidence, workload, and legal clarity, rather than as an ongoing monologue about market philosophy. Looking in the case law for a coherent framework addressing these classical judicial concerns is . . . quite fruitful. Looking in the case law for clear or consistent guidance about the conceptual foundations of economic integration is, as internal market lawyers know, a hopeless cause.[54]

[52] This point was outlined in Chapter 1, drawing from the empirical work on the free movement of goods undertaken by Woods, n24.

[53] Article 81(2) TFEU (judicial cooperation in civil matters); Article 113 TFEU (indirect taxation); Articles 114 and 115 TFEU (approximation of national laws); and Article 309 TFEU (the contribution of the European Investment Bank). Related obligations include e.g. the condition that any action taken under the enhanced cooperation procedure 'shall not undermine the internal market' (Article 326 TFEU).

[54] G Davies, 'The Court's jurisprudence on free movement of goods: Pragmatic presumptions, not philosophical principles' (2012) 2 *European Journal of Consumer Law* 25 at 27.

He later emphasizes the centrality of 'the goal of eliminating unjustified measures with a protectionist effect'.[55] That is itself a 'basic market philosophy' and whether it rationalizes the patterns shaping free movement case law will be considered in Chapter 7 in particular. But following the template of responsibility established in Chapter 1, the case law should not be the starting point for trying to find 'the conceptual foundations of economic integration'—instead, the primary signals must come from the constitution i.e. the Treaties.

The Preamble to the TEU provides some clues about the kind of market that the Union should aim to establish. It recalls the 'attachment' of the Member States to 'principles of liberty, democracy and respect for human rights and fundamental freedoms and of the rule of law' (including, in the next recital, fundamental social rights). It then outlines: a 'desire' to 'deepen solidarity' between their peoples; a 'resolution' to 'achieve the strengthening and the convergence of their economies'; and a determination to 'promote economic and social progress for their peoples ... and to implement policies ensuring that advances in economic integration are accompanied by parallel progress in other fields'. Similar threads appear in the Preamble to the TFEU.

Article 3(3) TEU formally confirms the establishment of an internal market as a Union objective, but continues as follows:

> [The Union] shall work for the sustainable development of Europe based on balanced economic growth and price stability, a highly competitive social market economy, aiming at full employment and social progress, and a high level of protection and improvement of the quality of the environment. It shall promote scientific and technological advance. It shall combat social exclusion and discrimination, and shall promote social justice and protection, equality between women and men, solidarity between generations and protection of the rights of the child. It shall promote economic, social and territorial cohesion, and solidarity among Member States. It shall respect its rich cultural and linguistic diversity, and shall ensure that Europe's cultural heritage is safeguarded and enhanced.[56]

That is quite a task list. And the EU internal market sounds like a nice place. But, crucially, its establishment in such an idealized and polygonal way comes without a more specific set of instructions for those tasked with its legal interpretation. What happens when, for example, the pursuit of technological advance clashes with safeguarding cultural diversity? How is the Court to decide where the balance between those values should lie?

The conclusiveness of a *shared* judge-led vision of the internal market was dismissed in Chapter 1. This impression is confirmed by reflecting on the different views expressed by Advocates General. For example, AG Tizzano in *CaixaBank*, discussing national measures that 'reduce the economic attractiveness' of a particular

[55] Davies, n54, 31.

[56] See also, Article 13 TFEU: '[i]n formulating and implementing the Union's ... internal market ... the Union and the Member States shall, since animals are sentient beings, pay full regard to the welfare requirements of animals, while respecting the legislative or administrative provisions and customs of the Member States relating in particular to religious rites, cultural traditions and regional heritage'.

activity, suggested that such measures should *not* come within the scope of freedom of establishment, since to decide otherwise would:

permit economic operators—both national and foreign—to *abuse* [Article 49 TFEU] to oppose any national measure that, *solely because it regulated the conditions for pursuing an economic activity*, could in the final analysis narrow profit margins and hence reduce the attractiveness of pursuing that particular economic activity. However, that would be *tantamount to bending the Treaty to a purpose for which it was not intended*: that is to say, not in order to create an internal market in which conditions are similar to those of a single market and where operators can move freely, but in order *to establish a market without rules*. Or rather, a market in which rules are prohibited as a matter of principle, except for those necessary and proportionate to meeting imperative requirements in the public interest.[57]

The Advocate General argued that Article 49 should only preclude national measures if they are discriminatory or they directly affect market access for economic operators from other Member States; and he left that determination to the national court. But the Court was more definitive, finding unequivocally that a restriction *did* exist and rejecting the justification arguments submitted. The importance of the substantive questions raised by the case will be returned to in Chapter 7; but the different outcomes supported by AG Tizzano and the Court demonstrate for now the potential for subjectivity inherent in attempts to elucidate the objectives and regulatory end-goals of the market.[58] Reflecting the limitations of case-based research outlined in Chapter 1, it is also important to remember that different market objectives are more dominant at different points in time. Spaventa finds a positive message in shifting perspectives on market objectives, describing the case law as 'a process of continuous self-reflection, and of continuous dialogue between regulators, traders and the Court'.[59] This conveys flexibility as an interpretative virtue, which can perhaps be balanced with the more negative potential for arbitrary subjectivity.

But the need to identify *overriding* market norms is tied to the objective of case law coherence in certain respects, especially in the search for more concrete answers to a fundamental question flagged in Chapter 1: coherent according to *what*? A conception of the nature and purpose of the internal market necessarily shapes the legal tests applied to deliver it. For example, if the relative merits of discrimination and market access are placed at the heart of the debate on the 'right' test to

[57] AG Tizzano in Case C-442/02 *CaixaBank France v Ministère de l'Économie, des Finances et de l'Industrie* [2004] ECR I-8961, paras 62–63 of the Opinion (emphasis added).

[58] This critique is often levelled at the EU in broader terms too; see AT Williams, 'Taking values seriously: Towards a philosophy of EU law' (2009) 29:3 OJLS 549; on the internal market, he comments that '[a]lthough we can deconstruct a degree of evolved appreciations of value that are prudential (in the sense that some valuable end—perhaps a single market—is being pursued for the good of the constituents of the EU) . . . these are generally incoherent and *so marked by contingency that they lack any substantive grounding*' (561, emphasis added).

[59] Spaventa, n16, 925; see similarly, E Spaventa, 'The outer limits of the Treaty free movement provisions: Some reflections on the significance of *Keck*, remoteness and *Deliège*' in C Barnard and O Odudu (eds.), *The Outer Limits of European Union Law* (Hart Publishing, 2008) 245 at 270: 'the rationale underpinning the interpretation of the free movement provisions is fluid: it evolves as our perception of the problems and aims of the internal market changes with time'.

apply to the scope of free movement law, then whether market regulation is about achieving more than equality or properly stops at the point of providing a shield against protectionism is the dominant question.[60] If the boundary between EU and Member State competence to regulate the market is the primary concern, then debates about the balance between market rule-uniformity and market rule-diversity become more prevalent.[61] Weatherill has remarked on the absence of 'a hard-edged superstructure of proper ends and standards' in the Treaty as a factor that tempers many of the Court's decisions from the perspective of legitimacy.[62] But he also acknowledges that the objectives shaping the EU internal market are profoundly 'imprecise' and that fact makes legal adjudication all the harder. In that light, Article 3(3) TEU suggests more questions than answers. Is the establishment of the internal market the 'first' objective there or of the same legal weight as the other values listed? Do the objectives included have a particularly special role in free movement law, or could the same be said of e.g. the requirement that the Union must respect national identities in Article 4(2) TEU?[63] Should these explicit policy areas be reflected in some way when States seek to justify restrictions on free movement rights, meaning that *other* arguments based on public interest reasoning would carry less weight? Where does the primary law status now accorded to the Charter of Fundamental rights by Article 6(1) TEU fit in the picture? And what about the instructions in Article 2 TEU that '[t]he Union is founded on the values of respect for human dignity, freedom, democracy, equality, the rule of law and respect for human rights, including the rights of persons belonging to minorities'?

All of these questions affect how the Court interprets and applies free movement law, and they become especially acute at the justification stage. As outlined in Chapter 1, the method that the Court (still) applies does privilege free movement as the overriding objective, against which justification arguments on different grounds of public interest must then be measured or compete. The fact that free movement objectives are translated into distinct primary rights in subsequent Treaty provisions—unlike, for example, the objective of a high level of environmental protection—supports that approach. A more nuanced interpretation would posit the different values and objectives now expressed in Article 3(3) as at least equal to free movement rights—something that takes on a heightened edge when the value competing with free movement also holds the status of a fundamental right.[64] But

[60] The internal market can also be analysed from e.g. the perspective of applicable economic models. For an overview, see Barnard, n12, chapter 1; and J Snell, 'Varieties of capitalism and the limits of European economic integration' (2010–11) 13 CYELS 415.

[61] See e.g. S Weatherill, 'Maximum versus minimum harmonization: Choosing between unity and diversity in the search for the soul of the internal market' in Nic Shuibhne and Gormley (eds.), n7, 175; and T Horsley, 'Subsidiarity and the Court of Justice: Missing pieces in the subsidiarity jigsaw?' (2012) 50:2 JCMS 267.

[62] Weatherill, n1.

[63] See further, A von Bogdandy and S Schill, 'Overcoming absolute primacy: Respect for national identity under the Lisbon Treaty' (2011) 48:5 CMLRev 1417.

[64] See e.g. AG Trstenjak in Case C-271/08 *Commission v Germany* [2010] ECR I-7091, para. 81 of the Opinion ('In the case of a conflict between a fundamental right and a fundamental freedom, both legal positions must be presumed to have equal status. That general equality in status implies, first, that, in the interests of fundamental rights, fundamental freedoms may be restricted. However, second, it

'equal' legal status does not signal an obvious way forward when values collide. In *Kadi*, the Court attached importance to the fact that respect for liberty, democracy, and respect for human rights is enshrined in Article 6 TEU as a foundation of the Union.[65] To add further complexity, however, the Charter recognizes only some of the objectives in Article 3(3) as fundamental or human rights on their own terms.[66]

Recalling Spaventa's reminder to adjust our perspectives over time, the Lisbon Treaty is now shaping the resolution of internal market disputes. At one level, as Davies has argued, it might be thought that '[t]he big ideational framework of the market is a done deal'.[67] However, in the 2010 Monti Report, addressing 'tensions between market integration and social objectives', it was suggested that:

> These are *even more vividly exposed*, now that the Lisbon Treaty has introduced, even formally, the objective of achieving a 'highly competitive social market economy'. If the market and the social components do not find an appropriate reconciliation, something has to give in. Following the crisis, with the declining appetite for the market and the increasing concern about inequalities, it is by no means clear that it would be the market, i.e. the single market, to prevail.[68]

implies also that the exercise of fundamental freedoms may justify a restriction on fundamental rights'); AG Poiares Maduro in Case C-438/05 *International Transport Workers' Federation and Finnish Seamen's Union v Viking Line ABP and OÜ Viking Line Eesti* [2007] ECR I-10779, para. 23 of the Opinion ('[n]either the Treaty rules on freedom of movement, nor the right to associate and the right to strike are absolute. Moreover, nothing in the Treaty suggests that the Community's social policy objectives must always take precedence over the objective of having a properly functioning common market. On the contrary, the inclusion of both policy objectives in the Treaty signifies the aim of the Community to bring these policies together. Therefore, the fact that a restriction on freedom of movement arises out of the exercise of a fundamental right or of conduct falling within the ambit of the social policy provisions does not render the provisions on freedom of movement inapplicable'). Also capturing the intertwined nature of the single market and its flanking objectives, see the speech by the EU Commissioner for Employment, Social Affairs and Inclusion at the FPC-Commission-TUC conference, 'Single market, equal rights? UK perspectives on EU employment and social law', London, 10 February 2012, available at <http://europa.eu/rapid/press-release_SPEECH-12-89_en.htm?locale=fr>. Developing the points noted in Chapter 1 about the significance of the *stage* at which fundamental rights are considered in the free movement case law paradigm, see E Spaventa, 'Federalisation versus centralisation: Tensions in fundamental rights discourse in the EU' in M Dougan and Currie (eds.), *50 Years of the European Treaties: Looking Back and Thinking Forward* (Hart Publishing, 2009) 343.

[65] Joined Cases C-402/05 P and C-415/02 P *Kadi and Al Barakaat International Foundation v Council and Commission* [2008] ECR I-6351, para. 303. See now, post-Lisbon, Article 2 TEU.

[66] E.g. Article 37 of the Charter provides only that '[a] high level of environmental protection and the improvement of the quality of the environment must be integrated into the policies of the Union and ensured in accordance with the principle of sustainable development' in contrast to the clear *prohibition* of different forms of discrimination in Article 21. Addressing the legal distinction between 'rights' and 'principles' in the Charter, see AG Trstenjak in Joined Cases C-411/10 and C-493/10 *N. S. v Secretary of State for the Home Department; M. E. and others v Refugee Applications Commissioner and Minister for Justice, Equality and Law Reform*, judgment of 21 December 2011, paras 171–174 of the Opinion.

[67] Davies, n54, 27.

[68] M Monti, *A New Strategy for the Single Market: At the Service of Europe's Economy and Society*, (2010) 26 (emphasis added), available at <http://ec.europa.eu/bepa/pdf/monti_report_final_10_05_2010_en.pdf>. See also 33 and esp. 70 on the decisions in Case C-341/05 *Laval un Partneri Ltd v Svenska Byggnadsarbetareförbundet, Svenska Byggnadsarbetareförbundets avdelning 1, Byggettan, Svenska Elektrikerförbundet* [2007] ECR I-11767 and *Viking Line*: 'The ECJ rulings pre-date the entry into force of the Lisbon Treaty, which explicitly sets out the social market economy as an objective for the Union and makes the European Charter of Fundamental Rights legally binding at Treaty level.

Similarly, the European Parliament's Committee on Constitutional Affairs, in a report on the Lisbon Treaty returned to below, considered that there is now 'a greater emphasis on policies that visibly benefit citizens', citing many of the objectives listed in Article 3(3) TEU. In para. 3.3 of the Explanatory Statement attached to its Report, it was also noted that '[t]hese objectives thus make up a basic political programme which was the well-spring for the establishment of the Union'. But any discussion of *how* to choose between the multiplicities of relevant virtues through law is completely absent. Interestingly, although its central goals were prominently detached from market idiom, the Treaty establishing a Constitution for Europe had in fact re-emphasized the *fundamental* character of the market freedoms after the process of their demotion to 'first among equals in a whole series of other objectives'[69] at Maastricht—although the latter, multi-string approach was eventually retained as the conceptual template for what is now Article 3(3) TEU.[70] The Constitution would also have brought about an internal reshuffle of the Treaty provisions on free movement more generally with, for the first time, the rules on persons preceding those on goods and capital.[71]

Can legal implications be read into the fact that the Lisbon Treaty—the agreed deal that has shaped the internal market's structure most recently—did *not* reflect the Constitution's proposed approach? Chalmers' depiction of market objectives as 'first among equals' conveys a canny significance: it seems to capture something about *both* the way in which Article 3(3) was drafted (*equals*) but also the inherited practice of the Court in resolving free movement disputes (*first*). The Committee on Constitutional Affairs stressed that the Lisbon Treaty 'establishes in a clearer and more visible way the values, common to all Member States, on which the Union is founded, as well as the objectives of the Union and the principles governing its action and its relations with Member States'.[72] This understanding of Union values and objectives is less about pitching the Union/free movement against the Member

These elements should shape a new legal context, in which the issues and the concerns raised by the trade unions should hopefully find an adequate response' (emphasis added).

[69] D Chalmers, 'The single market: From prima donna to journeyman' in J Shaw and G More (eds.), *New Legal Dynamics of European Union* (Clarendon Press, 1995) 55 at 68.

[70] Article 2 of the original Treaty of Rome stated that '[t]he Community shall have as its task, by establishing a common market and progressively approximating the economic policies of Member States, to promote throughout the Community a harmonious development of economic activities, a continuous and balanced expansion, an increase in stability, an accelerated raising of the standard of living and closer relations between the States belonging to it'. Cf. the multiple tasks and activities outlined in Articles 2 and 3 EC, following the ratification of the Maastricht Treaty (1992 OJ C224/31). Article I-3(2) of the Treaty establishing a Constitution (2004 OJ C310/1) stated more simply that '2. The Union shall offer its citizens an area of freedom, security and justice without internal frontiers, and an internal market where competition is free and undistorted' while Article I-4(1) ('fundamental freedoms and non-discrimination') provided that '[t]he free movement of persons, services, goods and capital, and freedom of establishment shall be guaranteed within and by the Union, in accordance with the Constitution'.

[71] See Articles I-4 and III-130(2); and from Article III-133 onwards.

[72] EP Committee on Constitutional Affairs, 2008 Report on the Lisbon Treaty (A6-0013/2008), available at <www.europarl.europa.eu/sides/getDoc.do?type=REPORT&reference=A6-2008-0013&language=EN>, para. 4.

States/other values—rather, it signals a more structural shift in the locus of value-balancing to Union level per se. Similarly, AG Mengozzi has also argued that the changes effected by the Lisbon Treaty were intended to be structural as well as conceptual:

> *As a result of the entry into force of the Treaty of Lisbon*, when working conditions constitute an overriding reason relating to the public interest justifying a derogation from the freedom to provide services, *they must no longer be interpreted strictly*. In so far as the protection of workers is a matter which warrants protection under the Treaties themselves, *it is not a simple derogation* from a freedom, still less an unwritten exception inferred from case-law. To the extent that *the new primary law framework* provides for a mandatory high level of social protection, it authorises the Member States, for the purpose of safeguarding a certain level of social protection, to restrict a freedom, and to do so *without European Union law's regarding it as something exceptional* and, therefore, as warranting a strict interpretation.[73]

The Advocate General's interpretation of the impact of the Lisbon Treaty retains the *formal* shape of the Court's three-step method in free movement case law; but it changes profoundly the *emphasis* that should be attached to public interest arguments in the second and third stages when the relevant objectives are themselves recognized by the Treaties. Weatherill makes an important related point about the interrelationship between the scope of *scope* (restrictions) and the scope of justification:

> Defining the scope of the Treaty provisions on the internal market is clearly a logically distinct issue from determining whether rules that fall within their scope are justified. And yet the issues cannot be sensibly kept fully separate. The broader the scope of application, the more crucial the *receptivity* under EU law to justification, for once the matter is wrenched out of the autonomy of the national regulator, practices may be maintained only where EU law standards of justification are met.[74]

In Chapter 7, some evidence of this greater degree of 'receptivity' will be traced in recent case law where the Court effected an expansion in the scope of Article 34 TFEU to include national rules regulating the use of goods.

More generally, and as argued in Chapter 1, the ability of the Court to realize conceptual shifts in internal market priorities contributes to its own significant influence—and responsibilities—as a Union policymaker. In his classic thesis on the scope of adjudication, Fuller suggested that 'the laying down of rules that will make a market function properly is one for which adjudication is well suited… The court gets into difficulty, not when it lays down rules about contracting, but when it attempts to write contracts'.[75] Many of the issues on which the Court adjudicates are located at the margins of EU law; and some are not legal questions at all. Determining whether a particular policy choice justifies a free movement

[73] AG Mengozzi in *Commission v Spain (Hospital Care)*, para. 53 of the Opinion (emphasis added). See also, J Snell, 'Varieties of capitalism and the limits of European economic integration', available at <www.jus.uio.no/ifp/forskning/prosjekter/markedsstaten/arrangementer/2011/free-movement-oslo/speakers-papers/jukka-snell.pdf>, 13–17.

[74] Weatherill, n1 (emphasis added).

[75] LH Fuller, 'The forms and limits of adjudication' (1978) 92 *Harvard Law Review* 353 at 403–4.

restriction is not really law. These are value judgments. As Fuller captured it, '[i]n working out the implications of federalism or of a regime of exchange, a court is not an inert mirror reflecting current mores but an *active participant* in the enterprise of articulating the implications of shared purposes'.[76] The idea of the Court acting relatively meekly in the precinct of negative integration is a misnomer in this context. The Court frequently resolves substantive questions that involve the application of intuition or common sense more than legal analysis. But the problem with common sense is, of course, that it is not necessarily 'common'.

If anything, the Lisbon Treaty has complicated further the already unreadable constitutional code that frames the internal market as well as the relationship between the pursuit of free movement and other objectives. In subsequent chapters, attention will be drawn to debates about the different interests shaping the post-Lisbon *legal* conception of the market and its associated values as well as rights where relevant. It is also important to remember the potential for subjectivity as well as flexibility. Where instances of case law fragmentation are identified, questions will be raised about the extent to which the fundamentally unsettled character of the market's values and objectives might be a relevant factor—drawing insight from the Opinions of the Court's Advocates General to try to understand the different perspectives that we can only assume are competing for prevalence within judicial deliberations and under the surface of particularly enigmatic judgment texts.

(c) Realizing the protection of fundamental rights

It may seem odd to characterize the protection of fundamental rights as a driver of case law fragmentation, especially now that the Charter of Fundamental Rights has the same binding legal effect as the EU Treaties.[77] As seen above, this is a critical factor in the apparent conceptual shift towards greater legal recognition for values and interests traditionally positioned 'after' free movement objectives. The protection of fundamental rights within the framework of free movement law raises a number of discrete questions too. As noted in Chapter 1, for example, should fundamental rights be treated just like any other justification arguments; or should they trigger a more consciously distinctive 'margin of appreciation' analysis?[78] How do free movement rights and fundamental rights relate to each other at the conceptual level? In *Bosman*, AG Lenz asserted that the rights conferred on trans-frontier workers by the Treaty are *themselves* fundamental rights, and that this fact merited the (then) differential approach in the case law on non-discriminatory

[76] Fuller, n75, 378 (emphasis added).

[77] See S. Iglesias Sánchez, 'The Court and the Charter: The impact of the entry into force of the Lisbon Treaty on the ECJ's approach to fundamental rights' (2012) 49:5 CMLRev 1565.

[78] The Court already acknowledges explicitly that States may claim a wider margin of appreciation in certain circumstances e.g. when regulating access to certain benefits (Case C-192/05 *Tas-Hagen and Tas v Raadskamer WUBO van de Pensioen- en Uitkeringsraad* [2006] ECR I-10451) or when regulating the spelling of names (Case C-391/09 *Runevič-Vardyn and Łukasz Paweł Wardyn v Vilniaus miesto savivaldybės administracija and others* [2011] ECR I-3787).

restrictions for workers as compared to goods.[79] In the final provisions of the Charter, however, and especially through Article 51(2), the Member States have made it very clear that the Charter cannot be used to *extend* the scope of EU law[80]—and this is a key driver of fragmentation that will be addressed in subsequent chapters.

The Member States do not see the Court of Justice as a human rights court—but it would seem, from the outcomes of some free movement case law, that the Court has at times perceived itself in that way. For example, the decision in *Carpenter* was controversial because the Court did not engage with the extent to which there was a material connection between the freedom exercised (provision of services) and the substantive right conferred (residence in the applicant's *home* State for his third country national spouse).[81] Linking *Carpenter* to *Bosman*—where the scope of the free movement of workers was extended significantly, but the applicant had a time-limited window within which he could continue to play professional football—Snell argued that '[a] prime duty of any court is to protect individuals against misuse of power ... in both of these cases any judge might have been inclined to disregard jurisdictional niceties in order to protect a vulnerable individual'.[82]

The tension between the integrity of protecting vulnerable individuals—discernible in the Court's pre-Lisbon case law in particular[83]—and the binding constitutional instructions codified in the Charter and the TEU demonstrates how the accommodation of protecting fundamental rights generates the potential for case law fragmentation i.e. because protecting fundamental rights cannot be measured by the *positive* impact of the Charter in isolation. The attribution of primary law status to the Charter is already producing remarkable results, demonstrating that the Lisbon Treaty did something that goes significantly beyond constitutional symbolism. In particular, the Court has, for the first time, annulled

[79] AG Lenz in Case C-415/93 *Union Royale Belge des Sociétés de Football Association ASBL v Bosman* [1995] ECR I-4921, para. 203 of the Opinion. Supporting the idea of movement rights as fundamental rights, the Universal Declaration on Human Rights includes a right to move and reside freely within the borders of a State and also to leave (and return to) one's own State (Article 13); see also, Protocol 4 to the ECHR and, for EU nationals, Article 45(1) of the Charter (protecting a right to move to and reside in other States). See also, S O'Leary, 'The relationship between Community citizenship and the protection of fundamental rights in Community law' (1995) 32:2 CMLRev 51 and G Neuman, 'Human rights and constitutional rights: Harmony and dissonance' (2003) 55 *Stanford Law Review* 1863.

[80] Article 51(2) provides that '[t]his Charter does not establish any new power or task for the Community or the Union, or modify powers and tasks defined by the Treaties'. See also, Article 6(1) TEU, which confirms similarly that '[t]he provisions of the Charter shall not extend in any way the competences of the Union as defined in the Treaties', and Case C-370/12 *Pringle v Government of Ireland, Ireland and The Attorney General*, judgment of 27 November 2012, para. 179.

[81] Case C-60/00 *Carpenter v Secretary of State for the Home Department* [2002] ECR I-6279.

[82] Snell, n18, 56. See similarly, Spaventa, n18.

[83] See e.g. AG Ruiz-Jarabo Colomer in Case C-228/07 *Petersen v Arbeitsmarktservice Niederösterreich* [2008] ECR I-6989, para. 17 of the Opinion, observing 'a tendency towards protecting individuals, a concern with the personal situation of those who exercise a right under the Treaties which in the past was much less evident'. However, other perceptions of the Court's emphasis on the rights of *individuals* raise broader questions about (transnational) solidarity and differing understandings of the common good; see generally, A Somek, *Individualism: An Essay on the Authority of the European Union* (OUP, 2008).

parts of EU legislation on fundamental rights grounds—on two separate occasions at the time of writing[84]—since the coming into force of the Lisbon Treaty in December 2009. But the general rule relevant to free movement law is that the Court of Justice can only protect fundamental rights when a substantive question of EU law is already established i.e. when the situation at issue falls within the scope of EU law.[85] For example, the right to respect for family life—protected by Article 7 of the Charter and by Article 8 ECHR—can normally only be invoked by an EU citizen to secure residence rights for their third country national spouse if the former has exercised free movement rights i.e. left their home State.

At times, the Court has seemed to struggle with this limit on its ability to protect the fundamental rights of EU citizens and it has, on the whole (and especially in cases drawing from the legal status of EU citizenship), seemed to reach for outcomes that accommodate due protection of those rights whenever it possibly can—however much the framework of free movement law was distorted in the process. But it has clearly held back in other cases. The fact that protection of fundamental rights makes a stronger imprint in some cases than in others is not something confined to recent case law.[86] But it *is* the message that seems to be hardening through references to Article 51 of the Charter in the post-Lisbon legal environment.[87] This *variable* emphasis on the limits of its own powers generates confusing case law, and this in turn generates a difficult constitutional choice from the perspective of coherence. Where the outcome of a case reflects genuine concern for the wellbeing of the claimant(s) involved, the scope of the provisions on free movement can, in consequence, be pushed right to (at least) the margins of the Treaties. However, when the emphasis on fundamental rights weakens in the face of competing forces—such as Article 51 of the Charter—the choices made seem to neglect the wellbeing of the claimants. The case law is therefore irreparably discordant in a systemic sense but, at different points in time, it respects different constitutional instructions. Which approach is at least *more* coherent, or more fair—and why?

The mixed, heterarchical messages offered by the constitutional texts are a real problem for the Court to manage in this context—since they speak with apparently equal force about the need to protect the rights of EU citizens on the one hand, but about the limits of that jurisdiction on the other. And that is hardly the Court's fault. But when it vacillates between rights and limits in reaching its own decisions—and when that is compounded by the absence of detailed reasoning and systematic engagement with conflicting authorities, even if only to overrule

[84] Case C-236/09 *Association Belge des Consommateurs Test-Achats ASBL and others v Conseil des ministers* [2011] ECR I-773; and Joined Cases C-92/09 and C-93/09 *Volker und Markus Schecke GbR and Eifert v Land Hessen* [2010] ECR I-11063.

[85] For a general overview of the post-Lisbon parameters within which the Court must consider the protection of fundamental rights, see Case C-400/10 PPU *McB v E* [2010] ECR I-8965, paras 50–53.

[86] E.g. compare the contrasting approaches of AG Alber and the Court in Case C-257/00 *Nani Givane and others v Secretary of State for the Home Department* [2003] ECR I-345.

[87] See e.g. the judgments in Case C-256/11 *Dereci and others v Bundesministerium für Inneres*, judgment of 15 November 2011, paras 70–72; and Case C-40/11 *Iida v Stadt Ulm*, judgment of 8 November 2012, paras 78–81. Both of these cases are discussed in Chapter 4.

them in light of the changed constitutional milieu post-Lisbon—the basic result is that the fundamental rights of certain EU citizens are sometimes protected more than those of others. It is difficult to reconcile that outcome with fairness, integrity, or coherence—with, in other words, the responsibilities of a constitutional court. These points will be fleshed out in Chapter 4 in particular, discussing case law that addresses the family reunification rights of both mobile and static EU citizens.

The long-running debate about the scope of the Charter with respect to Member State action is also relevant here. Pre-Charter case law established that national measures or practices *within the scope of* Union law could be reviewed to ensure their compliance with EU fundamental rights standards.[88] Critically, that formula embraced a review of Member State derogation actions using EU fundamental rights standards. The Charter seems to narrow that interpretation quite deliberately, by referring in Article 51(1) to measures *implementing* Union law. Several of the Court's Advocates General have reasoned that the broader pre-Charter understanding of scope should, nonetheless, continue to apply.[89] Instead of resolving the anomalies, however, post-Lisbon judgments to date have either: repeated the terms of Article 51(1) without further discussion;[90] cited pre-Charter case law without addressing whether the Charter has altered that threshold;[91] clouded the issue by introducing different wording, providing a good example of how the proliferation of principles can become problematic, as outlined in Section 3(a);[92] or introduced criteria that seem go beyond the limits of the Charter phrasing altogether.[93] What possible benefit comes from confusing an already too-complicated, under-explained yet fundamental constitutional boundary in these different ways? National courts are hardly at fault if they are struggling to understand what 'implementing' Union law actually means. Moreover, the relationship between fundamental rights as codified in the Charter and fundamental rights as general principles of EU law—arguably *not* constrained by the Charter's final provisions in the same way—is still being worked out.[94]

[88] E.g. Case C-309/96 *Annibaldi v Sindaco del Comune di Guidonia and Presidente Regione Lazio* [1997] ECR I-7493, paras 21–23; and Case C-260/89 *Elliniki Radiophonia Tileorassi AE (ERT) v Dimotiki Etairia Pliroforissis* [1991] ECR I-2925, paras 42–43.

[89] E.g. AG Trstenjak in *N.S.*, paras 74–83 of the Opinion; AG Bot in Case C-108/10 *Scattolon v Ministero dell'Istruzione, dell'Università e della Ricerca*, judgment of 6 September 2011, paras 116–120 of the Opinion. Cf. the more cautious approach of AG Cruz Villalón in Case C-617/10 *Åkerberg Fransson*, judgment of 26 February 2013.

[90] E.g. Case C-23/12 *Zakaria*, judgment of 17 January 2013, para. 39.

[91] E.g. *Iida*, para. 79, citing *Annibaldi*.

[92] E.g. *Dereci*, para. 72, referring to 'situations *covered by* Union law' (emphasis added).

[93] Case C-27/11 *Vinkov v Nachalnik Administrativno-nakazatelna deynost*, judgment of 7 June 2012, para. 59: 'it is not apparent from the order for reference that the national legislation constitutes a measure implementing EU law *or that it is connected in any other way with EU law*. Accordingly, the jurisdiction of the Court to rule on the reference for a preliminary ruling in so far as it relates to the fundamental right to an effective remedy is not established' (emphasis added).

[94] In *Iida*, the referring court had raised a series of questions on this point (see 2011 OJ C145/4). Arguing that general principles remain a distinct—and potentially wider—source of protection for fundamental rights, see e.g. AG Trstenjak in Case C-282/10 *Dominguez v Centre informatique du Centre Ouest Atlantique and Préfet de la région Centre*, judgment of 24 January 2012, para. 127.

The intricate balance between the scope of free movement law and the degree of protection afforded to fundamental rights, especially against the backdrop of recently revised constitutional instructions, will be traced in the chapters that follow. The discussion will also dwell on the different kinds of prices that have been paid for the legal effect now conferred on the Charter—by reflecting on the *level* of protection of fundamental rights prioritized at different points in time.

(d) The structure of the Court

The fragmentary impact of the Court's structure and working methods is difficult to measure with any degree of precision. However, it is increasingly asserted that these factors as well as relentless pressure to complete cases quickly mean that the quality of its judgments has suffered.[95] It will be argued here that, additionally, these factors are contributing to systemic case law fragmentation. This subsection considers, in particular, the extent to which the organization of the court might affect how it fulfils its constitutional functions.

The Court's judges (and Advocates General) are appointed for six-year terms through a process invoking the 'common accord of the governments of the Member States' (Article 19(2) TEU). Additionally, since the ratification of the Lisbon Treaty, a panel of 'former members of the Court of Justice and the General Court, members of national supreme courts and lawyers of recognised competence, one of whom shall be proposed by the European Parliament' must 'give an opinion on candidates' suitability to perform the duties of Judge and Advocate-General of the Court of Justice and the General Court before the governments of the Member States make the appointments' (Article 255 TFEU). Although the six-year term is renewable, that decision is taken by each Member State individually. Woods has drawn attention to the fact that the basic term is 'short, which may in itself give rise to issues about the quality of judicial decision-making'.[96] The importance of stability for the Court is reflected by the fact that there is a partial replacement of judges every three years (Article 9 of the Statute). Additionally, while Member State practice on reappointment does vary, several judges stay at the Court for more than one term.[97]

The Court's judges have sat together as the full court on just one occasion since the 2004 EU enlargement.[98] Normally, the Court is organized through a system of

[95] See e.g. Weatherill, n1. [96] Woods, n24, 343.

[97] In February 2013, for example, the majority of the judges had been at the Court for more than one six-year term (i.e. 13 years/one judge; 11 years/one judge; nine years/three judges; eight years/eight judges; seven years/two judges; six years/four judges; five years/one judge; three years/three judges; two years/two judges; one year/one judge; under one year/two judges. Additionally, two judges had also been Advocates General at the Court and three had been judges at the General Court.

[98] *Pringle* (27 judges); this was the first time that the 'exceptional importance' of the case triggered the full court formation (in accordance with Article 16 of the Statute of the Court of Justice, available at <http://curia.europa.eu/jcms/upload/docs/application/pdf/2012-10/staut_cons_en.pdf>; see also, press release No 154/12, available at <http://curia.europa.eu/jcms/upload/docs/application/pdf/2012-11/cp120154en.pdf>). The full court composition was also required by the Treaty provisions on which the proceedings in Opinion 1/09 (Draft Agreement on the European and Community

chambers. Since November 2012, the Grand Chamber consists of 15 (formerly 13) judges; but its decisions are valid with 11 judges sitting (Articles 16 and 17 of the Statute). However, ten chambers produce the majority of the Court's judgments, sitting as five-judge and three-judge formations.[99] The presidents of the five-judge chambers are elected for three years; the presidents of the three-judge chambers are elected for just one year. The presidents of five-judge chambers are members of those chambers only; however, all of the other judges belong to two chambers. Woods has commented positively on this structure from the angle of case law coherence, since it means that 'the chambers are not closed to each other'.[100] The legal complexity and/or the importance of a case more generally are the basic yardsticks that determine the size of the chamber to which a case will be assigned. The formal criteria for the assignment of cases to the Grand Chamber are expressed inversely in the Court's Rules of Procedure: '[t]he Court shall assign to the Chambers of five and of three Judges any case brought before it in so far as *the difficulty or importance of the case or particular circumstances* are *not* such as to require that it should be assigned to the Grand Chamber, unless a Member State or an institution of the European Union participating in the proceedings has requested that the case be assigned to the Grand Chamber, pursuant to the third paragraph of Article 16 of the Statute'.[101]

The Court undoubtedly has a heavy workload. As noted in Chapter 1, it faces the challenge of constructing judgments that are sufficiently *specific* to resolve the case at hand in an effective way and sufficiently *generic* to provide guidance at an appropriate level of abstraction so that the legal kernel can work across and within the Member States. The Court also faces persistent pressure to deliver its judgments as quickly and efficiently as it can. The current President of the Court, Judge Skouris, has been responsive to this mandate by adopting the speedy turnaround of cases as a strategic priority for the Court.[102] But speed is a double-edged goal. The positive value of timely justice is a fundamental element of the rule of law and Article 47 of the Charter guarantees the right to an effective remedy (as does Article 6 ECHR). On the other hand, as AG Sharpston has observed, '[e]xpediency,

Patents Court) [2011] ECR I-1137 (23 judges) and Case C-432/04 *Commission v Cresson* [2006] ECR I-6387 (17 judges) were based. Article 17 of the Statute provides that 17 judges will validly constitute the 'full' court.

99 In 2011, the Grand Chamber processed 11.4 per cent of the Court's completed cases; three-judge and five-judge chambers completed 32.54 per cent and 55.15 per cent of the cases respectively (see the Court's 2011 Annual Report, available at <http://curia.europa.eu/jcms/upload/docs/application/pdf/2012-06/ra2011_statistiques_cour_en.pdf>. The President of the Court issued an Order in 0.74 per cent of cases. The current membership of the Court's ten chambers is available at <http://curia.europa.eu/jcms/jcms/Jo2_7029/>.

100 Woods, n24, 348.

101 Article 60(1) of the Rules of Procedure of the Court of Justice, 2012 OJ L265/1 (emphasis added).

102 E.g. in the 2010 Annual Report, the President observed that the preceding 12 months had demonstrated the 'unflagging tempo of the institution's judicial activity' (5) and noted 'sustained productivity and a very significant improvement in efficiency as regards the duration of proceedings' (9) (available at: <http://curia.europa.eu/jcms/upload/docs/application/pdf/2011 05/ra2010_preface_final_en.pdf>).

however seductive, is not a valid legal argument'.[103] Neither is, for example, the 'increasing tendency of traders to invoke Article [34 TFEU] as a means of challenging any rules whose effect is to limit their commercial freedom'.[104]

A fast remedy is not necessarily going to be an effective one if the push for efficiency damages the quality of the outcome and contributes more systemically to case law breakdown. In the 2011 Annual Report, a change of tone can be detected:

> [The CJEU] is seeing a significant increase in the number of actions brought before and disposed of by its three judicial organs. The institution can only be gladdened by this trend which indicates the confidence of national courts and of litigants in the Courts of the European Union. Nevertheless, *this increase in the caseload demands a degree of vigilance* on the part of both the Court of Justice of the European Union and the European Union's legislative authorities *in order that the effectiveness of the European Union's judicial system is not jeopardised* and that European citizens continue to be served to the highest standards.[105]

The President then continued that, '[w]ith this in mind, the Court of Justice proposed in the past year a series of amendments to its Statute [in accordance with Article 281 TFEU] and a complete recasting of its Rules of Procedure, seeking, first, to improve its efficiency and productivity and those of the General Court and, second, to modernise its procedures'.[106]

The proposal that was most likely to affect case law coherence was the abolition of the automatic participation of the presidents of the chambers of five judges in the Grand Chamber. Before November 2012, the President of the Court and the presidents of the five-judge chambers were permanent members of the Grand Chamber; its remaining spaces were filled in accordance with rules laid down in the Rules of Procedure. This requirement ensured that a fixed core group of judges sat on cases assigned to the Grand Chamber, at least for a period of three years. The proposal for change was framed by arguments about the heavy workload of the five-judge chamber presidents (these chambers complete approx. 50 per cent of the Court's annual caseload). The President also expressed the view that the achievement of greater equality among judges was desirable, on the basis that a more fluid rotational composition 'provides for broader participation by the Judges in cases assigned to the Grand Chamber, allowing them to sit far more frequently than at

[103] AG Sharpston in Case C-196/09 *Miles and others v Écoles européennes* [2011] ECR I-5105, para. 82 of the Opinion.

[104] *Keck and Mithouard*, para. 14. The line between instrumental use and prohibited abuse of EU rights is discussed in Chapter 3.

[105] 2011 Annual Report, n99, President's Foreword (emphasis added).

[106] The draft amendments and explanatory notes are available at (for the Statute) <http://curia.europa.eu/jcms/upload/docs/application/pdf/2011-04/projet_en.pdf> and (for the Rules of Procedure) <http://curia.europa.eu/jcms/upload/docs/application/pdf/2011-05/en_rp_cjue.pdf>. Interestingly, the proposals also called for an increase in the number of General Court judges from 27 to 39 'in order to respond to the constant increase in its caseload' (2011 Annual Report, n99, President's Foreword); the issue is currently stalled—see Council Press Release No 17439/12, 11 December 2012, 7, available at <www.consilium.europa.eu/ueDocs/cms_Data/docs/pressData/EN/genaff/134235.pdf>. This would be a significant increase if the proposal is accepted, yet the caseloads at both Courts are not dramatically different: in 2011, the Court of Justice received 688 new cases and completed 550; the General Court's statistics are 714 and 579 respectively.

present (in almost half, instead of a third, of all cases)'. It was also suggested that the changes would 'have the advantage of enabling the Presidents of Chambers of five Judges to devote more time to managing their Chambers, which would help further to improve efficiency in the work of those Chambers, and to ensuring the harmonious development of the case-law'. Through the creation of a new post of Vice-President of the Court,[107] it was argued that '[t]he permanent presence of two persons, together with the more frequent participation of the other Judges in the work of the Grand Chamber, would ensure that its case-law is consistent'.

The unsustainable workload placed at present on the presidents of the five-judge chambers must be acknowledged. However, consider the formations of the Grand Chamber that heard two recent clusters of cases—the 2008/2009 decisions on rules regulating the use of goods and a 2011 trilogy on EU citizenship—that ignited particularly intensive debate. If we look at the composition of the Court in both sets of cases, the picture presented in Tables 2.1 and 2.2 emerges.

A more fluid Grand Chamber composition may reflect the good intention of ensuring that all of the judges gain more experience of Grand Chamber cases, which could in turn improve case law coherence in the round. But the crowded picture that emerges here does not remotely resemble what might be expected for a higher court determining questions of acute constitutional importance. Moreover, the Court's composition across the cases presented in Table 2.2—which reflects the proposed idea of two fixed Grand Chamber members—generated some of the most fiercely criticized judgments of recent years, discussed in Chapter 4. The Court's

Table 2.1 Use of goods (2008/2009)

Case	AG	Chamber	Composition	Rapporteur
C-265/06 *Comm. v Portugal* 10 April 2008	Trstenjak	Third	Rosas (P), Lõhmus, Klučka, Lindh, Arabadjiev	Lindh
C-110/05 *Comm. v Italy* 10 February 2009	Léger Bot	Grand	Skouris (P), Jann, Timmermans, Rosas, Lenaerts, von Danwitz, Tizzano, Cunha Rodrigues, Borg Barthet, Malenovský, Lõhmus Arabadjiev, Toader	Lõhmus
C-142/05 *Mickelsson and Roos* 4 June 2009	Kokott	Second	Timmermans (P), Makarczyk, Kūris, Arestis, Klučka	Arestis

* No Advocate General or judge involved in all three cases.

[107] In October 2012, Judge Lenaerts was elected to serve as the first Vice-President of the Court of Justice; see Press Release No 128/12, available at <http://europa.eu/rapid/press release_CJE-12-128_en.htm?locale=EN>.

Table 2.2 Citizenship (2011)

Case	AG	Chamber	Composition	Rapporteur
C-34/09 *Ruiz Zambrano* 8 March 2011	Sharpston	Grand	Skouris (P), Tizzano, Cunha Rodrigues, *Lenaerts*, Bonichot, Rosas, Ilešič, *Malenovský*, Lõhmus, Levits, Ó Caoimh, Bay Larsen, Berger	Cunha Rodrigues
C-434/09 *McCarthy* 5 May 2011	Kokott	Third	*Lenaerts* (P), Šváby, Silva de Lapuerta, Juhász, *Malenovský*	Silva de Lapuerta
C-256/11 *Dereci* 15 November 2011	Mengozzi	Grand	Skouris (P), Cunha Rodrigues, *Lenaerts*, Bonichot, *Malenovský*, Lõhmus, Silva de Lapuerta, Ilešič, Levits	Silva de Lapuerta

* Two judges involved in all three cases.

confidence in its ability to *enhance* case law coherence through the 2011 proposals thus seems completely misguided.

In November 2012, revised Rules of Procedure affecting the composition of the Grand Chamber came into effect—but the changes implemented were not as radical as the Court had proposed. Article 27 of the revised Rules of Procedure provides as follows:

> The Grand Chamber shall, for each case, be composed of the President and the Vice-President of the Court, *three Presidents of Chambers of five Judges*, the Judge-Rapporteur and the number of Judges necessary to reach 15. The last-mentioned Judges and the three Presidents of Chambers of five Judges shall be designated from the lists referred to in paragraphs 3 and 4 of this Article, following the order laid down therein. The starting-point on each of those lists, in every case assigned to the Grand Chamber, shall be the name of the Judge immediately following the last Judge designated from the list concerned for the preceding case assigned to that formation of the Court (emphasis added).

While the Grand Chamber has increased in size to 15 judges (but retaining the validity threshold of 11 judges from its former size of 13), three (of five) presidents of the five-judge chambers must also sit alongside the President and Vice-President of the Court—something that was absent from the draft originally proposed.[108]

Two further problems generated by the Court's chamber structure should also be noted: (1) questions raised by a judicial unit of the *size* of the Grand Chamber; and (2) what Woods calls the 'flat structure' of the Court more generally. Addressing, first, the size of the Grand Chamber, it would be a mistake to assume that criticism of how the Court articulates—or fails to articulate—its reasoning or to explain its use of authority is levelled at smaller chambers only. Remembering that all judgments of the Court are delivered in a single or collegiate format, specific

[108] See again, draft Article 27, <http://curia.europa.eu/jcms/upload/docs/application/pdf/2011-05/en_rp_cjue.pdf>.

concerns have been raised that the task of achieving agreement among the members of a group the size of the Grand Chamber makes it even more difficult to draft a detailed and persuasive text given the likelihood and/or extent of the disagreement feeding into the judges' deliberations. For example, Woods argues that 'in order to obtain agreement from a greater number of individuals, the judgments of the Grand Chamber may be drafted at an even greater level of abstraction than usual, especially give the difficulty or sensitivity of these cases'.[109]

The Court's eight Advocates General originally provided opinions in all proceedings before the Court. But now, according to Article 20 of the Statute, '[w]here it considers that the case raises no new point of law, the Court may decide, after hearing the Advocate-General, that the case shall be determined without a submission from the Advocate-General'.[110] Writing in a personal capacity, AG Sharpston has convincingly asserted the importance of the role performed by the Advocates General in a multi-chamber Court structure and, in particular, in a system that does not allow for dissenting judgments.[111] The task of keeping the overarching mainframe of EU law coherently together is frequently attributed as their particular responsibility, but it is a heavy burden to place on eight people. Moreover, they work essentially as individuals—they do not deliberate collegiately in the way that the judges do. According to Article 252 TFEU, the number of Advocates General may be raised to 11 on request from the Court, but that option is only now being animated.[112]

Second, as Woods reminds us, the Court of Justice has a 'flat structure'.[113] In particular, we have to remember that the tendency to dilute the significance of judgments from the smaller chambers is *not* formalized anywhere. In preliminary rulings, for example, confusion created by a judgment from a three-judge chamber that does not fit with established jurisprudence must still be dealt with as 'the law' by the national court—the referring judge is just as much bound to apply that ruling as a judgment from the Grand Chamber. Furthermore, while a smaller chamber can refer cases 'up' to a larger formation before judgment is delivered,[114] there is no appeal from *any* judgment of the Court once the adjudication process is complete.[115] In other words, notwithstanding the de facto precedence attributed

109 Woods, n24, 350.

110 In 2011, approx. 46 per cent of cases were completed *without* an Advocate General's opinion (2011 Annual Report, n99, 4; the figure was approx. 50 per cent in 2010).

111 E Sharpston, 'The changing role of the Advocate General' in A Arnull, P Eeckhout, and T Tridimas (eds.), *Continuity and Change in EU Law: Essays in Honour of Sir Francis Jacobs* (OUP, 2008) 20 at 32–3.

112 The President of the Court wrote to the Council of the European Union in January 2013 to request that effect should now be given to Article 252; the text of the letter is available at <http://register.consilium.europa.eu/pdf/fr/13/st05/st05737.fr13.pdf>.

113 See generally, Woods, n24.

114 See Article 60(3) of the Rules of Procedure.

115 Cf. Rule 73 of the ECtHR Rules of Court, para. 1 of which provides that '[i]n accordance with Article 43 of the Convention, any party to a case may exceptionally, within a period of three months from the date of delivery of the judgment of a Chamber, file in writing at the Registry a request that the case be referred to the Grand Chamber. The party shall specify in its request the serious question affecting the interpretation or application of the Convention or the Protocols thereto, or the serious issue of general importance, which in its view warrants consideration by the Grand Chamber'.

to the rulings of the Grand Chamber, there is no super-chamber that *formally* supervises the work of the smaller chambers or has appellate oversight over them.

A chamber structure is non-negotiable to ensure that the Court functions properly. But its current 'flat' organization is flawed. There are reforms that could be applied to ensure greater case law coherence yet stop short of introducing a formalized apex chamber with an explicit supervisory mandate. For example, the rules regulating both the composition and jurisdiction of the General Court contain flexible opportunities for further expansion, and there is always the possibility of creating new specialist courts.[116] Creative working methods could also be looked at e.g. a pool of *référendaires* working alongside the *lecteurs d'arrêts* in the President's chambers could be tasked specifically with ensuring that draft judgments fit logically in the existing system of the case law (or at least explain new or changed legal paths as clearly as possible) and that citation of authorities makes substantive and not just temporal sense.

But an even more fundamental shift in the way that the Court is conceived and structured is advocated here. Leaving aside its appellate jurisdiction, the *combination* of first instance and constitutional functions that the Court's jurisdiction confers on it necessitates a new apex court—or at least a formalized apex chamber—to take direct oversight responsibility of the development of EU law. This blend of functions occurs because, first, and most obviously, the Court has jurisdiction to hear certain direct actions at first instance (e.g. enforcement proceedings against Member States). But, second, as discussed in Chapter 1, it occurs also because the Court frequently pronounces so prescriptively in preliminary rulings that it is effectively deciding on the facts and not just articulating principled guidance at a more constitutional level. Because of the *erga omnes* effect of the Court's judgments, it is *not* just resolving the individual case in front of it, and it is thus deceptive to think about the impact of the Court and of its judgments in those terms. Additionally, the nature of some of the principles that it uses to resolve disputes on free movement law—notably proportionality—means that the individual situation being considered is in fact ultimately determinative.[117] However, when the Court fixates on the proportionality of a decision taken in respect of *one* applicant, it does not always consider the downstream systemic effects or implications of its decision for broader national regulatory priorities.

In the context of the Civilian tradition, Komárek observes that '[t]he highest courts on the European continent . . . were established in order not to adjudicate real-life disputes, as their common law counterparts originally were, but to say what

[116] See esp. Articles 254, 256, and 257 TFEU.

[117] Commenting on the interplay between proportionality and citizenship rights, for example, see Spaventa, n18, 40: '[t]he expansion of the personal and material scope of the Treaty, together with the ad hoc proportionality assessment required by the Court in (almost) any circumstance concerning the migrant, transforms the legislative act of general application, into a quasi administrative act where the authorities always have to exercise discretion in applying the black letter of the law to Union citizens . . . [A] piece of legislation which is found to be incompatible with [EU] law is incompatible with [EU] law in relation to all migrant economic operators [but] whether the denial of a right to residence for lack of resources and comprehensive health insurance is compatible with [EU] law will depend solely on the facts of the case and on the personal circumstances of the claimant'.

the law is and to control the application of law by lower courts. The separation of constitutional courts or the ECJ from ordinary or national courts follows the same pattern of separation of deciding disputes from making law in the context of adjudication'.[118] Contemporary supreme courts in common law jurisdictions are functionally separated from other courts as well. But for enforcement proceedings against Member States at the Court of Justice, there is only a one-judgment shot on the legal issues. The same is true de facto in preliminary rulings, since referring courts are obliged to apply the *legal* guidance provided. It is inconceivable to contemplate even suggesting a comparable architecture for a national judicial system. Moreover, as pointed out in Chapter 1, only the Court can, in real terms, review or revisit its own decisions. If it does not, its interpretations are otherwise locked into constitutional-level place without any checking mechanism short of the cumbersome (practically and politically) prospect of Treaty revision. This means that once the Court (i.e. any chamber of it) resolves a question of law, irrespective of its *actual* constitutional significance, the finding becomes a rigidly entrenched molecule of constitutional-level case law that must be respected by all judicial actors in all Member States and by all legislators—including the EU legislature—from then onwards. If any doubts persist about the character of the Court as a constitutional court, then the way in which its review power is framed cuts through them: assessing the actions of administrative and especially legislative actors against markers (usually) set down in a structuring document is exactly the task with which 'normal' constitutional courts are charged.

A too-large chamber cannot engage in the level of oversight—or debate—that the effective progression of constitutional law deserves. This problem is heightened at the Court of Justice because a single collegiate judgment must be drafted—as noted above, disagreement (on approach and/or outcome) demands a degree of concession that compromises the articulation of convincing reasoning. For particularly short judgments, what had to be taken out would perhaps be more telling than what is left in. The Court's recent success in raising the Grand Chamber formation to 15 judges makes no sense in this context. Moreover, a constantly rotating composition for that Chamber alongside multiple smaller chambers operating 'flatly' in parallel is not conducive to ensuring or sustaining case law coherence. A constitutional court needs to be smaller and its composition needs to be relatively static:

> Courts are not meant to be political institutions and there is thus no inherent requirement for them to be representative institutions . . . Whether or not the Court of Justice is called a supreme or constitutional court, it is the court with responsibility for ultimate oversight of the evolution and consistency of . . . Union law. That responsibility is immense, and the Court must be organised to enable its discharge appropriately and effectively . . . The court at the apex of [the EU judicial] structure needs . . . to sit around one table. And at that table,

[118] J Komárek, 'Reasoning with previous decisions: Beyond the doctrine of precedent', LSE Law, Society and Economy Working Papers 8/2012, available at <http://www.lse.ac.uk/collections/law/wps/WPS2012-08_Komarek.pdf>, 23.

the judges need to be able to have full and frank conversations; to see each other, to hear each other, and to sit together again the next day or next week, and the weeks after that.[119]

If we could leave to one side ideological and political debates about whether or not the EU should have a more obviously styled supreme court, the strongest arguments for it relate to the more prosaic but absolutely critical gauge of functionality. But of course we cannot; which means that the structure of the Court is unlikely to change so fundamentally and we must instead be alert to the constraints—the unorthodox structure, jurisdiction, and formations—within which this constitutional court has to operate, for now at least, when we evaluate the consistency of its case law.

4. Conclusion

In this chapter, the standard of case law coherence that will be applied to free movement case law in subsequent chapters was outlined. Legitimate differences shaping the way in which the principles determining the scope of free movement law should be applied or interpreted can be better accommodated by expectations based on coherence than by following models such as case law convergence or, more fundamentally, institutional legitimacy. Drawing from the work of the International Law Commission, emphasis was placed on finding a balance between an effective but also realistic standard. The quality and techniques of judicial reasoning, especially the appropriate use of and engagement with authority, proved to be as central in that respect as they were to the fulfilment of the constitutional responsibilities outlined more broadly in Chapter 1. An overview of four specific drivers of the opposing dynamic—case law fragmentation—was then presented: proliferation of principles and tests; the multiple and unsettled objectives of the internal market and free movement; the protection of fundamental rights; and the organizational dimension of the judicial function. These themes—many of which have been heightened by the Lisbon-changed constitutional framework—will now be tracked and developed through substantive analysis of case law on the scope of the Treaty's free movement provisions. In that discussion, the consequences as well as causes of fragmentation will also be considered.

[119] N Nic Shuibhne, 'A court within a court: Is it time to rebuild the Court of Justice?' (2009) 34:2 ELRev 173 at 174.

3

The Negative Scope of Free Movement Law: 'Who-Based' Exclusions

1. Introduction

To determine whether a rule or practice should be tested against free movement law, it must first be considered, as outlined in Chapter 1, whether the challenged measure comes within the scope of the Treaty. We tend to jump quickly to the critical question in that context: does the measure *restrict* free movement rights? But the Court has developed a series of principles that can have the effect of ending a challenge before either the existence or nature of a restriction becomes relevant—a stage of analysis recently reinvigorated as 'exclusionary rules' by Horsley.[1] Essentially, the application of exclusionary principles, a distinct subset of the framework principles that shape free movement law, provides mechanisms through which a connecting factor to EU law can be ruled out.[2]

It was also noted in Chapter 1 that framework principles share certain characteristics: for example, they emerge in cases concerning all of the Treaty freedoms, but they are not necessarily expressed through the same wording (either within or across the freedoms). Also, while these principles have the potential to constrain the scope of free movement law, they are not applied systematically or engaged with consistently. The *span* of exclusionary rules can be widely interpreted. Some of these rules are specified in the Treaty,[3] while others have emerged through the case law.[4] There are two main types of exclusionary rules in free movement law—'who-based'

[1] T Horsley, 'Unearthing buried treasure: Art 34 TFEU and the exclusionary rules' (2012) 37:6 ELRev 734.

[2] To distinguish the Court-based justification framework from Treaty-based derogation grounds, outlined in Chapter 1, the doctrine of mandatory requirements has also been conceptualized as exclusionary (e.g. E Spaventa, 'On discrimination and the theory of mandatory requirements' (2002) 3 CYELS 457).

[3] See e.g. Article 45(4) TFEU, excluding 'employment in the public service' from the scope of the free movement of workers; see similarly, Article 51 TFEU on freedom of establishment (which 'shall not apply ... to activities ... connected, even occasionally, with the exercise of official authority', extended to services through Article 62 TFEU). The Court has drawn the potential breadth of these exclusions narrowly: see e.g. Case C-405/01 *Colegio de Oficiales de la Marina Mercante Española v Administración del Estado* [2003] ECR I-10391 (Article 45(4) TFEU); Case C-61/08 *Commission v Greece* [2011] ECR I-4399 (Article 51 TFEU).

[4] For example, when the Court shapes 'where-based' rules connected to the geographical location of the activity (see e.g. Case C-452/04 *Fidium Finanz AG v Bundesanstalt für Finanzdienstleistungsaufsicht* [2006] ECR I-9521; Case C-214/94 *Boukhalfa v Bundesrepublik Deutschland* [1996] ECR I-2253).

principles (i.e. connected to the *actor* involved) and 'what-based' principles (i.e. connected to the *activity*)—and in chapters 3, 4, and 5, their application by the Court will be pushed through a filter of coherence, bearing in mind the threshold of realistic expectations developed in Chapters 1 and 2. Two related questions underpin the discussion: first, are differences in the interpretation or application of these principles properly rationalized; and, second, can we therefore construct a broadly coherent 'global' framework notwithstanding any disparities that do emerge?

This chapter will focus on the exclusionary rules that relate primarily to who is involved in a possible restriction of free movement law. It will first deal with literal or definitional exclusion from the scope of the Treaty (Section 2); and then examine the concept of abuse of EU rights (Section 3) and the horizontal reach of the Treaty provisions (Section 4). Chapter 4 will address a particularly controversial what- or activity-based rule i.e. the requirement of a cross-border connection; the principles of remoteness and *de minimis* will be discussed in Chapter 5.

2. Definitional exclusion from the scope of the Treaty

EU free movement law is premised on twin understandings of scope: personal scope i.e. the actor involved (e.g. exporters of goods) and material scope, which relates to the activity or area at the heart of the claim (e.g. a mandatory inspection system the costs of which are imposed on exporters). Definitional rules attach to both personal and material scope. They can be set explicitly by the Treaty (e.g. Article 57 TFEU defines 'services') but, more commonly, they are developed through the Court's interpretation of the relevant terms and phrases. Although this section will focus mainly on rules connected to personal scope, the basic principles that determine material scope will be outlined briefly in subsection (a), in order, first, to illustrate the wider context within which definitional questions on personal scope (subsection (b)) are located and, second, in recognition of the fact that, as will then be argued in more detail in subsections (c) and (d), actor- and activity-based rules cannot always be neatly detached.

(a) Material scope

The subject of material scope is linked to broader questions about substantive competence. Essentially, if the substance of a claim can be connected to the substance of the Treaties, then the claim will be considered to fall within the material scope of EU law.[5] The scope of the Treaties in turn subsumes the scope of secondary legislation and, in fact, most case law discussions on material scope (or scope *ratione materiae*) are about whether a set of facts falls within the parameters of an EU regulation or directive, or not.

[5] The distinct requirement of a cross-border connection is addressed separately in Chapter 4.

As a general rule, the material scope of the Treaties is interpreted very broadly. For example, as will be illustrated in more detail below, there is no need to establish a *direct* connection between personal and material scope. Additionally, weaker forms of Union competence can suffice to bring policy areas within material scope as issues 'covered' by EU law. Even policies that appear to fall exclusively within the competence of the Member States do not escape EU-level constitutional review. Where the Union does not have (or is unlikely, usually for political reasons, to exercise) competence to act in a particular policy field, the Court will still test national measures against the requirements of free movement and the general principles of EU law (especially non-discrimination and proportionality). The regulation of direct taxation and access to Member State nationality are two sensitive areas where this obligation of 'having due regard' to EU law is often applied.[6]

Importantly, the material scope of the Treaty is not static. It changes each time the Treaty is amended: most obviously, when new policy areas are added but also in a way that shows how the personal and material scope of the Treaty interlace. This point is well illustrated by the decision in *Bidar*, where the Court stated expressly that the exclusion of student maintenance grants from the material scope of the Treaty was no longer sustainable since the Maastricht Treaty had introduced, first, what is now Title XII TFEU (by which the EU is empowered to act in the field of education, but only to adopt non-harmonizing incentive measures) and, second, the personal status of EU citizenship.[7]

The student case law can also be used to flag an instance of definitional fragmentation, however, with respect to the source of remuneration for the underpinning activity. Before Maastricht, students came within the personal scope of the Treaty through the Court's wide interpretation of vocational training.[8] Notwithstanding the interim legal evolution (or arguably because of it, since citizenship introduced an alternative source of free movement rights), the Court has never revised its view that students who attend publicly funded institutions are not service recipients. In *Humbel*, that conclusion was based on the fact that 'the State, in establishing and maintaining [a national education system], is not seeking to engage in gainful activity but is fulfilling its duties towards its own population in the social, cultural and educational fields. Secondly, the system in question is, as a general rule, funded from the public purse and not by pupils or their parents'.[9] The fact of remuneration for the services provided—an essential definitional criterion according to Article 57 TFEU—was not sufficient. Instead, the Court engaged in a level of review that came close to exploring the underlying *motivation* for the

[6] E.g. Case C-135/08 *Rottmann v Freistaat Bayern* [2010] ECR I-1449, para. 41 (regulation of nationality). On direct taxation, see e.g. Case C-446/03 *Marks & Spencer plc v Halsey (Her Majesty's Inspector of Taxes)* [2005] ECR I-10837, para. 29: 'although direct taxation falls within their competence, Member States must none the less exercise that competence *consistently with* [Union] law' (emphasis added).

[7] Case C-209/03 *Bidar v London Borough of Ealing; Secretary of State for Education and Skills* [2005] ECR I-2119, paras 38–42.

[8] Case 293/83 *Gravier v City of Liège* [1985] ECR 593.

[9] Case 263/86 *Belgium v Humbel and Edel* [1988] ECR 5365, para. 18.

provision of the service—an important vector that will resurface throughout this chapter in different contexts.

Meanwhile, in case law on access to cross-border healthcare services, the provision of remuneration from the public purse was considered to be immaterial. Before the Court ruled on this point, AG Saggio had reasoned in *Vanbraekel* that '[i]f [the *Humbel*] conditions are transposed to a national system of health-care, it follows that services which, on the one hand, are an integral part of the public health-care system, in the sense that they are established and organised by the State, and, on the other hand, are financed by public funds, must be excluded from the provisions on freedom of movement'.[10] In *Geraets-Smits and Peerbooms*, the Court expressly acknowledged submissions that drew the same analogies with the education case law.[11] But then, that logic was not so much reversed as completely ignored.[12] In *Watts*, AG Geelhooed placed a minor question mark over the continuing status of *Humbel* as 'good law' precisely because of the developments on healthcare services.[13] In *Commission v Austria*, AG Jacobs outlined both synergies and differences between publicly funded infrastructures for education and healthcare; and he mentioned the *Humbel* distinction as an illustration of difference.[14] But now, even in case law on education services specifically, the Court continues to cite *both* the restrictive paradigm for publicly funded education from *Humbel* and the more general principle from the healthcare case law that the Treaty 'does not require that the service be paid for by those for whom it is performed'.[15] It is astonishing that the Court has not tackled the disparity directly; it could either reverse *Humbel* or explain clearly why public funding should be treated differently in the fields of education and healthcare. Instead, two strands of conflicting case law are somehow both 'good law'—epitomizing the claims made in Chapters 1 and 2 about incompleteness of reasoning and the selective citation of existing authority. The example also illustrates the role of the Court in shaping policy as well as legal choices.

(b) Personal scope: the basic framework

The personal scope of free movement law can be expressed as one fundamental question: to whom do the Treaty provisions apply? Certain elements of the answer

10 AG Saggio in Case C-368/98 *Vanbraekel and others v Alliance nationale des mutualités chrétiennes (ANMC)* [2001] ECR I-5363, para. 21 of the Opinion.

11 Case C-157/99 *B.S.M. Geraets-Smits v Stichting Ziekenfonds VGZ and H.T.M. Peerbooms v Stichting CZ Groep Zorgverzekeringen* [2001] ECR I-5473, paras 48–49.

12 Ibid paras 58–59; all the Court says is that 'the payments made by the sickness insurance funds ... are indeed the consideration for the hospital services and *unquestionably represent remuneration* for the hospital which receives them and which is engaged in an activity of an economic character' (emphasis added). It did not address the *Humbel* proviso at all.

13 AG Geelhoed in Case C-372/04 *Watts v Bedford Primary Care Trust and Secretary of State for Health* [2006] ECR I-4325, para. 60 of the Opinion. See also, AG Stix-Hackl in Case C-76/05 *Schwarz and Gootjes-Schwarz v Finanzamt Bergisch Gladbach* [2007] ECR I-6849, esp. paras 32–40 of the Opinion.

14 AG Jacobs in Case C-147/03 *Commission v Austria* [2005] ECR I-5969, esp. paras 31–35 of the Opinion.

15 *Schwarz and Gootjes-Schwarz*, para. 41.

are technical or specific to the context of the relevant Treaty freedom. For example, there is extensive case law on the incorporation of legal persons in other States for strategic reasons, which shapes the outer limits of freedom of establishment from the perspective of personal scope. Some of these issues are discussed in Section 3, on the concept of abuse of rights, and in Chapter 7, considering the extent to which conditions developed in the case law have qualified the principle of market access. But the general principles are that: (1) companies established in one Member State are not precluded from establishing subsidiary branches in another State in order to take advantage of more favourable tax regimes; but (2) such subsidiaries must be *genuinely* established in the host State i.e. they must pursue genuine economic activity there.[16] The relevance of intention or motivation, suggested by the second criterion, has already been flagged as a general concern and will be returned to below.

More generally, the critical definitional threshold for personal scope is Member State nationality, the holding of which conclusively determines access to some—but not all—free movement rights. The Treaty requires the following:

Citizenship: Member State nationality—directly (Article 20 TFEU)

Goods: [No personal scope conditions]

Workers: Member State nationality—indirectly (Article 45(2) TFEU, 'abolition of any discrimination based on nationality between *workers of the Member States*')

Establishment: Member State nationality—directly (Article 49 TFEU)

Services: Member State nationality—directly (Article 56 TFEU; for service providers)

Capital: [No personal scope conditions]

The variable significance of Member State nationality was used in Chapter 2 as an argument against the convergence-by-citizenship thesis. For the free movement of goods and capital, the nationality of the actors involved is completely irrelevant: a connecting factor to EU law can be established so long as the relevant goods or payments cross from one Member State to another. Here, for that reason, the questions on personal scope discussed in this subsection relate to Articles 21, 45, 49, and 56 TFEU only.

Starting with Article 21, the exclusion of third country nationals from the status of EU citizenship is widely criticized in the literature,[17] but the Member States have not adjusted this condition through the Treaty revision process. This means that

[16] E.g. Case C-196/04 *Cadbury Schweppes v Commissioners of Inland Revenue* [2006] ECR I-7995, esp. paras 36 and 54. For a comprehensive overview of relevant case law, see V Edwards and P Farmer, 'The concept of abuse in the freedom of establishment of companies: A case of double standards?' in A Arnull, P Eeckhout, and T Tridimas (eds.), *Continuity and Change in EU Law: Essays in Honour of Sir Francis Jacobs* (OUP, 2008) 205 at 215–20; and C Barnard, *The Substantive Law of the EU: The Four Freedoms*, 3rd edn (OUP, 2010) 329–33 and 345–7.

[17] See e.g. A Wiesbrock, 'Granting citizenship-related rights to third-country nationals: An alternative to the full extension of European Union citizenship?' (2012) 14:1 EJML 63; H de Waele, 'EU citizenship: Revisiting its meaning, place and potential' (2010) 12:3 EJML 319; C Murphy, 'Immigration, integration and citizenship in European Union law: The position of third country nationals' (2008–09) 8 *Hibernian Law Journal* 155; M Hedemann-Robinson 'Third-country nationals, European Union citizenship, and free movement of persons: A time for bridges rather than divisions' (1996) 16 YEL 321.

the rights of third country national family members of a Union citizen, for example, continue to be conceptualized as derivative vis-à-vis the empowering Member State national.[18] However, Directive 2004/38 generates quasi-autonomous rights for third country national family members in certain circumstances:[19] initial rights of entry, residence, and movement continue to depend on having defined ties to a Union citizen,[20] but family members retain an independent right of residence (subject to meeting specified conditions) in the event of the death or departure of the Union citizen (Article 13) or divorce, annulment, or termination of a registered partnership (Article 14). They are also eligible for the right of permanent residence (Article 16), the acquisition of which then displaces the triggering family connection to a Union citizen in legal terms.

The language of the Treaty in Article 45 TFEU is more ambiguous about the threshold condition of Member State nationality: Article 45(1) states simply that '[f]reedom of movement for workers shall be secured within the Union'. The reference to 'workers of the Member States' in Article 45(2) has been construed as a nationality requirement, however, a reading supported by the specific legislative competence in Article 202 TFEU for regulating the movement for workers from associated overseas countries and territories. Finally, Articles 54 and 56 TFEU confirm the equivalence of national and legal persons for the purpose of applying the condition of Member State nationality to freedom of establishment and service provision respectively.

Aside from the judgment in *Martínez Sala*, which established that EU citizenship brings *all* Member State nationals within the personal scope of the Treaty as a starting point at least, there have been few recent judgments addressing the scope of free movement through isolated questions about nationality.[21] The contrasting reasoning in the Opinion of AG Léger and the decision of the Court in *FKP Scorpio* is an interesting exception.[22] The EU legislature extended the personal scope of Article 56 TFEU i.e. the Treaty rules on service provision to include the converse activity of service *receipt*.[23] *FKP Scorpio* concerned liability for income tax, but the

[18] The Member States have, however, transferred incremental but increasingly significant regulatory competence to the EU in the general field of immigration (see Title V TFEU).

[19] Directive 2004/38/EC on the right of citizens of the Union and their family members to move and reside freely within the territory of the Member States, 2004 OJ L158/77.

[20] See esp. Articles 2–3, 5–11, and 22–33 of Directive 2004/38.

[21] Case C-85/96 *Martínez Sala v Freistaat Bayern* [1998] ECR I-2691. Most questions about the personal scope (or field of application *ratione personae*) of the Treaty provisions were ironed out in the foundational case law. See e.g. Case C-292/89 *R v Immigration Appeal Tribunal, ex parte Antonissen* [1991] ECR I-745 (confirming that job-seekers come within the scope of Article 45 TFEU); and Case 152/73 *Sotgiu v Deutsche Bundespost* [1974] ECR 153 (narrowing the scope of Article 45(4) with respect to 'public service').

[22] Case C-290/04 *FKP Scorpio Konzertproduktionen GmbH v Finanzamt Hamburg-Eimsbüttel* [2006] ECR I-9461.

[23] A (positive) right to reside in another Member State for the purpose (and duration) of receiving a service was established in Article 4(2) of Directive 73/148, while a (negative) right to protection against expulsion from a host State was extended to service recipients through Directive 64/221. Both measures, which have since been repealed and replaced by Directive 2004/38, were referred to by the Court in para. 12 of its judgment in Joined Cases 286/82 and 26/83 *Luisi and Carbone v Ministero del Tesoro* [1984] ECR 377, confirming that service recipients also fell within the scope of the primary rights conferred directly by Treaty.

key issue for present purposes related to the nationality of the service provider. The service *recipient* was FKP Scorpio, a concert-organizing company 'whose registered office is in Germany'[24] i.e. a German national, in accordance with Article 54 TFEU. The service provider was described by the Court as 'a natural person trading under the name of Europop ... established in the Netherlands'—but despite the use of the language of establishment here, the Court then observed that '[t]he national court states that it does not know Europop's nationality' and it had thus framed one of its questions around the relevance of the nationality of service providers, on the presumption that Europop did not hold the nationality of an EU Member State.[25] The Court first confirmed that the Treaty confers rights on service recipients as well as service providers (including in situations where neither the service provider nor the service recipient actually moves).[26] Looking at the wording of Article 56 TFEU, however, it held that the Treaty 'does not extend the benefit of those provisions to providers of services who are nationals of non-member countries, even if they are established within the [Union] and an intra-[EU] provision of services is concerned'.[27] This position is supported by the competence expressly provided for in Article 56 to extend service provision rights to third country nationals 'established within the Union' through the ordinary legislative procedure.

In his Opinion on the case, AG Léger took a distinctly different approach. From the same starting points engaged by the Court—the extension of primary rights to service recipients; the protection of the movement of the *service*—he argued that 'the purpose of liberalising trade pursued by the Treaty in order to achieve an internal market explains the extent of the meaning attributed by the Court to the concept of provision of services'.[28] On the specific nationality question raised by the case, the Advocate General addressed the scope of service provision and service receipt on their own terms, rather than constructing a bridge of dependency between them:

> [I]t does not follow either from the wording of [Article 56] or from the case-law of the Court that enjoyment by a service provider of the freedom provided for in that article is conditional upon the service provider showing that his contractual partner who is the recipient of the services is a national of a Member State. Nor does such a view hold good where it is the recipient of services who is relying on that article ... [T]he right of entry as a tourist into another Member State to receive services without being exposed to discrimination cannot, in my view, be conditional upon the recipient of services demonstrating that the service providers, the owners of a hotel for example, are nationals of a Member State. Also, as the Commission observes, it is *unjustified and unreasonable* to distinguish according to the nationality of the service provider, because that would require the recipient of the service systematically to obtain, and check, information concerning the nationality of his trading partners established in another Member State ... [T]o accept that protection of a recipient of services depends on the nationality of his contractual partner would amount to *depriving freedom to provide services of a significant part of its effects*.[29]

[24] *FKP Scorpio*, para. 18. [25] *FKP Scorpio*, para. 18 (see also, para. 26).
[26] *FKP Scorpio*, paras 63–64. [27] *FKP Scorpio*, para. 68.
[28] AG Léger in *FKP Scorpio*, para. 107 of the Opinion.
[29] AG Léger in *FKP Scorpio*, paras 118–122 of the Opinion (emphasis added, citations omitted).

AG Léger clearly invoked an internal market philosophy to frame his reasoning and he also articulated a view on its flanking principles, focusing especially on the value of effectiveness. The Court, in contrast, relied on a literal reading of Article 56 TFEU: but without telling us why and resulting in the irony that a core premise of the reasoning it *did* outline—the rights of service recipients—is not mentioned in the Treaty at all.

Although mindful of the caution about investing undue significance in one judgment, the arguments submitted by the Commission and the Advocate General in *FKP Scorpio* should be considered, since the decision of the Court might seem on the face of it to bring about a fundamental change in how the rights of service recipients are protected. However, there are two key reasons why this is not actually the case. First, the decision in *Martínez Sala* demonstrates a point introduced briefly in Section 2(a): that personal and material scope have been decoupled in free movement case law. In other words, it is not necessary to establish a direct link between the status enjoyed (in that case, citizenship) and the benefit or right being claimed (a child-raising allowance: considered by the Court to fall within the scope of EU social security legislation, which is normally associated with the status of worker). The two issues are often connected in a given case—e.g. someone who is looking for work and claiming job-seeker benefits—but they do not *have* to be. In the tourism example given by AG Léger, the nationality of the hotel owner (the service provider) will not cancel out the tourist's status as a service recipient if the latter becomes involved in a legal dispute with the host State authorities that is not substantively connected to the accommodation services received.[30] Second, as discussed in Section 4, claims that service receipt has been restricted within the meaning of EU law cannot generally be made against private actors—i.e. private service providers—anyway. This means that the nationality of the hotel owner in the tourism example is irrelevant because of a prior stumbling block on basic admissibility.

The choice made by the Court in *FKP Scorpio* was certainly a narrow one, but it does not shatter the general coherence of the scheme of free movement law. It can be flagged, however, as an example of a relatively unusual phenomenon: where the Court chooses to constrict the scope of primary free movement rights when a more liberal interpretation is at least *possible*—something clearly shown in this case by AG Léger's analysis. No overt reasons are given in the judgment, but note the time span of the case: it was lodged at the Court in July 2004—four months after the controversial proposal for the Bolkestein Directive on services in the internal market was published—and the judgment was delivered in October 2006, two months before the significantly curtailed Services Directive was finally adopted.[31]

[30] See e.g. Case C-411/98 *Ferlini v Centre hospitalier de Luxembourg* [2000] ECR I-8081; Case 186/87 *Cowan v Trésor public* [1989] ECR 195.

[31] Directive 2006/123/EC of the European Parliament and of the Council of 12 December 2006 on services in the internal market, 2006 OJ L376/36. The original proposal presented by Commissioner Bolkestein was published in March 2004 (COM(2004) 2 final/3). See generally, C Barnard, 'Unravelling the Services Directive' (2008) 45:1 CMLRev 323.

(c) Personal scope: the substantive dimension

The personal scope of the Treaty has an important substantive dimension i.e. determining personal scope is inherently connected to the nature and extent of the relevant definitional *activity* too. In this connection, the core Treaty nationality conditions have been overlaid with a matrix of case law principles. For example, as noted in Chapter 2, being a worker within the meaning of Article 45 TFEU means that 'the person performs services for and under the direction of another person in return for which he receives remuneration'.[32] On the whole, the Court has also interpreted the scope of *work* (and thus workers) very broadly, developing the following explanatory criteria:

> [T]he concept of worker has a specific [Union] meaning and *must not be interpreted narrowly*. It must be defined in accordance with *objective criteria* which distinguish an employment relationship by reference to the rights and duties of the persons concerned. In order to be treated as a worker, a person must pursue an activity which is *genuine and effective*, to the exclusion of activities on such a small scale as to be regarded as *purely marginal and ancillary*... [N]either the *sui generis* nature of the employment relationship under national law, nor the level of productivity of the person concerned, the origin of the funds from which the remuneration is paid or the limited amount of the remuneration can have *any consequence* in regard to whether or not the person is a worker for the purposes of [EU] law.[33]

Four reasons that support this expansive approach were provided in *Levin*: the need to ensure a *uniform* approach throughout the Member States; the general principle that rights conferred by the Treaty should be interpreted *broadly* (or, conversely, that their field of application should not be construed restrictively); securing conformity with the achievement of broader *Union objectives* (the removal of obstacles in general and, more specifically for workers, 'harmonious development of economic activities and a raising of the standard of living'); and maximizing the *effectiveness* of free movement rights.[34]

The criteria extracted above are consistently reaffirmed as the essential features of work, but the *nature* of the relevant economic activity has been treated in different ways. In *Grogan*, for example, the provision of abortion was held to constitute a service within the meaning of Article 57 TFEU.[35] That judgment reflects the dominant approach in free movement law: definitions tend to be applied in a

[32] Case 66/85 *Lawrie-Blum v Land Baden-Württemberg* [1986] ECR 1741, para. 17.

[33] Case C-18/00 *Kurz, né Yüce v Land Baden-Württemberg* [2002] ECR I-10691, para. 32 (emphasis added). AG Geelhoed discussed the advantages of this broad approach and the need for a nuanced understanding of the effects of and intentions behind different types of work in Case C-456/02 *Trojani v Centre public d'aide sociale de Bruxelles (CPAS)* [2004] ECR I-7573, esp. at paras 26–31 of the Opinion. *De minimis* questions with respect to the *level* of work undertaken are discussed in Chapter 5.

[34] Case 53/81 *Levin v Staatssecretaris van Justitie* [1982] ECR 1035, paras 12–13 and 15.

[35] Case C-159/90 *Society for the Protection of Unborn Children Ireland Ltd (SPUC) v Stephan Grogan and others* [1991] ECR I-4685, para. 21. However, applying a remoteness test, the Court did not consider that service provision had been restricted (see further, Chapter 5).

neutral way without an express accommodation of associated value debates, however sensitive. In other words, the Court rarely excludes activity from the scope of the Treaty at the level of definition.[36] Instead, it more properly navigates moral and other complexities at the justification and proportionality stages. For example, neither gambling activities nor prostitution fall outside the scope of the free movement provisions per se.[37] If an activity is unlawful in *all* of the Member States, it will not be treated as economic activity at all, precluding individuals from relying on the Treaty to challenge restrictions on that activity e.g. the distribution of narcotic drugs outwith strictly controlled channels for medical and scientific use.[38] This is an objective yardstick that can be measured empirically, and it avoids the need for unhelpfully subjective decisions. Taking the empirical approach even further, the claimant in *Josemans*, a coffee shop owner in the Netherlands, was considered to fall within the scope of freedom of establishment on the grounds that somewhere between 2.5 and 7.1 per cent of his turnover was generated not by the sale and consumption of cannabis but through the marketing of non-alcoholic beverages and food. The challenge failed at the justification stage, but the existence of a *restriction* on free movement rights was first upheld. That decision also illustrates the general absence of *de minimis* considerations in free movement law, discussed in Chapter 5.

Just two years before the decision in *Grogan*, however, work performed 'merely as a means of rehabilitation or reintegration' was excluded from the Treaty's scope in *Bettray*.[39] In that case, the claimant was participating in a work programme in the course of recovery from drug addiction. The Court did not explain *why* work that met the remuneration and supervision conditions of *Lawrie-Blum* but was performed as part of a social employment programme was not effective and genuine.[40] The applicant was seeking a residence permit only, and not claiming any financial benefits: in contrast to the situation in *Levin*, where recourse to

[36] See Case 279/80 *Criminal proceedings against Webb* [1981] ECR 3305, para. 10: 'the special nature of certain services does not remove them from the ambit of the rules on the freedom to supply services'. This approach has influenced the development of case law on e.g. sporting activities, where the general principle is that the Treaty provisions 'do not affect rules concerning questions which are of purely sporting interest and, as such, have nothing to do with economic activity'—meaning that sporting rules outwith this narrowly interpreted band *do* fall within the scope of EU law (see e.g. Case C-519/04 P *Meca-Medina and Majcen v Commission* [2006] ECR I-6991, para. 25 and cf. Joined Cases C-51/96 and C-191/97 *Deliège v Ligue francophone de judo et disciplines associées ASBL, Ligue belge de judo ASBL, Union européenne de judo, and Pacquée* [2000] ECR I-2549).

[37] See e.g. Case C-275/92 *Her Majesty's Customs and Excise v Schindler* [1994] ECR I-1039: '[e]ven if the morality of lotteries is at least questionable, it is not for the Court to substitute its assessment for that of the legislatures of the Member States where that activity is practised legally' (para. 32); Case C-268/99 *Jany and Others v Staatssecretaris van Justitie* [2001] ECR I-8615 'prostitution is a provision of services for remuneration which . . . falls within the concept of economic activities' (para. 49).

[38] See e.g. the authorities cited in Case C-137/09 *Josemans v Burgemeester van Maastricht* [2010] ECR I-13019, para. 41.

[39] Case 344/87 *Bettray Staatssecretaris van Justitie* [1989] ECR 1621.

[40] The Court considered that work 'cannot be regarded as an effective and genuine economic activity if it constitutes merely a means of rehabilitation or reintegration for the persons concerned and the purpose of the paid employment, which is adapted to the physical and mental possibilities of each person, is to enable those persons sooner or later to recover their capacity to take up ordinary employment or to lead as normal as possible a life' (*Bettray*, para. 17).

supplementary income allowances did not defeat the applicant's status as a (part-time) worker under EU law.[41]

The approach of the Court in *Bettray* again comes close to exploring questions in the realm of motivation: and at the definition rather than justification stage of free movement law, as we saw similarly in case law on publicly funded education. In *Birden*, the Court acknowledged that the decision in *Bettray* 'does not follow the general trend of the case-law concerning the interpretation of [the concept of worker] in [EU] law' and 'can be explained only by the particular characteristics of that case'[42]—not altogether helpful, and exemplifying the concerns expressed in Chapter 2 about the Court's dual functioning as a de facto first instance but also constitutional court. Six years later, in *Trojani*, the Court expanded on the 'particular characteristics' of *Bettray* as 'concern[ing] the situation of a person who, by reason of his addiction to drugs, had been recruited on the basis of a national law intended to provide work for persons who, for an indefinite period, are unable, by reason of circumstances related to their situation, to work under normal conditions'.[43] Significantly, AG Geelhoed, following considerable discussion of *Bettray*, did not consider that Mr Trojani *could* be considered as a worker. The Court confirmed that he met the basic conditions of remuneration and supervision through 'various jobs' performed under the direction of the Salvation Army, while receiving 'benefits in kind and some pocket money... as *part of a personal reintegration programme*'.[44] But critically, whether or not he reached the required threshold of effective and genuine activity was left, this time, for determination by the national court.

This is an appropriate delegation of the decision-making function to the national court in a framework of constitutional responsibility; but the lack of a clear steer from the Court on the continuing legal force of *Bettray* undercuts the *utility* of that trust overall. Looking at the decisions in *Bettray* and *Trojani* together, the coherence of the case law was affected in the narrower sense of authority-fit but also against the wider gauge of the Court's well-rationalized preference for an expansive understanding of work and workers—an objective linked to the realization of an effective internal market. Like *Humbel*, *Bettray* is an odd decision that has never been properly explained yet continues to cast an exclusionary interpretative shadow. Its effects were softened in *Trojani*, but why not reverse *Bettray* definitively by engaging support from post-*Bettray* Treaty commitments? The exclusion of work that meets the essential characteristics of the Court's definition purely because it is linked to rehabilitation objectives does not fit with the TEU objective of promoting 'economic and social progress' and it does not affirm 'as the essential objective of [Member States'] efforts the constant improvements of the living and working conditions of their peoples'. It also jars with almost all of the objectives listed in Article 9 TFEU, especially with the fight against social exclusion. At a

[41] See generally, C O'Brien, 'Social blind spots and monocular policy making: The ECJ's migrant worker model' (2009) 46:4 CMLRev 1107.

[42] Case C-1/97 *Birden v Stadtgemeinde Bremen* [1998] ECR I 7747, para. 31.

[43] *Trojani*, para. 19.

[44] *Trojani*, paras 20, 23, and 24 (emphasis added).

general level, *Bettray* remains good law because the Court continues to cite it—but, ironically, the paragraphs that tend to be referenced relate to the obligation to interpret the concept of a worker *broadly*, leaving the narrow outcome in *Bettray* itself at the edges of free movement law. This case law was also flagged here in respect of an inclination towards exploring the motivation of the actor involved when determining personal scope; a theme that will be developed further in Section 3 on abuse of EU rights.

(d) Is there a hierarchy of rights in free movement law?

A final issue to consider is whether there is a legally relevant hierarchy of free movement rights. Like the substantive dimension discussed above, this question brings an activity-based angle to delimiting personal scope, by asking whether there are different *categories* of actors within the free movement framework (and whether that, in turn, has implications for *what* they are entitled to claim). As a starting point, it was noted in Chapter 2 that the Treaty defines services as a residual or sweeper freedom vis-à-vis goods, workers, establishment, and capital, and that the Court has developed principles to determine which Treaty provision(s) apply in specific factual circumstances (e.g. is an iPhone contract about goods or services, or both?). Additionally, the Court has been flexible when the centre of activity-gravity is not particularly obvious, aided by the convergence of many of the principles that frame free movement law in a general sense. But two particular questions beyond this basic, Treaty-set hierarchy will now be considered: first, the hybrid category of 'citizen-workers' and, second, general implications from the perspective of protecting fundamental rights.

(i) The citizen-worker

Although not mandated by the Treaty, and at odds with the conception of EU citizenship as the 'fundamental status' of Member State nationals,[45] it could be suggested that the Court considers the rights to move and reside in Article 21 TFEU as residual even to services: where the Treaty provisions on economic activity *can* be used, the Court says that they should be.[46] On one view, this convention can be seen as a formal one, first developed in the twilight zone before the autonomous qualities of Articles 20 and 21 were animated through the case law beginning with *Martínez Sala*. It does not, in other words, detract from the substantive legal force of either provision, a claim examined further in Chapter 4. It was noted in Chapter 2, however, that the Court has created a distinctive 'citizen-worker' category that is taking root as a discrete form of personal

[45] The phrase was first used by the Court in Case C-184/99 *Grzelczyk v Centre public d'aide sociale d'Ottignies-Louvain-la-Neuve* [2001] ECR I-6193, para. 31; 'fundamental *legal* status' (emphasis changed) had been used by AG La Pergola in *Martínez Sala*, paras 18–19 of the Opinion.

[46] See e.g. Case C-56/09 *Zanotti v Agenzia delle Entrate—Ufficio Roma 2* [2010] ECR I-4517, para. 24; Case C-318/05 *Commission* v *Germany* [2007] ECR I-6957, paras 32–37; Case C-92/01 *Stylianakis v Elliniko Dimosio* [2003] ECR I-1291, para. 18.

scope. The also-distinctive material rights that can stem from this hybrid status are particularly apparent in case law on access to benefits for job-seekers.[47] In *Collins* and *Vatsouras and Koupatantze*, and in line with previous case law,[48] AG Ruiz-Jarabo Colomer proceeded on the basis that job-seekers come within the scope of Article 45 TFEU, then discussing relevant provisions of Directive 2004/38. The same Advocate General delivered the Opinion in *Ioannidis*, focusing there, however, on Article 21 TFEU, having ruled out the possibility that the applicant was a migrant worker and stressing that '[t]he status of citizen of the Union is set to become the fundamental legal status of Member State nationals, entitling them—irrespective of their nationality and without prejudice to certain special provisions—to enjoy the same treatment in law as that accorded to the nationals of those Member States who find themselves in the same situation'.[49]

In all three Opinions, then, the rights of the applicants were discussed as relating to *either* migrant workers *or* the status of citizenship. But in *Collins*, the Court conjoined the two lines of argument: 'in view of the establishment of citizenship of the Union and the interpretation in the case-law of the right to equal treatment enjoyed by citizens of the Union, it is no longer possible to exclude from the scope of Article [45(2) TFEU] . . . a benefit of a financial nature intended to facilitate access to employment in the labour market of a Member State'.[50] The critical implication of the citizen-worker fusion then follows: '[b]enefits of a financial nature which, independently of their status under national law, are intended to facilitate access to the labour market *cannot be regarded as constituting "social assistance"* within the meaning of Article 24(2) of Directive 2004/38'[51]—meaning that migrant job-seekers may become eligible to receive them during the first three months of residence in a host State, and for as long as they 'can provide evidence that they are continuing to seek employment and that they have a genuine chance of being engaged' (Article 14(4)(b)). More generally, for an initial three-month period, Article 6 of the Directive confirms that Union citizens (and their family members, as defined by Article 2) have a right of residence in a host State 'without any conditions or any formalities other than the requirement to hold a valid

[47] Joined Cases C-22/08 and C-23/08 *Vatsouras and Koupatantze v Arbeitsgemeinschaft (ARGE) Nürnberg 900* [2009] ECR I-4585; Case C-258/04 *Office national de l'emploi v Ioannidis* [2005] ECR I-8275; Case C-138/02 *Collins v Secretary of State for Work and Pensions* [2004] ECR I-2703.

[48] See esp. *Antonissen*.

[49] AG Ruiz-Jarabo Colomer in *Ioannidis*, para. 54 of the Opinion.

[50] *Collins*, para. 63; confirmed in *Vatsouras and Koupatantze*, para. 37.

[51] *Collins*, para. 45 (emphasis added). Article 24(2) of Directive 2004/38 provides as follows: '1. Subject to such specific provisions as are expressly provided for in the Treaty and secondary law, all Union citizens residing on the basis of this Directive in the territory of the host Member State shall enjoy equal treatment with the nationals of that Member State within the scope of the Treaty. The benefit of this right shall be extended to family members who are not nationals of a Member State and who have the right of residence or permanent residence. 2. By way of derogation from paragraph 1, the host Member State shall not be obliged to confer entitlement to social assistance during the first three months of residence or, where appropriate, the longer period provided for in Article 14(4)(b), nor shall it be obliged, prior to acquisition of the right of permanent residence, to grant maintenance aid for studies, including vocational training, consisting in student grants or student loans to persons other than workers, self-employed persons, persons who retain such status and members of their families'.

identity card or passport'. But Article 7(1)(b) requires that, for migrant Member State nationals who are *not* working, self-employed or studying there, two conditions must thereafter be met i.e. sufficient resources not to become a burden on the host State social assistance system; and comprehensive sickness insurance cover. What the Court has done, in effect, is also to remove migrants *seeking* work from the reach of these conditions. The rights of citizen-workers are thus greater than the sum of their parts.

The Court has used the citizen-worker logic implicitly in other contexts too. In its decisions in *Ibrahim* and *Teixeira*, for example, it held that the applicants acquired derivative lawful residence rights in the United Kingdom through Article 12 of Regulation 1612/68 because they were the primary carers of children being educated there.[52] Mrs Ibrahim, a Somali national, was married to but separated from a Danish national who had briefly worked in the UK (from October 2002 to May 2003). The applicant in *Teixeira*, a Portuguese national, had herself worked there in the past (intermittently between 1989 and 2005). In both cases, the lawfulness of their continued residence in the UK was questioned because the applicants had applied for housing benefits—i.e. becoming a burden on the host State social assistance system. But the Court was adamant that no prior requirements of self-sufficiency could be read into what is now Regulation 492/2011. The rights conferred by the Regulation on the children of migrant workers—to complete their education in the host State—were paramount; the right to respect for family life then kicked in to ensure that the children's primary carers could reside in the UK with them. Both judgments are framed in the language of workers, but the actual level of work undertaken surely skirts close to the marginal/ancillary threshold discussed above[53]—a test that was cited in the Opinion, but not the judgment, in *Teixeira*. It is submitted that the fact of work was used instrumentally to achieve something else in *Ibrahim* and *Teixeira*: enabling two families otherwise outwith the scope of Directive 2004/38 to continue to live in the State where they had settled, with support from that State if needed.[54] The fundamental rights dimension of this objective will be returned to in Section 2(d)(ii).

Citizen-worker hybrid rights do not apply to economic activity generally: for example, the Court has confirmed that the rights conferred on the children of migrant workers by Regulation 492/2011—and, more specifically, the residence rights then derived by their primary carers—cannot be extended to self-employed

[52] Case C-310/08 *London Borough of Harrow v Ibrahim and Secretary of State for the Home Department* [2010] ECR I-1065; Case C-480/08 *Teixeira v London Borough of Lambeth and Secretary of State for the Home Department* [2010] ECR I-1107. Regulation 1612/68 has since been replaced by Regulation 492/2011 on freedom of movement for workers within the Union (2011 OJ L141/1), Article 10 of which is identical to the earlier measure's Article 12 on the right to host State education for the children of migrant workers.

[53] See e.g. *Trojani*, para. 15. See further, C O'Brien, case comment on *Ibrahim* and *Teixeira*, (2011) 48:1 CMLRev 203 at 214. There was no discussion of *de minimis* thresholds in these cases; see further, Chapter 5.

[54] The problematic way in which the Directive has been implemented by the Member States should also be borne in mind; see e.g. European Commission, Communication on guidance for better transposition and application of Directive 2004/38/EC, COM(2009) 313.

persons.[55] Even in the context of work, however, the Court has set limits. The downside of taking citizen-workers outside the span of Directive 2004/38 in some circumstances became starkly apparent in AG Bot's Opinion in *Alarape and Tijani*, a case that further explores the rights of primary carers. It is interesting first to note that, addressing four of the five questions sent by the national immigration tribunal, which were aimed at fleshing out the characteristics of the primary care relationship, AG Bot considered that he should not answer questions that would 'require [the Court] to depart from the area of law and venture into the area of fact, which is a matter for the national court, whose freedom in assessing the evidence laid before it cannot and must not be restricted by the definition of precise criteria'.[56] This approach reflects the arguments presented in Chapters 1 and 2 at one level; it is submitted, however, that the Advocate General could have extracted from the facts-based questions that relate very directly to the family situations at issue more general questions that do seek to understand the meaning of the status of 'primary carer' in law—something that is not yet clearly settled in existing case law. It will be seen in Chapter 4, for example, that dependency has been interpreted very narrowly in another strand of case law, focusing on material and not emotional support: does the same threshold apply to primary carers or not? It is not the role of the Court of Justice to consider, for example, the depth or evidence of the ties involved in the actual family situations in this case; but it does need to advise the referring court whether such an inquiry should form part of the latter's remit or not.

In the substantive part of his analysis, addressing the fifth question referred, AG Bot reaffirmed the linkages between different parts of the overall scheme of Directive 2004/38. Article 16 of the Directive created a significant new status in EU law: Article 16(1) establishes that 'Union citizens who have resided legally for a continuous period of five years in the host Member State shall have the right of *permanent residence* there' (emphasis added). Critically, the self-sufficiency conditions set out in Article 7 of the Directive will then no longer apply. Article 16(2) confirms that the possibility of acquiring permanent residence rights 'shall apply also to family members who are not nationals of a Member State and have legally resided with the Union citizen in the host Member State for a continuous period of

[55] Joined Cases C-147/11 and C-148/11 *Secretary of State for Work and Pensions v Czop and Punakova*, judgment of 6 September 2012, paras 30–33.

[56] AG Bot in Case C-529/11 *Alarape and Tijani v Secretary of State for the Home Department*, judgment of 8 May 2013, para. 35 of the Opinion. The first four questions probed various aspects of financial, material and emotional dependence in the context of primary care: '1. [f]or a parent to qualify as a "primary carer" so as to derive a right of residence from a child over 21 exercising a right of access to education under Article 12 Regulation No 1612/68 . . . , is it necessary for that child to be (i) dependent on such a parent; (ii) residing in that parent's household; and (iii) receiving emotional support from that parent? 2. If in order to qualify for such a derived right of residence it is unnecessary for a parent to show that all three of the above circumstances obtain, is it sufficient to show that only one obtains or that only two obtain? 3. In relation to [(ii) in the first question], can there continue to be residence on the part of an adult student child in a common household with his parent(s) even when the former is living away from home for the duration of his studies (save for holidays and occasional weekends)? 4. In relation to [(iii) in the first question], is it necessary for the emotional support provided by the parent to be of a particular quality (viz. close or physically proximate) or is it sufficient if it consists in a normal emotional tie between a parent and an adult child?' (para. 21 of the Opinion).

five years'. But in *Alarape and Tijani*, AG Bot argued that periods of residence derived exclusively from education rights conferred by the Regulation should *not* count towards the five-year period of lawful residence required by Article 16 of the Directive if the Article 7 conditions of self-sufficiency were not met during the material time—a position confirmed by the Court.[57] He reasoned this conclusion as a consequence of the fact that residence rights based on Regulation 492/2011 had been 'freed by the case-law' from the Article 7 conditions;[58] but he also acknowledged the oddity of the result:

> Since the children and the parents caring for them may be entitled to a right of residence of more than three months which corresponds to that provided for in Article 7 of Directive 2004/38, but the implementation of which is independent of the conditions set out in that article, the reintroduction of those conditions for the acquisition of the status of permanent resident is paradoxical, which is all the more striking because the principle of the autonomy of the right of residence, conceived to benefit the child by relieving him of any requirement of financial autonomy, *finally rebounds against its beneficiary* by depriving him of access to the status of permanent resident.[59]

The main rationale for this outcome was considered by AG Bot to be 'the need to preserve the balance, desired by the Union legislature, between, on the one hand, requirements of freedom of movement and integration and, on the other, the financial interests of the Member States'.[60]

In *Förster*, prioritizing the same objective can be used to explain, if not defend, a similarly constricted outcome.[61] The case concerned a German national who had resided in the Netherlands since 2000 as a third-level student and had also engaged in various forms of employment there; in particular, she participated in a paid placement connected to her studies from October 2002 to June 2003. After that date, she did not take up further paid employment until, after her graduation in 2004, she accepted a position as a social worker. Ms Förster was awarded a maintenance grant for her studies but the relevant public authority sought to reclaim it for the period from July to December 2003, arguing that she had been awarded the grant as an EU worker but that she was not, in fact, working at the time in question; neither did she retain the status of worker under applicable EU rules. National regulations otherwise required at least five years of continuous residence in the Netherlands before the award of maintenance to a migrant student per se.

The applicant was found *not* to come within the scope of Article 45 TFEU during the material time, but she instead invoked EU citizenship rights and the more fluid 'certain degree of integration' reasoning applied to a student

[57] AG Bot in *Alarape and Tijani*, esp. para. 77 of the Opinion onwards; citing, in particular, Joined Cases C-424/10 and C-425/10 *Ziolkowski and Szeja and others v Land Berlin*, judgment of 21 December 2011.

[58] AG Bot in *Alarape and Tijani*, para. 74 of the Opinion.

[59] AG Bot in *Alarape and Tijani*, para. 74 of the Opinion (emphasis added).

[60] AG Bot in *Alarape and Tijani*, para. 80 of the Opinion.

[61] Case C-158/07 *Förster v Hoofddirectie van de Informatie Beheer Groep* [2008] ECR I-8507.

maintenance claim in *Bidar*.[62] The test developed in that case—whether the applicant had 'established a genuine link with the society of [the host] State'—reflects the Court's dominant approach in free movement law generally: it requires that the particular circumstances of each individual should be assessed on a case-by-case basis.[63] Unexpectedly, however, the Court held in *Förster* that 'a residence requirement of five years . . . does not go beyond what is necessary to attain the objective of ensuring that students from other Member States are to a certain degree integrated into the society of the host Member State'.[64] The national restrictions were considered to be 'appropriate'[65] and not 'excessive'[66]—a very one-dimensional proportionality assessment considering, on the other hand, the short duration of the period for which reimbursement was being sought against the much longer period of integration into the host State, as both a student and a worker, that Ms Förster had already built up and continued to deepen. For those very reasons, AG Mazák had proposed a proportionality-softened solution that built on the decision in *Bidar*. In the judgment, however, the Court quietly repackaged the subjective and flexible 'degree of integration' test from *Bidar* as an objective and fixed temporal benchmark.[67]

Crucially, the five-year rule in the national regulations mirrored the wording of Article 24(2) of Directive 2004/38: the student maintenance case law was thus being future-proofed to ensure a better fit with the (then) adopted but not yet in force Directive.[68] This example illustrates an important constitutional constraint under which the Court must operate in the development of EU citizenship rights: Articles 20 and 21 TFEU provide that the rights to move and reside freely are subject to the limits and conditions laid down not just in the Treaties but also *by the measures adopted to give them effect*[69]—by secondary legislation, in other words, which inverts the normally applicable Treaty/legislation hierarchy.[70] If the decision

[62] *Bidar*; see generally, paras 51–63.

[63] 'Real link' tests are used in other areas of free movement law too e.g. for resolving questions concerning the State of residence and State of employment in case law on frontier workers; see A Tryfonidou, 'In search of the aim of the EC free movement of persons provisions: Has the Court of Justice missed the point?' (2009) 46:5 CMLRev 1591. Similarly, in the case law on benefits for job-seekers, applicants can be required to demonstrate that 'a genuine link exists between the person seeking work and the employment market of [the host] State' (*Collins*, para. 69).

[64] *Förster*, para. 58.

[65] *Förster*, para. 52.

[66] *Förster*, para. 54, going on (in para. 55) to cite Article 24 of the Directive 'in that connection'. For critique, see S O'Leary, 'Equal treatment and EU citizens: A new chapter on cross-border educational mobility and access to student financial assistance' (2009) 34:4 ELRev 612.

[67] Comparing case law in which the circumstances of the individual were emphasized with decisions where more detached, blanket rules were instead approved, see M Dougan, 'Judicial activism or constitutional interaction? Policymaking by the ECJ in the field of Union citizenship' in H Micklitz and B de Witte (eds.), *The European Court of Justice and the Autonomy of the Member States* (Intersentia, 2012) 113 at 131 ff.

[68] Both *Bidar* and *Förster* were heard by the Grand Chamber, with different rapporteurs but five judges in common.

[69] Article 21 TFEU; Article 20 refers similarly to 'measures adopted [under the Treaties]'.

[70] For further discussion of this point, see N Nic Shuibhne, 'The third age of EU citizenship: Directive 2004/38 in the case law of the Court of Justice' in P Syrpis (ed.), *The Judiciary, The Legislature and The EU Internal Market* (CUP, 2012) 331 at 336–7.

in *Förster* seems to unsettle the coherence of the case law that preceded it, it can at least be rationalized on one level by the constitutional message in Article 21 that the limits set by the legislature have to be observed. The Court has recently confirmed that Article 24(2) must nevertheless, as a derogation from the principle of equal treatment, be interpreted narrowly: this means that the more flexible 'genuine link' approach continues to apply in cases involving financial aid for students that is *not* considered to constitute 'student grants or student loans'.[71] But the decision in *Förster* also underscores a more difficult point: that weaker rights can attach to citizens than to citizen-workers (or just workers generally).[72] Looking at the decision in *Alarape and Tijani*, however, the opposite statement is equally true: citizen-workers can in turn be excluded from some of the benefits of EU citizenship. In seeking to reconcile these apparently conflicting bases, what *is* the intended hierarchy of rights for the personal scope of the Treaty, and how can the underpinning case law be rationalized from the premise of coherence?

The Court's approach to work is not straightforwardly about self-sufficiency. The case law on job-seekers fits with the decisions in *Ibrahim* and *Teixeira* if we prioritize not the contribution made through economic activity but, instead, the value of achieving the most favourable outcome in individual cases by harnessing the conceptual power of EU citizenship—whether the relevant Treaty provisions are directly engaged or not.[73] But the dangers of overemphasizing individual situations when developing principles of law at the constitutional level must be restated here: applicants who are unlucky enough to bring their claims at points when the case law snaps back on itself in the pursuit of varying goals will unfairly bear negative consequences. It is unlikely that good betting-odds would have been given post-*Bidar* for predicting that Ms Förster would lose; but then, it seemed equally unlikely to expect judgments like *Ibrahim* and *Teixeira* after *Förster*. These points will be picked up again in Chapter 4.

The relevant broader goals also seem to be pursued inconsistently. In *Förster*, for example, the result was compliant with the legislature's intentions, as expressed through Directive 2004/38, and with the deference to legislative limits explicitly built into Articles 20 and 21 TFEU. But the citizen-worker case law subverts those very same factors, calling into question more pluralist explanations that suggest, as discussed in Chapter 1, an ongoing judicial/political dialogue. Furthermore, the Court attached decisive weight to (limited) past work undertaken in *Teixeira* and *Ibrahim*, but not to work undertaken in both the past *and* the present in *Förster*, raising questions about the imperfect rationales that shape judicial responses to claims about access to benefits. In the majority of these cases, the Court has tried to find a way to help individual claimants, by isolating Directive 2004/38 and its express self-sufficiency limits, notwithstanding the express convergence intention

[71] Case C-75/11 *Commission v Austria*, judgment of 4 October 2012, confirming that reduced student fares on public transport did not come within the scope of Article 24(2) of the Directive.

[72] Cf. the decision in *Förster* with the tougher stance in Case C-542/09 *Commission v Netherlands*, judgment of 14 June 2012, which *was* based on Article 45 TFEU.

[73] See e.g. E Spaventa, 'Seeing the wood despite the trees? On the scope of Union citizenship and its constitutional effects' (2008) 45:1 CMLRev 13.

that informs the Directive's preamble and the undoubted inclusion of workers (and other economically active migrants) in the personal scope of the Directive more generally.

The legitimacy of supplementing self-sufficiency through partial or 'reasonable' recourse to host State resources long predates EU citizenship and Directive 2004/38.[74] But it could be argued that the general force of the self-sufficiency conditions in Article 7 of the Directive requires *all* migrant EU citizens residing in a host State for longer than three months to meet them—including those who work or engage in other forms of economic activity. There is another crucial point here: the housing assistance claims of Ms Teixeira and Ms Ibrahim would be no less real if their children were *not* in education, but neither work nor citizenship could help them then.[75] Is this framework of personal scope, which clearly links *who* you are with *what* you do and what, in material terms, you *have*, properly compliant with other constitutional imperatives such as the protection of fundamental rights?

(ii) The human (rights) dimension

In Chapter 2, the Opinion of AG Ruiz-Jarabo Colomer in *Petersen* was flagged as a reflection on directions of travel in case law on the free movement of persons. Discussing the interplay between work and citizenship, he described the application of Article 45 TFEU to disputes involving employed persons only as the 'more orthodox approach' but then suggested, commenting on the simultaneous application of the Treaty provisions on citizenship and work outlined above, that while the orthodox approach 'is consistent with the case-law . . . the outcome reached is not always clear or convincing'.[76] These remarks reflect the caveat, acknowledged in Chapters 1 and 2, that sustaining case law coherence is a necessary but not necessarily sufficient constitutional objective. AG Ruiz-Jarabo Colomer noted that in *Carpenter*, for example, there was an acute disconnect between personal and material scope, illustrated by the securing of a long-term right of residence in the applicant's *home* State for his third country national spouse on the basis that he provided services in *other* Member States from time to time.[77] But, by stepping back from individual decisions, he considered that the Court's judgments collectively 'demonstrate a tendency towards protecting individuals, a concern with the personal situation of those who exercise a right under the Treaties which in the past was much less evident. Thus, the free movement of persons acquires its own identity, imbued with an essential nature that is *more constitutional than statutory*,

[74] See e.g. the decision in *Levin* and, in the specific context of education, see Joined Cases 389/87 and 390/87 *Echternach and Moritz v Minister van Onderwijs en Wetenschapp* [1989] ECR 723.

[75] Unless it could be claimed that the family would otherwise be forced to leave the territory of the Union, as discussed in Chapter 4.

[76] AG Ruiz-Jarabo Colomer in Case C-228/07 *Petersen v Arbeitsmarktservice Niederösterreich* [2008] ECR I-6989, para. 18 of the Opinion.

[77] The use of an inherently temporary freedom to establish long-term residence rights was later rejected by AG Tizzano in Case C-200/02 *Zhu and Chen v Secretary of State for the Home Department* [2004] ECR I-9925, paras 57–61 of the Opinion.

transforming it into a freedom akin to the dynamics of the fundamental rights'.[78] Can this fundamental concern with the individual as a rights-bearing citizen compensate in more systemic terms for the points of friction that have been identified in the case law on personal scope?

As emphasized in Chapter 2, the Court can only protect fundamental rights in a secondary sense; a substantive question 'within the scope of EU law' must be identified first. The decision in *Givane*, delivered just seven months after the judgment in *Carpenter*, illustrates this point very well. At the time, the right to remain in a host State following the death of a migrant worker was governed by Regulation 1251/70, Article 3(2) of which addressed situations where the worker died during his working life.[79] In the context of continuing residence rights for family members, Article 3(2) required that the worker, on the date of his or her decease, had resided continuously in the territory of the host State for at least two years. Mr Givane was a Portuguese national. He first arrived in the UK in 1992, where he resided and worked until he travelled to India, staying there from April 1995 to February 1996. He then returned to the UK with his wife and three children, who were Indian nationals, but died there 21 months later in November 1997.

Drawing from the 'purpose and scheme of the rules of which [Article 3(2)] forms part',[80] the Court held that that the critical period of 'at least two years' had to be interpreted as *immediately* preceding the worker's death—thus not requiring the UK to extend a right to remain to Mr Givane's widow or children on the basis of EU law. It reached this conclusion by assessing the scheme of the Regulation itself but also the objectives of Article 45 TFEU. In that context, citing *Carpenter*, the Court acknowledged the importance of the right to respect for family life and the fact that '[i]t is in the interest of the worker and his family that, should that worker die prematurely, his family members should, *as a rule*, be entitled to reside in the territory of the host Member State'.[81] But the Court then emphasized that such rights were 'subject to the limitations and conditions laid down by the EU Treaty and by the measures adopted for its application'.[82] Here again, we see hybridization; but the other way around: the Court limits the rights conferred on *workers* through the formula that appears in the Treaty provisions on *citizenship* only. In *Givane*, the human dimension was clearly more decisive for AG Alber, who had argued as follows:

> The subsequent arrival of family members generally entails considerable changes for that family, such as, for example, leaving their homeland and social environment, giving up the home to which they have become accustomed, a possible transfer of school-age children to another school, establishment of a reasonable standard of accommodation and living in the host State, etc. It therefore seems entirely justified that—where the worker has already

[78] AG Ruiz-Jarabo Colomer *Petersen*, para. 17 of the Opinion (emphasis added).

[79] These situations are now regulated by Articles 12 and 17 of Directive 2004/38.

[80] Case C-257/00 *Givane and others v Secretary of State for the Home Department* [2003] ECR I-345, para. 37.

[81] *Givane*, para. 45 (emphasis added).

[82] *Givane*, para. 46.

acquired an established right—family members who have taken this step should not be faced with a period of legal uncertainty with respect to their right to remain. This applies particularly where the worker dies since this is most often an unforeseeable stroke of fate for the family.[83]

Echoing the student maintenance case law, the Court considered that host States are entitled to expect a 'certain level of integration in society' from migrant workers before an obligation to confer a right to remain on family members can be triggered. Crucially, however, the Court equated that expectation with its narrow interpretation of the Regulation's two-year requirement. In other words, *Givane* reflects *Förster*, not *Bidar*. Recalling the discussion in Chapter 2 about the impact of the Court's working methods on case law coherence, it can also be noted that *Carpenter* was heard by the full Court while *Givane* was resolved by the Fifth Chamber; only two judges were involved in both cases.

Even accepting the logic of the Court's point that '[t]he existence of a significant connection between the host Member State and the worker concerned could not be ensured if the right of residence... provided for by [Article 3(2) of the Regulation] were to be acquired as soon as a worker had resided for at least two years in that State at some stage of his life, even in the distant past',[84] there is not even a mention of proportionality in this judgment—the mitigating principle typically applied where clear legislative language appears to determine a particular outcome.[85] The Court in *Givane* appeals convincingly to the legal certainty created by applying legislation strictly: but the problem is that it does not always do that *itself*.

In *Petersen*, AG Ruiz-Jarabo Colomer proposed a 'more refined legal method' for resolving cases on personal free movement rights. The core premises of his reasoning are worth quoting in full:

The concept of citizenship, which entails *a legal status for individuals*, means that the Member States must pay *particular attention to individual legal situations*. The fundamental rights play a vital role in the performance of that task... Holding their fundamental rights as prerogatives of freedom, citizens of the Union afford their claims greater legitimacy. Moreover, in some cases, where a fundamental right is not at stake but a clear injustice has been committed, a stringent review of proportionality may be carried out... Thus, the *free movement of persons* becomes the *movement of free citizens*. That change of perspective is not insignificant, because, rather than falling on the concept of movement, the focus of attention has shifted to the individual... [T]he importance of the responsibilities and obligations of States of origin is noticeably waning in favour of the responsibilities and obligations of host States... When the ties of identity with a single State are broken so that they may be shared with others, a connection is woven in a wider sphere. As a result, the notion of European belonging is created, which the Treaties seek to strengthen. Justice Benjamin Cardozo expressed it superbly in *Baldwin v GAF Seelig*, in connection with the Constitution of the United States of America, when he pointed out that the Constitution

83 AG Alber in *Givane*, para. 64 of the Opinion. 84 *Givane*, para. 47.

85 For example, this was how the Court relieved an applicant of the requirement to have fully *comprehensive* sickness insurance in accordance with Article 7 of Directive 2004/38 in Case C-413/99 *Baumbast and R v Secretary of State for the Home Department* [2002] ECR I-7091.

'was framed upon the theory that the peoples of the several states must sink or swim together, and that in the long run prosperity and salvation are in union and not division'.[86]

In this passage, the Advocate General defended the method of focusing on the circumstances of the individual by using the normative weight of the status of citizenship and the protection of fundamental rights—which he conceptualizes as distinct but complementary objectives, bringing a different complexion to the risks of overemphasizing the situation of the individual identified more generally in Chapter 2. He also located this objective in broader ideas of community and solidarity: not in the top-down way currently prevalent in discourse on the Eurozone crisis,[87] but through more organic processes sparked by the contributory actions of the citizens themselves. The latter approach is not only more appealing; it is also more likely to create something *real*. But it is also more fragile; it takes time, and it exposes another constitutional choice that has yet to be settled definitively: does the protection of the individual through EU citizenship only come on stream in the context of migration? The Advocate General argues that protection of fundamental rights properly shifts our focus from the concept of movement, but his thesis is rooted primarily in the changing nature of duties imposed on *host* States—meaning that movement has already occurred. These critical questions will be picked up in Chapter 4.

(e) Definitional exclusion from the scope of the Treaty: interim conclusions

An overview of case law on exclusion from the personal scope of free movement rights at the level of basic definitions might be expected to uncover splinters of fragmentation driven mostly by the application of multiple concepts and tests. Instead, questions of a less technical, more thematic nature have emerged. First, the relationship between personal and material scope is complicated. In one sense, the Court has severed the need to establish a direct connection between who you are and what you are seeking; but in other respects, what you do or what you have clearly shapes how you come within the scope of the Treaty in a personal sense. Second, there is no coherent hierarchy among different categories of personal scope; in particular, citizenship is not *always* the 'fundamental status' of Member State nationals. Third, there are clear examples of conflicting lines of authority on the same issue that the Court has not addressed. The relevance of motivation was distinguished in that context and will be picked up in Section 3.

The tension between developing constitutional principles at the systemic level and resolving disputes necessarily shaped by individual facts and circumstances

[86] AG Ruiz-Jarabo Colomer in *Petersen*, paras 27–34 of the Opinion (emphasis in original), citing *Baldwin v GAF Seelig, Inc.*, 294 U.S. 522, 523 (1935).

[87] E.g. Amtenbrink has argued that the Eurozone crisis has exposed the thinness rather than resilience of transnational solidarity (F Amtenbrink, 'Europe in times of economic crisis: Bringing Europe's citizens closer to one another?' in M Dougan, N Nic Shuibhne, and E Spaventa (eds.), *Empowerment and Disempowerment of the European Citizen* (Hart Publishing, 2012) 171.

became particularly apparent. As argued in Chapters 1 and 2, 'preliminary ruling proceedings combine the specific features of a particular case with the requirements of case-law which has been laid down for a Community of 500 million citizens who seek responses that are both individual and universal'.[88] The case law on personal scope adds further questions in this context. On the one hand, judgments defying the liberalizing dynamic that dominates the free movement case law are usually compatible with a higher-order coherence that appeals to specific constitutional objectives e.g. respecting the limits established by legislation. But then, two problems arise. First, why do *different* broader objectives matter more at some times than at others, and which conceptual or structural factors are really driving the Court's oscillation between them? Second, how can the restrictive implications of narrower judgments be rationalized from the perspective of the actual impact on the individuals affected? In such cases, the rights of citizens and traders are too easily pushed to the side. We can engage analytical tools from discourse on judicial law-making more generally here, thinking especially of the distinction between process and outcome as useful analytical pivots.[89] But these devices serve only to illustrate the instances of fragmentation uncovered in this section; they do not resolve them, and that is why a paradigm grounded in constitutional responsibility can bring concrete added value. These themes will be discussed again in Chapter 4, which addresses the continuing relevance of requiring a cross-border connection against the indices of citizenship and fundamental rights introduced here.

3. Abuse of (EU free movement) rights

It is not clear whether abuse of rights functions purely as an interpretative principle or operates as a fully-fledged general principle of EU law.[90] But that question does not need to be resolved for present purposes. Here, the concept of abuse is assessed as an exclusionary framework principle because it can preclude factual situations that would otherwise fall within the scope of the Treaty from being addressed through the application of free movement rights.[91] In the case law to date, abuse of rights has been defined primarily in negative terms: in other words, the Court usually determines that factual situations have *not* reached the threshold of abusing

88 AG Ruiz-Jarabo Colomer in *Petersen*, para. 24 of the Opinion.

89 See e.g. J Waldron, 'The core of the case against judicial review' (2006) 115 Yale LJ 1346.

90 The Court referred to the 'principle of prohibiting abusive practices' in Case C-255/02 *Halifax and others v Commissioners of Customs and Excise* [2006] ECR I-1609 (para. 70) but to 'the *general Community law principle* that abuse of rights is prohibited' in Case C-321/05 *Kofoed v Skatteministeriet* [2007] ECR I-5795, para. 38 (emphasis added). On the credibility of abuse of rights as a general principle of EU law, see generally, R de la Feria and S Vogenauer (eds.), *Prohibition of Abuse of Law: A New General Principle of EU Law?* (Hart Publishing, 2011).

91 The preliminary nature of questions about abuse of EU law is evident in *Cadbury Schweppes*, para. 34: '[*b*]*efore* examining the legislation... in the light of Articles [49 and 54 TFEU], it is important to answer the national court's initial question seeking to ascertain whether the fact that a company established in a Member State establishes and capitalises companies in another Member State solely because of the more favourable tax regime applicable in that Member State constitutes an abuse of freedom of establishment' (emphasis added).

EU rights but has rarely confirmed that they actually have.[92] Picking up on the theme of motivation introduced in Section 2, abuse of rights is treated as an element of personal scope here because of the critical imprint of the relevant *actor(s)* on the activity undertaken. The guiding rule is that merely *using* rights conferred by the Treaty does not amount to *abuse* of free movement law, however self-serving the exercise of that activity might be. An element of deceptive intent seems to be central to displacing that presumption.[93] It is less clear if or when purposive or instrumental use of EU law can cross the abuse line. In the following subsections, the origins, development, and impact of abuse of rights in free movement law will first be traced. Three main sticking points will then be discussed—deliberate circumvention of national rules; the relevance of subjective criteria; and the sub-fraud threshold—to assess whether or not abuse of rights is operating coherently.

(a) Abuse of rights in free movement law: the emergence of a concept

The notion of abuse of rights is well developed in some parts of EU law, especially competition and trademark law. But in early free movement case law, most submissions on abuse reflected a more general concern: uneasiness with the fact that EU law could override national rules. Member States tended to raise the prospect of abuse in an effort to constrain the embryonic scope of free movement rights—most commonly, in the context of evading mandatory national professional standards by engaging in cross-border economic activity.[94] The Court did—and continues to[95]—acknowledge the legitimacy of a Member State's interest in protecting against abuse of rights situations, but it rarely agreed that the measures taken could actually defeat the contested free movement right. Instead, the Court sought to entrench a wide reading of the Treaty freedoms while narrowly demarcating the space allocated for Member State derogation arguments.[96] It is simply a consequence of primacy—of conflict between sources—that the exercise of EU

[92] E.g. A Kjellgren, 'On the border of abuse: The jurisprudence of the European Court of Justice on circumvention, fraud and abuses of Community law' in M Andenas and W-H Roth (eds.), *Services and Free Movement in EU Law* (OUP, 2002) 245 at 277 ('stunningly low practical application value'); B Hofstotter, 'A cascade of rights, or who shall care for little Catherine? Some reflections on the *Chen* case' (2005) 30:4 ELRev 548 at 558 ('a frequently tested but ineffective argument').

[93] E.g. Article 35 of Directive 2004/38: 'Member States may adopt the necessary measures to refuse, terminate or withdraw any right conferred by this Directive in the case of abuse of rights or fraud, such as marriages of convenience'. See also, recitals 15 and 28 of the Preamble; and Article 54 of the Charter of Fundamental Rights ('[n]othing in this Charter shall be interpreted as implying any right to engage in any activity or to perform any act aimed at the destruction of any of the rights and freedoms recognised in this Charter or at their limitation to a greater extent than is provided for herein').

[94] E.g. Case 33/74 *Van Binsbergen v Bestuur van de Bedrijfsvereniging voor de Metaalnijverheid* [1974] ECR 1299, para. 12; Case 115/78 *Knoors v Staatssecretaris van Economische Zaken* [1979] ECR 399, para. 27.

[95] E.g. Case C-524/04 *Test Claimants in the Thin Cap Group Litigation v Commissioners of Inland Revenue* [2007] ECR I-2107, paras 71–77; but cf. the less sympathetic approach in *Commission v Netherlands*, paras 68–69.

[96] See e.g. AG Mancini in Case 352/85 *Bond van Adverteerders and others v The Netherlands* [1988] ECR 2085 at 2121.There were some flickers of abuse of rights in earlier case law (e.g. Case 2/67 *De Moor v Caisse de pension des employés privés* [1967] ECR 197 at 207).

rights must displace national rules in most circumstances. As will be shown below, however, the Court does sometimes consider the objectives behind national measures that seek to prevent circumvention of national rules at the justification stage.[97] This variable exclusion from scope/justification of a restriction approach to abuse of rights—which has significant consequences for how States should then shape their public interest defences—can already be flagged from the perspective of coherence.

It is clear that questions about abuse of EU rights are increasing in volume and complexity.[98] This can be partly explained by the hardening definition of abuse in the case law. But it is difficult to disconnect the trend from the expanding scope of Treaty-caught restrictions more generally: if free movement law applies in more situations, then arguments grounded in exclusionary principles will also be attempted more often.[99] Abuse of rights is argued most commonly in the areas of immigration rules for natural persons and, for legal persons, the incorporation and taxation of companies. Although different formulas have been used,[100] the Court has long acknowledged the possibility that abuse of free movement rights might remove situations from the ambit of the Treaty altogether. For example, in *Lair*, the Court held that 'where it may be established *on the basis of objective evidence* that a worker has entered a Member State for the *sole purpose* of enjoying, after a very short period of occupational activity, the benefit of the student assistance system in that State', that worker would not come within the scope of EU law.[101] This approach seemed to signal that instrumental exercise of free movement rights would be frowned upon, but Ziegler has recast the judgment as a 'harbinger' of the genuine link tests that emerged later in the case law on citizenship.[102] In *Lair*, the relevant period of employment was undoubtedly brief, undermining the applicant's consequential eligibility for study finance on the face of it. But she had resided in the host State for several years, with periods of involuntary unemployment explaining gaps in her overall work profile. She *had* established genuine links, in other words, with the host State, explaining why the Court was more preoccupied with uncovering the purpose behind her *original* entry.

In the 1990s, case law on national regulatory standards for professional activities continued to build on *van Binsbergen* and *Knoors*, targeting economic actors 'whose

[97] See generally, Edwards and Farmer, n16, 208–15; and K Engsig Sørensen, 'Abuse of rights in Community law: A principle of substance or merely rhetoric?' (2006) 43:2 CML Rev 423 at 433.

[98] On the burgeoning of case law on abuse of rights, see R de la Feria's 'Introduction' in de la Feria and Vogenauer (eds.), n90, xv at xxv.

[99] See Engsig Sørensen, n97, 423–4.

[100] '[F]or many years, the Court used words such as "avoidance", "evasion", "circumvention", "fraud" and "abuse", in an apparently interchangeable fashion' (R de la Feria, 'Prohibition of abuse of (Community) law: The creation of a new general principle of EC law through taxation' (2008) 45:1 CMLRev 395 at 395–6). On the potential substantive significance of different terms, see also, Kjellgren, n92, and Engsig Sørensen, n97, 431–2. The Court has made a more conscious effort to standardize its treatment of abuse in recent case law, as will be seen below: it will be argued that spots of incoherence now arise more through substantive gaps in reasoning than the application of different terminology.

[101] Case 39/86 *Lair v Universität Hannover* [1988] ECR 3161, para. 43 (emphasis added).

[102] KS Ziegler, '"Abuse of law" in the context of the free movement of workers' in de la Feria and Vogenauer (eds.), n90, 295 at 311.

activity is entirely or principally directed towards . . . exercising the [relevant Treaty] freedom . . . in order to avoid the provisions regulating the relevant occupational activity'.[103] Echoing the evasion theme of the early case law, the Court held in *Kraus* that EU law 'does not preclude a Member State from adopting, in the absence of harmonization, measures designed to prevent the opportunities created under the Treaty from being abused in a manner *contrary to the legitimate interests of the State*' and it made particular reference to protecting the public from the consequences of abuse.[104] Here, we find confirmation that Member States may be alert to potential abuse of EU rights and legitimately retain the option of taking appropriate safeguards. The Court has also consistently emphasized, however, that abuse of rights must be determined on a case-by-case basis. As a corollary, it has been specified that counter-abuse measures taken by Member States must have 'the *specific purpose* of preventing wholly artificial arrangements'.[105]

In other cases from the 1990s, there is a more noticeable emphasis on fraud. But it was not clear whether fraud *was* abuse, or whether fraud and abuse bred conceptually distinct thresholds. For example, in *Singh*, addressing spousal residence rights under EU law, the Court held that '[a]s regards *the risk of fraud* . . . it is sufficient to note that . . . the facilities created by the Treaty cannot have the effect of allowing the persons who benefit from them to evade the application of national legislation and of prohibiting Member States from taking the measures necessary to prevent *such abuse*'.[106] However, we can also trace the emergence of another moderating obligation at this time i.e. to consider potential regulatory evasion situations against the broader objectives of relevant Treaty provisions, suggesting that a finding of abuse should be more the exception than the rule.[107]

The Opinion of AG Lenz in *TV10* was the first extensive discussion of abuse of rights in free movement law. Considering the 'specific purpose' element of *Kraus*, he noted that the Commission had initially 'described this aspect as a subjective criterion, but ceased to do so at the hearing . . . [T]he question arises as to how the "avoidance" must come about and on the basis of what circumstances it may be determined. It turns in particular on whether subjective criteria are involved—which especially in the case of legal persons are scarcely susceptible of proof—or avoidance determined on the basis of objective circumstances'.[108] The Advocate General concluded that '[c]ircumvention of a law or an abuse of law is regularly

[103] AG Lenz in Case C-23/93 *TV10 SA v Commissariaat voor de Media* [1994] ECR I-4795, para. 53 of the Opinion (for an overview of relevant case law, see paras 50–52).

[104] Case C-19/92 *Kraus v Land Baden-Württemberg* [1993] ECR I-1663, paras 34–35 (emphasis added).

[105] Case C-324/00 *Lankhorst-Hohorst GmbH v Finanzamt Steinfurt* [2002] ECR I-11779, para. 37 (emphasis added); see further, *Thin Cap*, para. 72 ff.

[106] Case C-370/90 *R v Immigration Appeal Tribunal and Singh, ex parte Secretary of State for the Home Department* [1992] ECR I-4265, para. 24 (emphasis added).

[107] Case C-206/94 *Brennet AG v Paletta (Paletta II)* [1996] ECR I-2357, para. 25. Confirmed in e.g. Case C-373/97 *Diamantis v Elliniko Dimosio (Greek State) and Organismos Ikonomikis Anasygkrotisis Epicheiriseon AE (OAE)* [2000] ECR I-1705, para. 33; Case C-456/04 *Agip Petroli SpA v Capitaneria di porto di Siracusa and others* [2006] ECR I-3395, para. 19.

[108] AG Lenz in *TV10*, para. 57 of the Opinion.

characterized by an *intention* to circumvent or abuse, which is undoubtedly a subjective factor'.[109] He then reiterated the distinction between legal persons and natural persons in this context, noting that it is 'possible to take account of intention and motives'—and therefore to consider subjective criteria—in situations involving natural persons only.[110]

The Advocate General's analysis of 'specific purpose' revives questions about the relevance and feasibility of deciphering motivation, critiqued for different reasons in Section 2 with respect to *Humbel* and *Bettray*. For legal persons, AG Lenz confined his proposed framework to a review of objective criteria.[111] He also took a creative stance on the appropriate division of functions between national courts and the Court of Justice: 'although the national court makes the findings of fact, it is the task of the Court of Justice to assess them in the light of [EU] law. Determining whether a law has been circumvented or evaded is *a legal assessment of facts* which cannot be entirely withdrawn from the appreciation of the Court of Justice'.[112] The Court followed the logic of the Opinion; but it applied a more implicit abuse test and it did this at justification rather than exclusion stage, finding that 'a Member State may regard as a domestic broadcaster a radio and television organization which establishes itself in another Member State in order to provide services there which are intended for the first State's territory, since the aim of that measure is to prevent [such] organizations . . . from being able, by exercising the freedoms guaranteed by the Treaty, *wrongfully to avoid obligations under national law*'.[113] The Court's treatment of the alleged abuse here at justification stage reflects a broader concern: when is it legitimate for a Member State to assert its regulatory preferences on those operating on the national market?[114] The question then raised is whether those concerns are properly dealt with at the justification stage or whether it is possible—or desirable—to formulate a more general, principled test that operates as an exclusionary rule while still retaining the functionality of enabling evidenced, case-by-case assessment. The former approach would situate discussion of abuse of rights at the exclusion stage only in clear cases of fraud. The latter—favoured in submissions by the Member States—opens up the possibility of sharper cut-off points at the preliminary stages of a dispute, and retains latitude for material consideration of the circumvention of national rules as an impugned practice: not just an offshoot of primacy.

The Court's decision in *Centros* marked a significant turning point in the case law narrative on abuse of rights.[115] Danish nationals had established a private limited

[109] AG Lenz in *TV10*, para. 59 of the Opinion (emphasis added).

[110] AG Lenz in *TV10*, para. 59 of the Opinion; cf. his analysis of legal persons from the perspective of intention (para. 60).

[111] AG Lenz in *TV10*, para. 65 of the Opinion (e.g. 'the time of the commencement, the substance and orientation of the company's business operations. Corporate relationships may also play a part in the assessment').

[112] AG Lenz in *TV10*, para. 58 of the Opinion (emphasis added).

[113] *TV10*, para. 21 (emphasis added).

[114] I am grateful to Thomas Horsley for raising this point.

[115] Case C-212/97 *Centros Ltd v Erhvervs- og Selskabsstyrelsen* [1999] ECR I-1459; although some Advocates General have distinguished *TV10* on its specific facts rather than viewing *Centros* as a

company in the United Kingdom deliberately to take advantage of the considerably lower share capital requirements there relative to Danish law. The company's trading activities were directed exclusively at the Danish market—it had never traded in the UK at all—leading the Danish authorities to refuse to register Centros in Denmark as a branch of a foreign company and seeking instead to force it to register its principal establishment there. In an Opinion rooted firmly in the single market objectives of freedom of establishment, AG La Pergola stated that '[this] situation, whether one likes it or not, is the logical consequence of the rights guaranteed under the Treaty... [I]n the absence of harmonisation, competition among rules must be allowed free play in corporate matters'.[116] The Advocate General distinguished the facts from evasion cases like *van Binsbergen* in a footnote; he did not engage with the question of instrumental use of free movement rights more generally.

The Court dealt with the concept of abuse more directly. First, citing a string of relevant judgments, it confirmed that 'a Member State is entitled to take measures designed to prevent certain of its nationals from attempting, undercover of the rights created by the Treaty, improperly to circumvent their national legislation or to prevent individuals from *improperly or fraudulently* taking advantage of provisions of [EU] law'.[117] Next, it combined the requirement for objective evidence of abuse or fraudulent conduct on a case-by-case basis with the *Paletta II* emphasis on the objectives underpinning the Treaty freedoms. Applying these criteria to the circumstances in *Centros*, the Court concluded that 'the fact that a national of a Member State who wishes to set up a company chooses to form it in the Member State whose rules of company law seem to him the least restrictive and to set up branches in other Member States cannot, *in itself*, constitute an abuse of the right of establishment'.[118] The Court stated specifically that absence of trade in the Member State of establishment was not *in itself* a sufficient indicator of improper or fraudulent conduct. The applicants had merely taken advantage of differential market conditions. Legitimate concerns about the protection of the public were, again, shifted forward to scrutiny of justification and proportionality.

(b) A widening gap between concept and impact?

The development of abuse of rights outlined above is an example of incremental legal evolution rather than case law fragmentation since the shifting parameters of the definition and content of the principle were, on the whole, explained through the reasoning of the Court and supported by the comprehensive citation of existing

dramatic turning point e.g. AG Alber in Case C-167/01 *Kamer van Koophandel en Fabrieken voor Amsterdam v Inspire Art Ltd* [2003] ECR I-10155, para. 120 of the Opinion.

[116] AG La Pergola in *Centros*, para. 20 of the Opinion. He argued that place of incorporation was an 'exercise of the freedom of choice, guaranteed to individuals under the Treaty, as to the company instrument best suited to their purposes of all the instruments available under the various national systems of the Member States'.

[117] *Centros*, para. 24 (emphasis added).

[118] *Centros*, para. 27 (emphasis added); confirmed in e.g. *Inspire Art*.

authorities. De la Feria has shown how the decision in *Centros* can also be linked to broader policy choices, reflecting the discussion on market objectives in Chapter 2:

> [S]o long as no harmonization rules apply within the internal market, persons and businesses alike are *entitled to choose the most beneficial regulatory regime*; thus, if regulatory discrepancy continues to be the norm across the EU, regulatory competition would increase, with potential economic benefits for EU competitiveness as a whole; if, on the other hand, Member States are dissatisfied with the regulatory status quo, then further harmonization of company law constitutes the only alternative which is compatible with the internal market principles. Either way—increased competition or further harmonization—there are potential gains for the European integration cause. Seen in this context, the Court's new approach to abuse adopted in *Centros* was probably, not only a calculated policy choice, but equally, a rational one.[119]

That analysis fits with the market-opening philosophy more generally apparent in case law across the freedoms at the time—with the exception of the (still) awkward decision in *Keck* for Article 34 TFEU, discussed in Chapter 7.

The Court's sanctioning of the instrumental use of EU law short of fraudulent conduct—i.e. simply taking advantage of the possibilities created by free movement—was widely transposed from *Centros* to the case law on personal free movement. While some Advocates General did consider the relevance of intention or motivation,[120] the Court's approach became more consciously consistent with the view that instrumental exercise (or 'legitimate circumvention'[121]) of free movement rights does not constitute abuse. For example, in *Ninni-Orasche*, the applicant—an Italian national living in Austria and married to an Austrian national—had worked for a short period in order to generate eligibility for study finance benefits in the host State.[122] To determine whether she was a worker within the meaning of EU law, the national court was empowered by the Court of Justice to determine whether the relevant activity was purely marginal and ancillary. It was also emphasized that 'factors relating to the *conduct* of the person concerned before and after the period of employment are not relevant in establishing the status of worker'.[123] However, the Court nevertheless felt the need to reiterate the *Lair* emphasis on *sole* purpose: here, the applicant moved to Austria to live with

[119] De la Feria, n100, 407–8 (emphasis added).

[120] E.g. AG Stix-Hackl in Case C-60/00 *Carpenter v Secretary of State for the Home Department* [2002] ECR I-6279, paras 74–75 of the Opinion (referring to 'the possible risk that national rules on residence concerning the legal position of spouses of nationals who are nationals of non-member countries *could be evaded* by the spouse who is a national being tempted to create a [Union] connection. Thus it might be argued that nationals of a Member State might, for example, take up employment—even only for a short term—in another Member State *precisely in order thereby to bring themselves and the non-member-country spouse within the scope of [EU] law*... On this point, it must be observed that there is *no evidence of such an intention to evade* in the present case, since Mr Carpenter already operated his business and offered services across frontiers before the marriage' (emphasis added).

[121] De la Feria, n100, 403: 'the idea that circumvention of national rules can be legitimate, and not abusive, rests on the assumption that, even when there is circumvention, the free movement provisions should still apply'.

[122] Case C-413/01 *Ninni-Orasche v Bundesminister für Wissenschaft, Verkehr und Kunst* [2003] ECR I-13187.

[123] *Ninni-Orasche*, para. 28 (emphasis added).

her husband, not for the sole purpose of claiming study finance (or even studying per se).[124]

The developing profile of abuse of rights was thus only superficially coherent. In *Akrich*, AG Geelhoed sought to map its post-*Centros* features by reflecting on how the concept was applied across free movement law. He first noted that an 'intention on the part of the person concerned to obtain an advantage from [EU] rules' was a relevant consideration in the context of 'misuse' of EU law.[125] But he then stressed that 'the intentions of the person making use of the [EU] right may not be inquired into'.[126] The question to be resolved in *Akrich* was whether Regulation 1612/68 generated a right of residence in the UK (the applicant's home State) for her third-country national spouse; he had never resided lawfully in the UK, but he did live with her in Ireland for a period of six months while she worked there. The fact that the applicant had travelled to and worked in Ireland deliberately to glaze her situation with a cross-border dimension was acknowledged by all of the parties involved: the purpose of her move was solely to regularize her husband's residence *in the UK* after their return. Drawing from the logic of *Centros*, AG Geelhoed concluded:

> The installation of Mr and Mrs Akrich in Ireland must be viewed as a use of [EU] law for a purpose not contemplated by the [Union] legislature but which is inherent in [EU] law. The [EU] legislature did not intend to create a right that can be used in order to evade national immigration laws but did create a right in favour of a national of a Member State to install himself in another Member State together with his spouse. Installation in that other Member State constitutes the key element of the freedom given by [EU] law to nationals of the Union.[127]

Building on decisions such as *Singh*, AG Geelhoed reasoned that a worker in Mrs Akrich's circumstances retained EU rights when she returned to her home State; and any concerns that the UK might have about the immigration status of her third-country national spouse were shifted forwards to the sphere of justification and proportionality. The Advocate General identified three problems with the practical application of a more broadly conceived doctrine of 'misuse' of EU law: first, opacity in the case law about the significance of subjective criteria; second, the fact that objective criteria can also be circumvented; and, third, that 'the dividing line between abuse and use for a purpose not contemplated by the legislature is hard to define'.[128]

[124] *Ninni-Orasche*, paras 45–47. See similarly, AG Jacobs in Case C-111/91 *Commission v Luxembourg* [1993] ECR I-817, para. 25 of the Opinion, suggesting that that a Member State was 'entitled . . . to require that women receiving childbirth allowance are resident [there] at the time of birth, since otherwise expectant mothers resident elsewhere might arrange to give birth [there] merely in order to collect the benefit'.

[125] AG Geelhoed in Case C-109/01 *Secretary of State for the Home Department v Akrich* [2003] ECR I-9607, para. 96 of the Opinion. See subsequently, AG Poiares Maduro in *Halifax*, paras 62–71 of the Opinion.

[126] AG Geelhoed in *Akrich*, para. 102 of the Opinion.

[127] AG Geelhoed in *Akrich*, para. 180 of the Opinion.

[128] AG Geelhoed in *Akrich*, para. 173 of the Opinion, further elaborated in paras 174–183.

The Court did not find a right of residence for Mr Akrich under Regulation 1612/68, holding that a precondition of prior lawful residence in an EU Member State could be attached to the spousal residence rights derived from that measure.[129] But it did not override AG Geelhoed's understanding of abuse of rights in order to reach that decision. If anything, the Court was even clearer about the irrelevance of motivation in the legal framework that regulates the free movement of workers and (re)turned to fraudulent behaviour to provide a concrete example of abuse.[130] On the other hand, however, it did not explain how its reasoning here fits with the *Lair/Ninni-Orasche* 'sole purpose' test.[131]

Similarly, in *Chen*, AG Tizzano summarized the facts of the case as follows, referring to the UK Government's submissions: 'Mr and Mrs Chen had arranged for their daughter to be born in Northern Ireland with the *manifest intention* of ensuring that she would acquire Irish nationality and thereby the right of residence in [the UK]... Catherine's Irish nationality is therefore "contrived", being the result of *a specific plan put into effect by her parents* in order to acquire a right of residence in the [Union]'.[132] In response, he appealed to 'the scheme of the relationship between Union law and the laws of the Member States [which] necessarily implies that it is *only in exceptional circumstances* that the exercise of a right conferred by the Treaty can constitute an abuse, because the non-application of a national provision as a result of reliance on a right conferred by [EU] law constitutes *the normal consequence of the principle of the supremacy of [EU] law*'.[133] His sense of the transition from use to abuse was linked to 'betraying the spirit and scope' of EU law.[134] Furthermore, he considered that the purpose of Article 21 TFEU was *precisely* to eliminate restrictions on movement and residence for Union citizens (subject to becoming a financial burden). He added that the family should not be criticized just because they availed of opportunities created, after all, by Ireland's nationality laws.[135]

129 This finding was later reversed in Case C-127/08 *Metock and others v Minister for Justice, Equality and Law Reform* [2008] ECR I-6241, on the basis of Directive 2004/38. In Case C-1/05 *Jia v Migrationsverket* [2007] ECR I-1, the Court took the interim step of categorizing the assessment of prior lawful residence requirements per *Akrich* as permissive rather than prescriptive.

130 *Akrich*, para. 57 (i.e. 'if the facilities afforded by [EU] law in favour of migrant workers and their spouses were invoked in the context of marriages of convenience entered into in order to circumvent the provisions relating to entry and residence of nationals of non-Member States').

131 National courts continue to refer questions about the relevance of intentional movement; see e.g. Case C-46/12 *LN v Styrelsen for Videregående Uddannelser og Uddannelsesstøtte*, judgment of 21 February 2013, confirming the approach taken in *Ninni-Orasche*.

132 AG Tizzano in *Zhu and Chen*, para. 108 of the Opinion (emphasis added).

133 AG Tizzano in *Zhu and Chen*, para. 112 of the Opinion (emphasis added). The Advocate General also expressed 'reservations of a general nature prompted by the transposition to [EU] level of a concept whose existence is a matter of dispute in national systems of law and of which the definition is even less certain' (para. 111).

134 AG Tizzano in *Zhu and Chen*, para. 112 of the Opinion; he phrased this as 'a distortion of the purposes and objectives of the [EU] provision which grants the right in question' (para. 115, emphasis removed).

135 AG Tizzano in *Zhu and Chen*, para. 126 of the Opinion (since tightened by the Irish Nationality and Citizenship Act 2004). With respect to Belgian law, see AG Sharpston in Case C-34/09 *Ruiz Zambrano v Office national de l'emploi (ONEm)* [2011] ECR I-1177, paras 104–106 of the Opinion.

A final point to note: the peripheral nature of fundamental rights discourse in these cases is striking. Even in case law on personal free movement, the practical difficulties associated with applying an abuse of rights test are addressed in much more detail than any human/trade dichotomy. Essentially, securing the objectives of free movement law is paramount, and this is just as evident in *Chen* as it was in *Centros*.

(c) Three points of discord

As will be shown below, the Court's carving of a more principled approach to abuse of rights has intensified in recent case law: it has clearly endeavoured to 'make' a principle and to build a standard definition that can be applied across different free movement situations. But several issues continue to distort the coherence of its *application*. First, case law on the circumvention of national regulatory standards (e.g. *van Binsbergen*; *TV10*) remains live notwithstanding the parallel elaboration of the *Centros* doctrine. In *Fidium Finanz*, AG Stix-Hackl explained the resulting divergence as follows: '[i]n the context of Article [49 TFEU], the Court has not withdrawn the circumvention of national provisions from potential allegations of abuse generally, but only because the freedom of establishment is specifically intended to enable companies having their registered office in the [EU] to pursue activities in other Member States through a branch'.[136] In other words, it could be suggested that the persisting validity of both lines of case law hinges on the very *specific* nature of the regulation *and* circumvention in cases like *van Binsbergen* compared to the *generic* quality of both of those aspects in *Centros*.[137] However, this point of discord has been overtaken by more recent case law, which suggests that the implications of the decision in *Centros* have now been curtailed; this point is picked up again below.

Second, the extent to which both objective and subjective factors are necessary to substantiate a finding of abuse has never been properly resolved.[138] The *Centros* doctrine—in which the Court emphasized (1) the need for objective criteria based on evidence, to be (2) considered on a case-by-case basis, but also (3) against the broader objectives of the relevant free movement provisions—had solidified as the dominant authority on the instrumental use of free movement law, reinforced by the *Akrich* and *Chen* judgments in the area of personal free movement rights. But in *Emsland-Stärke*—now described as the definitive authority on abuse of rights[139]—the Court also referred to 'a subjective element consisting in the *intention* to obtain an advantage from the [EU] rules *by creating artificially* the conditions laid down for obtaining it'.[140] Determination of these criteria is explicitly designated for the

[136] AG Stix-Hackl in *Fidium Finanz*, para. 91 of the Opinion.

[137] See e.g. Kjellgren, n92, 273–4.

[138] See similarly, D Weber, 'Abuse of law–European Court of Justice, 14 December 2000, Case C-110/99, *Emsland-Stärke*' (2004) 34 LIEI 43 at 51–2.

[139] E.g. De la Feria, n100, 407.

[140] Case C-110/99 *Emsland-Stärke GmbH v Hauptzollamt Hamburg-Jonas* [2000] ECR I-11569, para. 53 (emphasis added).

national court.[141] The condition of artificiality has also been suggested as a mediatory way to make sense of the *van Binsbergen/Centros* deviation (although that is not, as explained below, a solution without its own problems).[142]

Emsland-Stärke concerned the export of products from Germany to Switzerland, for which the applicant company received an export refund under the applicable EU scheme[143]—notwithstanding their immediate re-importation to another Member State (Italy). Different formulations of abuse of rights for free movement and agriculture law would not be a problem per se,[144] except that the latter definition is now cited in free movement case law too—most notably (given the significance of *Centros*) in a decision on freedom of establishment; but, to date at least, at the stage of justification only i.e. after the existence of a restriction was already established.[145] This unfortunate step thus ends up tangling several threads of fragmentation together in an undoubtedly well-intentioned attempt to create a test that works across free movement law.

Outwith the context of the CAP, *Emsland-Stärke* is raised most frequently in cases on direct and indirect taxation.[146] In *Halifax*, a case concerning VAT, AG Poiares Maduro sought to demystify the subjective element of the test in *Emsland-Stärke,* arguing that it was not about 'a search for the elusive subjective intentions of the parties'. Instead, he suggested that the purpose of the subjective limb was to determine 'the artificial character of the situation to be assessed' i.e. '[w]hat matters is not the actual state of mind of A, but the fact that the activity, objectively speaking, has no other explanation but to secure a tax advantage'.[147] But how does that logic then translate to the blessing of moving temporarily to Ireland from the UK to generate spousal residence rights; or from choosing where to give birth purely to take strategic advantage of permissive nationality laws? These situations are also 'artificial' and they were contrived 'to secure an advantage'. They were saved by another formula—the underlying objectives of free movement law—but that is not sufficient to deliver the substantive coherence that the language of *Emsland-Stärke* suggests might be possible: after all, preventing restrictions on freedom of establishment is a Treaty objective too.

The Court's approach to abuse of free movement rights for natural persons has been relatively consistent on its own terms. The overlaying of movement rights

[141] Affirming the merits of this division of functions for constitutional reasons, see P Koutrakos, 'The *Emsland-Stärke* abuse of law test in the law of agriculture and free movement of goods' in de la Feria and Vogenauer (eds.), n90, 203 at 215–16.

[142] After thorough analysis of several possible explanations for the divergence, Engsig Sørensen concludes that the older and newer strands of case law are 'not easy to reconcile' (n97, 443–7).

[143] Commission Regulation (EEC) 2730/79 on the application of the system of export refunds on agricultural products, 1979 OJ L317/1.

[144] E.g. AG Geelhoed in *Akrich*, who acknowledged the test invoking subjective criteria in *Emsland-Stärke* but pointed out that it related to 'a different area of law' (fn66) and argued that such considerations should not be applied in free movement law (paras 96–105 of the Opinion).

[145] *Cadbury Schweppes*, para. 64 (freedom of establishment and direct taxation). See also, the Opinion of AG Stix-Hackl in *Fidium Finanz*, para. 97 (free movement of capital).

[146] On the significance of these cases for taxation, see De la Feria, n100, 418–34.

[147] AG Poiares Maduro in *Halifax*, paras 64–71 of the Opinion. In its judgment, the Court focused on the artificiality test and avoided subjective/objective terminology altogether.

with the protection of fundamental rights and the objectives of EU citizenship vindicates an absolving mindset. But even in that more singular sphere, uncertainty still characterizes the *sometimes*-relevance of intention or motivation. Again, it is the variability of this concern that resonates with *Bettray* and *Humbel*, and delivers a point of thematic fragmentation that is not freedom- or issue-specific.[148] The parallel development of abuse in the fields of agriculture and taxation has also been internally consistent. But the emphasis on artificiality in *Cadbury Schweppes* does seem to have tempered the *Centros* doctrine in freedom of establishment case law too.[149] Confirmation of that point would be helpful, but then the circular argument would resume: how could the Court retreat from *Centros* more explicitly without undermining its own concurrent emphasis on the realization of Treaty objectives?[150] There are bounteous statements about the fundamental importance of the internal market generally, and not just the free movement of (natural) persons, throughout the Court's case law. At the very least, then, explicit reconciliation of the different strands of case law addressing the relevance of subjective criteria and motivation (broadly speaking: *Centros/Chen* 'versus' *Emsland-Stärke/Cadbury Schweppes*) would bring useful clarification and resolve coherence problems brought about by the Court's apparent ambition to bring about convergence in this area of law.

Finally, the third point of discord is that the sub-fraud threshold—the point of transition from use to abuse—has yet to be pinned down more concretely.[151] Ziegler argues that 'fraud refers to a deception about a condition of a right being met, where the condition is not formally fulfilled' whereas 'abuse might be taken to refer to the situation where *pro forma* requirements are met, giving otherwise rise to a right, but there is a flaw in the motive or purpose'.[152] She uses the examples of forgery of a marriage certificate[153] and marriages of convenience respectively to illustrate the difference between the two concepts. Member State authorities are

[148] See e.g. AG Mazák in *Förster*, first confirming the decision in *Lair* (para. 78 of the Opinion) but going on to dissolve the relevance of motivation when defining an EU worker, even where someone comes to a Member State 'principally to study' (para. 80 ff.).

[149] *Cadbury Schweppes*, esp. para. 54 ff. See also e.g. AG Poiares Maduro in Case C-210/06 *Cartesio Oktató és Szolgáltató bt* [2008] ECR I-9641, para. 29 of the Opinion.

[150] In the context of workers, Ziegler captures the dilemma as follows: '[o]n the one hand, the Court of Justice merges abuse with the conditions of the free movement right. On the other hand, the very right is given such importance that it outweighs any allegations of abuse which are made by the Member States' (n102, 306).

[151] In the case law on the CAP, evidence of 'collusion between the exporter receiving the refunds and the importer of the goods' can constitute abuse of EU law (Case C-279/05 *Vonk Dairy Products BV v Productschap Zuivel* [2007] ECR I-239, para. 33). For free movement law, the difficult circumstances in Case C-303/08 *Land Baden-Württemberg v Bozkurt* [2010] ECR I-13445 are illustrative of the high threshold that needs to be met; see esp. AG Sharpston, para. 68 of the Opinion.

[152] Ziegler, n102, 296, writing in the context of Directive 2004/38. See similarly, Engsig Sørensen, n97, 431.

[153] See similarly, the decision in Case C-285/95 *Kol v Land Berlin* [1997] ECR I-3069, para. 28: 'employment under a residence permit issued as a result of fraudulent conduct which has led, as in this case, to a conviction, cannot give rise to any rights in favour of the Turkish worker, or arouse any legitimate expectation on his part'.

generally under an obligation to recognize documents issued and findings made by authorities in other States.[154] But even for clear-cut cases of fraud, the knock-on effects of a finding of abuse have yet to be worked out.[155] This is especially complex given the meshed nature of residence rights that can be acquired under EU law. In *Kol*, for example, there was a direct connection between the fraud committed—false declarations by a Turkish national about the status of his marriage to a German woman; she had in fact initiated divorce proceedings and the couple no longer lived together—and the rights claimed i.e. the right to stay in Germany since the period of lawful employment required under the Association Agreement framework had now been achieved. The Court was clear that 'employment under a residence permit issued as a result of fraudulent conduct which has led, as in this case, to a conviction, cannot give rise to any rights in favour of the Turkish worker, or arouse any legitimate expectation on his part'.[156] But what if a Union worker's third country national spouse claimed an initial (derived) right of residence in a host State on the basis of a forged document; could that individual be denied residence rights under EU law several years later if, for example, he or she is the primary carer of the couple's children, the latter are in education in the host State, and the documentary fraud becomes apparent only at that point?[157]

To assist Member State authorities in the application of Directive 2004/38, the Commission has developed interpretative guidelines.[158] It emphasizes the mobility objectives underpinning EU citizenship, the principle of proportionality, and the need to investigate all assertions of abuse on a case-by-case basis; and it uses the benchmark of 'genuine and effective' use of EU rights. The Commission also expressly adopts the definition of abuse developed in *Emsland-Stärke* and articulates more detailed guidelines on marriages of convenience (paragraph 4.2) and family reunification rights (paragraph 4.3). The implications of *Emsland-Stärke* become especially apparent when, in paragraph 4.2, the Commission states that 'Member States may define a set of indicative criteria suggesting the ***possible intention to abuse the rights*** conferred by the Directive for the ***sole purpose*** of contravening national immigration laws' (emphasis added). But how does the subjective element condoned here fit with the judgments in *Chen*, *Akrich*, and *Metock*, especially given the Commission's emphasis on the 'sole purpose' test? What is the significance of the express linkage between intention and *abuse* not *use*? Arguably, the Commission has confused rather than clarified the position. To be fair, however, the jurisprudence has not provided a helpful starting-point.

[154] E.g. *Paletta II*, paras 26–27. [155] See further, Kjellgren, n92, 247.

[156] *Kol*, para. 28.

[157] On abuse of rights and EU citizenship generally, see C Costello, 'Citizenship of the Union: Above abuse?' in de la Feria and Vogenauer (eds.), n90, 321.

[158] Communication from the Commission to the European Parliament and the Council on guidance for better transposition and application of Directive 2004/38/EC on the right of citizens of the Union and their family members to move and reside freely within the territory of the Member States, (2009)COM 313 final.

(d) Abuse of rights: interim conclusions

In the first *Paletta* case, AG Mischo spoke plainly about the legitimacy of 'prevent-[ing] [EU] law from being applied in a way which went against common sense and ignored obvious and undeniable realities'.[159] Similarly, commenting on *Emsland-Stärke*, Edwards and Farmer considered that 'the company's situation seemed to fall within the scope of the provisions of secondary [EU] law *on any normal interpretation*, and yet it had somehow contrived to defeat the purpose of the provisions in a manner that was *so blatant and damaging for the [Union] regime* that the Court felt constrained *to prevent it from benefitting from its ingenuity*'.[160] These insights reflect the fact that abuse of rights is essentially an *intuitive* determination, which has to be situated in a highly contained space given that the internal market regulatory system operates on primacy-based conflict rules more generally. In *Kofoed*, the Court sought to bring its case law on abuse of rights together and to create an ordered definition. It categorized abuse of rights as a general principle of EU law, which requires that '[i]ndividuals must not *improperly or fraudulently* take advantage of provisions of [EU] law. The application of [EU] legislation cannot be extended to cover abusive practices, that is to say, transactions carried out not in the context of normal commercial operations, but *solely for the purpose* of *wrongfully obtaining advantages* provided for by [EU] law'.[161] But that definition—which clearly produces convergence across different areas of law—raises important concerns about formal coherence that does *not* deliver substantive results. Commentators can make best sense of the case law when they separate the issues into three distinct strands: circumvention or evasion of national standards; situations involving fraud; and other instances of abuse. In its eagerness to streamline jarring precedents and deliver a neater holistic definition, the Court has ended up welding enduring dissonances together rather than unpacking and addressing them in their different contexts.

To try to resolve some of these issues, perhaps the most important question to ask is whether the concept of abuse contributes something of actual *value* to free movement law in the first place. The prevailing mood veers from sceptical to cautious on this point; and most commentators tend to reflect the practical concerns highlighted by AG Geelhoed in *Akrich*, as well as raising difficulties at the normative level[162] and querying the wisdom of equipping national judges with a tool that could considerably narrow the scope of directly effective EU rights if

[159] AG Mischo in Case C-45/90 *Paletta and others v Brennet AG* [1992] ECR I-3423, para. 34 of the Opinion.

[160] Edwards and Farmer, n16, 227. (emphasis added).

[161] *Kofoed*, para. 38 (emphasis added).

[162] Spaventa notes that 'the transformation from legality to illegality happens via means of judicial interpretation in the case at issue and therefore might raise problems of legal certainty as well as democratic accountability' ('Comments on abuse of law and the free movement of workers' in de la Feria and Vogenauer (eds.), n90, 315 at 316.

misapplied.[163] Additionally, the *scale* of the perceived problem that needs to be addressed specifically by an abuse of rights doctrine is questioned.[164] And it is also difficult to convey the difference between treating something as an abusive practice and recognizing that free movement rights were never intended to grant the advantage sought in the first place.[165] Abuse of rights seems to contribute most worth as, ironically, an exemplar of the intended *breadth* of scope of free movement rights for both natural and legal persons. It is perhaps also a sort of comfort blanket for the Member States, in that the consequences and implications of the market of their own creation are occasionally drawn in softer focus at least. We should not underestimate the value of this kind of salve at the political level; but the solace granted in principle will almost certainly either be dissolved in the process of adjudication, through recourse to the objectives of free movement law more widely or, for justification-stage arguments, to the requirements of proportionality.

In *Chen*, AG Tizzano emphasized that exploiting benefits created by non-harmonized regulatory frameworks—there, the specifics of Irish nationality law—could, once uncovered, be curtailed by revisiting those frameworks: either collectively at the Union level where appropriate (i.e. assuming Union competence, and a collective political appetite, to regulate the issue); or, as happened post-*Chen*, by the affected State unilaterally. Perhaps the same logic applies more generally too: meaning that, actually, what the situation in *Emsland-Stärke* demonstrated was that the Regulation governing the export scheme needed to be amended to deal more effectively with the anomalies caused by re-importation.

It is thus worth considering—because of the difficulties surrounding its definition, application, and corroboration—whether abuse of rights should function as an exclusionary rule in clear cases of fraud only, transferring all sub-fraud questions in the lesser sphere of misuse to the justification and proportionality stages as a rule. Edwards and Farmer propose that formalizing this distinction would be a useful recalibration in conceptual terms but also a pragmatic solution, given the increasing tendency in the case law to address questions of abuse through discussion of justification and proportionality already.[166] A justification stage analysis recognizes that Member States may legitimately aim to prevent abuse of rights, but then assesses the suitability and necessity of the measures actually taken through the well-established premises of a proportionality test. Persisting questions about the

[163] D Triantafyllou, 'Abuse of rights *versus* primacy? Comment on Case C-376/96 *Kefalas*' (1999) 36:1 CMLRev 157 at 161–2.

[164] E.g. AG Tesauro in Case C-367/96 *Kefalas and Others v Elliniko Dimosio (Greek State) and Organismos Oikonomikis Anasygkrotisis Epicheiriseon AE (OAE)* [1998] ECR I-2843, para. 23 of the Opinion.

[165] The different routes taken by AG Poiares Maduro (who analysed the facts through the prism of abuse and concluded (at para. 56 of the Opinion) that 'the arrangements undertaken appear very likely to be artificial') and the Court (taking a more existential approach to the right in question) in Case C-311/06 *Consiglio Nazionale degli Ingegneri v Ministero della Giustizia and Cavallera* [2009] ECR I-415 are illustrative here; the dispute concerned the status of a certificate of homologation in other Member States of professional qualifications acquired in home States.

[166] Edwards and Farmer, n16, 227.

relevance of intention or motivation would need still, however, to be addressed by the Court head-on.

4. The horizontal scope of free movement law

With the exception of the rights conferred by Article 21 TFEU and the rules on capital payments, the Court has confirmed that the Treaty freedoms catch the actions of private as well as public actors to some extent at least. The reach of free movement law extends furthest for the protection of workers. The provisions on establishment and services capture rules the regulatory impact of which is felt collectively, and the logic of that case law has now been extended to Article 34 TFEU too. Whether the Treaty should catch private actors at all is not the main concern here; for present purposes, that ship has sailed. The discussion is instead premised on the fact that the horizontal scope of free movement law is characterized by divergence: does it follow that the case law is also fragmented?

In this section, the way in which the Court has applied different personal scope limits to different free movement rights will be examined. Whether the boundaries of horizontality have been whittled down so much that it no longer functions as an exclusionary principle will also be considered. Following an outline of the applicable frameworks in subsection (a), the discussion will then address two core themes—*discrimination* and *autonomy*—in subsections (b) and (c) respectively.

(a) How horizontal? The different reaches of the Treaty freedoms

The case law on horizontal scope is part of the broader construction of direct effect—of the Court's attribution of enforceable rights to individuals, overriding the basic tenets of dualism as a framework for the reception of external law into domestic legal systems, and feeding into the systemic objective of enhancing the effectiveness and uniformity of EU law.[167] The basic question is: if private actors can benefit from directly effective free movement *rights*, are they in any sense bound by the Treaty's free movement *obligations*? All of the provisions conferring core free movement rights have vertical direct effect.[168] And the classic understanding of free movement law is that it curtails the actions of public authorities, while competition

[167] The implications of direct effect stem from the reasoning in Case 26/62 *NV Algemene Transport- en Expeditie Onderneming van Gend en Loos v Administratie der Belastingen* [1963] ECR 1. More recently, the horizontal scope of general principles of EU law, following the decision in Case C-144/04 *Mangold v Helm* [2005] ECR I-9981 on age discrimination, have generated fresh discussion see e.g. Editorial comments, 'The scope of application of the general principles of Union law: An ever expanding Union?' (2010) 47:6 CMLRev 1589.

[168] E.g. *Baumbast*, para. 84 (Article 21 TFEU); Case 74/76 *Iannelli & Volpi SpA v Ditta Paolo Meroni* [1977] ECR 557, para. 13, (Articles 30 and 34 TFEU); Case 167/73 *Commission v France* [1974] ECR 359, para. 41 (Article 45 TFEU); Case 2/74 *Reyners v Belgian State* [1974] ECR 631, para. 26 (Article 49 TFEU); *Van Binsbergen*, para. 27 (Article 56 TFEU); Joined Cases C-163/94, C-165/94 and C-250/94 *Criminal proceedings against Sanz de Lera and others* [1995] ECR I-4821, para. 41 (Article 63 TFEU).

rules manage the behaviour of private market actors above agreed market-impact thresholds.[169] But this line is clearly blurring in the case law.[170] The following preliminary conclusions can be drawn from what the relevant Treaty provisions say about their intended addressees:

Citizenship: Ambiguous (Article 20(2) TFEU: 'Citizens of the Union shall enjoy the rights and be subject to the duties provided for in the Treaties'; see also Article 21(1) TFEU)

Goods: Ambiguous (Article 30 TFEU: 'Customs duties on imports and exports and charges having equivalent effect shall be prohibited between [not *by*] Member States'; similarly, Article 34 TFEU: 'Quantitative restrictions on imports and all measures having equivalent effect shall be prohibited between Member States')[171]

Workers: Ambiguous (Article 45(2) TFEU: 'freedom of movement shall entail the abolition of any discrimination based on nationality between workers of the Member States as regards employment, remuneration and other conditions of work and employment')

Establishment: Ambiguous (Article 49 TFEU: 'restrictions on the freedom of establishment of nationals of a Member State in the territory of another Member State shall be prohibited')

Services: Ambiguous (Article 56 TFEU: 'restrictions on freedom to provide services within the Union shall be prohibited in respect of nationals of Member States who are established in a Member State other than that of the person for whom the services are intended')

Capital: Ambiguous (Article 63(1): 'all restrictions on the movement of capital between Member States and between Member States and third countries shall be prohibited')[172]

Additionally, Article 18 TFEU states simply that '*any* discrimination on grounds of nationality shall be prohibited' (emphasis added).

The wording of the Treaty does not, therefore, provide a clear signpost either way with respect to its scope—not, at least, in the rights-conferring provisions themselves. If we look at the context in which those rights are situated, however, there are strong signals that the Treaty's free movement provisions are addressed to the Member States only—especially since all of the accompanying exception provisions articulate derogations connected to *public* policy, *public* security, and

[169] See e.g. AG Poiares Maduro in Case C-438/05 *International Transport Workers' Federation and Finnish Seamen's Union v Viking Line ABP and OÜ Viking Line Eesti* [2007] ECR I-10779, paras 31–35 of the Opinion.

[170] See similarly, C Semmelmann, 'The European Union's economic constitution under the Lisbon Treaty: Soul-searching among lawyers shifts the focus to procedure' (2010) 35:4 ELRev 516 at 528–30.

[171] Snell stresses, however, that now-deleted provisions of the Treaty clearly indicated that Member States were the addressees of what is now Chapter 3 of the TFEU ('Prohibition of Quantitative Restrictions between Member States'); J Snell, 'Private parties and the free movement of goods and services' in Andenas and Roth (eds.), n92, 211 at 211.

[172] The scope of restrictions on the free movement of capital will not be considered further in this Chapter; as Barnard has remarked, '[s]ince the majority of cases concern challenges to national legislation . . . the difficult questions as to the potential horizontal application of Article 63 have not been broached' (n16, 566).

public health. Can the extension of horizontal effect sit comfortably with that system, or even taking into account the broader opportunities for justification of restrictions that are not directly discriminatory? Four arguments suggest that it can. First, the Court has ruptured the idea that all of the provisions attached to Treaty freedom pockets need to be applied in the same way i.e. it differentiates the effects of specific Treaty provisions even where they relate to the same freedom.[173] Second, the Court has reasoned that 'the fact that certain provisions of the Treaty are *formally* addressed to the Member States does not prevent rights from being conferred *at the same time* on any individual who has an interest in compliance with the obligations thus laid down'.[174]

Third, the fact that private actors may not be in a position *positively* to shape policy on matters of public interest does not mean that they cannot take responsibility for respecting or delivering those interests nonetheless. This point raises two further questions, however: whether there has to be some attribution of responsibility for the delivery of the relevant public interest objective to the private body by the State;[175] and whether the particular case of free movement for workers—where, as will be shown below, even individual private employers have obligations under the Treaty—should be treated differently from situations where the relevant private bodies have a more collectively felt regulatory impact. Finally, AG Trstenjak has suggested that recognition of a distinct justification category for private actors—special grounds in the *private* interest—may also be developing.[176]

As noted earlier, the Court has effected three different levels of horizontality in the free movement case law to date: collective regulatory impact (goods, establishment, services, and workers); assigning Member State responsibility for private actions that impede free movement (goods); and full horizontal reach (workers). In the absence of unequivocal guidance from the wording of the Treaty, the Court has justified its extensions of horizontal scope with direct appeals to the fundamental nature of the Treaty's free movement provisions and the latter's status as fundamental objectives of the EU more generally. Each of the three levels will now be looked at in turn.

[173] E.g. in Case 36/74 *Walrave and Koch v Association Union cycliste internationale, Koninklijke Nederlandsche Wielren Unie and Federación Española Ciclismo* [1974] ECR 1405, the Court acknowledged that while some of the Treaty provisions on services relate specifically 'to the abolition of measures *by the State*, this fact does not defeat the general nature of the terms of Article [56], which makes no distinction between the source of the restrictions to be abolished' (para. 20, emphasis added).

[174] In the context of gender discrimination, see Case 43/75 *Defrenne v Société anonyme belge de navigation aérienne Sabena (Defrenne II)* [1976] ECR 455, para. 31 (emphasis added); confirmed for free movement law in e.g. Case C-281/98 *Angonese v Cassa di Risparmio di Bolzano SpA* [2000] ECR I-4139, para. 34.

[175] As in e.g. Case C-309/99 *Wouters and others v Algemene Raad van de Nederlandse Orde van Advocaten, intervener: Raad van de Balies van de Europese Gemeenschap* [2002] ECR I-1577, esp. para. 100 ff (connected to free movement law by para. 122).

[176] AG Trstenjak in Case C-171/11 *Fra.bo SpA Deutsche Vereinigung des Gas- und Wasserfaches eV (DVGW)—Technisch-Wissenschaftlicher Verein*, judgment of 12 July 2012, para. 38 of the Opinion, citing Case C-415/93 *Union royale belge des sociétés de football association ASBL v Bosman* [1995] ECR I-4921, para. 106 ff. and Case C-325/08 *Olympique Lyonnais SASP v Olivier Bernard and Newcastle UFC* [2010] ECR I-2177, para. 38 ff.

(i) Collective regulatory impact

The threshold of collective regulatory impact marks the level of horizontal scope that is longest established, most comprehensively and consistently reasoned, and most widely applied across the span of free movement law. In its ground-breaking decision in *Walrave*, the Court emphasized the prohibition of discrimination in Article 18 TFEU and its sectoral reflection in the Treaty provisions on workers and service providers:

> Prohibition of such discrimination does not only apply to the action of public authorities but extends likewise to rules of any other nature aimed at *regulating in a collective manner gainful employment and the provision of services*. The abolition as between Member States of obstacles to freedom of movement for persons and to freedom to provide services, *which are fundamental objectives of the Community*... would be compromised if *the abolition of barriers of national origin could be neutralized* by obstacles resulting from the exercise of their legal autonomy by associations or organizations which do not come under public law. Since, moreover, working conditions in the various Member States are governed sometimes by means of provisions laid down by law or regulation and sometimes by agreements and other acts concluded or adopted by private persons, to limit the prohibitions in question to acts of a public authority would risk creating inequality in their application.[177]

These principles have been repeatedly confirmed in cases involving sporting associations.[178] They have also been extended to collective regulation by professional bodies generally[179] and to actions taken by trade unions.[180] Notwithstanding the reference to 'aim' in the extract above, the Court targets the *effect* rather than the origin or intention of the disputed rule or action.[181] The nucleus of its reasoning is directed at ensuring the maximum effectiveness of EU law and the prevention of disparity or inequality. The latter objective has emerged more strongly in the case law over time; for example, in his Opinion in *Viking Line*, AG Poiares Maduro observed that the horizontality of free movement law 'follow[s] logically from the Treaty... to enable market participants throughout the [Union] to have equal opportunities to gain access to any part of the common market'.[182]

[177] *Walrave and Koch*, paras 17–19 (emphasis added). This finding was extended to freedom of establishment in *Wouters*, para. 120; and, in more limited form (as explained further below) to the free movement of goods in *Fra.bo*, paras 31–32.

[178] E.g. Case 13/76 *Donà v Mantero* [1976] ECR I-1333, para. 18; *Bosman*, paras 83–84; *Deliège*, para. 47; and Case C-176/96 *Lehtonen and Castors Canada Dry Namur-Braine ASBL v Fédération royale belge des sociétés de basket-ball ASBL (FRBSB)* [2000] ECR I-2681, para. 35.

[179] E.g. *Wouters*, para. 120.

[180] *Viking Line*, para. 33; Case C-341/05 *Laval un Partneri Ltd v Svenska Byggnadsarbetareförbundet, Svenska Byggnadsarbetareförbundets avdelning 1, Byggettan and Svenska Elektrikerförbundet* [2007] ECR I-11767, para. 98.

[181] On the extension of the scope of *Walrave and Koch* brought about by the inclusion of collective action, see AG Mengozzi in *Laval*, paras 158–159 of the Opinion.

[182] AG Maduro in *Viking Line*, para. 35 of the Opinion.

(ii) Member State responsibility

The second approach to horizontality—assigning Member State responsibility for the behaviour of private actors—has so far been confined to case law on the free movement of goods. The founding decision is *Commission v France (Spanish strawberries)*.[183] The facts concerned a lengthy period of protest that included intimidation of traders and carriers, and the destruction of agricultural products imported from Spain into France; these actions were carried out repeatedly by private individuals over several years. Eventually, the Commission sought to challenge the passivity of the French authorities, claiming that the latter had failed to take appropriate action to address the situation and had therefore failed to fulfil their obligations to facilitate the free movement of goods in accordance with Article 34 TFEU. Sidestepping the *Walrave* template, AG Lenz constructed a framework of State responsibility for the market-obstructing behaviour of private actors by connecting Article 34 with the loyalty obligation in (now) Article 4(3) TEU. The resulting responsibility, which could apply to any sphere of free movement, required Member States to 'take all appropriate measures, whether general or particular, to protect the freedom in question against attacks by private individuals'.[184] The central principle was *enforcement*; but the Advocate General referred to 'protection of the practical *effectiveness* of Article [34]' too.[185] He also cited a decision of the Court on charges having the effect of a customs duty imposed by private actors, which had attributed horizontal responsibility more directly; but added that he was more persuaded by the enforcement approach applied by AG La Pergola in the same case.[186]

The Court in *Spanish strawberries* followed the path laid by AG Lenz. Its initial depiction of the free movement of goods as an 'indispensable instrument for the realisation of a market without internal frontiers' is reminiscent of *Walrave*.[187] However, the Court then adopted the Advocate General's responsibility and enforcement paradigm in the substantive part of its judgment.[188] Framing its decision with the language of constitutional responsibility, the Court emphasized the discretion granted to the Member States to regulate public order, but confirmed

[183] Case C-265/95 *Commission v France (Spanish strawberries)* [1997] ECR I-6959. It has been suggested that earlier seeds for horizontal effect in the free movement of goods can be linked to decisions on intellectual property rights e.g. Case 58/80 *Dansk Supermarked A/S v A/S Imerco* [1981] ECR 181, para. 17 ('it is impossible in any circumstances for agreements between individuals to derogate from the mandatory provisions of the Treaty on the free movement of goods'); and AG Geelhoed in Case C-253/00 *Muñoz y Cia SA and Superior Fruiticola SA v Frumar Ltd and Redbridge Produce Marketing Ltd* [2002] ECR I-7289, para. 44 of the Opinion). See further, G Marenco and K Banks, 'Intellectual property and the Community rules on free movement: Discrimination unearthed' (1990) 15:3 ELRev 224.

[184] AG Lenz in *Spanish strawberries*, para. 41 of the Opinion.

[185] AG Lenz in *Spanish strawberries*, para. 43 of the Opinion (emphasis added).

[186] AG Lenz in *Spanish strawberries*, para. 44 of the Opinion, citing Case C-16/94 *Dubois and Général Cargo Services* [1995] ECR I-2421, para. 20; cf. paras 9–12 of the Opinion of AG La Pergola.

[187] *Spanish strawberries*, para. 30. See similarly, Case C-112/00 *Schmidberger, Internationale Transporte und Planzüge v Republik Österreich* [2003] ECR I-5659, para. 51 ff.

[188] *Spanish strawberries*, paras 31–32.

that it had a general power of review over the appropriateness of actions taken in order to ensure that free movement rights have been respected.[189] Several paragraphs of the Opinion and also of the judgment focused on the multiple defences raised by France; but the severity and duration of this 'structural situation of non-compliance'[190] prevailed.

If the severe circumstances of the *Spanish strawberries* case were perceived in some way as an indication of *when* the enforcement principle might be applied to private actions restricting the free movement of goods,[191] the adoption of Regulation 2679/98 and especially the subsequent decision in *Schmidberger* corrected any misapprehension.[192] In *Schmidberger*, Austria had to justify the decision of a public authority to allow an environmental protest even though it meant that the Brenner motorway had to be closed for almost 30 hours. This was a one-off road closure: appreciably different, in other words, from the events in *Spanish strawberries*. However, both AG Jacobs and the Court emphasized the fact that the motorway in question is a 'major' cross-border transit route.[193] Linking back to the discussion in Sections 2 and 3, and addressing the lawfulness of the authorized protest under Austrian law, AG Jacobs considered that '[t]he *intentions* of those responsible for a restriction or the classification of a restriction within categories of national law *are in principle not relevant*'.[194]

In *Viking Line*, AG Poiares Maduro remarked that the decisions in *Spanish strawberries* and *Schmidberger* 'rely fundamentally on the reasoning that private action can jeopardise the objectives of the provisions on freedom of movement'.[195] Why, then, did the case law on goods develop initially along a distinctive enforcement rather than effectiveness/inequality track? One point to consider is that by dealing with the actions of private individuals through the channel of Member State responsibility, the Court could leave to one side other case law clearly indicating that Article 34 *is* addressed to the Member States—especially since it had expressly commented on the ambiguity of the wording of the Treaty in case law on the horizontal scope of workers, services, and establishment.[196] This view also fits with

[189] *Spanish strawberries*, para. 35.

[190] AG Geelhoed in Case C-494/01 *Commission v Ireland* [2005] ECR I-3331, para. 45 of the Opinion.

[191] Which would have fit with earlier case law too: in *Spanish strawberries*, AG Lenz pointed to authority for the premise that 'for an administrative practice to constitute a measure prohibited under Article 30 that practice must show a certain degree of consistency and generality' (para. 17 of the Opinion, referring to Case 21/84 *Commission v France* [1985] ECR 1355, para. 13).

[192] See *Schmidberger*, esp. paras 58–59; and Council Regulation (EC) 2679/98 on the functioning of the internal market in relation to the free movement of goods among the Member States, 1998 OJ L337/8, referring to 'serious disruption' and 'serious loss' (Article 1).

[193] *Schmidberger*, para. 63; and paras 77–81 and 83 of the Opinion.

[194] AG Jacobs in *Schmidberger*, para. 80 of the Opinion (emphasis added).

[195] AG Maduro in *Viking Line*, para. 38 of the Opinion; see also para. 40, where he considers that indirect horizontal effect in cases like *Schmidberger* and the direct horizontal effect achieved in e.g. *Defrenne* differ only in form and not in substance, and reflects on the implications of this conclusion for national judicial review procedures.

[196] E.g. Case 311/85 *Vereniging van Flaamse Reisbureaus* [1987] ECR 3801, para. 30 (i.e. Article 34 TFEU 'concern[s] only public measures and not the conduct of undertakings'); Case C-159/00 *Sapod Audic v Eco-Emballages SA* [2002] ECR I-5031, para. 74 ('[s]uch a contractual provision cannot be

Snell's observation that the Member States were the direct addressees of the original provisions of the Treaty of Rome on quantitative restrictions.[197] But a close reading of the judgment in *Spanish strawberries* shows that, in fact, the Court did not rule out more general private reach for Article 34, applying the State responsibility dimension *in that case* because of the boundary-setting focus of the Commission's enforcement proceedings. This interpretation is drawn from paragraph 30 of the judgment, where the Court held that 'Article [34] therefore *does not prohibit solely measures emanating from the State* which, in themselves, create restrictions on trade between Member States. It *also applies* where a Member State abstains from adopting the measures required in order to deal with obstacles to the free movement of goods *which are not caused by the State*' (emphasis added).[198] In *Viking Line*, seeds of reconciliation are also apparent—there, the Court referred to the case law on goods to support the finding that 'restrictions [on free movement] may be the result of actions by individuals or groups of such individuals rather than caused by the State'.[199] In the same case, AG Poiares Maduro developed an extended framework for horizontality that attributed different *functions* to both strands of the case law but also recognized that both served the same *objective*: ensuring the proper functioning of the market against the parameters set by free movement law. His ideas are discussed in more detail in Section 4(c).

In *Fra.bo*, the case law on horizontality was pulled together more consciously by AG Trstenjak, to determine 'whether a private-law association which inter alia draws up technical standards for products used in the drinking water supply sector and certifies products, or has products certified, on the basis of those technical standards must comply with the principle of the free movement of goods when undertaking those activities'.[200] But the fact that it was 'virtually impossible to market pipes and accessories for drinking water supply in Germany' without the relevant body's certification was clearly influential for the Advocate General;[201] she concluded that '*in these circumstances*, there are *no fundamental objections* to the application of the argument developed in case-law on the limited horizontal effect of the freedom of movement for [workers, establishment and service provision] to a case . . . in which the applicability of the principle of the free movement of goods to a private-law association with *de facto rule-making competence* is at issue'.[202] In its judgment, the Fourth Chamber was even more cautious. It too emphasized the singularity of the certification process under review in this case[203] and arguably constricted the broader *Walrave* threshold of 'regulating in a collective manner' by

regarded as a barrier to trade for the purposes of Article [36 TFEU] since it was not imposed by a Member State but agreed between individuals').

197 Snell, n171, 212–13.

198 A similar ambiguity can be read into AG Jacobs' Opinion in *Schmidberger* at para. 84.

199 *Viking Line*, para. 62.

200 AG Trstenjak in *Fra.bo*, para. 1 of the Opinion.

201 AG Trstenjak in *Fra.bo*, para. 41 of the Opinion; see also, para. 50.

202 AG Trstenjak in *Fra.bo*, para. 45 of the Opinion (emphasis added).

203 E.g. 'only possibility'; 'other procedure of little or no practical use'; 'considerable restriction on the marketing of the products concerned on the German market' (*Fra.bo*, paras 28–30).

stating that the body in question here '*in reality holds the power to regulate* the entry into the German market of products'.[204] The Court concluded that Article 34 TFEU catches 'activities of a private-law body, where the national legislation considers the products certified by that body to be compliant with national law and that has the effect of restricting the marketing of products which are not certified by that body'.[205]

The tentative shift into *Walrave* territory in *Fra.bo* brings more coherence to the horizontality of free movement law in one sense, since it finally infuses a basic threshold of collective regulation into goods as well. But the Court was careful to confine the language and thus the scope of its decision as narrowly as possible: this was a very specific 'private-law body' performing legislatively designated public functions. As if to underscore the distinctiveness of these circumstances, the Court did not cite either the *Walrave* or *Schmidberger* lines of case law in any part of its judgment.

The outcome in *Fra.bo* and especially the Opinion of AG Trstenjak nevertheless fit with a surging wave of case law discussion on horizontal scope more generally, leading several Advocates General to make cross-references between free movement judgments and case law on the horizontal application of general principles of EU law. For example, reflecting on *Walrave* in a case on age discrimination, AG Sharpston observed that 'one should be slow to exclude the possibility that a general principle of [EU] law may, in appropriate circumstances, be applied horizontally'.[206] Working out the contours of the 'appropriate circumstances' is precisely the zone of interpretative contention that shapes the debate on horizontality. It is not yet clear if the collective regulation threshold is as far as the Court will go with respect to goods, or indeed other freedoms, a point picked up again in Section 4(c).

(iii) Full horizontal reach

Finally, for the free movement of workers, the Court authorized full horizontal effect in *Angonese* i.e. individual employers are directly bound by the prohibition of discrimination in Article 45(2) TFEU.[207] The referring court explicitly framed its question around the extent to which a bank governed by private law could be

[204] *Fra.bo*, para. 31 (emphasis added). [205] *Fra.bo*, para. 32.

[206] AG Sharpston in Case C-427/06 *Bartsch v Bosch und Siemens Hausgeräte (BSH) Altersfürsorge GmbH* [2008] ECR I-7245, para. 85 of the Opinion. In *Kücükdeveci*, AG Bot considered that 'recognising that provisions of the Treaty containing specific expressions of the general principle of equal treatment and non-discrimination have horizontal direct effect' was in fact a 'more significant step' than applying a general principle of EU law in national proceedings between private parties (Case C-555/07 *Kücükdeveci v Swedex GmbH & Co. KG* [2010] ECR I-365, para. 85 of the Opinion). Taking the cross-fertilization from free movement law further still, AG Trstenjak has argued that 'the direct application of fundamental rights in the form of general principles in relationships between private individuals cannot be ruled out in principle' (Case C-282/10 *Dominguez v Centre informatique du Centre Ouest Atlantique and Préfet de la région Centre*, judgment of 24 January 2012, para. 126 of the Opinion).

[207] Case C-281/98 *Angonese v Cassa di Risparmio di Bolzano SpA* [2000] ECR I-4139.

subject to Article 45, and relevant provisions of Regulation 1612/68, given the bank's insistence that it would only accept a language competence certificate issued by the public authorities in Bolzano as part of its employment competitions. The applicant was seeking to demonstrate that he had acquired the necessary level of competence in German through other channels, mainly while studying in Austria. AG Fennelly concentrated on whether those studies could be characterized as a *qualification* within the meaning of EU law. Having concluded that they could not, he touched on horizontal scope only briefly at the end of the Opinion. Although he acknowledged that full horizontal reach was 'not excluded' by the Court's approach in the cases about collective regulatory impact, all of which had involved sporting associations at that time, AG Fennelly did not offer any further analysis on a speculative basis.[208]

However, after first recalling its reasoning in the *Walrave* line of case law, the Court went on to state very plainly that the prohibition of discrimination in Article 45 'must be regarded as applying also to private persons'.[209] Although the Court engaged the full horizontal scope of the Treaty provisions on equal pay for equal work by analogy, it is perhaps not insignificant that the decision in *Walrave* in fact pre-dated the judgment in *Defrenne*.[210] The approach taken in *Angonese* was confirmed in *Raccanelli*, where the Court held that Article 45 TFEU applied to contracts between individuals, including private-law associations.[211] Moreover, that decision was reached without an Advocate General's opinion, demonstrating the extent to which the scope of Article 45 is regarded as a settled legal question. Whether the full horizontal reach of free movement law should stop at the boundary of workers is examined in Section 4(c).

(b) Distilling the Treaty's objectives: the catalyst of discrimination

Discrimination is critical but, as will be shown in subsequent chapters, not sufficient when describing the scope of restrictions on free movement rights in a general sense. However, the basic premises of horizontal reach, as expressed in *Walrave* and affirmed consistently since then, were overtly reasoned through the logic of discrimination. In her Opinion in *Casteels*, for example, AG Kokott, addressing *Angonese* and *Raccanelli,* confirmed that the Court had stretched the application of Article 45 TFEU to 'employment relationships governed by private law . . . *or at any rate* the prohibition of discrimination contained therein'.[212] This case law exposes the interconnected nature of EU objectives in Russian doll format: the

[208] AG Fennelly in *Angonese*, para. 40 of the Opinion; however, he seemed sceptical of the feasibility of full horizontal effect (para. 41). For a contrasting, pre-*Angonese* view of the potential scope of Article 45, see AG Cosmas in *Ferlini*, paras 71–79 of the Opinion.

[209] *Angonese*, para. 36.

[210] The original analogy to *Walrave* was drawn by AG Trabucchi in *Defrenne* (at 489).

[211] Case C-94/07 *Raccanelli v Max-Planck-Gesellschaft zur Förderung der Wissenschaften eV* [2008] ECR I-5939, paras 45–46; confirmed in Case C-172/11 *Erny v Daimler AG—Werk Wörth*, judgment of 28 June 2012, para. 36.

[212] AG Kokott in Case C-379/09 *Casteels v British Airways plc* [2011] ECR I-1379, fn62 of the Opinion (emphasis added).

creation of an internal market is a central objective of the Union; free movement is a central objective of the internal market; and non-discrimination is a central objective of free movement.[213]

In *Bartsch*, however, AG Sharpston observed that while the decisions in *Laval* and *Viking Line* both concerned the extent to which the actions of trade unions are caught by EU free movement law, only *Laval* followed the familiar 'specific expression of discrimination' formula for the provision of services.[214] In *Viking Line*, the Court just stated that 'Articles [45, 49, and 56 TFEU] do not apply only to the actions of public authorities but extend also to rules of any other nature aimed at regulating in a collective manner gainful employment, self-employment and the provision of services'.[215] Both judgments were delivered by the Grand Chamber (*Viking Line* on 11 December 2007; *Laval* one week later), with different rapporteurs and different Advocates General, but exactly the same composition for the Grand Chamber. In *Laval*, AG Mengozzi had argued for the decoupling of horizontal scope from the prohibition of discrimination embodied in the Treaty's free movement provisions. Reviewing the Court's analysis in *Deliège* and *Wouters*, he suggested that the exclusion of the relevant restrictions from the scope of services in those cases had *not* hinged on their non-discriminatory nature.[216] He then outlined a normative argument based on the objectives of free movement law:

> [I]n so far as a fundamental Treaty freedom is involved, *any attempt to delimit the horizontal effect of the obligation it imposes according to whether the obstacles raised against it are or are not discriminatory* is in my opinion somewhat misconceived. If such an approach were upheld, there would then be complex debates as to whether a particular action or set of rules adopted by private persons should be seen as indirect discrimination based on nationality, a restriction, a barrier or a deterrent to the freedom to provide services. As is already apparent from the case-law, since the line of demarcation between those different classifications is in practice far from being entirely clear, to impose such a delimitation of the horizontal scope of Article [59] would affect the legal certainty of operators.[217]

The collapsing of restrictions into a more generic pool, irrespective of whether they are discriminatory or not, was already seen in Chapter 1 in the context of the Court's expanding justification framework. In a more general sense, this question is addressed again in Chapter 6. It is not clear whether the Court in *Viking Line* intended to subsume AG Mengozzi's broader point in *Laval*. But it is astonishing that no one thought to synchronize the narrower approach ultimately taken in *Laval* with the broader judgment being developed concurrently, by the same

[213] In *Angonese*, AG Fennelly suggested that 'an allegation of *indirect discrimination* on grounds of nationality . . . may present *special problems and difficulties* in the case of private economic actors' (para. 41 of the Opinion, emphasis added). He did not elaborate further, and the issue has not been picked up in subsequent case law.

[214] AG Sharpston in *Bartsch*, fn83 of the Opinion.

[215] *Viking Line*, para. 33. Cf. para. 55 in *Laval*, confirming Article 59 TFEU as a 'specific expression' of the non-discrimination prohibition in Article 18.

[216] AG Mengozzi in *Laval*, paras 225–226 of the Opinion.

[217] *Laval*, para. 228 (emphasis added), citing e.g. Case C-76/90 *Säger v Dennemeyer & Co. Ltd* [1991] ECR I-4221, para. 13.

judges, for *Viking Line*—especially since these were the first occasions on which collective action was brought within the scope of free movement law, something that was never going to pass uncontested.[218]

The intentions of the Court became clearer in *Olympique Lyonnais* and *Casteels*. In the latter case, considering an employment relationship governed by rules with collective regulatory impact, the Court held that 'Article 45 TFEU militates against any measure which, *even though applicable without discrimination* on grounds of nationality, is capable of hindering or rendering less attractive the exercise by European Union nationals of the fundamental freedoms guaranteed by the Treaty'.[219] Given the open-ended expression of this principle, it is not unreasonable to assume that the same approach will be extended to individual employers. Even if not, the detachment of horizontal scope from discrimination at the level of collective regulatory impact is itself a fundamental interpretive shift. It does fit with the Court's approach to non-discriminatory restrictions on free movement law more generally. But whether these developments should be welcomed in a more global sense will be considered in Chapter 7.

(c) The curbing of private autonomy

In *Laval*, AG Mengozzi raised an interesting question about the logic of limits. Leaving the discrimination point to one side, what is the reason for limiting full horizontal reach to workers? If a landlord refuses to offer a tenancy agreement to migrant EU students but not to home State students, does that action not 'neutralize' the rights to move and reside conferred on the former by Union citizenship? Is there not 'inequality of application' if individual traders can discriminate as much and as openly against imported products as they like, subject only to the unlikely imposition of home State sanctions? In his Opinion in *Viking Line*, AG Poiares Maduro posed the question as follows: 'does the Treaty imply that, in order to ensure the proper functioning of the common market, the provisions on freedom of movement protect the rights of market participants, not just by limiting the powers of the authorities of the Member States, but also *by limiting the autonomy of others*?'[220] The decisions of associations or organizations that have collective regulatory impact and, for nationality discrimination at the very least, the employment powers of private-law associations and private individuals are increasingly subject to a Treaty signed by States. Capturing obstacles to free movement that result from

[218] See A Dashwood '*Viking* and *Laval*: Issues of horizontal direct effect' (2007–2008) 10 CYELS 525; J Krzeminska-Vamvaka, 'Horizontal effect of fundamental rights and freedoms—much ado about nothing? German, Polish and EU theories compared after *Viking Line*', Jean Monnet Working Paper 11/09, available at <http://centers.law.nyu.edu/jeanmonnet/papers/09/091101.pdf>. Snell supports the catching of 'private non-undertakings' in this way since they are unlikely to come within the scope of the competition rules (n171, 233–4).

[219] *Casteels*, para. 19 (emphasis added). See similarly, *Olympique Lyonnais* paras 33–37. The two cases had different Advocates General (AG Trstenjak and AG Sharpston respectively). *Olympique Lyonnais* was a Grand Chamber decision, sharing four judges with *Laval* and *Viking Line*. The Third Chamber delivered the judgment in *Casteels*. Only one judge sat on all four cases.

[220] AG Poiares Maduro in *Viking Line*, para. 36 of the Opinion (emphasis added).

the *exercise* of their legal autonomy steers the case law on horizontal scope.[221] But the propriety of *limiting* their autonomy in consequence—a major sticking point in the academic debate[222]—has not been addressed directly by the Court.

In *Viking Line*, AG Poiares Maduro reconceptualized the balancing exercise that the Court undertook in *Schmidberger* as an exploration of the curbing of autonomy: weighing the demonstrators' right to freedom of expression against the right of the transport company to move goods between Member States. He concluded that 'private individuals must not be allowed to act without appropriate concern for the rights that other private individuals draw from the rules on freedom of movement'.[223] He went on, however, to propose a sliding scale for the horizontal reach of free movement law, contrasting the 'normative and socio-economic power inherent in State authorities'—since they have 'significant potential to thwart the proper functioning of the common market'—with the fact that 'in many circumstances, private actors simply do not wield enough influence successfully to prevent others from enjoying their rights to freedom of movement'.[224] Addressing the example of the individual shopkeeper who refuses to sell goods imported from other Member States, AG Poiares Maduro considered that normal marketplace competition would ensure that both suppliers and consumers could still participate in the market for those imported goods. He thus proposed that 'the rules on freedom of movement apply directly to any private action that is capable of *effectively restricting others from exercising their right* to freedom of movement'—a test that he acknowledged did not provide a 'simple answer'.[225] He developed the idea as follows:

> [T]he finding that certain private actors are subject to the rules on freedom of movement does not spell the end of their private autonomy. Nor does it necessarily mean that they must be held to exactly the same standards as State authorities. The Court may apply *different levels of scrutiny*, depending on the *source and seriousness* of the impediment to the exercise of the right to freedom of movement, and on the *force and validity* of competing claims of private autonomy. In other words, private actors may often still do things that public authorities may not.[226]

[221] Conversely, early case law on the meaning of 'public' authority concentrated more on demonstrating that various bodies did *not* exercise sufficient autonomy to detach them from State control (e.g. Case 249/81 *Commission v Ireland (Buy Irish)* [1982] ECR 4005, para. 15). Even an individual's actions are capable of being attributed to the State (e.g. Case C-470/03 *A.G.M.-COS.MET Srl v Suomen valtio and Lehtinen* [2007] ECR I-2749).

[222] See P Pescatore, 'Public and private aspects of European Community law' (1987) 10 Fordham Int'l L.J. 373 and G Marenco, 'Competition between national economies and competition between businesses—a response to Judge Pescatore' (1987) 10 Fordham Int'l L.J. 420; see also, J Baquero Cruz, 'Free movement and private autonomy' (1999) 24:6 ELRev 603 and M Kumm, 'Who's afraid of the total constitution? Constitutional rights as principles and the constitutionalization of private law' (2006) 7:4 *German Law Journal* 352.

[223] AG Poiares Maduro in *Viking Line*, para. 38 of the Opinion; considering the implications of this approach, he noted (in para. 40) that '[i]f *Schmidberger* were to have been decided as a private suit between the transport company and the demonstrators, the Court would still have had to weigh the right to freedom of movement of the former against the right to demonstrate of the latter'.

[224] AG Poiares Maduro in *Viking Line*, paras 41–42 of the Opinion.

[225] AG Poiares Maduro in *Viking Line*, para. 43 of the Opinion (emphasis added).

[226] AG Poiares Maduro in *Viking Line*, para. 49 of the Opinion (emphasis added).

This might at first glance resemble a *de minimis* threshold for market intervention, but the test is arguably more concerned with levels of market power. For example, citing *Angonese*, the Advocate General rationalized the full reach of free movement law into the private employment sphere through the 'particular significance' of working conditions and access to employment, since the conditions set by the employer raised 'an obstacle that [the worker] cannot reasonably circumvent'.[227] He also proposed a theoretically sound reconciliation of the *Walrave* and *Schmidberger* case law, in which State responsibility provides a sweeper function when Treaty provisions cannot be applied to private action more directly.[228] But his sliding-scale framework does not resolve a fundamental niggle identified by Snell: 'it is logically a rather curious move to place a Member State under an obligation to adopt appropriate measures to ensure that private individuals do not create obstacles to the free movement of goods, when those private individuals do not have any duty not to create those obstacles in the first place'.[229] It also fails to address the often significantly different degrees of market power that shape trading relationships more generally.

Where does this leave our student tenants? Does the Advocate General's test seize the reluctant landlord by analogy, on the basis that '[t]he possibility that, in the long run, economic incentives will undercut such discriminatory recruitment practices is of little comfort to the individual who seeks employment [accommodation?] today'?[230] The example shows that a neatly convergent approach to horizontality across the freedoms does not take into account differences in their functioning that have become important in the case law.[231] Similar problems of disconnect were discussed in Chapter 2, in the context of efforts to conceptualize trade freedoms as citizenship rights. The human/trade fault-line discussed there may differentiate situations empirically and also normatively.[232] But a finding of direct effect must be based on the capacity for direct enforcement suggested by the relevant Treaty *provision*—not the functional aspects of it.

In *van Gend en Loos*, the imposition of obligations—and not just the conferring of rights—on private individuals was pitched as a defining feature of the EU legal order:

[T]he [Union] constitutes a new legal order of international law for the benefit of which the states have limited their sovereign rights, albeit within limited fields, and *the subjects of which*

[227] AG Poiares Maduro in *Viking Line*, paras 46 and 48 of the Opinion. See similarly, AG Trstenjak in *Fra.bo*, para. 34 of the Opinion, suggesting that since 'horizontal effect concerns private individuals *only in the context of a well-defined rule-making activity*, it is limited in its impact' (emphasis added).

[228] AG Poiares Maduro in *Viking Line*, para. 50 of the Opinion: 'the provisions on freedom of movement do not always provide a specific solution for each case, but merely set certain boundaries within which a conflict between two private parties may be resolved'.

[229] Snell, n171, 237.

[230] AG Poiares Maduro in *Viking Line*, para. 47 of the Opinion.

[231] E.g. contrast the examples discussed by Snell, n171, 228, relating to services provided by undertakings and, therefore, aligning more closely with goods than with situations involving workers.

[232] See e.g. Krzeminska-Vamvaka, n218, who argues that horizontal effect is a mechanism for the guarantee of fundamental rights as well as fundamental freedoms. She also emphasizes, however, that horizontal effect should be *exceptional* (see esp. 52–4).

comprise not only Member States but also their nationals. Independently of the legislation of Member States, [EU] law therefore *not only imposes obligations on individuals* but is also intended to confer upon them rights which become part of their legal heritage. These rights arise not only where they are expressly granted by the Treaty, *but also by reason of obligations which the Treaty imposes in a clearly defined way upon individuals* as well as upon the Member States and upon the institutions of the [Union].[233]

We saw in Section 4(a) that, on the basis of the wording of the provisions alone, full horizontal effect is possible for all of the Treaty freedoms. But that does not mean that it is desirable. It was perhaps a mistake for the Court to go there for workers, since the consequences of that step inevitably reverberate beyond Article 45 TFEU. Because it did go there, however, the Court will be faced with cases involving private restrictions on the other freedoms, and it will have to make choices—and rationalize those choices.

So far, there has been a formal emphasis on the Treaty provision engaged but a more material concern with the *effect* of the restriction being challenged. This may have worked out well to date, but the next set of cases will be more complicated. Continuing to resolve the issues by reference to the relevant Treaty provision, which is what the general scheme of direct effect requires, may lead to situations that are both too rigid—e.g. deciding that services should follow either goods or workers misses crucial nuances—and too intrusive e.g. the clarity of Article 34 TFEU and its centrality to the internal market makes an *Angonese* claim difficult to rule out; if the protest in *Schmidberger* had occurred without the interim step of official permission, would respect for private autonomy be enough to defeat the legitimacy of the transit company's claim against the demonstrators directly? AG Poiares Maduro has suggested that it might not be.[234] Because the *effect* on the company's business would have been the same.

The question of practical workability has to be borne in mind too. As Snell points out, '[i]t would be impossible, not to mention ridiculous, to demand a justification for every decision not to buy imported goods or services'.[235] The Court could engage citizenship and fundamental rights more consciously in the future to shore up the deeper reach of its case law for workers. But then it will have to face challenging scenarios under services and establishment that would seem to require splitting the freedoms along a human/trade fault-line—an approach that, in turn, cannot be squared with the principles and application of direct effect more generally.

5. Conclusion

The exclusionary principles considered in this chapter are at different stages of conceptual development. For example, the refining and pleading of abuse of rights

233 *Van Gend en Loos*, 12 (emphasis added).
234 See again, AG Poiares Maduro in *Viking Line*, para. 40 of the Opinion.
235 Snell, n171, 230.

has intensified, but the exclusionary potential of horizontal scope is dissolving. However, analysis of different who-based principles that narrow the scope of free movement rights reveals common thematic trends that surface in quite distinctive contexts. First, there is evidence of increasing awareness of the need to aim for consistency, especially at the level of *definition*. Second, however, the judgments of the Court often fail to *explain* the definitions that are being developed and, more fundamentally, to *deal with existing case law* that does not fit with the interpretative choices now being made. The Court seems slow to reverse its own judgments definitively, even if they distort the overall symmetry of the case law. The relevance of intention or motivation was shown to be an example of this problem across a series of quite different who-based principles. Third, there are inconsistencies at the level of *application*. Some principles are applied methodically (e.g. the horizontal scope of the Treaty for rules with collective regulatory impact), but a discernible tendency toward overly individualized outcomes causes discord at the systemic level i.e. when trying to understand the applicable constitutional principles at more distance from the particular facts of each case.

Recalling the drivers of fragmentation identified in Chapter 2, the *proliferation of tests and principles* is not as acute a problem in the case law considered here as might have been expected. As noted above, the Court has made conscious efforts to streamline the definitions it applies when determining personal scope. But that process is not going to be effective if the Court fails to provide comprehensive reasoning in its judgments—and that includes either reconciling or departing from obviously conflicting authorities. The Court has also been consistent in its use of *internal market objectives* to reinforce its decisions. At the level of exclusionary rules, however, the engagement of these objectives is relatively straightforward: the rights-conferring Treaty provisions at issue are essentially about free movement; the Court is not yet immersed in the trickier task of weighing multiple competing interests. As will be seen in Chapter 4, showcasing movement as *the* core internal market objective brings problems in other aspects of free movement law. Finally, the Court rarely engaged overtly with *fundamental rights* in the case law considered in this chapter. But the pull of the human/trade fault-line is clearly evident beneath the surface of many of its judgments—acting both to reduce the impact of abuse of rights for natural persons and to extend the horizontal reach of (some of) the Treaty provisions that affect them.

4

The Negative Scope of Free Movement Law: Cross-Border Connections and the Significance of Movement

1. Introduction

The principles considered in Chapter 3 were thematically linked by a focus on *who* can fall outside the scope of free movement law. Attention shifts here to the *what*-based dimension. Generally speaking, the free movement framework privileges inclusion, but two broad parameters mark the outer boundaries of its substance. First, the EU must have competence to deal with the material issue or subject matter. Second, the Court has emphasized that EU law will not be concerned with 'disparities in treatment, for persons and undertakings subject to the jurisdiction of the [Union], which may result from divergences existing between the various Member States, so long as they affect all persons subject to them in accordance with objective criteria and without regard to their nationality'.[1] When you move, in other words, you must generally accept the regulatory content of the host State as you find it. In reality, the constraining effects of these rules are more anaemic, since the Court can review national measures for compliance with general principles of EU law even where the measures regulate areas for which the EU lacks regulatory competence itself.[2] Also, as developed in later chapters, the philosophy of market access and the corollary expansion of Treaty-relevant restrictions make it difficult to draw lines around rules and practices that *cannot* be challenged by invoking EU rights. However, a critically important what-based principle that can limit the scope of free movement law will be examined here: the requirement of demonstrating a cross-border connection. The converse expression of the rule is that free movement law is not normally relevant to situations that are purely internal to one Member State. The extent to which EU law *should* be relevant in such situations is a pivotal

[1] Case C-403/03 *Schempp v Finanzamt München V* [2005] ECR I-6421, para. 34.

[2] Or where the EU does have competence in certain respects (e.g. in accordance with the conditions set down in Articles 114 and 115 TFEU) but the political will to engage it is lacking. See e.g. Case C-446/03 *Marks & Spencer plc v Halsey (Her Majesty's Inspector of Taxes)* [2005] ECR I-10837, para. 29 (direct taxation); Case C-369/90 *Micheletti and others v Delegación del Gobierno en Cantabria* [1992] ECR I-4239, para. 10 (regulation of nationality).

constitutional question connected to locating the appropriate limits of Union regulatory authority.

Like the principles of *de minimis* and remoteness, considered in Chapter 5, the application of the purely internal rule can have sharply decisive effects in individual cases, but its impact on the case law in systemic terms is less straightforward. In this chapter, three complex and interlinked case law tensions surface repeatedly. First, the protection of fundamental rights emerges as a strong driver of fragmentation in the context of the purely internal rule. In particular, recent case law acutely demonstrates the mixed constitutional signals emanating from the Charter of Fundamental Rights outlined in Chapter 2. Much attention to date has been focused on 'implementing' Union law for the purposes of Article 51 of the Charter. But the discussion here seeks also to reflect on the meaning of two other phrases: 'new power or task' in the same provision and 'extend in any way the competences of the Union' in Article 6(1) TEU. Second, there is a tension between, on the one hand, the *depletion of the fact of movement* in the case law in many respects alongside the contrasting *scale and depth of substantive protection* that can ensue when that threshold is crossed. Third, a fundamental tension bridges the discussion here with the analysis of discrimination and market access in later chapters: how can we ensure that the exclusionary application of a purely internal rule in *some* cases is not arbitrary, given that the free movement framework also accepts a *potential* impact on movement as a legitimate factor for the purposes of connecting a situation to EU law?

The foundations of the purely internal rule will first be outlined in Section 2. The idea and causes of the depletion of movement will be addressed in Section 3 and, in Section 4, the constitutional challenges provoked by the tensions noted above will be considered in more detail. It will be argued that reconceptualizing the requirement of cross-border movement as a marker of arbitrary or differential treatment appropriately downplays the mere fact of movement, which, paradoxically, seems both to matter profoundly and not to matter much at all in the case law at present. The domain of equal treatment provides a more solidly constitutional basis for internal situation piercings by the case law—if desired—and it also sets up the discussion about what the application of a market access principle is really tying to achieve in the chapters that follow.

2. What does movement mean and why does it matter (so much)?

The Court has consistently confirmed that the material scope of the Treaty cannot be extended to 'internal situations which have no link with [Union] law'.[3] This does not mean that situations that are purely internal to one State can never come within the scope of the Treaty. But it does mean that a 'link' with Union law must be established. For free *movement* law, a cross-border connection provides the

[3] Case C-499/06 *Nerkowska v Zakład Ubezpieczeń Społecznych Oddział w Koszalinie* [2008] ECR I-3993, para. 25.

relevant link: achieved usually, but not necessarily,[4] through the exercise of movement in some form. This in turn means that, in certain circumstances, Member States may withhold from their own (static) nationals substantive benefits that they are obliged to extend to lawfully resident (migrant) EU nationals. The regimes governing family reunification provide an important example of how different rights can apply to static and migrant citizens in otherwise comparable material situations.[5] Resulting differences in treatment are typically articulated through the language of reverse discrimination, raising related questions about the regulatory level—EU, national, both, or neither—at which any anomalies should be tackled. All of these issues are debated extensively in the literature.[6] They will be considered here through the specific framing lenses of responsibility and coherence.

The Court has established the relevance of cross-border connections in all of the main domains of free movement law i.e. for Article 21 TFEU/citizenship,[7] Article 34 TFEU/goods,[8] Article 45 TFEU/workers,[9] Article 49 TFEU/establishment,[10] Article 56 TFEU/services,[11] and Article 63 TFEU/capital.[12] The Court has also established that crossing borders *within* a State is not—generally—enough to displace the purely internal rule.[13] Is it the Treaty that requires movement

[4] E.g. holding the passport of a Member State other than the State against which the material claim is being made can be sufficient to trigger the relevance of the Treaty, even if the claimant has never been in (i.e. moved to) the first State; see Case C-200/02 *Zhu and Chen v Secretary of State for the Home Department* [2004] ECR I-9925, esp. paras 36–41.

[5] In EU law, residence and other (e.g. eligibility to work) rights for third country national family members are regulated by three main systems: national immigration law for static home State nationals; EU citizenship and free movement law for migrant EU nationals (primarily through Directive 2004/38 on the right of citizens of the Union and their family members to move and reside freely within the territory of the Member States, 2004 OJ L158/77); and EU immigration law for lawfully resident third country nationals (Directive 2003/86/EC on the right to family reunification, 2003 OJ L251/12).

[6] E.g. E Cannizzaro, 'Producing "reverse discrimination" through the exercise of EC competences' (1997) YEL 29; C Dautricourt and S Thomas, 'Reverse discrimination and free movement of persons under Community law: All for Ulysses, nothing for Penelope?' (2009) 34:3 ELRev 433; D Hanf, '"Reverse discrimination" in EU law: Constitutional aberration, constitutional necessity or judicial choice?' (2011) 18:1–2 MJ 29; S Kon, 'Aspects of reverse discrimination in Community law' (1981) 6:1 ELRev 75; N Nic Shuibhne, 'Free movement of persons and the wholly internal rule: Time to move on?' (2002) 39:4 CMLRev 731; S O'Leary, 'The past, present and future of the purely internal rule in EU law' in M Dougan, N Nic Shuibhne, and E Spaventa (eds.), *Empowerment and Disempowerment of the European Citizen* (Hart Publishing, 2013) 37; DMW Pickup, 'Reverse discrimination and freedom of movement for workers' (1986) 23:1 CMLRev 135; M Poiares Maduro, 'The scope of European remedies: The case of purely internal situations and reverse discrimination' in C Kilpatrick, T Novitz, and P Skidmore (eds.), *The Future of European Remedies* (Hart Publishing, 2000) 117; E Spaventa, 'Seeing the wood despite the trees? On the scope of Union citizenship and its constitutional effects' (2008) 45:1 CMLRev 13; A Tryfonidou, *Reverse Discrimination in EC Law* (Kluwer Law International, 2009).

[7] Joined Cases C-64/96 and C-65/96 *Land Nordrhein-Westfalen v Uecker; Jacquet v Land Nordrhein-Westfalen* [1997] ECR I-3171, para. 23.

[8] Case 286/81 *Criminal proceedings against Oosthoek's Uitgeversmaatschappij BV* [1982] ECR 4575, para. 9.

[9] Case 175/78 *R v Saunders* [1979] ECR 1129, para. 11.

[10] Case 115/78 *Knoors v Staatssecretaris van Economische Zaken* [1979] ECR 399, para. 24.

[11] Case 52/79 *Procureur du Roi v Debauve and others* [1980] ECR 833, para. 9.

[12] Case C-483/99 *Commission v France* [2002] ECR I-4781, paras 35 and 40.

[13] Case C-212/06 *Government of the French Community and Walloon Government v Flemish Government* [2008] ECR I-1683, para. 33. But cf. the discussion below on Article 30 TFEU.

as a precondition for its application or, counter-intuitively, could rights normally associated with movement also be relevant in situations that are confined to one State?

Citizenship: Ambiguous (Article 21(1) TFEU: 'Every citizen of the Union shall have the right to move *and reside* freely *within the territory of the Member States*'; see also Article 20(2)(a) TFEU, 'Citizenship of the Union is hereby established')

Goods: Cross-border connection required (Article 30 TFEU: 'Customs duties on imports and exports and charges having equivalent effect shall be prohibited *between Member States*'; Article 34 TFEU: 'Quantitative restrictions on imports and all measures having equivalent effect shall be prohibited *between Member States*')

Workers: Cross-border connection required (Article 45(2) TFEU: '*Such freedom of movement* shall entail the abolition of any discrimination based on nationality between workers of the Member States as regards employment, remuneration and other conditions of work and employment')[14] (Cf. Article 157 TFEU, '*Each Member State* shall ensure that the principle of equal pay for male and female workers for equal work or work of equal value *is applied*' i.e. no reference to movement)

Establishment: Cross-border connection required (Article 49 TFEU: 'restrictions on the freedom of establishment of nationals of a Member State *in the territory of another Member State* shall be prohibited')

Services: Cross-border connection required (Article 56 TFEU: 'restrictions on freedom to provide services within the Union shall be prohibited in respect of nationals of Member States who are established *in a Member State other than that of the person for whom the services are intended*')

Capital: Cross-border connection required (Article 63(1): 'all restrictions on the movement of capital *between Member States* and between Member States and third countries shall be prohibited')

This overview shows why and where movement matters i.e. almost everywhere. According to Article 4(2) TFEU, the Treaty conceives of the internal market as a space for which regulatory competence is shared. Cross-border market situations demonstrate precisely the rationale and *added* value of EU regulation, reinforcing the presumption that purely internal situations should be regulated by the Member States themselves in line with explicit constitutional instructions such as conferral of powers and subsidiarity.

In the case law to date, however, two exceptions to the purely internal rule have been established. First, the Court has realized the potential latent in the ambiguity of the citizenship provisions by finding that situations involving (1) loss of Member State nationality (*Rottmann*) or (2) the citizen's forced departure from the territory of the Union (*Ruiz Zambrano*, read in the light of *Dereci*) engage the protection of

[14] In his Opinion in *Saunders*, however, AG Warner emphasized that Article 45(3) TFEU speaks more broadly of the right to accept offers of employment while 'mov[ing] freely *within the territory* of the Member States', which mirrors the phrasing now used in Article 21 TFEU (*Saunders*, at 1142–3, emphasis added).

EU law even if the material facts are confined to one State.[15] In *Rottmann*, the referring court had queried 'whether it is contrary to [EU] law... for a Member State [Germany] to withdraw from a citizen of the Union the nationality of that State acquired by naturalisation and obtained by deception inasmuch as that withdrawal deprives the person concerned of the status of citizen of the Union and of the benefit of the rights attaching thereto by rendering him stateless, acquisition of that nationality having caused that person to lose the nationality of his Member State of origin [Austria]'.[16] Confirming the admissibility of the case, AG Poiares Maduro pointed to the applicant's move from Austria to Germany, through which he had established a cross-border connection that 'had an impact on the change in his civil status'.[17] The Court seemed to attach no weight to this factor in its judgment. Looking more closely, however, it does seem to take both the fact and relevance of the available cross-border link into account:

It is clear that the situation of a citizen of the Union who, like the applicant in the main proceedings, is faced with a decision withdrawing his naturalisation, adopted *by the authorities of one Member State*, and placing him, after he has lost the nationality *of another Member State* that he originally possessed, in a position capable of causing him to lose the status conferred by Article [20 TFEU] and the rights attaching thereto falls, by reason of its nature and its consequences, within the ambit of European Union law.[18]

The decision in *Rottmann* established a foreseeable (from *Micheletti*) albeit controversial further layer of review over the exercise of a fundamental stream of national regulatory competence. But it was not a purely internal situation. Where possible loss of nationality relates to two Member State nationalities, as it did here, a cross-border dimension is present. In a case involving a dual national where just one Member State passport is held, however, the principle established in *Rottmann* could be applied in an otherwise internal situation: since to lose that Member State nationality would clearly deprive the individual concerned of the status of EU citizenship altogether.

The bond to movement was fractured more definitively in *Ruiz Zambrano*, where the presumed forced departure of infant Union citizens from the territory of the Union—in consequence of their home State, Belgium, refusing to grant

[15] Case C-135/08 *Rottmann v Freistaat Bayern* [2010] ECR I-1449, Case C-34/09 *Ruiz Zambrano v Office national de l'emploi (ONEm)* [2011] ECR I 1177, and Case C-256/11 *Dereci and others v Bundesministerium für Inneres*, judgment of 15 November 2011. This case law has already been analysed extensively in the literature e.g. S Adam and P Van Elsuwege, 'Citizenship rights and the federal balance between the European Union and its Member States: Comment on *Dereci*' (2012) 37:2 ELRev 176; K Hailbronner and D Thym, 'Comment on Case C-34/09 *Ruiz Zambrano*' (2011) 48:4 CMLRev 1253; N Nic Shuibhne, '(Some of) the kids are all right: Comment on Case C-434/09 *McCarthy* and Case C-256/11 *Dereci*' (2012) 49:1 CMLRev 349; H van Eijken and SA dee Vries, 'A new route into the Promised Land? Being a European citizen after *Ruiz Zambrano*' (2011) 36:5 ELRev 704; P van Elsuwege and D Kochenov, 'On the limits of judicial intervention: EU citizenship and family reunification rights' (2011) 13:4 EJML 443; A Wiesbrock, 'Disentangling the "Union citizenship puzzle"? The *McCarthy* case' (2011) 36:6 ELRev 861.

[16] *Rottmann*, para. 36.

[17] AG Poiares Maduro in *Rottmann*, para. 13 of the Opinion.

[18] *Rottmann*, para. 42 (emphasis added).

residence rights, and work permits, to their Colombian national parents—was characterized as 'depriving citizens of the Union of the *genuine enjoyment of the substance of the rights* conferred by virtue of their status as citizens of the Union'.[19] While the content of this new test was not yet clear at the time, what *was* clear was that no cross-border connection was identified or projected. In other words, the Court established a substantive role for the status of Union citizenship in a situation that was, and was acknowledged to be, purely internal to one State.

Soon afterwards, however, the *Ruiz Zambrano* deprivation test was tightly qualified in *McCarthy* and *Dereci*. In both cases, the withholding of family reunification rights from Union citizens in purely internal situations who could (presumably) either continue to reside in their home States without their third country national family members or leave their home States and live with their families in other EU Member States—i.e. citizens not *forced* to leave the territory of the Union in either scenario—was found not to engage the protection of EU law. The Court emphasized material dependency over emotional dependency, even though the former can clearly be transmitted more readily across State borders than the latter.[20] The line of authority that had seemed to privilege the right to respect for family life as a fundamental concern, introduced in Chapter 3 and exemplified by the decision in *Carpenter*,[21] was not discussed. These issues will be picked up in Section 4. More fundamentally, the Court confirmed first, in all three cases, that holding the nationality of a Member State is enough to bring someone within the personal scope of the Treaty. Looking then at the question of material scope, the Court utilized the ambiguous wording of both Article 20 (in *Ruiz Zambrano*)—which

[19] *Ruiz Zambrano*, para. 42 (emphasis added). In its subsequent judgment in *O, S and L*, the Court clarified that the test in *Ruiz Zambrano* is not 'confined to situations in which there is a blood relationship between the third country national for whom a right of residence is sought and the Union citizen who is a minor from whom that right of residence might be derived' but could include 'persons on whom those citizens are legally, financially or emotionally dependent . . . it is the relationship of dependency between the Union citizen who is a minor and the third country national who is refused a right of residence that is liable to jeopardise the effectiveness of Union citizenship, since it is that dependency that would lead to the Union citizen being obliged, in fact, to leave not only the territory of the Member State of which he is a national but also that of the European Union as a whole, as a consequence of such a refusal'; (Joined cases C-356/11 and C-357/11 *O and S Maahanmuuttovirasto; Maahanmuuttovirasto v L*, judgment of 6 December 2012, paras 55 and 56).

[20] Cf. AG Mengozzi in *Dereci*, paras 45–48 of the View. In *O, S and L* (n19), the Court referred to other forms of dependency solely in the context of *forced* departure; AG Bot distinguished between forced and voluntary departure as follows: 'it is possible that S and L might choose to follow their respective spouses to their countries of origin in order to preserve the unity of their family life. The fact that their children have Union citizenship cannot amount to putting them "under house arrest" in the territory of the European Union, when they have been invested with full parental authority by the judicial authorities of the Union itself. In any event, if they chose to leave . . . the young children who are Union citizens would indeed have no other choice but to leave the territory of the Union and, consequently, lose the enjoyment of the rights conferred on them as citizens of the Union. However, in my view, departure from the territory of the Union would be *freely decided* by their mother for a reason linked to the preservation of family life and *would not be imposed* under the implementation of national legislation' (paras 41–42 of the Opinion, emphasis added). The parameters of emotional dependency were also under consideration in Case C-529/11 *Alarape and Tijani v Secretary of State for the Home Department*, judgment of 8 May 2013, in the context of rights of residence for the third country national primary carers of Union citizens.

[21] Case C-60/00 *Carpenter v Secretary of State for the Home Department* [2002] ECR I-6279.

denotes the rights held as 'inter alia' and thus suggests a potential corpus of unenumerated citizenship rights—and Article 21 (in *McCarthy*), which refers to movement and residence rights *within the territory of the Member States* (as does Article 20 too).

From a literal perspective, the Court did nothing in *Ruiz Zambrano* that overstepped the lines of the Treaty text when it put the requirement of a cross-border connection to the side. In contrast, however, Article 30 TFEU provides that '[c]ustoms duties on imports and exports and charges having equivalent effect shall be prohibited *between Member States*' (emphasis added). But, in *Lancry*, the Court held that the Treaty prohibits the imposition of a customs duty at any frontier—including one *within* a State.[22] The Court considered—against the views of AG Tesauro, who reasoned that the situation was purely internal—that '[t]he *unity of the [Union] customs territory* is undermined by the establishment of a regional customs frontier *just the same*, whether the products on which a charge is levied by reason of the fact that they cross a frontier are domestic products or come from other Member States'.[23] Rejecting most of the logic presented by the Court, Oliver did accept the significance of one particular factor: in 1992, customs documents were abolished for almost all goods moving within the Union, meaning that 'in practice it would be very difficult, if not impossible, to distinguish between products of domestic origin and those originating in other Member States'.[24]

But the position taken in *Lancry* has gained wider significance over time. Despite repeated cautions and even objections from several Advocates General, the Court continues to interpret the scope of Article 30 in the same way, articulating the frontier-less character of the market in more value-laden than pragmatic terms to develop a line of authority.[25] Because the objectives shaping the internal market are so pliable, a point discussed in Chapter 2, they neither help nor force the Court to distil more definitive choices. In *Jersey Potatoes*, AG Léger argued for a narrower approach. He considered that 'by defining the internal market as "an area without internal frontiers", the authors of the Single European Act did not intend to call in question the framework that had been clearly laid down by the EEC Treaty for application of the rules on the free movement of goods, persons, services and capital, which had already been highlighted by the case-law of the Court'.[26] In

22 Joined Cases C-363, 407-11/93 *Lancry v Direction Générale des Souanes and others* [1994] ECR I-3957.

23 *Lancry*, para. 29 (emphasis added).

24 P Oliver, 'Some further reflections on the scope of Articles 28–30 (EX 30–36) EC' (1999) 36:3 CMLRev 783 at 785.

25 Joined Cases C-485/93 and C-486/93 *Simitzi v Kos* [1995] ECR I-2655, Case C-72/03 *Carbonati Apuani Srl v Comune di Carrara* [2004] ECR I-8027, and Case C-293/02 *Jersey Produce Marketing Organisation Ltd v States of Jersey and Jersey Potato Export Marketing Board* [2005] ECR I-9543. In *Jersey Potatoes*, AG Léger argued that this line of case law 'depart[s] significantly from the traditional case-law of the Court regarding the territorial scope of the Treaty rules on the free movement of goods' (para. 90 of the Opinion); in *Carbonati Apuani*, AG Poiares Maduro considered its foundations to be 'fragile' having regard to the wording of the relevant Treaty provisions (para. 45 of the Opinion).

26 AG Léger in *Jersey Potatoes*, para. 129 of the Opinion. See similarly, A Tryfonidou, 'In search of the aim of the EC free movement of persons provisions: Has the Court of Justice missed the point?'

Carbonati Apuani, however, the Court used the same provision to make precisely the opposite point: 'Article [26(2) TFEU] defines the internal market as "an area without internal frontiers in which the free movement of goods, persons, services and capital is ensured", without drawing any distinction between inter-State frontiers and frontiers within a State'.[27]

The *Lancry* reasoning reinforces a more general point about discord between general and specific Treaty provisions. As seen, the economic freedoms clearly stipulate cross-border thresholds. But the Treaty's guidelines are less clear-cut when looked at in the round. For example, does the reference to '*any* discrimination on grounds of nationality' (Article 18 TFEU) also prohibit reverse discrimination? Similarly, as emphasized by the Court in *Lancry*, Article 26 TFEU defines the internal market as 'an area *without internal frontiers* in which the free movement of goods, persons, services and capital is ensured'; does the proviso then attached—that this is to be ensured 'in accordance with the provisions of the Treaties'—import the cross-border conditions built into the economic freedoms or not? Additionally, messages about equality, inclusion, justice, and the protection of rights are repeated across the TEU, TFEU, and the Charter of Fundamental Rights. But so too are principles that determine and seal the boundaries of exclusively national concern.[28]

We saw in Chapter 2 that the Treaties reflect a polity template built on diverse messages, housing varied objectives, and reflecting the patchwork nature of successive Treaty revisions. The core free movement provisions have never been changed at all: the status of citizenship and multiplying references to values and fundamental rights have been strapped *around* them. Those additions deepen the political and constitutional purpose as well as functions of the Union. But that process also exposes the need to rationalize conflicting approaches to the role of EU law in static situations more convincingly. With particular resonance for the coherence thesis, AG Poiares Maduro cautioned as follows in *Carbonati Apuani*:

> [T]he judgment in *Lancry*... and the ensuing case-law expose the Court to the risk of inconsistency. After all, the '*Lancry* solution' could have been expected to be extended to *all matters* connected with the provisions on free movement. There seemed no reason why the reasoning applied in that case should not be reproduced in relation to other barriers to trade.

(2009) 46:5 CMLRev 1591 at 1612 ('the aim of establishing an internal market in labour is not furthered by protecting the rights of Member State nationals who are economically active *but* in a purely domestic context', emphasis in original); AG Geelhoed in Case C-109/01 *Secretary of State for the Home Department v Akrich* [2003] ECR I-9607, para. 179 of the Opinion ('[i]t is precisely the objective of [EU] law to promote mobility'); and AG Poiares Maduro in *Marks & Spencer*, para. 37 of the Opinion ('[j]udicial review of measures likely to prohibit, impede or render less attractive the exercise of the freedoms of movement rather seeks to ensure that those choices take account of the impact which they may have *on transnational situations*', emphasis added).

[27] *Carbonati Apuani*, para. 23.

[28] Esp. the principle of attributed powers (Articles 4(1) and 5(1)–(2) TEU, and 2–6 TFEU), respect for the national identities of the Member States (Article 4(2) TEU), subsidiarity (Article 5(3) TEU) and proportionality (Article 5(4) TEU). As noted at the beginning of this chapter, it is also made clear that the Charter per se cannot extend the competences of the Union (Articles 6(1) TEU and 51(2) of the Charter).

Instead of detriment to the unity of the Community customs territory, detriment to the internal market or even to the economic unity resulting from Economic and Monetary Union would have been sufficient grounds on which to challenge such barriers. Those circumstances could, in theory, have the same practical effects. However, that was not the solution adopted by the Court. In all those areas, it chose to maintain the traditional principle of the inapplicability of the rules on free movement to purely internal situations. *There therefore remains a seemingly unjustifiable contradiction* between the line taken in relation to charges having equivalent effect and the line generally taken by the Court in other areas.[29]

As the Advocate General emphasized, the requirement of a cross-border connection had been set aside *expressly* for customs duties only at that time; this has since been extended to very limited situations connected to Union citizenship. In Section 3, however, the ways in which movement is tempered in other strands of the case law will be outlined, raising questions about the tenacity with which the Court continues to articulate the formal relevance of the purely internal rule. As noted in Section 1, systemic questions about the application of the rule—given the broader convention in free movement law that potential effects can legitimately constitute a sufficient link with EU law, and thereby a Treaty-caught restriction—need to be considered too.

3. The incredible shrinking concept: does movement matter less?

The ways in which people, companies, products, services, or money can move across borders have been utterly revolutionized since the inception of the internal market. Both technological advances, especially the rise and normalcy of online activity, and low-cost transport have completely transformed the way that we trade and travel. It is now infinitely easier to purchase things, to go to, or to transact business (with traders established) in other States than it was even a decade ago, never mind in the 1950s. These developments have opened up all of the Treaty freedoms, but they have impacted particularly on the transfer of capital payments and the evolution of the service industry. The Court's case law had to respond to and accommodate the ways in which movement changed in the real world, since an overly rigid approach would have left a massive volume of cross-border transactions outside the scope of the Treaty altogether. Moreover, EU law already contained most of the regulatory tools needed. For example, it has long been the case that neither the service provider nor service recipient have to move so long as the service per se crossed a Member State border;[30] but that principle becomes even more relevant in the domain of online services.

[29] AG Poiares Maduro in *Carbonati Apuani*, paras 47–48 of the Opinion (emphasis added).

[30] E.g. Case C-18/93 *Corsica Ferries Italia v Corpo dei Piloti del Porto di Genova* [1994] ECR I-1783, para. 30; Case C-384/93 *Alpine Investments BV v Minister van Financiën* [1995] ECR I-1141, para. 21.

But even though movement became easier, it is still the pivot of the EU market framework. Aside from the two exceptions outlined in Section 2, the Court consistently reasserts the centrality of the purely internal rule to free movement law more generally.[31] At the same time, however, there has been a significant dilution of the nature or type of movement that is actually required to establish that a cross-border connection has been activated. When this fact is joined with the expansive approach taken to what constitutes a restriction in a positive sense, shown in Chapter 7, the scope of free movement rights is strikingly broad. Two factors that contribute to that momentum notwithstanding the retention of the purely internal rule will be outlined further here: first, the Court's intermittent use of fudging formulas when dealing with questions of admissibility; and, second, the changing nature of movement *in law*.

(a) Admissibility of (internal) national disputes under Article 267 TFEU

In some Member State jurisdictions, national law requires that purely internal situations must be treated in the same way as similar situations that have a cross-border dimension. If courts or tribunals refer questions of law to the Court of Justice in such circumstances, the Court invokes the critical role of those institutions in the preliminary rulings procedure to provide a response, even if the referring court will be applying the interpretation of EU law to facts relating exclusively to the national context.[32] This approach properly reflects the law/facts division built into the preliminary rulings procedure, discussed in Chapter 1. In *Angonese*, the Court observed that '[a] reference for a preliminary ruling from a national court may be rejected only if it is quite obvious that the interpretation of Community law sought by that court bears no relation to the actual nature of the case or the subject-matter of the main action'.[33]

However, the Court has also admitted cases where the fact that national law might require internal and cross-border situations to be treated similarly was projected rather than established. In *Anomar*, for example, a case concerning licensing rules for gaming machines and the consequential impact on service provision rights, the Court agreed that the facts of the case were confined to one State but added: 'it is not obvious that the interpretation of [EU] law requested is

[31] E.g. Case C-250/08 *Commission v Belgium*, judgment of 1 December 2011, para. 41: 'European Union law cannot be applied to such a purely internal situation where there has been no question of the exercise of freedom of movement within the European Union'.

[32] E.g. Case C-371/11 *Punch Graphix Prepress Belgium NV v Belgische Staat*, judgment of 18 October 2012, para. 27: 'where domestic legislation adopts for purely internal situations the same solutions as those adopted by European Union law, it is for the national court alone, in the context of the division of judicial functions between national courts and the Court of Justice under Article 267 TFEU, to assess the precise scope of that reference to European Union law, the jurisdiction of the Court of Justice being confined to the examination of provisions of that law'. This reasoning reflects a line of case law built on Joined Cases C-297/88 and C-197/89 *Dzodzi v Belgian State* [1990] ECR I-3763, paras 41–42.

[33] Case C-281/98 *Angonese v Cassa di Risparmio di Bolzano SpA* [2000] ECR I-4139, para. 18.

not necessary for the referring court. Such a reply might be useful to it *if its national law were to require* that a Portuguese national must be allowed to enjoy the same rights as those which a national of another Member State would derive from [EU] law in the same situation'.[34] Such a reply 'might be useful' but does that mean that the Court should be giving it? From the perspective of constitutional responsibility, does it empower or confuse national courts when they receive a definitive interpretation of the substantive point of EU law they have raised, but no reflection on whether or not they should actually apply it in the case before them? A coherence-based question also arises: if the Court takes this approach in some cases, then why not do so in *all* cases involving apparently internal situations?

Relatedly, the Court frequently recasts the questions sent to it by referring courts. This is normally done to extract the relevant questions of EU law more succinctly from lengthy, overlapping, or confusingly drafted references. Sometimes, however, the Court introduces completely new questions through this process and changes the whole focus of the case. For example, in *McCarthy*, the national court referred questions about whether or not a dual national EU citizen who had always resided in the State of her birth, without any instances of cross-border movement, came within the scope of Directive 2004/38.[35] The Court gave a negative answer; but it then considered whether the applicant could claim rights under Article 21 TFEU—a question that had not been asked by the national court. The Court does not point to any written or oral observations on this question; and AG Kokott confined her Opinion to the provisions of the Directive highlighted by the referring court. The Court also made legally decisive assumptions about Mrs McCarthy's ability to move to another Member State or remain in her home State without her husband that did not take into account potentially significant facets of her personal situation, a point picked up in Section 4.

The Court considers that it should 'provide the national court with all those elements for the interpretation of [EU] law which may be of assistance in adjudicating on the case pending before it, *whether or not* that court has specifically referred to them in its questions'.[36] But that is not a risk-free approach. In *Sbarigia*, a case about national rules that regulated the opening times of pharmacies, AG Jääskinen first went through the issues raised by the national court, which related to services.[37] He then observed that some of the parties had submitted written observations on freedom of establishment and the free movement of goods, but he argued that 'the Court should not rule on those two provisions, on which the

[34] Case C-6/01 *Associação Nacional de Operadores de Máquinas Recreativas (Anomar) and others v Estado português* [2003] ECR I-8621, para. 41 (emphasis added). See similarly, Case C-448/98 *Criminal proceedings against Guimont* [2000] ECR I-10663, para. 23 (goods) and Joined Cases C-515/99, C-519/99 to C-524/99, and C-526/99 to C-540/99 *Reisch and Others* [2002] ECR I-2157, para. 26 (capital).

[35] Case C-434/09 *McCarthy v Secretary of State for the Home Department* [2011] ECR I-3375, para. 21.

[36] Case C-336/07 *Kabel Deutschland Vertrieb und Service GmbH & Co. KG v Niedersächsische Landesmedienanstalt für privaten Rundfunk* [2008] ECR I-10889, para. 47 (emphasis added).

[37] Case C-393/08 *Sbarigia v Azienda USL RM/A and others* [2010] ECR I-6337.

referring court did not ask any questions'.[38] He rationalized his conclusion as follows, in a passage worth extracting in full:

> First, it is for the referring court to identify the provisions of European Union law of which an interpretation seems to it necessary in order to resolve the case in the main proceedings. In its order for reference, it did so in a way that seems to me to be exhaustive, referring explicitly to the specific principles that underlie a fairly significant number of provisions of European Union law. In such a case, *it is not for the Court to seek out all the other provisions* of European Union law the interpretation of which might prove useful to the referring court. The power which the Court has taken upon itself to reformulate referred questions is intended, in my view, to allow the Court to assist the referring court in finding the *precise expression* of a problem of interpretation of European Union law that is relevant for the purposes of the proceedings. On this view, it is for the Court *to clarify, and not to expand*, the problem raised by the reference for a preliminary ruling. Secondly, this restrictive interpretation is also supported by the Statute of the Court of Justice of the European Union. The order for reference as formulated by the national court is notified, under the Statute of the Court, to the Member States and institutions of the European Union in particular. It is on the basis of this document that the latter determine whether or not it would be useful to submit written observations and to participate in the proceedings before the Court. For the Court as well, this is *a document of reference*. It is clear that a reformulation would *require* the Court to have available *all the necessary and relevant material*, including that relating to the facts and the national legal framework.[39]

Both the side-stepping of purely internal barriers and the significant rephrasing or even genesis of questions recall several of the concerns identified in Chapters 1 and 2: about consistency in the use of tests or formulas; the blending of constitutional and first instance functions; the consequential implications for evaluating relevant evidence; and the Court's general approach to reasoning when more than one line of authority might be relevant. As devices, they are applied sometimes to widen and sometimes to narrow the scope of the Court's own jurisdiction in cases before it. What we do not know, however, is what lies *behind* decisions to apply them. This presents an image, fairly or otherwise, of arbitrary application: because if the Court is willing to take these steps in some cases, is it not then obliged to take the same steps in all of them?

(b) The changing significance of movement in law

The changing nature of movement in the real world was underlined above, but the definitional breadth of free movement law exceeds the baseline of real-world situational reflection. For example, in *Alpine Investments*, the Court confirmed that '[t]he freedom to provide services would become illusory if national rules were at liberty to restrict offers of services. The prior existence of an identifiable recipient

[38] AG Jääskinen in *Sbarigia*, paras 77–78 of the Opinion.

[39] AG Jääskinen in *Sbarigia*, paras 79–80 of the Opinion (emphasis added). In its judgment, however, the Court went through all of the potentially relevant provisions 'for the sake of completeness' (para. 35).

cannot therefore be a condition for application of the [relevant] provisions'.[40] More generally, it is essential to emphasize that the Court recognizes *all kinds of movement* for the purposes of activating a cross-border connection, including: transit movement;[41] past movement;[42] potential or future movement;[43] movement by others;[44] movement undertaken deliberately to open up Treaty rights;[45] contract movement;[46] and passport movement.[47] These strands of case law have been particularly significant for EU citizens and traders claiming Treaty rights against their own Member States. When this definitional permissiveness is combined with the types of impediment to movement that can be sufficient to constitute a restriction—addressed in later chapters on positive scope, but including situations that e.g. cause disadvantage, or deter or discourage someone from moving—the potency of the Treaty framework becomes apparent. Additionally, as seen in Chapter 3, while personal and material connections to EU law are both required, there does not need to be a *direct* connection between the two. In *Eind*, for example, a Dutch national went to the UK to work and was joined there directly by his Surinamese daughter.

[40] *Alpine Investments*, para. 19. The Court confirmed the same point for potential service *providers* in Case C-355/00 *Freskot AE v Elliniko Dimosio* [2003] ECR I-5263, para. 63.

[41] E.g. Case 266/81 *Società Italiana per l'Oleodotto Transalpino (SIOT) v Ministero delle finanze, Ministero della marina mercantile, Circoscrizione doganale di Trieste and Ente autonomo del porto di Trieste* [1983] ECR 731, para. 16 ('[free movement of goods] could not itself be complete if it were possible for the Member States to impede or interfere in any way with the movement of goods in transit. It is therefore necessary, as a consequence of the Customs Union and in the mutual interest of the Member States, to acknowledge the existence of a general principle of freedom of transit of goods within the [Union]').

[42] E.g. Case C-370/90 *R v Immigration Appeal Tribunal and Singh, ex parte Secretary of State for the Home Department* [1992] ECR I-4265, para. 19 ('[a] national of a Member State might be deterred from leaving his country of origin in order to pursue an activity as an employed or self-employed person . . . in the territory of another Member State if, on returning to the Member State of which he is a national in order to pursue an activity there as an employed or self-employed person, the conditions of his entry and residence were not at least equivalent to those which he would enjoy under the Treaty or secondary law in the territory of another Member State').

[43] E.g. Case 8/74 *Procureur du Roi v Dassonville* [1974] ECR 837, para. 5 ('[a]ll trading rules enacted by Member States which are capable of hindering, directly or indirectly, actually or potentially, intra-Community trade are to be considered as measures having an effect equivalent to quantitative restrictions'); *Chen*, para. 19 ('[t]he situation of a national of a Member State who was born in the host Member State and has not made use of the right to freedom of movement cannot, for that reason alone, be assimilated to a purely internal situation'); Case C-348/96 *Criminal proceedings against Calfa* [1999] ECR I-11, para. 18 ('expulsion for life from the territory . . . clearly constitutes an obstacle to the freedom to provide services . . . since it is the very negation of that freedom').

[44] E.g. Case C-255/99 *Humer* [2002] ECR I-1205 (movement to another State by dependent child in the context of social security benefits).

[45] E.g. Case C-109/01 *Secretary of State for the Home Department v Akrich* [2003] ECR I-9607, discussed in Chapter 3.

[46] E.g. Case C-214/94 *Boukhalfa v Bundesrepublik Deutschland* [1996] ECR I-2253, para. 22 (EU law 'applies to a national of a Member State who is permanently resident in a non-member country, who is employed by another Member State in its embassy in that non-member country and whose contract of employment was entered into and is permanently performed there, as regards all aspects of the employment relationship which are governed by the legislation of the employing Member State').

[47] E.g. Case C-138/02 *Collins v Secretary of State for Work and Pensions* [2004] ECR I-2703, in the context of dual nationality. The Court's generous approach is also apparent in cases involving acquired naturalization (e.g. Joined Cases C-7/10 and C-9/10 *Staatssecretaris van Justitie v Kahveci and Inan*, judgment of 29 March 2012, on the Association Agreement with Turkey); but cf. the hardening approach in *McCarthy* for dual EU citizens with two EU passports, discussed in Section 4.

The following year, he returned to the Netherlands with his daughter where, because of ill health, he was no longer in or able to seek employment. Supporting a right of residence for Mr Eind's daughter in the Netherlands, the Court reasoned as follows:

> A national of a Member State *could be deterred* from leaving that Member State in order to pursue gainful employment in the territory of another Member State if he does not have the certainty of being able to return to his Member State of origin, *irrespective of whether he is going to engage in economic activity in the latter State*. That deterrent effect would also derive *simply from the prospect*, for that same national, of not being able, on returning to his Member State of origin, to continue living together with close relatives, *a way of life which may have come into being in the host Member State* as a result of marriage or family reunification. Barriers to family reunification are therefore liable to undermine the right to free movement which the nationals of the Member States have under [EU] law, as the right of [an EU] worker to return to the Member State of which he is a national cannot be considered to be a purely internal matter.[48]

In effect, Mr Eind gained family reunification rights when he came back to his home State that he never had there before leaving it—a significant development beyond the situation in *Singh*,[49] where a couple had resided together in the UK before moving to Germany together (where Mrs Singh, a British national, exercised economic activity); Mr Singh, an Indian national, successfully claimed a derived right of residence on the couple's return to the UK (where Mrs Singh continued to exercise economic activity).

Whether the Court has stretched the meaning of movement too far will be considered in Section 4. It is important to reiterate that these developments are connected more generally to the breadth of the Court's understanding of restrictions on free movement law, which plainly covers potential as well as actual impediments.[50] However, the sheer force of that case law momentum, considered in its wider context in Chapters 5–7, raises three distinct questions in the more specific context of cross-border connections and purely internal situations. First, if the requirement of movement is potentially so *easily* satisfied, is its formal retention as a precondition for the exercise of Treaty rights arbitrary in application or, at least, redundant in effect? Second, because the requirement of movement *is* formally preserved, can the exclusion of a shrinking pool of static situations from EU protection, and resulting reverse discrimination, still be justified? Third, who, institutionally speaking, is best placed to resolve these questions?

On the first question, it was demonstrated above that the Treaty provisions establishing all EU free movement rights—with the exception of citizenship rights—

[48] Case C-291/05 *Minister voor Vreemdelingenzaken en Integratie v Eind* [2007] ECR I-10719, paras 35–37 (emphasis added).

[49] Case C-370/90 *R v Immigration Appeal Tribunal and Singh, ex p Secretary of State for the Home Department* [1992] ECR I-4265.

[50] See e.g. for Article 34 TFEU, Joined Cases C-321-24/94 *Criminal Proceedings against Pistre, Barthes, Milhau and Oberti* [1997] ECR I-2343, paras 43–45 (cf. the stricter approach of AG Jacobs, paras 32–42 of the Opinion, who emphasized (at para. 41) the value of ensuring coherence in the case law).

require a cross-border connection and that the exercise of some form of movement remains the way in which most cross-border connections are formed. At the same time, the Court has incrementally depleted the substance of movement while retaining it as a formal requirement—staying within the boundaries of the Treaty but approaching the edges of lawfulness nonetheless. In *Ruiz Zambrano*, AG Sharpston depicted the consequences of both formally *requiring* movement but also *depleting* its substance in vivid terms:

If one insists on the premiss that physical movement to a Member State other than the Member State of nationality is required before residence rights as a citizen of the Union can be invoked, the result risks being both strange and illogical. Suppose a friendly neighbour had taken Diego and Jessica on a visit or two to Parc Astérix in Paris, or to the seaside in Brittany. They would then have received services in another Member State. Were they to seek to claim rights arising from their 'movement' it could not be suggested that their situation was 'purely internal' to Belgium. Would one visit have sufficed? Two? Several? Would a day trip have been enough; or would they have had to stay over for a night or two in France?[51]

There is a coherent dynamic evident at one level in the case law, in that the Court normally finds a way to bring the relevant situation within the scope of the Treaty. But sometimes, of course, it does not. In *Government of the French Community and Walloon Government*, for example, the Court affirmed the significance of an *inter*-State connection for the free movement of workers. But in doing so, it ignored AG Sharpston's arguments about frontiers within a State—drawing from *Lancry*—and whether that approach had to be applied to workers by analogy. The Court did not confront these two opposing currents of live case law, or rationalize why it picked one over the other in the circumstances of the case—patterns we have seen too many times already.

Turning to the second, related, question, should the Court retreat from its erosion of the substance of movement and align the case law more strongly with the cross-border expectations programmed into the Treaty; or should it detach the case law from the clear wording of the Treaty more radically, drawing support from wider objectives such as the border-free market and the imperative of protecting fundamental rights? Taking the second alternative first, the constitutional messages embedded in the Treaty are not internally consistent. Even so, it is difficult to see how a more deliberate overturning of the purely internal rule would sit with the Lisbon-heightened principle of attributed powers. Additionally, is an enhanced register for EU law within national legal orders what the EU Member States and citizens actually want? The personal/trade dichotomy discussed in Chapter 2 is helpful on one level to defend more intensive protection of the rights of EU citizens—furthermore, as shown in Section 2, the Treaty's citizenship provisions do not specify a cross-border dimension.[52] But the fusion problem discussed in

[51] AG Sharpston in *Ruiz Zambrano*, para. 86 of the Opinion.

[52] See esp. Spaventa, n6; see also, A Tryfonidou, 'Reverse discrimination in purely internal situations: An incongruity in a Citizens' Europe' (2008) 35:1 LIEI 43 and 'In search of the aim of the EC free movement of persons provisions: Has the Court of Justice missed the point?' (2009) 46:5

Chapter 3 resurfaces here when EU citizens are exercising economic activity: since the Treaty provisions that govern economic free movement rights *do require* a cross-border connection, should EU legal protection be extended in internal situations to citizens who are *not* economically active only? Such a distinction would only exacerbate already awkward disparities: and, ironically, in pursuit of a solution to secure equality for all Union citizens. On what may have seemed like an unlikely first alternative i.e. *replenishing* the substance of movement in law, there are recent signs that the Court is, to some extent at least, in just such a phase of retreat. The implications of this *contracting* case law dynamic will be addressed in Section 4; it will also be contrasted with the *inflating* dynamics concurrently shaping other free movement contexts in Chapter 7.

Finally, third, what about the institutional responsibility placed not only on the Court but also on EU and national political processes? On the one hand, the Member States have remained silent on the controversies of the purely internal issue through sequential Treaty revision processes. At the level of secondary legislation, a key question has been whether family reunification rights should be extended to static Member State nationals through the channels of EU law. On the grounds that 'Union citizenship is indivisible', the Commission initially proposed but later withdrew such an extension in its original draft of Directive 2003/86, which regulates family reunification rights for lawfully resident third country nationals.[53] In its amended proposal for the Directive, the Commission stated that '[t]he alignment of the rights of all Union citizens to family reunification will be reviewed later' i.e. once work on Directive 2004/38 was completed, since that measure is distinctly about movement.[54] But Directive 2004/38 has long since been adopted. And still we wait.

4. Standing at the constitutional crossroads: the specific case of citizenship and purely internal situations

For the economic freedoms, the Treaty stipulates that rights are conferred in cross-border situations. For that reason, though noting the fragmenting effects of the *Lancry* anomaly, the questions that relate to movement as a linking factor in the context of economic activity will be returned to in later chapters addressing the positive scope of Treaty restrictions and the question of potential restrictions in particular. The discussion in the remainder of this chapter focuses on the specific interplay between cross-border connections and EU citizenship rights, given the ambiguity of the wording of Articles 20 and 21 TFEU in this respect.

CMLRev 1591; and the Opinions of AG Sharpston in *Government of the French Community and Walloon Government* and *Ruiz Zambrano*.

53 See Articles 3(1)(c) and 4 of the draft directive published as part of the original proposal (COM (1999) 638 final); on the indivisibility of Union citizenship, see p14.

54 COM(2002) 225 final, para. 2.4.

As a polity, the EU is founded on the principle of conferred powers but it is also committed, both textually and through sustained jurisprudence, to protecting the rights of its citizens. Precisely because of the ambiguity noted above, describing a role for EU law in internal *citizenship* situations—i.e. situations that can be linked to Articles 20 and 21—as an aberration of competence is a misplaced characterization. On the other hand, prioritizing an extensive role for the EU in internal situations could, as O'Leary has cautioned, 'give rise to the highly questionable proposition that Member State nationals resident in their own Member State do so as a matter of EU law'.[55]

Mindful of that complex constitutional backdrop, the discussion here has two main objectives. First, in subsection (a), the developing relationship between citizenship rights, movement, and the protection of fundamental rights will be examined in more detail, with specific emphasis on recent case law suggesting that a constitutional retreat is underway. That analysis relates to tensions noted in Section 1: the mixed constitutional objectives of the Charter; and the inverse relationship between the depletion of movement in substance and the strength of the legal protection it can nevertheless evoke. Questions about the different levels or types of coherence affected will also be considered. For example, is the Court's *greatest* responsibility owed to the text of the Treaties or to the constitutional standards established by its own previous case law? More concretely, in responding to its obligations towards constitutional subjects, should the Court in e.g. a family reunification dispute privilege the claims of the citizen or the politically mandated immigration choices being imposed by the Member State? In subsection (b), a more constitutionally entrenched concept of movement will be developed, setting any discrimination encountered because movement is being or has been exercised as a marker of differential treatment that infringes the general principle of equality to which the EU is constitutionally committed. If movement really is at the heart of the internal market, questions about case law that offsets it as a *meaningful* linking factor have to be faced more seriously. Moving beyond citizenship, that part of the discussion also creates a bridge to the *positive scope* of the Treaty, considered more overtly from Chapter 5 onwards.

(a) A changing matrix? Citizenship, movement, and the protection of fundamental rights

In Chapter 2, the assertion that protection of fundamental rights through the prism of EU citizenship properly shifts the focus of the case law away from *movement* and onto the *individual* was questioned.[56] In the case law on internal situations, this shift has happened explicitly only once: in *Ruiz Zambrano*.[57] The continuing

[55] O'Leary, n6, 64.

[56] AG Ruiz-Jarabo Colomer in Case C-228/07 *Petersen v Arbeitsmarktservice Niederösterreich* [2008] ECR I-6989, esp. paras 27–34 of the Opinion (further discussed in Chapter 3).

[57] On the decoupling of citizenship from the movement-driven logic of the internal market, see D Kochenov and R Plender, 'EU Citizenship: From an incipient form to an incipient substance? The discovery of the Treaty text' (2012) 37:3 ELRev 369.

significance of migration more generally was underlined soon afterwards by the decisions in *McCarthy*, *Dereci*, and *Iida*.[58] The reasoning of the Court in *McCarthy* and *Dereci* will be outlined in more detail below; but to frame the discussion and further illustrate the tensions characterizing the case law on internal situations at present, the contrast between the Opinion and the judgment in *Iida* provides a useful starting point. It should be emphasized that this case was not about a purely internal situation: Union citizens had clearly moved to and were residing in another State. The question at the heart of the national dispute was whether EU law could be used to establish a right of residence in Germany for the Japanese father of an infant German national now residing in Austria with her German mother; the couple had separated but not divorced. It was confirmed that 'Mr Iida regularly visits his daughter in Vienna for one weekend a month, and she spends most of her holidays with her father in Ulm'.[59]

In its judgment, the Court first ruled out the application of Directive 2004/38, since the applicant 'neither accompanied nor joined in the host Member State the member of his family who is a Union citizen who exercised her right of freedom of movement'.[60] The potential relevance of Articles 20 and 21 TFEU was then considered. The Court pointed out that on the basis of the information provided, it seemed that the applicant could reside in Germany, in accordance with national law, until such time as he could, in principle, be granted long-term residence status under Directive 2003/109—something he had applied for but then not pursued. It also observed that, in the meantime, 'the absence of a right of residence under European Union law [had not] discouraged his daughter or his spouse from exercising their right of freedom of movement by moving to Austria'—thus raising no question of either forced departure from the Union or an impediment to the Union citizen's exercise of free movement rights, the two standard tests now applied in case law on the scope of citizenship rights.[61] Given that his situation was not, therefore, 'governed by EU law' (paragraph 80), the Court ruled out any obligation to consider the right to respect for family life or the rights of the child in Articles 7 and 24 of the Charter respectively—explicitly pointing out the post-Lisbon constitutional limits by which it is now bound:

> [I]n accordance with Article 51(1) of the Charter, its provisions are addressed to the Member States only when they are implementing European Union law. Under Article 51 (2) . . . it does not extend the field of application of European Union law beyond the powers of the Union, and it does not establish any new power or task for the Union, or modify powers and tasks as defined in the Treaties. Accordingly, the Court is called on to interpret, *in the light of the Charter*, the law of the European Union *within the limits of the powers conferred on it*.[62]

[58] Case C-40/11 *Iida v Stadt Ulm*, judgment of 8 November 2012.

[59] *Iida*, para. 26.

[60] *Iida*, para. 65.

[61] *Iida*, para. 74; the evolution of the tests over the decisions in *Ruiz Zambrano*, *McCarthy*, and *Dereci* is addressed below. Directive 2003/109/EC concerning the status of third-country nationals who are long-term residents, 2003 OJ L16/44.

[62] *Iida*, para. 78 (emphasis added); see generally, paras 78–81.

It was also emphasized that since the purely hypothetical prospect of exercising free movement rights does not establish a sufficient connection with EU law, a threshold test discussed in Chapter 5, '[t]he same applies to purely hypothetical prospects of that right being obstructed'.[63] The overall tone of the judgment is practical and the reasoning of the Court is made clear. But the approach taken by AG Trstenjak was distinctly more *familiar*. In an Opinion reminiscent of the decision in *Carpenter*, she first confirmed that a link—here, a mobility connection—to EU law was established, so that the real question underpinning the case from her perspective—facilitating respect for family life—then took centre stage. She argued as follows:

> [A] parent who has a right of custody and is a third-country national can, *in order to maintain a personal relationship and direct parental contact on a regular basis*, have a right of residence in the Member State of origin of his child who is a Union citizen under Articles 20 TFEU and 21 TFEU, *if the child has moved from there to another Member State*, exercising his right of free movement. For such a right of residence to exist, the denial thereof must have a restrictive effect on the child's right to freedom of movement and must be regarded as amounting to a disproportionate interference with fundamental rights.[64]

The way in which the Advocate General championed the right to family life for Mr Iida's daughter might seem understandable and even laudable from the perspective of protecting fundamental rights per se. But her approach also provides a strong example of how the *fact* of movement can be constitutionalized above and beyond the actual *substance* of the family life situation at issue: was Mr Iida's residence in Germany through one particular legal route really essential to his maintaining a family relationship with his daughter in the terms outlined above, given that his residence there seemed to be secure through other legal means and that she was now, in any event, residing in Austria? Moreover, when AG Trstenjak's openness is juxtaposed with the Court's comparably harsh dismissal of the suggestion that the families in *McCarthy* and *Dereci* might wish to live together in the *same* State—never mind simply to facilitate occasional visits to or from another State as in *Iida*—it becomes difficult to defend the *extent* of the privilege that might have been extended to Ms Iida *purely* because she was lucky enough to have moved: or more accurately, to benefit passively from her mother's wish *and ability* to move—and recalling, once again, the critical point that neither Article 20 nor Article 21 TFEU require the imposition or satisfaction of cross-border conditions at all. It is precisely the near randomness of these kinds of outcomes that led AG Sharpston to declare in *Ruiz Zambrano* that '[l]ottery rather than logic would seem to be governing the exercise of EU citizenship rights'.[65] A conceptual switch that puts equal treatment at the centre of the analysis, treating movement as a second-level criterion or exemplar of differential treatment, would prioritize *the citizen* over *the citizen's choices* or *capacities*. The elements that can be used to build such a framework will be outlined in subsection (b).

[63] *Iida*, para. 77. [64] AG Trstenjak in *Iida*, para. 88 of the Opinion (emphasis added).
[65] AG Sharpston in *Ruiz Zambrano*, para. 88 of the Opinion.

Another critically important question stems from comparing the judgment and the Opinion in *Iida*. In its consideration of the relevance of Articles 20 and 21 TFEU and also the Charter, the Court focused solely on the fact that the applicant's daughter had already moved to another Member State without impediment. But AG Trstenjak considered impediments in a prospective sense too: 'if it were to transpire in a particular case that denying a right of residence would rule out the possibility of maintaining regular personal relations, this could constitute interference with a fundamental right, the justification for which would have to be assessed from the standpoint of proportionality. In that context, it would be necessary to consider, among other things, whether the child's father who is a third-country national also actually exercises his right of custody and endeavours to fulfil his parental duties'.[66] She left the determination of these questions to the referring court, but her raising of the issue reflects an acutely grey area between *potential* and *hypothetical* effects. This issue will be considered in a more global free movement sense in Chapter 5, but it is clear that the Court and the Advocate General were sitting on opposite sides of the dividing line in *Iida*. It is also fair to note at this stage that the Court invokes prospective restrictions on movement rights, as AG Trstenjak did in *Iida*, far more frequently than it applies the exclusionary threshold of hypothetical effects, raising broader questions about how the decision in *Iida* fits into case law on the right to family life more generally.

It was noted at the beginning of this subsection that the circumstances in *Iida* did involve a clear cross-border connection i.e. a Union citizen's movement from Germany to Austria. The decisions in *Ruiz Zambrano*, *McCarthy*, and *Dereci* are also about recognition of the right to respect for family life through EU law, but in purely internal situations. As outlined in Section 2, the situation in *Ruiz Zambrano* concerned a refusal by Belgian authorities to grant residence and work permits to the Colombian national parents of children born in Belgium who held only Belgian nationality. The forced departure of the family from the territory of the Union that would result in consequence was found to deprive the children of the genuine enjoyment of the substance of their rights as Union citizens and thus to infringe Article 20 TFEU. The Court did not discuss the right to family life or the Charter in its judgment at all.

In *McCarthy*, a British national who had always resided in the UK but who also held an Irish passport was seeking recognition of a residence right in the UK under Directive 2004/38, on the basis of which her Jamaican husband could then claim derivative residence rights there as her spouse. Because she could always continue to reside in the UK herself, the Court (Third Chamber) did not consider that the genuine enjoyment of the substance of her citizenship rights was affected; but neither did it find any impediments to her right to move and reside elsewhere in the Union. Addressing the scope of Article 21 rather than 20 TFEU, the Court confirmed that Article 21 'is not applicable to a Union citizen who has never exercised his right of free movement, who has always resided in a Member State of

[66] AG Trstenjak in *Iida*, para. 85 of the Opinion.

which he is a national and who is also a national of another Member State, *provided that* the situation of that citizen does not include the application of measures by a Member State that would have the effect of depriving him of the genuine enjoyment of the substance of the rights conferred by virtue of his status as a Union citizen *or* of impeding the exercise of his right of free movement and residence within the territory of the Member States'.[67] As in *Iida*, the Court did not explore any potential impediments to those rights and, as in *Ruiz Zambrano*, there was no discussion of the right to respect for family life . However, exhibiting the concerns expressed in Chapter 1 about full and complete consideration of all relevant evidence, the Court seemed to be unaware of the fact that the applicant was the full-time carer of her disabled child, a factor that could obviously hamper her ability to leave her home State.[68] Of course, a considerable degree of responsibility for the failure to have this factor properly discussed must rest with the lawyers involved in the case. But the Court bears a degree of responsibility here too. As noted in Section 3(a), it alone reframed the scope of the *McCarthy* case by addressing the applicant's status under Article 21 TFEU even though the national court referred questions about Directive 2004/38 only. More fundamentally, it appeared to make presumptions about the family circumstances in *Ruiz Zambrano* in that family's favour, but to the opposite effect in *McCarthy*—it should have done so in neither case, leaving facts-based questions to the national court and neither substituting nor suggesting its own perception of the facts in such definitive tones.

In *Dereci*, we do see a clearer, and welcome, delegation to the national court in this respect. An array of different family situations was presented to the Court; the common theme was that at least one Austrian citizen who had never resided in another Member State was involved in all of the disputes, and all of the cases involved the compatibility with the right to respect for family life under EU law of refusals by the relevant authorities to grant residence permits in Austria to third country national family members.[69] Mr Dereci, for example, is a Turkish national who had entered Austria illegally in 2001; but in 2003, he married an Austrian national with whom he has three children (also Austrian nationals). In its judgment, the Court (Grand Chamber) first confirmed that deprivation of the genuine enjoyment of the substance of citizenship rights is triggered when a Union citizen 'has, in fact, to leave not only the territory of the Member State of which he is a national but also the territory of the Union as a whole'.[70] The Court continued as follows:

> [T]he the mere fact that it might appear desirable to a national of a Member State, for economic reasons or in order to keep his family together in the territory of the Union, for the members of his family who do not have the nationality of a Member State to be able to reside with him in the territory of the Union, is not sufficient in itself to support the view that the Union citizen will be forced to leave Union territory if such a right is not granted.[71]

67 *McCarthy*, para. 56 (emphasis added).

68 See further, Nic Shuibhne, n15, 370–1.

69 For an overview of all of the situations relevant to the judgment, see the View of AG Mengozzi at paras 5–10.

70 *Dereci*, para. 66.

71 *Dereci*, para. 68.

As noted earlier, the Court focused on material and not emotional dependency in this case: if the Union citizen can stay within the territory of the Union without their third country national family member(s), then the *Ruiz Zambrano* threshold of *forced* departure is not met. The financial self-sufficiency of the families without the input of the third country national applicants was emphasized in that context. In contrast to the judgment in *McCarthy*, the Court did go on in *Dereci* to consider whether the right to respect for family life affected those conclusions. But it focused on Article 51 of the Charter, and advised the national court that it should first establish whether any of the disputes fell within the scope of Union law before evaluating whether respect for family life had in fact been undermined. The Court then noted, arguably giving a steer that the facts of the different family situations were outside the scope of Union law, that '[a]ll the Member States are, after all, parties to the ECHR'.[72] Interpreting this advice in the kindest light—since no direct legal responsibility can be invoked in this context[73]—it could be said that the Court was simply recognizing the fact of intertwined legal orders and encouraging a pluralist understanding of the dynamics driving contemporary constitutional obligations.

A theme raised above in respect of *Iida* links that decision with the outcome in both *McCarthy* and *Dereci*: it would seem that the Court is struggling to sustain its long-standing approach to the protection of fundamental rights while also managing the express limits effected by the final provisions of the Charter. Recent choices made by the Court suggest that a more restrictive case law phase has materialized. The judgments in *McCarthy* and *Dereci* appear to follow the letter of Article 51 of the Charter. But the Court has, in the process, reduced its own established standards on the relevance of prospective impediments to movement rights and on the substantive—sometimes distinctive—levels of fundamental rights protection that had been developed for the EU legal order. For example, the right to respect for family life was first recognized as a general principle of EU law in *Carpenter*, drawing on Article 8 ECHR. In *Ruiz Zambrano*, AG Sharpston summarized the key features of relevant European Court of Human Rights (ECtHR) case law, noting that 'removal of a person from his family members is permissible only when it is shown to be "necessary in a democratic society, that is to say justified by a pressing social need and, in particular, proportionate to the aim pursued"'.[74] Critically, however, the ECHR protects a family's right to live

[72] *Dereci*, para. 73.

[73] In *Kamberaj*, the Court confirmed that 'the reference made by Article 6(3) TEU to the ECHR does not require the national court, in case of conflict between a provision of national law and the ECHR, to apply the provisions of that convention directly, disapplying the provision of national law incompatible with the convention' (Case C-571/10 *Kamberaj v Istituto per l'Edilizia sociale della Provincia autonoma di Bolzano (IPES) and others*, judgment of 24 April 2012, para. 63). In his view on *Dereci*, AG Mengozzi reflected similarly on the 'complementary' dynamics of the national, Union, and ECHR legal orders, while noting that respect for family life in purely internal situations must be managed through the first and third of those orders only (see para. 40 of the View).

[74] AG Sharpston in *Ruiz Zambrano*, para. 55 of the Opinion, citing relevant ECtHR case law; see generally, paras 54–60 of the Opinion.

somewhere—not somewhere *in particular*.[75] That became the benchmark applied implicitly in *McCarthy* and overtly in *Dereci* for families in purely internal situations. But is it the right benchmark for Union as distinct from ECHR law? Put plainly: why has the Court decided that preventing families from living together does *not* deprive Union citizens of the genuine enjoyment of the substance of their citizenship rights, whether a cross-border connection can be established or not?

In *Carpenter*, the Court held that if the UK did not grant a residence permit to Mrs Carpenter, the couple's separation 'would be detrimental to their family life and, therefore, to the *conditions under which* Mr Carpenter exercises a fundamental freedom. That freedom *could not be fully effective* if Mr Carpenter were to be deterred from exercising it by obstacles raised in his country of origin to the entry and residence of his spouse'.[76] Mr Carpenter had submitted that the impact on his freedom to provide services would be felt through the fact that Mrs Carpenter cared for his children from a previous marriage when he travelled occasionally to other States. But the extent to which this function influenced the decision of the Court is not clear, as the material paragraph, extracted above, does not hinge on or even refer to any particular contribution on Mrs Carpenter's part. Even more significantly for present purposes, the Court acknowledged that '[e]ven though no right of an alien to enter or to reside *in a particular country* is as such guaranteed by the Convention, the removal of a person from *a country where close members of his family are living* may amount to an infringement of the right to respect for family life as guaranteed by Article 8(1) of the Convention'.[77]

In subsequent case law—notably *MRAX*,[78] *Baumbast*,[79] and *Metock*[80]—the Court continued to insist that in situations governed by EU law, due regard had to be given by national authorities to proper respect for the right to family life. In *Metock*, the Court emphasized that 'if Union citizens were not allowed to lead a normal family life in the host Member State, the exercise of the freedoms they are guaranteed by the Treaty would be seriously obstructed'.[81] However, the disputes in these cases were not about family members residing in *host* States: they all concerned the Union citizen's *home* State. In effect, the Court substantiated the right to family life as protecting a *home* State right of residence—as the State of residence by *choice*—for EU market actors (widely construed). In *Ruiz Zambrano*, it crossed a new line by protecting the same right for static Union citizens in certain circumstances.

And yet, in *Ruiz Zambrano* and *McCarthy*, there is no discussion of fundamental rights at all. This was problematic in *Ruiz Zambrano* because, there, drawing again

[75] See further, the case law cited by Wiesbrock, n15, at note 52.

[76] *Carpenter*, para. 39 (emphasis added).

[77] *Carpenter*, para. 42 (emphasis added).

[78] Case C-459/99 *Mouvement contre le racisme, l'antisémitisme et la xénophobie ASBL (MRAX) v Belgian State* [2002] ECR I-6591.

[79] Case C-413/99 *Baumbast and R v Secretary of State for the Home Department* [2002] ECR I-7091.

[80] Case C-127/08 *Metock and others v Minister for Justice, Equality and Law Reform* [2008] ECR I-6241.

[81] *Metock*, para. 62; in para. 56, the Court cites six authorities for the same point, beginning with *Carpenter*—a home State case. The origins of the reasoning can be also be seen in *Singh*.

from the formula used by the Advocate General in *Petersen*, the Court overtly shifted the focus of the case law away from *any* requirement of movement outside the home State and onto the material situation of the family involved. If that decision was driven by the right to respect for family life, could the Court reconcile it with the limits in Article 51 of the Charter? However slight the reasoning in the judgment, the substantive decision in *Ruiz Zambrano* can nevertheless be defended in the sense that, first, it is a Treaty-compliant step beyond movement, since, looking at the wording of Article 20 TFEU, the Court did not actually *need* to consider prospective impediments to movement anyway; and, second, the outcome did reflect the pre-existing case law standard of protecting the Union citizen's right to reside with his or her family members in the home State.

The family life silence was more problematic in *McCarthy* because, there, the Court overtly raised the legal relevance of possible impediments to the applicant's right to move i.e. it did not just consider the deprivation/genuine enjoyment test in isolation, as it had in *Ruiz Zambrano*. More problematically still, the Court assumed that the McCarthy family could reside elsewhere in the Union, but the reasons for that view were never explained in the judgment. And then, should it not have offered the same advice to the Ruiz Zambrano family? Was there really no feasible possibility that the family could live in any of the other Member States, remembering that, under Directive 2004/38, they could stay in any of them for up to three months without the need to meet any conditions other than valid passports or identity cards? The national court was never asked to contemplate this. The judgment also wavers between referring to permits (both residence and work) for Mr Ruiz Zambrano alone and speaking about the children's *parents*. What is the position, in law, of Mrs Ruiz Zambrano? It is difficult to avoid feeling that, exemplifying concerns introduced in Chapter 1, the case law had become so facts-driven as to raise accusations of arbitrariness; in so many respects, the decision in *Ruiz Zambrano* marked the high- (or low-) point of this dynamic in the citizenship jurisprudence.

The protection of fundamental rights goes a long way towards redressing the balance of concern with respect to charges of undue judicial activism, especially in a legal order that also confers and protects a distinctive status of citizenship. But then, fundamental rights have to be protected *consistently*, or their engagement as an appropriate motivation, even in explanatory terms, will weaken a more sustainable claim to legitimacy.[82] The effort made to imprint retrospective judicial restraint in *McCarthy* and *Dereci*, surely driven by the criticism that had been levelled at the

[82] See further, N Nic Shuibhne, 'Seven questions for seven paragraphs (editorial)' (2011) 36:2 ELRev 161 at 162: 'there is a family at the heart of [the *Ruiz Zambrano*] case, a family living under constant strain for almost a decade . . . But however much the Court of Justice might want to help, and I believe this to be the motivation underpinning its judgment, it is simply not constitutionally possible or legitimate for the Court to resolve every breach of fundamental rights that occurs. Or, if it is truly serious about pushing the constitutional reach of EU law this far, then be open about it, be thorough, be direct, and persuade us as to why this must be the outcome . . . The Court is trying to do good things in individual cases; but it cannot continue to ignore the systemic legitimacy—and credibility—consequences of this choice'.

Court for the cryptic nature and extensive substitutive—of national immigration decisions—regulatory potential of the judgment in *Ruiz Zambrano*, brought those concerns into sharp relief. The coherence problem we are left with can be summarized in the following way. The decisions in *Carpenter*, *MRAX*, *Baumbast*, and *Metock* form a coherent line of authority about the high level at which respect for family life is protected in the EU legal order, which had been about protecting residence in the citizen's home State as a matter of choice. The decisions in *McCarthy*, *Dereci*, and *Iida* also make sense when read together given their emphasis on Article 51 of the Charter and limited exploration of impediments—especially prospective impediments—to movement rights. The problems are, first, that the two lines of case law do not sit easily together; and, second, that the limited exploration of impediments to movement in *McCarthy*, *Dereci*, and *Iida* does not sit easily with voluminous case law on potential Treaty restrictions more generally.

If we take the constraining approach in *McCarthy*, *Dereci*, and *Iida* as reflecting current judicial choices, can we save the fragmentary reasoning, and outcomes, as reflections of post-Lisbon changes to the underpinning constitutional signals? However close the case law may seem to have come in the past to a general or standalone fundamental rights jurisdiction for the Court of Justice or the EU more broadly, such an extreme—in competence terms—mandate is simply not legally permissible. Ideas that suggest the adjustment of that competence barrier have to date centred on exceptional circumstances only. In *Centro Europa 7*, for example—before the coming into effect of the Lisbon Treaty (and thus the Charter) and also before the decision in *Ruiz Zambrano*—AG Poiares Maduro proposed a reimagining of the case law that shapes the role of the Court in protecting fundamental rights, but he stopped short of proposing a full-scale fundamental rights jurisdiction in purely internal situations.[83] Focusing on the commitments to fundamental rights that the Member States make as an 'indispensable condition of EU membership', he proposed that 'serious and persistent violations which highlight a problem of systemic nature in the protection of fundamental rights in the Member State at issue, would . . . qualify as *violations of the rules on free movement*, by virtue of the direct threat they would pose to the transnational dimension of European citizenship and to the integrity of the EU legal order'.[84] In her Opinion for *Ruiz Zambrano*, AG Sharpston proposed a different template: 'the clearest rule would be one that made the availability of EU fundamental rights protection dependent neither on whether a Treaty provision was directly applicable nor on whether secondary legislation had been enacted, but rather on *the existence and scope of a material EU competence*... [P]rovided that the EU had competence (whether exclusive or shared) in a particular area of law, EU fundamental rights should protect the citizen of the EU *even if such competence has not yet been exercised*'.[85] But

[83] See e.g. AG Poiares Maduro in Case C-380/05 *Centro Europa 7 Srl v Ministero delle Comunicazioni e Autorità per le garanzie nelle comunicazioni and Direzione generale per le concessioni e le autorizzazioni del Ministero delle Comunicazioni* [2008] ECR I-349, esp. paras 17–23 of the Opinion.

[84] AG Poiares Maduro in *Centro Europa 7*, para. 22 of the Opinion (emphasis added).

[85] AG Sharpston in *Ruiz Zambrano*, para. 163 of the Opinion (emphasis in original).

she too acknowledged that the 'necessary constitutional evolution in the foundations of the EU' that would be needed to accommodate the radical nature of her proposal, which 'would involve introducing *an overtly federal element* into the structure of the EU's legal and political system', simply has not happened yet.[86]

Comparably speaking, AG Sharpston's analysis of free movement law in the same Opinion was more traditional, but it does make the essential relevant links to *existing* case law. The discussion demonstrates how case law concepts on the economic freedoms and citizenship rights are innately fused, but it also emphasizes the particular implications stemming from the latter. The Advocate General first provided a comprehensive overview of the case law on potential restrictions for both personal and trade free movement rights.[87] Turning to the case law on citizenship, she then acknowledged the depletion of the substance of movement in a way that reflects the arguments outlined in Section 3(b), stating bluntly that there are already cases 'in which the element of true movement is either barely discernable or frankly non-existent'.[88] She outlined three options that could be drawn from to find a right of residence for the Ruiz Zambrano parents through the application of EU law. First, the Court could continue to have plausible but ultimately disingenuous recourse to the case law on potential restrictions on free movement, which had the advantage of contributing to coherence overall but did not face up to the interpretative elasticity involved. Second, the Court could articulate overt EU competence to tackle instances of reverse discrimination in certain circumstances. Or third, as outlined above, the Court could claim a radically enhanced jurisdiction to secure protection of fundamental rights in internal situations.

The Court took none of these routes in its judgment. The national court had framed its questions in terms of both citizenship and the protection of fundamental rights. The Court stayed firmly in the terrain of the former, which adds legitimacy to its decision on one view, given that the open-ended wording of those Treaty provisions permits excursions into purely internal situations. However, once the step of bringing the children's situation within the scope of Article 20 TFEU was already taken, then the protection of fundamental rights that implicitly followed would *not* have been problematically standalone i.e. it was not an *autonomous* exercise of fundamental rights jurisdiction contra Article 51(2) of the Charter; it does not *in and of itself* 'establish any new power or task for the Union, or modify powers and tasks as defined in the Treaties'. Instead, it was the usual *secondary* obligation of protection attaching to a situation that was already grounded in the Treaty and is thus legitimately 'governed by EU law'. This interpretation may induce constitutional shivers regarding judicial activism and conferred powers, but it does reflect the actual wording of the Treaty.

[86] AG Sharpston in *Ruiz Zambrano*, paras 172–175 of the Opinion (emphasis added).

[87] AG Sharpston in *Ruiz Zambrano*, paras 69–74 of the Opinion.

[88] AG Sharpston in *Ruiz Zambrano*, para. 77 of the Opinion, discussing *Chen* and Case C-148/02 *Garcia Avello v Belgian State* [2003] ECR I-11613, as well as *Rottmann*. On *Chen*, see the discussion on abuse of rights in Chapter 3; the judgments in *Garcia Avello* and *Rottmann* are returned to below.

We saw above that the genuine enjoyment test developed in *Ruiz Zambrano* is confined thus far to wholly exceptional circumstances: loss of Member State nationality and a citizen's forced departure from the territory of the Union are the only examples in the case law to date. Had the Court taken the purely internal piercing further, and considered that the family life risks at issue in *McCarthy* and *Dereci* also affected the genuine enjoyment of the citizenship rights of those citizens, this would have been an undoubtedly bold but legally permissible step: legally permissible having regard to the Court's previous case law and the permissiveness built into the Treaty (Articles 20 and 21 TFEU). Instead the Court has chosen to focus more deliberately on the limits of both the Treaty (Article 6 TEU) and the Charter. In essence, that is its reading of the admittedly confusing constitutional instructions provided by the Member States through the Lisbon Treaty process, a big part of which sought to effect the explicit delimitation of respective EU/Member State powers. The Court faced an unenviable task: how best to contain the implications of the case law on purely (or tangentially) internal situations, in a broader political environment dominated by the Eurozone crisis, bitter EU budget negotiations, a national constitutional court declaring a Court of Justice ruling to be ultra vires,[89] and the prospect in principle at least of the withdrawal of the United Kingdom from the Union altogether. And so the Court pulled back.

But even if it did so for good reasons, trying not to aggravate already volatile EU polity dynamics, at what point does the Court's responsiveness to the political pass from being a commendable marker of appropriate dialogue with other constitutional actors to a dereliction of its own distinct obligations? A stark consequence of its choice was flagged in Chapter 2: the fundamental rights of some EU citizens are sometimes protected more than those of others; and it is simply difficult to reconcile that result with fairness, integrity, or coherence—with, in other words, the values and responsibilities of a constitutional court. Is defending the protective standards already established, notwithstanding political strains, pressures, or even outright hostilities, not part of what constitutional courts are there precisely to do? The often-overlooked responsibilities of the States to *support* this constitutional court will be emphasized again in the Conclusion chapter. Meanwhile, either give all of these families the right to live together in the Union citizen's home State or give it to none of them. Because there is a critical point that needs to be faced up to here: no one forced the Court to take the radical step effected in *Ruiz Zambrano* in the first place. Decades of case law on the purely internal rule would have enabled it to decline jurisdiction; and its own reminder in *Dereci* that the States are all parties to the ECHR may have had to satisfy its genuine concern for the family involved.

In many respects, the choice of wording about *genuine enjoyment* of the *substance* of citizenship rights is not helpful in trying to answer criticism that protection of fundamental rights should surely be a part of the 'substance' of Union citizenship.

[89] Czech Republic Constitutional Court, Judgment No PL. ÚS 4/06: Slovak Pensions, 14 February 2012 (available in English at <http://www.usoud.cz/view/pl 04 06>), concerning Case C 399/09 *Landtová v Česká správa sociálního zabezpečení*, judgment of 22 June 2011.

Legal tests created through the judicial law-making function evolve and become refined over time; their reach and scope solidify through new sets of facts and questions against which they are tested. We know now that what the Court is concerned with in purely internal situations are consequences of *national* decisions, and not those taken by citizens themselves, that take Member State nationals to the very precipice of *losing* their 'additional' citizenship status—which Article 20 of the Treaty makes clear that it must be—either literally (*Rottmann*) or in a comparably serious way (*Ruiz Zambrano*). Wording closer to literal loss or preclusion of citizenship rights, or inability to exercise rather than enjoy, would have been a better way to convey the intended extremity of circumstances more clearly. It would also render the piercing of the purely internal perimeter more defensible and more palatable, given the constitutional consequences of accepting a material role for EU law in any *truly* internal situations at all.

The more difficult problem to overcome is that the Court's concern to contain the implications of the genuine enjoyment test has also leached into the way in which the other half of the citizenship test was applied in *McCarthy*, *Dereci*, and *Iida* i.e. declining to consider the implications of prospective impediments to free movement as a way to establish a material link with EU law. It is undoubtedly the case that legal recognition of potential impediments to movement opens up the scope of the Treaty to an enormous extent. But the coherence point is that it has already happened; and if it is a problem, it is a problem of the Court's own making. The applicants in *McCarthy* and *Dereci* paid a regrettable price for coming just after the significant but overly individualized response in *Ruiz Zambrano*. It is also worrying to see a constitutional court still working out its thinking in public over three successive judgments released (rushed?) over a very short space of time. That is not the same thing as the normal evolution of ideas through the narrative of case law.

Reflecting on the idea of residual situations that are generated by the partial impact of EU law on national law, AG Poiares Maduro developed some generalizable ideas about the role of discrimination in *Carbonati Apuani*. In particular, he extricated the potential of discrimination as a general principle of EU law:

> These principles are in the nature of fundamental rules of the [EU] legal order. They provide an objective framework for all the rules and situations capable of falling within the scope of [EU] law. They therefore serve either as criteria for assessing the validity of [EU] acts, or as criteria for interpreting acts and situations falling within the scope of [EU] law... The principles applicable in such circumstances include, in particular, the general principle of non-discrimination, established by the Court as a fundamental principle of [EU] law. That principle has traditionally been seen as nothing more than a "functional extension" of the rules on free movement. In fact, when the [EU] judicature uses that principle, it is generally to protect the freedoms established by the Treaty... It seems appropriate now for that principle to be given *an independent existence and an independent scope*.[90]

[90] AG Maduro in *Carbonati Apuani*, paras 65–68 of the Opinion (emphasis added).

It will be argued below that applying non-discrimination as a general principle of EU law could bring greater coherence and much needed normative weight to this messy sphere of case law. For this to be practically useful as well as conceptually persuasive, however, two factors need to be worked out in particular: the marker of differential treatment at issue, and the existence of an appropriate comparator. Both of these issues will now be considered.

(b) Recalibrating the weight of movement

Non-discrimination requires that comparable situations must not be treated differently and, conversely, that different situations must not be treated in the same way. In the context of EU free movement law, the classic marker of differential treatment is nationality. Article 18 TFEU prohibits 'any discrimination on grounds of nationality' and is now mirrored by Article 21(2) of the Charter. The case law has always made it clear that the Article 18 prohibition includes both direct and indirect discrimination, but only 'within the scope of application of the Treaties'. In other words, while Article 18 is a powerful, directly effective prohibition, and while it can apply independently of the free movement provisions, a material connecting factor with EU law must still be established: Article 18 is not a standalone source of rights and it is not a standalone form of action.[91] It shares these limitations with the way in which fundamental rights are relevant within EU law more generally.

But it has also been emphasized throughout this chapter that it is important to join the discussion on purely internal situations with the fact that free movement law has progressed *beyond* discrimination more generally. In *Bosman*, for example, a UEFA requirement that transfer fees had to be paid before a professional footballer could take up a new contract of employment was found to restrict the free movement rights conferred on migrant EU workers by Article 45 TFEU.[92] The critical point for present purposes is that the transfer fee applied irrespective of whether a player was moving to a club 2 miles away or two States away, which is why these kinds of rules are often described as 'genuinely' non-discriminatory. But, as we saw in Section 2, it is only the actual or potential encumbering of the *cross-border* worker that attracts the protection of EU law.

The argument developed here is premised initially on the Treaty-based distinction followed above. First, for situations connected to the provisions governing economic activity, the wording of the Treaty dictates that a cross-border connection needs to be forged; case law that evades this requirement (e.g. through recourse to the dispute-framing authority of referring courts and tribunals) was argued in Section 3 not to reflect an appropriate discharge of constitutional responsibility;

[91] See e.g. Case C-450/09 *Schröder v Finanzamt Hameln* [2011] ECR I-2497, para. 28: 'Article 18 TFEU, which lays down a general prohibition of all discrimination on grounds of nationality... applies independently only to *situations governed by European Union law* for which the Treaty does not lay down any specific rules of non-discrimination' (emphasis added).

[92] Case C-415/93 *Union Royale Belge des Sociétés de Football Association ASBL v Bosman* [1995] ECR I-4921.

neither does the overtly defiant persistence of the *Lancry* exception in case law on the free movement of goods. Establishing whether there is a cross-border connection in cases at the margins of movement is also bound up with the limited development and application of threshold rules in free movement law more generally, a problem examined in Chapter 5. Second, however, for situations connected to Articles 20 and 21 TFEU, it will be argued in the remainder of this chapter that the case law has moved beyond *nationality* discrimination; that Article 21 plus non-discrimination as a general principle of EU law could be reconceptualized as *migration discrimination*; and that Article 20 plus non-discrimination could provide deeper constitutional authority for greater protection of the rights, especially family reunification rights, of even static EU citizens than we have seen in recent case law.

In titling Part Two of the TFEU as 'Non-discrimination and Citizenship of the Union', the Lisbon Treaty codified an established conceptual link between citizenship and the principle of equality. Article 19 TFEU provides a legislative competence for the Union to tackle discrimination based on 'sex, racial or ethnic origin, religion or belief, disability, age or sexual orientation', with the Council acting unanimously under the special legislative procedure. The inability of this provision to generate directly effective rights has been superseded by the prohibition-format of Article 21(1) of the Charter (including, additionally, the criteria of colour, social origin, genetic features, language, political or any other opinion, membership of a national minority, property, and birth) and by case law conceptualizing the prohibition on age discrimination (at least) as a general principle of EU law.[93]

Articles 20–25 TFEU go on to outline the rights attached to EU citizenship, with limited further references to equal treatment.[94] It is also interesting to look at the Preamble to Directive 2004/38 to get a sense of the profile and priorities of EU citizenship. Here, the early recitals emphasize the 'primary and individual right to move and reside freely within the territory of the Member States' (recital 1), noting that EU citizenship 'should be the fundamental status' of Member State nationals when they exercise those rights (recital 3) and be 'exercised under objective conditions of freedom and dignity' (recital 5, in the context of extending movement and residence rights to family members). Equal treatment with nationals of the host State does not really feature until recital 20. A more general commitment to non-discrimination is not articulated until recital 31; this is also the Preamble's only reference to respect for fundamental rights. Article 24 of the Directive then establishes a commitment to non-discrimination in a substantive sense. But in Article 24(2), derogations are immediately listed.[95]

[93] Case C-144/04 *Mangold v Helm* [2005] ECR I-9981; Case C-555/07 *Kücükdeveci v Swedex GmbH & Co. KG* [2010] ECR I-365.

[94] On the rights to vote and stand as a candidate in European Parliament and municipal elections, see Articles 20(2)(b) and 22 TFEU; on consular protection in third countries, see Articles 20(2)(c) and 23 TFEU. In December 2011, the Commission finally published its proposal for a directive on consular protection for citizens of the Union abroad; see COM(2011) 881 final.

[95] '[T]he host Member State shall not be obliged to confer entitlement to social assistance during the first three months of residence or, where appropriate, the longer period provided for in Article 14

The way in which the framework of the Directive is constructed suggests, overall, that the rights to move and reside are the nuclear legal content of Union citizenship.[96] The right to equal treatment is, on this view, an add-on: it is a critical add-on, but it is not the defining principle of citizenship law. Two further questions should be asked, however: first, does the prohibition of discrimination in fact drive EU citizenship rights, in an empirical sense; and, second, does it drive their development more abstractly, providing the framing objectives and purposes? Taking the second question first, the judicial mission-formula for Union citizenship centres on its 'fundamental status'.[97] But this objective is almost always tied to the intention of 'enabling those who find themselves in the same situation to enjoy the same treatment in law *irrespective of their nationality*' (emphasis added). The prohibition of nationality discrimination has therefore been, and remains, the dominant paradigm in the citizenship case law. Because the rights to move to or reside in *other* Member States were the central concern around which the development of citizenship rights actually happened, securing protection against discrimination necessarily became the case law's defining legal principle—thus providing a provisional answer, at least, to the first question above too.

We saw in Chapter 3 that the status of citizenship brought important additional elements to case law developed for the economic freedoms. First, it broadened the *personal* scope of the Treaty and, importantly, it did this at the level of *primary* Union law.[98] Second, it accelerated the decoupling of personal scope from the *material* claims being grounded in EU rights. But it did not initially displace the rule that purely internal situations could not come within the scope of EU law; and thus it did not initially raise the prospect of a more transformative constitutional shift in the boundaries of competence between the Union and the Member States. Furthermore, the majority of early citizenship cases were clear instances of direct discrimination i.e. additional burdens or conditions placed *only* on the nationals of other Member States. For the purposes of discrimination analysis, this also meant that the necessary comparator group—host State nationals—was easily identified. Reflecting the broader ecosystem of free movement rights, the case law progressed swiftly to dealing with indirect discrimination. Most commonly, this kind of differential treatment is effected through the setting of nationality-blind conditions such as residence requirements, compliance with which is obviously less burdensome

(4)(b), nor shall it be obliged, prior to acquisition of the right of permanent residence, to grant maintenance aid for studies'.

96 This interpretation is reflected in several AG Opinions; see e.g. AG Sharpston in *Ruiz Zambrano*, para. 80 of the Opinion; AG Ruiz-Jarabo Colomer in Joined Cases C-11 and 12/06 *Morgan and Bucher* [2007] ECR I-9161, para. 67 of the Opinion.

97 The phrase was first used by the Court in Case C-184/99 *Grzelczyk v Centre public d'aide sociale d'Ottignies-Louvain-la-Neuve* [2001] ECR I-6193, para. 31; but '*fundamental* legal status' (emphasis in original) had been used by AG La Pergola in Case C-85/96 *Martínez Sala v Freistaat Bayern* [1998] ECR I-2691; see paras 18 and 19 of the Opinion.

98 The 1990s Residence Directives (repealed and replaced by Directive 2004/38) had already started this process.

for home State nationals.[99] If the Court finds that there is no differential treatment within the meaning of EU law—i.e. if the alleged differential treatment is linked to objectively different *situations*—it confirms that the relevant issue falls outside the scope of the Treaty altogether.[100]

Turning to rights beyond discrimination, it was noted above that the language of restrictions is a broad one, including, for example, 'obstacles' and 'disadvantages'. In *Ruiz Zambrano*, AG Sharpston incisively exposed the consequences of the Court's willingness to accept that virtually any potential or future restriction might 'deter' or 'discourage' free movement or make it 'less attractive'. It is submitted here that we need to begin to conceptualize restriction-based case law more convincingly. The argument being proposed—starting with citizenship in this chapter—is that just because we go beyond *nationality* discrimination, it does not follow that we have to go beyond discrimination per se. The starting point is *D'Hoop*, which involved the imposition of what is described here as a *migration penalty* i.e. the applicant was treated less favourably in law (deemed ineligible for a social security benefit) by her home State because she had exercised free movement rights in the past; she had completed part of her secondary education in another Member State. The Court reasoned as follows:

> In that a citizen of the Union must be granted in all Member States *the same treatment in law as that accorded to the nationals of those Member States who find themselves in the same situation*, it would be incompatible with the right of freedom of movement were a citizen, in the Member State of which he is a national, to receive *treatment less favourable* than he would enjoy if he had not availed himself of the opportunities offered by the Treaty in relation to freedom of movement. Those opportunities could not be fully effective if a national of a Member State could be deterred from availing himself of them by obstacles raised on his return to his country of origin by legislation penalising the fact that he has used them.[101]

The deterrence philosophy that emerges in the final sentence, which builds coherently on an established line of case law that can be traced to *Singh*, is the primary

[99] See e.g. Case C-503/09 *Stewart v Secretary of State for Work and Pensions*, judgment of 21 July 2011; Case C-73/08 *Bressol and others v Gouvernement de la Communauté française* [2010] ECR I-2735; Case C-103/08 *Gottwald v Bezirkshauptmannschaft Bregenz* [2009] ECR I-9117; Joined Cases C-22/08 and C-23/08 *Vatsouras and Koupatantze v Arbeitsgemeinschaft (ARGE) Nürnberg 900* [2009] ECR I-4585; Case C-158/07 *Förster v IB-Groep* [2008] ECR I-8507; Case C-209/03 *Bidar v London Borough of Ealing; Secretary of State for Education and Skills* [2005] ECR I-2119; Joined Cases C-502/01 and C-31/02 *Gaumain-Cerri and Barth* [2004] ECR I-6483; Case C-138/02 *Collins v Secretary of State for Work and Pensions* [2004] ECR I-2703.

[100] See e.g. Case C-391/09 *Runevič-Vardyn and Łukasz Paweł Wardyn v Vilniaus miesto savivaldybės administracija and others* [2011] ECR I-3787: 'when a citizen of the Union moves to another Member State and subsequently marries a national of that other State, the fact that the surname which that citizen had prior to marriage, and her forename, cannot be changed and entered in documents relating to civil status issued by her Member State of origin except using the characters of the language of that latter Member State cannot constitute treatment that is less favourable than that which she enjoyed before she availed herself of the opportunities offered by the Treaty in relation to free movement of persons' (para. 69).

[101] Case C-224/98 *D'Hoop v Office national de l'emploi* [2002] ECR I-6191, paras 30–31 (emphasis added).

ratio extracted from the judgment since then. The justification offered, i.e. ensuring the *effectiveness* of Treaty rights, is also very familiar to EU lawyers.[102] But for present purposes, the opening lines of the extract are more relevant. Here, the Court seems to be extrapolating a general principle of equal treatment from the starting point of nationality discrimination. The basic marker of discrimination analysis—identification of a comparator—is then attached: 'national legislation introduces a difference in treatment between Belgian nationals who have had all their secondary education in Belgium and those who, having availed themselves of their freedom to move, have obtained their diploma of completion of secondary education in another Member State'.[103] In their analysis of the judgment, Iliopoulou and Toner commented as follows:

> [T]he Court [focused] on *migration discrimination as a separate category of equal treatment*, but did not wish to exclude the application of the concept of non-discriminatory obstacles entirely. This is right because the two grounds can be used cumulatively to strengthen the case against *discrimination based on migration*. Both free movement and equal treatment constitute principles worthy of protection and are the main axes [of EU citizenship]. *D'Hoop* echoes [discrimination-based] case law but takes it a step further: a citizen who avails himself/herself of mobility opportunities must be guaranteed the same treatment in law. Consequently, after *D'Hoop*, *nationality is not the only forbidden ground of discrimination*, the only 'suspect class', according to the principles underpinning EU citizenship.[104]

As we saw also in the judgment of the Court, the analysis applied above is rooted at one level in Article 18 TFEU, but important markers of a more novel concept of 'migration discrimination' can be clearly distinguished too.[105]

Several migration penalty cases, in which the treatment of home State claimants who had exercised free movement rights was compared to the entitlements of nationals of the same State who had not moved anywhere, followed *D'Hoop*.[106] In all of these judgments, common threads of deterrence, being penalized, suffering disadvantage, and then of effectiveness, are reiterated and reinforced in line with standard interpretations of the economic freedoms i.e. that the Treaty should catch non-discriminatory obstacles to movement however tangential or prospective.[107]

[102] On effectiveness as a general principle of EU law, see e.g. Case C-312/93 *Peterbroeck and others v Belgium* [1995] ECR I-4599.

[103] *D'Hoop*, para. 33. In keeping with a discrimination approach, it was also stressed that any restrictions identified could only be applied if they were justifiable and proportionate.

[104] A Iliopoulou and H Toner, 'A new approach to discrimination against free movers?' (2003) 28:3 ELRev 389 at 395 (emphasis added).

[105] The extent to which this concept can be identified in free movement case law more generally will be addressed in Chapters 6 and 7.

[106] E.g. Case C-56/09 *Zanotti v Agenzia delle Entrate—Ufficio Roma 2* [2010] ECR I-4517; Case C-499/06 *Nerkowska v Zakład Ubezpieczeń Społecznych Oddział w Koszalinie* [2008] ECR I-3993; *Morgan and Bucher*; Case C-192/05 *Tas-Hagen and Tas v Raadskamer WUBO van de Pensioen- en Uitkeringsraad* [2006] ECR I-10451; Case C-76/05 *Schwarz and Marga Gootjes-Schwarz v Finanzamt Bergisch Gladbach* [2007] ECR I-6849; Case C-406/04 *De Cuyper v Office national de l'emploi* [2006] ECR I-6947; Case C-224/02 *Pusa v Osuuspankkien Keskinäinen Vakuutusyhtiö* [2004] ECR I-5763.

[107] With respect to *justifying* differential treatment, we saw in Chapter 3 that the Court developed 'proxies' in citizenship case law (see F de Witte, 'The end of EU citizenship and the means of non-discrimination' (2011) 18:1–2 MJ 86 at 106) i.e. various real link tests, which ensure that (i) codified

But the prevailing focus on mere 'disadvantage'[108] opens the Court too easily to the same damaging critiques of case law on the economic freedoms discussed in Chapter 7: essentially, it fuels a presumption that *all* national rules or practices are vulnerable to challenges grounded in EU law, a degree of regulatory interference that collides with expectations about a market structured formally around shared competence.[109] More specifically for present purposes, the breadth of that approach is also difficult to reconcile with the Treaty-set benchmark of EU citizenship as an 'additional' legal status.[110] Critically, and building on the discussion in Section 3, the restriction-based approach also privileges movement to an extraordinary degree: the priorities of the Court no longer seem to be about *facilitating* Treaty rights, but actually *inciting* them in a super-charged way. The decisions in *McCarthy* and *Dereci*, for example, oblige and even positively encourage Union citizens to move temporarily but instrumentally to another State in order to achieve residence rights for family members when back in their own States—protected from charges of abuse of rights, as we saw in Chapter 3.

In a special edition of the *Maastricht Journal of European and Comparative Law*, which focused specifically on the principle of non-discrimination in EU law, van der Mei argued as follows:

> The principle of non-discrimination rests on comparability, but in itself does not provide guidance as to which situations must be compared and when situations must be labelled as comparable. As such, equality is a skeleton concept that has no legal life for as long as no flesh has been put on its bones. That flesh must be provided by courts and consist of criteria or factors determining what to compare and how to compare... [EU citizenship] may entitle [migrant and static citizens] to equality of treatment in comparable situations, *but does not imply that they must be regarded as being in the same position.*[111]

residence requirements can be conceptualized as legitimate in principle but (ii) their application to individual situations is reviewed against the general principles of EU law, notably proportionality. See also, C O'Brien, 'Real links, abstract rights and false alarms: The relationship between the ECJ's "real link" case law and national solidarity' (2008) 33: ELRev 643.

[108] See *Bosman*, para. 94 ('the provisions of the Treaty relating to freedom of movement for persons are intended to facilitate the pursuit by Community citizens of occupational activities of all kinds throughout the Community, and preclude measures which might place Community citizens at a disadvantage when they wish to pursue an economic activity in the territory of another Member State'), confirmed in e.g. Case C-464/02 *Commission v Denmark* [2005] ECR I-7929, para. 34.

[109] See e.g. AG Jacobs in *Pusa*, para. 21 of the Opinion: 'freedom of movement entails more than simply the abolition of restrictions on a person's right to enter, reside in or leave a Member State. Such freedom cannot be assured unless *all measures of any kind* which impose an unjustified burden on those exercising it are also abolished. Whatever the context in which it may arise—including leaving or returning to the home Member State, or residing or moving elsewhere within the Union—*no such burden* may be imposed' (emphasis added). See generally, T Horsley, 'Subsidiarity and the Court of Justice: Missing pieces in the subsidiarity jigsaw?' (2012) 50:2 JCMS 267.

[110] See AP van der Mei, 'The outer limits of the prohibition of discrimination on grounds of nationality: A look through the lens of Union citizenship' (2011) 18:1–2 MJ 62 at 85: '[n]ational citizenship also gives an entitlement to equal treatment and fundamental rights and it is not readily apparent why these national rights must be substituted by their EU equivalents. Union citizenship objects to "depriving citizens of the Union of the genuine enjoyment of the substance of the rights" conferred by virtue of Union citizenship, not to enjoyment of rights flowing from national citizenship'.

[111] Van der Mei, n110, 77 (emphasis added).

Can we find more substantive 'legal life' for the important but indeterminate ideas about differential treatment that inform restriction-based case law on citizenship rights? In *Pusa*, the Court held that '[n]ational legislation which places at a disadvantage certain [home State] nationals simply because they have exercised their freedom to move and to reside in another Member State would give rise to inequality of treatment, *contrary to the principles which underpin the status of citizen of the Union*, that is, the guarantee of the *same treatment in law* in the exercise of the citizen's freedom to move'.[112] This invocation of equality as a principle *underpinning* EU citizenship offers a different order of rationality than justification based on *effective* law alone. Similarly, in *Tas-Hagen*, AG Kokott first confirmed that there was no question of nationality discrimination—direct or indirect—at issue in the case. Nevertheless, she then argued that '[l]egislation which results in a Union citizen who exercises his right to free movement being afforded *less favourable treatment* than if he had not exercised that right *must also be assessed* in the light of Article [21 TFEU]'.[113]

These case law pieces are all on-point, but they never quite take the next conceptual step that would better rationalize both the application and as yet unexploited potential of non-discrimination. One way to achieve this is to knit two separate strands of case law more consciously together—the advantage/deter/discourage cases outlined above and jurisprudence on non-discrimination as a general principle of EU law per se i.e. the line of authority which confirms that 'the prohibition of discrimination laid down in [Article 18 TFEU] is merely a specific enunciation of the *general principle of equality* which is one of the fundamental principles of [Union] law'.[114] The general principle of equality is already applied widely in the case law.[115] In *Kücükdeveci*, reflecting the views of AG Poiares Maduro in *Carbonati Apuani*, AG Bot characterized equal treatment as 'one of the fundamental rights whose observance the Court ensures'.[116] He then outlined the principle's main functions: '[i]t permits the [EU] judicature to *fill gaps* which might appear in secondary legislation. It is also an *instrument of interpretation* capable of clarifying the meaning and scope of provisions of [Union] law, and a *means of reviewing* the validity of [Union] acts'.[117]

In cases like *D'Hoop* and *Tas-Hagen*, home State claimants were treated differently purely because they had *moved*. Moreover, the Court always points to a

[112] *Pusa*, para. 20 (emphasis added).

[113] AG Kokott in *Tas-Hagen*, para. 49 of the Opinion (emphasis added).

[114] Joined Cases 117/76 and 16/77 *Ruckdeschel & Co. and Hansa-Lagerhaus Ströh & Co. v Hauptzollamt Hamburg-St. Annen; Diamalt AG v Hauptzollamt Itzehoe* [1977] ECR 1753, para. 7 (emphasis added).

[115] See e.g. AG Stix-Hackl in *MRAX*, para. 59 of the Opinion (extending the scope of the principle to evaluations of differential treatment of two groups of third country nationals). In *Defrenne II*, the Court observed that the principle of equal pay 'represents the application of a general principle of equality which forms part of a philosophy common to the Member States' (Case 43/75 *Defrenne v Société anonyme belge de navigation aérienne Sabena (Defrenne II)* [1976] ECR 455 at 478).

[116] AG Bot in Case C-555/07 *Kücükdeveci v Swedex GmbH & Co. KG* [2010] ECR I-365, para. 79 of the Opinion.

[117] AG Bot in *Kücükdeveci*, para. 80 of the Opinion.

relevant comparator group in its decisions i.e. home State nationals who did not move. So these cases are about discrimination: it is just that they are not about *nationality* discrimination. The Court has at times tried to use Article 18 TFEU as a starting point for its analysis in cases involving seemingly non-discriminatory restrictions. Not only is this not necessary, it is a mistaken conflation of different treatment and nationality in cases where the two markers do not actually connect. If the more general principle of non-discrimination is animated, then movement per se is a sufficient causal trigger—the *criterion* or *reason* underpinning either different treatment of citizens in a similar position or similar treatment of citizens in a different position. Importantly, movement is not the conceptual driver in this construction: it does not, in other words, constitute something approaching the status of a general principle of EU law on its own terms. As argued above, the contrasting approaches in the Opinion and judgment in *Iida* illustrate why we should avoid elevating the *idea* of movement to that extent.

In his landmark work on the *General Principles of EU Law*, Tridimas describes non-discrimination as a principle that 'transcends the specific provisions of the Treaty' and he continues as follows:

> In declaring equal treatment as a general principle of law the Court does not endorse any particular theory of equality. It does not seek to advance a particular idea of the social good. Rather, the principle is seen as a democratic guarantee which prevents community and national authorities from imposing differential treatment without good reason . . . *[I]t does not seek to resolve the issues but rather to act as a check on the decision-makers.* The principle thus does not dictate a single result: more than one policy choice may be compatible with it . . . as a general principle of [EU] law, equality is *consistency and rationality.*[118]

In this extract, and especially in its final line, we can find 'legal life' for a citizenship-relevant principle of equal treatment. The distinction between equality as a substantive principle that encapsulates preferred outcomes (and is thus more suited to the manifestation of the principle in specific Treaty provisions e.g. nationality discrimination) and equality as a more generic public law principle, which primarily serves to trigger a justification burden when differential treatment has occurred, is particularly relevant for present purposes. It provides a rationalized explanation of what the Court should require from national authorities when home State nationals are treated differently purely because they have moved. The application of discrimination analysis is often criticized on the basis that the challenged burden must 'affect nationals of other Member States more significantly than those of the State imposing it'.[119] But that is not how the Court actually engages with comparators in the *D'Hoop* jurisprudence, where the existence of a comparator is a simpler question of fact that demonstrates the existence of differential treatment at a very basic empirical level.

[118] T Tridimas, *The General Principles of EU Law*, 2nd edn (OUP, 2006) 62 (emphasis added). See generally, K Lenaerts and JA Gutiérrez-Fons, 'The constitutional allocation of powers and general principles of EU law' (2010) 47:4 CMLRev 1629.

[119] AG Jacobs in *Pusa*, para. 22 of the Opinion; this critique resonates keenly with arguments connected to the free movement of goods case law, discussed in Chapters 5 and 7 in particular.

The situation in *Garcia Avello* demonstrates the problems inherent in overstretching the capacity of a disadvantage-based framework.[120] The disadvantage there concerned the hypothesized movement of two dual national children (born in Belgium to Spanish and Belgian parents) from Belgium to Spain at some undetermined point in the future. That possibility was then found to justify an overruling of Belgian rules on the registration of the children's surnames in favour of their father's choice, Garcia Weber, to reflect Spanish surname conventions, because the Belgian rules might amount to an obstacle to free movement.[121] This degree of intrusion into national regulatory choices is problematic, to say the least, given the wholly uncertain character of the future movement intentions of two children; but also because of the very subjective test that the Court applied to determine the existence of the impediment to movement: future or potential 'serious inconvenience'.[122] Adding ballast to its reasoning, the Court engaged Article 18 TFEU too, since the children held dual nationality. The comparison drawn was between Belgian nationals holding only that nationality and Belgian nationals also holding the nationality of another EU Member State. In *Grunkin and Paul*, however, the relevance of dual nationality was displaced so long as a cross-border connection could be established in another way: '[i]t matters little in that regard whether the discrepancy in surnames is the result of the dual nationality of the persons concerned or of the fact that, in the State of birth and residence, the connecting factor for determination of a surname is residence whilst, in the State of which those persons are nationals, it is nationality'.[123]

The classic discrimination formula in paragraph 31 of the Court's judgment in *Garcia Avello*—'the principle of non-discrimination requires that comparable situations must not be treated differently and that different situations must not be treated in the same way'—is particularly interesting for present purposes because, here, the Court cited the more equality-generic judgment in *National Farmers' Union*, and not citizenship or free movement authority, in support.[124] A more widespread reconceptualization of case law involving restrictions that do not engage *nationality* discrimination as still engaging *discrimination* could go some way towards filling a normative gap in some of the Court's case law on citizenship. The idea of migration discrimination appears in both case law and academic commentary, but without the conceptual value that the general principle of equal treatment could add. A more principled construction of restriction-based citizenship case law reflects the centrality of migration rights in EU law generally. Crucially, it also takes proper account of the relevance of movement written into

[120] Case C-148/02 *Garcia Avello v Belgian State* [2003] ECR I-11613.

[121] This approach was confirmed in Case C-353/06 *Grunkin and Paul* [2008] ECR I-7639; for an example of justifiable national restrictions in the context of surname regulation, however, see Case C-208/09 *Sayn-Wittgenstein v Landeshauptmann von Wien* [2010] ECR I-13693.

[122] *Garcia Avello*, para. 36. In *Runevič-Vardyn*, the Court hardened its stance, charging the referring court with making a more empirical determination of the 'serious inconvenience' at issue (see paras 74–78).

[123] *Grunkin and Paul*, para. 24.

[124] See Case C-354/95 *National Farmers' Union and Others* [1997] ECR I-4559, para. 61.

the Treaty but dilutes the significance attached to it relocating it more appropriately as a second-order concern—as a marker of differential treatment. It provides arguments that can respond to challenges created by the widespread push 'beyond discrimination'. It also steers judicial analysis to questions that are more about substantive disparities in treatment than situations that simply result from moving per se. A more overt discrimination method will not resolve all of the problems. It will not, for example, rationalize marginal cases that rely *solely* on prospective movement. But perhaps it should not. Maybe the problem there lies in the fact that we cannot predict the future and so we should be wary of hitching our 'legal life' to it quite so extensively. This point is picked up again below and in subsequent chapters.

Turning to the application of this argument to situations of reverse discrimination, we saw in subsection (a) that the decision in *Ruiz Zambrano* was not about movement within the EU. It is also the only case to date in which the Court's articulation of the 'fundamental status' principle was *not* immediately followed by the 'find themselves in the same situation' migration formula. Much has been made of the Court's use of Article 20, and not 21, TFEU in its judgment, even though, as seen above, there is a degree of textual ambiguity in both provisions. Article 20 TFEU was used in early citizenship case law, as the basic starting point for inclusion within the personal scope of the Treaty.[125] In *My*, the Court emphasized that '[Article 20], whilst establishing citizenship of the Union, merely provides that citizens of the Union enjoy the rights conferred by the Treaty and are subject to the duties imposed thereby. It cannot therefore be applied independently of the specific provisions of the Treaty which govern the rights and duties of the citizens of the Union'.[126] This interpretation has never been repeated. No other *Treaty* provision was mentioned in *Ruiz Zambrano*, so we have to assume that the proviso in *My* has been overruled. Since Article 20 is enough to bring an EU citizen within the personal scope of the Treaty for the purposes of requiring nationality discrimination to be justified—something we know since the decision in *Martínez Sala*—the same logic must also extend to the general principle of equal treatment with respect to other criteria or markers of differential treatment.

Before *Ruiz Zambrano*, some form of past or prospective movement was then engaged to prompt a differential treatment analysis in cases involving an applicant's home State. But possible equal treatment comparators still exist in the absence of mobility. Recalling the facts of *Ruiz Zambrano*, Belgian citizens with third country national parents are necessarily in a different position from both other-State-EU citizens with third country national parents residing in Belgium and Belgian citizens with Belgian parents: a threat of forced departure from the Union is

[125] See e.g. C Timmermans, '*Martínez Sala* and *Baumbast* revisited' in M Maduro and L Azoulai (eds.), *The Past and Future of EU Law: The Classics of EU Law Revisited on the 50th Anniversary of the Rome Treaty* (Hart Publishing, 2010) 345, who points out (at 351–4) that Articles 18 and 20 TFEU were used in *Martínez Sala*, *Bidar* and Case C-456/02 *Trojani v Centre public d'aide sociale de Bruxelles (CPAS)* [2004] ECR I-7573, whereas Articles 18 and 21 TFEU were applied in *Pusa*, *Chen*, *de Cuyper*, and *Tas-Hagen*; see also, the discussion in E Spaventa, n6, 16–22.

[126] Case C-293/03 *My v Office national des pensions (ONP)* [2004] ECR I-12013, para. 32.

unlikely to be relevant in the former scenario and is impossible in the latter under international law. Thus while the genuine enjoyment test was adopted instead of a mobility test, an overarching protection against differential treatment can still be argued into focus: Belgian nationals with Belgian parents face no such threat of deprivation of the genuine enjoyment of the substance of their EU citizenship rights. Applying discrimination-based analysis to *Ruiz Zambrano* does, at one level, reconcile the substantive outcome in the case with the Court's subsequent decisions in *McCarthy* and *Dereci*—none of the claimants there was in the more precarious position of the Ruiz Zambrano children since there was at least one EU national parent involved.[127] The Opinion of AG Kokott in *McCarthy* is also worth including in this context. Consistently with *Garcia Avello*, AG Kokott recognized the legal relevance of Mrs McCarthy's dual nationality but continued as follows:

> [T]he issue is whether ... the position of Union citizens differs, in view of their dual nationality, in a legally relevant way from the situation of other Union citizens who are nationals of the host Member State only ... The right at issue here, namely the right of residence of Union citizens, for themselves and their family members, serves to facilitate free movement of Union citizens within the territory of the Member States. In this connection, *no particular factors arise from the dual nationality of a Union citizen in Mrs McCarthy's position*. From the point of view of the law on residence, *she is in the same situation as all other British nationals who have always lived in England and never left their country of origin*: she does not exercise her right of free movement.[128]

I have argued above and elsewhere[129] that there are critical flaws in both the *McCarthy* and *Dereci* judgments; and the application of discrimination analysis would not have saved the claimants in either case. But if the Court did believe (even wrongly, recalling the incomplete picture of Mrs McCarthy's family situation, in particular) that no *differential* treatment existed—compared to a static British national holding just one passport, in that case—that would bring a sort of coherence, at least, to a troubled turn in the case law. Given what was at stake for the Union citizens actually involved, however, it is cold comfort.

Equal treatment thus brings a valuable added dimension to EU citizenship, but it is still not enough to overcome the systemic fragmentary effects of recent case law. In fact, in some ways, the discussion in this subsection highlights the unfairness of some of the outcomes presented in subsection (a) even more strongly: the Court has failed to explain why possible 'serious inconvenience' caused by surname format that *might* be experienced in the future is somehow more injurious than the serious inconvenience actually being faced by Mrs McCarthy, since she must now decide either to leave her home State or to remain there but without her husband. Linking back to the discussion in Chapter 3 on instrumental use of EU law, it is also worth asking: even if Mrs McCarthy or any of the Union citizens in *Dereci* are in a

[127] A fundamental flaw in any attempt to read *Ruiz Zambrano* through a lens of differential treatment must be acknowledged, however—no mention of possible justification arguments was made anywhere in the judgment.

[128] AG Kokott in *McCarthy*, paras 35 and 37 of the Opinion (emphasis added).

[129] Nic Shuibhne, n15.

position to reside temporarily in another Member State without much inconvenience at all, and thereby to effect purely instrumental movement by relocating temporarily to another State, is it really better to urge EU citizens to animate the protection of their rights through this patently staged route? Why must we continue pretending that never residing in another Member State and residing elsewhere 'on purpose' for a brief period of time are materially different? On a more practical note, how long would any of them need to stay away from their home States: would the three-month window for unconditional residence provided by Article 6 of Directive 2004/38 be enough? Would less time suffice? The Court may have been trying to contain the impact of *Ruiz Zambrano* in *McCarthy* and *Dereci*, but it is actually more likely that further facts-specific questions will come through multiple preliminary references instead.

As a final reflection, it should be asked whether the two conditions recognized in the case law to date—loss of Member State nationality and forced departure from the territory of the Union—set an appropriate threshold for review of otherwise internal situations. With respect to more systematic piercing of the purely internal shield, van der Mei rightly reminds us of the landslide constitutional consequences:

> The command not to discriminate would harmonise national rules and policies in areas in which they have not empowered the EU to harmonise or not yet accepted common norms. The EU ban on nationality discrimination was never meant to play such a 'harmonizing' role. It was, and is, merely meant as an instrument to curtail Member States' freedom of decision-making and to fight national protectionism, in whatever form.[130]

The conceptual awkwardness and potential futility of reverse discrimination in a Union framed by citizenship—the tension that opposes van der Mei's view—brings us back to the driver of protecting fundamental rights. It is the de facto benchmark against which the altered scope of EU citizenship is contemplated and it is the pivotal issue around which the next phase in the evolution of EU citizenship rights and free movement law more generally will be played out.[131] It is certainly a significant part of the context within which national courts and tribunals are framing citizenship questions.[132] But it is not, as emphasized repeatedly, a straightforward dynamic. The citizenship case law has reached a point where the scope of

[130] Van der Mei, n110, 80.

[131] See e.g. O'Leary, n6, who concludes her chapter as follows (at 122): '[t]he combination of Union citizenship and the EU's general commitment to fundamental rights has already . . . proved to be a potent one. If one adds to that combination a general principle of equality which is proving to have far-reaching substantive and procedural effects and a comprehensive, loosely-framed Charter which is now recognised as having equal legal value to the Treaties, the difficulties which the Court will face in future in determining the confines of EU law and applying the purely internal rule become patent. It is, in this context, both reductive to think of the status of Union citizenship purely in terms of free movement and excessive to suppose that its introduction mandates the Court abandoning a rule whose *raison d'être* remains valid, if not essential, in a legal order based on attributed competences'.

[132] At the time of writing, see e.g. Case C-87/12 *Ymeraga and others v Minister for Labour, Employment and Immigration*, judgment of 8 May 2013; Case C-86/12 *Alopka v Ministre du Travail, de l'Emploi et de l'Immigration*, pending (which includes a specific question on the scope of the 'genuine enjoyment' test; Opinion of AG Mengozzi delivered on 21 March 2013); Case C-45/12 *ONAFTS v Ahmed*, pending; and Case C-300/11 *ZZ v Secretary of State for the Home Department*, pending.

primary rights is increasingly infused with a parallel concern about articulating constitutional limits. The triangular relationship between these overlapping dynamics—citizenship, fundamental rights, and general principles of EU law—is now being reconstituted in the case law. In many respects, what you think of the results is intimately bound up with what you think about courts and their functions too.

5. Conclusion

The case law on purely internal situations can be summarized as follows. First, for all of the freedoms governing economic activity except the prohibition of customs duties, the case law formally aligns with the premise of the Treaty provisions, all of which require a cross-border i.e. *inter*-State element. Second, the Court has not reconciled its case law on Article 30 TFEU, which recognizes *intra*-State frontiers, with that more general approach; but neither has it extended the Article 30 rationale to other seams of free movement law. Third, the fact that past, present, *and* prospective movement can engage the Treaty has contributed along with other dynamics to the depletion of the substance of movement, meaning that it can be relatively easy to generate sufficient cross-border relevance for the purposes of defeating the purely internal rule. Finally, in limited and exceptional circumstances, the Court has recognized that EU citizenship rights can be relevant even in purely internal situations, an interpretation that is compatible with the Treaty but is deeply constitutionally sensitive.

The lines of case law that strain systemic coherence most intensely reflect the influence of two of the main fragmentation drivers. For the Article 30 case law, the key dynamic is the unsettled objectives of the internal market—Article 26 TFEU has been used to site the purely internal argument in directly opposing registers, depending on the interpretation applied to an underpinning market vision. The recent case law on citizenship powerfully illustrates the mixed constitutional signals coded into the Charter and the Court's conflicted attitude towards preserving the fundamental rights standards it had already established. The difficult trajectory unfolding at present thus raises difficult questions about who *owns* constitutional case law.

It is irrefutable that the Treaty demands a cross-border connection in almost all circumstances. Whether the thresholds set for the exceptions to that rule in connection with Union citizenship rights are the right ones is an important but discrete question. The broader concern is that if the substance of the cross-border condition has been depleted to the extent that the law reaches too far into de facto static situations, that momentum must be corrected. Recalibrating the purpose and function of movement as a marker of differential treatment was advocated as a partial solution. The untapped potential of discrimination as a general principle of EU law will feature again in Chapters 6 and 7, drawing thematic links between what should be excluded from and what should fall within the meaning of restrictions on free movement rights. The third tension identified in Section 1 thus merits restating as a bridge to the opening up of that discussion in Chapter 5: how do we ensure that the exclusionary application of a purely internal rule in *some* cases is not arbitrary, given that the free movement framework also accepts a *potential* impact on movement as a legitimate factor for the purposes of connecting a situation to EU law?

5

Between Negative and Positive Scope? The Principles of *De Minimis* and Remoteness

1. Introduction

Up to this point, while the shape of the positive scope of the Treaty has been coming into focus, the discussion has concentrated on its negative scope i.e. on principles that can take situations possibly impinging on free movement rights beyond the Treaty's reach. The principles of *de minimis* and remoteness raise questions about whether a situation conceivably restricting free movement rights amounts to *enough* to warrant the Treaty's prohibitive force. A *de minimis* test would set a quantitative appreciability threshold below which free movement law could not be engaged even if the elements otherwise required to constitute a free movement restriction are in place. Remoteness questions the adequacy of the link between cause and effect: is the alleged restriction of EU rights properly *connected* to the national rule or practice being challenged? In other words, *de minimis* would apply when a situation is connected to EU law but is too minor for EU law to bother with; but remoteness is about situations that are not connected to EU law in the first place.

This chapter looks at the development and extent of application of both tests in the free movement case law. The Court does use an inadvisable multiplicity of adjectives, phrases, and tests in both contexts, but that practice is not the main cause of case law fragmentation—it will be argued that a relatively consistent understanding of the remoteness test, in particular, can still be distilled. What is more problematic is that, first, both tests tend to be applied erratically or inconsistently in a more substantive sense; and, second, there is a problem at the level of 'conceptual spillage' i.e. an appropriate conceptual distinction between the purposes of the principles has not been properly maintained. It will then be argued that these problems raise broader systemic concerns when trying to understand how *de minimis* and remoteness delimit the positive scope of the free movement provisions. For example, how does the generally established preclusion of a *de minimis* rule in free movement law sit with the convention that a reduction in the volume of imports is not usually sufficient to attract the Article 34 TFEU prohibition on quantitative restrictions? Similarly, how are the discouragement, deterrence, and dissuasion strands of free movement law, prevalent in the sphere of prospective or potential movement, reconciled with the remoteness benchmark of uncertainty? The main objective of the chapter is to flesh out the principles of *de minimis* and remoteness on their own terms before then addressing these systemic questions more fully in Chapters 6 and 7.

De minimis and remoteness are distinguished from the exclusionary rules considered in Chapters 3 and 4 through the suggestion that they sit in an intermediate conceptual space between negative and positive scope: they are neither fully fledged, what-based exclusionary rules, nor exclusively inherent elements of the pivotal restrictions test that stems from *Dassonville*.[1] They share the delimiting impulse of the purely internal rule (Chapter 4). But their place and function as principles in the framework of free movement law also needs to be reframed within the current trajectories of case law on the positive scope of free movement rights (Chapters 6 and 7). In Section 2, it will be shown that the Court preserves a general presumption against the operation of a *de minimis* rule in free movement, but concurrently applies what do seem to be appreciability thresholds in some case law pockets. The fact and implications of conceptual spillage are then introduced, showing that quantitative elements of *de minimis* are frequently merged with remoteness-type concerns. The main features of remoteness are examined in Section 3, with particular focus on its dominant expression as an 'effects too uncertain and indirect' test. Setting up Chapter 6, Section 4 then addresses whether *de minimis* and remoteness (should) have independent case law life as what-based exclusionary rules[2] or whether their extraction from the determination of positive scope is neither possible nor useful.[3] In order to move beyond the intermediate space described above, it will be argued that *de minimis,* remoteness, and the interplay between them need to be rationalized more coherently; and that this is better done in the context of positive scope i.e. as part of the work needed to refine the definition of a restriction on free movement rights.

2. Too little: is there a *de minimis* test in EU free movement law?

In this section, an overview of the basis for the presumption that a *de minimis* threshold does *not* apply in free movement law will first be presented. Two issues will then be addressed in more detail: first, empirical challenges to that received wisdom; and, second, the blurring of *de minimis* and remoteness—introducing the idea of conceptual spillage but also its practical implications.

(a) Free movement and *de minimis*: the case against

The application of a *de minimis* test is most commonly associated with case law on the competition rules and with the economic and statistical thresholds applied in

[1] Case 8/74 *Procureur du Roi v Dassonville* [1974] ECR 837.

[2] E.g. T Horsley, 'Unearthing Buried Treasure: Art 34 TFEU and the Exclusionary Rules' (2012) 37:6 ELRev 734.

[3] E.g. P Oliver, 'Of trailers and jet skis: Is the case law on Article 34 TFEU hurtling in a new direction?' (2009) 33 Fordham Int'l L.J. 1423 at 1432.

that case law, primarily for the purposes of market definition.[4] In the context of Article 101 TFEU, the Court first articulated the *de minimis* principle as a threshold of appreciability in *Société Technique Minière*,[5] but its subsequent expression in *Völk* works particularly well for comparison with the development of free movement law:

If an agreement is to be capable of affecting trade between Member States it must be possible to foresee with a sufficient degree of probability on the basis of a set of objective factors of law or of fact that the agreement in question *may have an influence, direct or indirect, actual or potential, on the pattern of trade between Member States in such a way that it might hinder the attainment of the objectives of a single market between States.* Moreover the prohibition in Article [101](1) is applicable only if the agreement in question also has *as its object or effect the prevention, restriction or distortion* of competition within the Common Market. Those conditions must be understood by reference to the actual circumstances of the agreement. Consequently an agreement falls outside the prohibition in Article [101] when it has *only an insignificant effect on the markets,* taking into account the *weak position which the persons concerned have on the market* of the product in question. Thus an exclusive dealing agreement, even with absolute territorial protection, may, having regard to the weak position of the persons concerned on the market in the products in question in the area covered by the absolute protection, escape the prohibition laid down in Article [101](1).[6]

This passage provides the DNA not just for the rules on distortion of competition but also for the fundamentals of free movement law: with one critical difference. In *Dassonville*, the Court imported (for Article 34 TFEU) the idea that '[a]ll trading rules enacted by Member States which are capable of hindering, *directly or indirectly, actually or potentially*, intra-Community trade are to be considered as measures having an effect equivalent to quantitative restrictions'.[7] But that judgment was silent with respect to the market power dimension of the competition framework for the purposes of delimiting the scope of free movement law.[8]

The next step was the decision in *Groenveld*, where the Court also brought the 'object or effect' criterion from *Völk* into free movement law.[9] But it then took a

[4] Guidance on market share thresholds can be found in the Commission notice on agreements of minor importance which do not appreciably restrict competition under Article 81(1) of the Treaty establishing the European Community (*de minimis*), 2001 OJ C368/13.

[5] Case 56/65 *Société Technique Minière (L.T.M.) v Maschinenbau Ulm GmbH (M.B.U.)* [1966] ECR 337.

[6] Case 5/69 *Völk v S.P.R.L. Ets J. Vervaecke* [1969] ECR 295, para. 5 (emphasis added).

[7] *Dassonville*, para. 5 (emphasis added).

[8] The market power angle of *Völk* finds further resonance in the discussion on the horizontal scope of free movement rights, outlined in Chapter 3. Although the *Dassonville* test was formulated for Article 34 and the free movement of goods specifically, the 'direct or indirect, actual or potential' formula will be used here as shorthand for how the Court defines restrictions on free movement rights more generally; see e.g. AG Sharpston in *Ruiz Zambrano*, who discussed the scope of restrictions on free movement rights in a similar way, drawing from both personal and 'classic economic' case law (Case C-34/09 *Ruiz Zambrano v Office national de l'emploi (ONEm)* [2011] ECR I-1177, paras 69–78 of the Opinion).

[9] Case 15/79 *PB Groenveld BV v Produktschap voor Vee en Vlees* [1979] ECR 3409, para. 7. At the time, the phrase was explicitly tied to *discriminatory* effects but that limitation has fallen away (see e.g. Case C-110/05 *Commission v Italy (Trailers)* [2009] ECR I 519, para. 37; this point is discussed further in Chapter 7).

definitively different view on the relevance of appreciability in *van de Haar*. To establish whether national legislation that imposed fixed pricing on the sale of tobacco products was a quantitative restriction within the meaning of Article 34, the referring court framed its questions explicitly around the similarities between the definition of a quantitative restriction in *Dassonville* and agreements affecting trade in the case law on Article 101, asking inter alia whether the threshold of appreciability applied as part of the latter framework should also be applied in free movement law. The Commission, noting the shared—and fundamental—objectives of competition and free movement law, observed initially (on the 'may affect trade' limb of the Article 101 test) that 'the terms, purpose and context of the provisions in question militate against the application of different criteria for determining whether it is a question of a measure having equivalent effect hindering intra-Community trade or a measure affecting trade between Member States within the meaning of Article [101] of the Treaty'.[10] But then, specifically addressing the *de minimis* question and noting the Court's consistent emphasis on the wide scope of Article 34 TFEU, it submitted that 'in such a system there is no place for a *de minimis* rule whereby Article [34] would not be applied to an existing *and ascertainable* restrictive effect on imports because it was so slight. It must also be remembered that to define a slight effect is extremely difficult'.[11]

Following that premise, and distinguishing between the intended private and public reach of the competition and free movement rules respectively,[12] the Court confirmed a different preference for free movement law:

Article [34] of the Treaty does not distinguish between measures having an effect equivalent to quantitative restrictions according to the *degree* to which trade between Member States is affected. If a national measure is *capable of hindering imports* it must be regarded as a measure having an effect equivalent to a quantitative restriction, *even though the hindrance is slight* and even though it is possible for imported products to be marketed in other ways.[13]

That decision has been reinforced in case law on the scope of free movement restrictions ever since, with a strong degree of consistency and using either the same[14] or essentially similar[15] language. The irrelevance of *de minimis* across the

[10] Joined Cases 177/82 and 178/82 *Criminal proceedings against van de Haar and Kaveka de Meern BV* [1984] ECR 1797 at 1805.

[11] *Van de Haar*, 1807 (emphasis added; the reference to 'ascertainable effect' is an early remoteness point).

[12] The extent to which private reach is relevant for Article 34 TFEU is discussed in Chapter 3.

[13] *Van de Haar*, para. 13 (emphasis added). Reflecting concern for systemic coherence, AG Reischl had also pointed out (at 1823) that no *de minimis* rule had been applied in case law on customs duties and charges having equivalent effect, citing Joined Cases 52 and 55/65 *Federal Republic of Germany v Commission of the European Economic Community* [1966] ECR 159 and Case 2/73 *Riseria Luigi Geddo v Ente Nazionale Risi* [1973] ECR 865.

[14] E.g. Case C-463/01 *Commission v Germany* [2004] ECR I-11705, para. 63.

[15] E.g. on Article 34 TFEU, Case 16/83 *Criminal proceedings against Prantl* [1984] ECR 1299, para. 20 ('it is sufficient that the measures in question are liable to impede, directly or indirectly, actually or potentially, trade between the Member States. It is not necessary that they should have an appreciable effect on intra-Community trade'), Case C-105/91 *Commission v Greece* [1992] ECR I-5871, para. 20 ('a Member State is guilty of a failure to fulfil its obligations under the Treaty regardless of the frequency or the scale of the circumstances complained of'), and Case C-126/91

entire span of free movement law—arguably entrenching its character as a what-based exclusionary rule—was emphasized by the Court in *Corsica Ferries*: 'the articles of the . . . Treaty concerning the free movement of goods, persons, services and capital are fundamental [Union] provisions and *any restriction, even minor*, of that freedom is prohibited'.[16] The circumstances of the *Bluhme* case—involving a national decision on the keeping of bees on the Danish island of Læsø, the effects of which concerned just 0.3 per cent of the national territory—are frequently cited as the archetypal demonstration of the absence of an appreciability threshold in free movement law.[17] In its decision, the Court focused more on submissions about the hypothetical and uncertain nature of the alleged restrictions on free movement law, but AG Fennelly had drawn from the reasoning in *van de Haar* and, importantly, cautioned against 'confus[ing] scale with remoteness': against conflating, in other words, the principles of *de minimis* and remoteness.[18] In the *Spanish strawberries* case, discussed in Chapter 3, AG Lenz touched upon *de minimis* questions in a way that had perhaps blended the considerations that AG Fennelly was later concerned to separate out:

It is beyond question that the violent acts at issue here directly obstructed imports of goods from other Member States. The fact that the volume of those imports may nevertheless have remained constant is therefore irrelevant. Moreover, it equally cannot be ruled out that those imports would have reached a higher volume if the acts of violence in question had not occurred. At the hearing before the Court, the French Government's representative stated that, in 1994, of 170000 tonnes of strawberries imported into France from Spain, only eight tonnes were destroyed, which was equivalent to 0.005%. However, that does not in any way alter the fact that the acts of violence *directly obstructed* imports of goods from other Member States. The seriousness of the incidents alone means that no importance whatsoever can be attached to the fact that the volume of goods actually destroyed may have been *relatively insignificant.*[19]

Schutzverband gegen Unwesen in der Wirtschaft eV v Yves Rocher GmbH [1993] ECR 1-2361, para. 21 ('Article [34] of the Treaty does not make a distinction between measures which can be described as measures having equivalent effect to a quantitative restriction according to the magnitude of the effects they have on trade within the Community'); on Article 49 TFEU, Case 270/83 *Commission v France (avoir fiscal)* [1986] ECR 273, para. 21 ('Article 52 prohibits all discrimination, even if only of a limited nature'); and on Article 56 TFEU, Case C-76/90 *Säger v Dennemeyer & Co. Ltd* [1991] ECR I-4221, para. 12 ('Article [56] requires not only the elimination of all discrimination against a person providing services on the ground of his nationality but also the abolition of any restriction').

[16] Case C-49/89 *Corsica Ferries France v Direction générale des douanes françaises* [1989] ECR 4441, para. 8 (emphasis added); confirmed in e.g. Case C-212/06 *Government of the French Community and Walloon Government v Flemish Government* [2008] ECR I-1683, para. 52.

[17] Case C-67/97 *Criminal proceedings against Bluhme* [1998] ECR I-8033.

[18] AG Fennelly in *Bluhme*, para. 19 of the Opinion. In his subsequent Opinion in *Imperial Tobacco*, AG Fennelly argued that '*harmonising* action should relate to national rules which have *more than trivial effects* on trade' (AG Fennelly in Case C-74/99 *The Queen v Secretary of State for Health and Others, ex parte Imperial Tobacco Ltd and others* [2000] ECR I-8599, para. 104 of the Opinion, emphasis added); cf. the approach of the Court in e.g. Joined Cases C-465/00, C-138/01 and C-139/01 *Rechnungshof, Neukomm and Lauermann v Österreichischer Rundfunk and others* [2003] ECR I-4989, para. 41.

[19] AG Lenz in Case C-265/95 *Commission v France (Spanish strawberries)* [1997] ECR I-6959, para. 16 of the Opinion (emphasis added).

The statistical kernel of this extract reflects the reasoning in *Bluhme*; but the Advocate General's concern with the *directness* of the obstruction is connected more to questions about remoteness, a point picked up in Section 3.[20]

It was shown in Chapter 3 that in order to be considered as a worker within the meaning of EU law, a person must pursue 'effective and genuine activities, with the exception of those . . . on such a small scale as to be regarded as purely marginal and ancillary'.[21] That test was examined in Chapter 3 from the perspective of the relevance of the worker's motivation. But can the prescribed criteria be reconciled with the Court's rejection of a *de minimis* test in free movement law generally? There is an imprint of *van de Haar* spirit, at least, in the relevant case law, since a low volume of either hours or remuneration would not be sufficient per se to preclude someone from being treated as a worker.[22] The Court normally leaves determination of the facts in these cases to the referring court, though it has derived a presumption that someone *was* a worker because it was provided with no steer to the contrary.[23] In two cases where the quantitative make-up of the applicants' employment profiles was explicitly questioned by the referring courts, the Court engaged in more extensive discussion of the *qualitative* factors of the employment relationships at issue, emphasizing that quantitative factors alone could not determine whether persons were workers or not. In other words, the Court dodged the issue by focusing on the 'real and genuine' and not the 'marginal and ancillary' angle.[24]

As a final preliminary point, it can be recalled that questions about the level of work undertaken were classified in Chapter 3 as who-based exclusionary rules, as they necessarily have to be addressed before consideration of whether or not a restriction on the relevant worker's rights then exists. In that sense, they are *entry-portal criteria*. The application of *de minimis*, on the other hand, becomes relevant after (or at least alongside) establishing that the elements needed to constitute a restriction are otherwise in place—making it more of an *exit-portal criterion*. This distinction demonstrates how the *de minimis* test thus has some relevance as *both* an exclusionary rule and an inherent element of the positive definition of a restriction on free movement rights—a point developed further below.

[20] For a critique of the way in which the limited geographical scope of the measure in *Bluhme* seemed, however, to be relevant for AG Fennelly in his discussion of the justification of the restriction, see P Oliver, 'Some further reflections on the scope of Articles 28–30 (ex 30–36) EC', (1999) 36:4 CMLRev 783 at 792–3.

[21] Case C-213/05 *Geven v Land Nordrhein-Westfalen* [2007] ECR I-5347, para. 16.

[22] See e.g. Case 53/81 *Levin v Staatssecretaris van Justitie* [1982] ECR 1035, paras 15–16; Case 139/85 *Kempf v Staatssecretaris van Justitie* [1986] ECR 1741, paras 2 and 16.

[23] See e.g. Case C-337/10 *Neidel v Stadt Frankfurt am Main*, judgment of 3 May 2012, para. 24.

[24] Case C-444/93 *Megner and Scheffel v Innungskrankenkasse Vorderpfalz* [1995] ECR I-4741 and Case C-14/09 *Genc v Land Berlin* [2010] ECR I-931. In situations where it might be considered that the relevant activities *are* marginal and ancillary, it has been suggested that individuals could nevertheless be brought within the scope of EU law as job-seekers; see e.g. the discussion by AG Cruz Villalón in Case C-367/11 *Prete v Office national de l'emploi*, judgment of 25 October 2012, paras 19–26 of the Opinion.

(b) Challenges to the status quo

Two main challenges to the prevailing presumptions outlined in subsection (a) will be considered here: the explicit argument in favour of a *de minimis* test developed by AG Jacobs in *Leclerc-Siplec*;[25] and more scattered case law examples that, together, suggest an obliquely operative *de minimis* test.

The most significant questioning of the preclusion of *de minimis* considerations from free movement law came from AG Jacobs in the aftermath of the decision in *Keck*.[26] In *Keck*, the Court sought to reorient the centre of gravity of Article 34 TFEU around inter-State trade and the prevention of protectionism.[27] It thus redrew the outer limits of the *Dassonville* test by stating that 'certain selling arrangements' fell outwith the scope of Article 34 'so long as those provisions apply to all relevant traders operating within the national territory and so long as they affect in the same manner, in law and in fact, the marketing of domestic products and of those from other Member States'.[28] The Court observed that the application of such rules does 'not by nature... prevent... access to the market or... impede access any more than it impedes the access of domestic products'.[29] The brief reference to market access here did not override the decision's primary emphasis on catching discriminatory measures—against the trajectory of case law on the other sectors of free movement and arguably against the foundational decision of *Dassonville* itself. The decision in *Keck* thus hardened a binary rift both within and beyond the Court: distinguishing those who supported the judgment's renewal of the significance and import of discrimination, and those who critiqued it as a retrograde step that improperly prevented the application of the market access principle to Article 34.

More nuanced debates on the scope of free movement law will be addressed in Chapters 6 and 7, but the summary above provides a backdrop for AG Jacobs' Opinion in *Leclerc-Siplec*, delivered just under a year after the judgment in *Keck* and in which he argued strongly for the (re)instatement of a market access approach to the free movement of goods. Crucially, he also accepted that the introduction of a *de minimis* test was 'of course' the corollary of his proposal on the basis of 'a need to limit the scope of Article [34] in order to prevent excessive interference in the regulatory powers of the Member States'[30]—thereby capturing both the delimiting influence of *de minimis* and the constitutional risks of *unchecked* market access as a foundational principle for free movement law. The framework he sketched was

[25] Case C-412/93 *Société d'Importation Edouard Leclerc-Siplec v TF1 Publicité SA and M6 Publicité SA* [1995] ECR I-179.

[26] Joined Cases C-267/91 and C-268/91 *Criminal Proceedings against Keck and Mithouard* [1993] ECR I-6097.

[27] *Keck and Mithouard*, para. 14, in which the Court referred to 'the increasing tendency of traders to invoke Article [34] as a means of challenging any rules whose effect is to limit their commercial freedom even where such rules are not aimed at products from other Member States'.

[28] *Keck and Mithouard*, para. 16. [29] *Keck and Mithouard*, para. 17.

[30] AG Jacobs in *Leclerc-Siplec*, para. 42 of the Opinion.

(and still is) supported by academic commentators.[31] But it also engaged concerns; for example, apart from noting that 'it will be necessary to define carefully the circumstances in which [a *de minimis* test] should apply',[32] AG Jacobs did not suggest the actual thresholds that would need to be met for his own proposed test.[33] However, he did emphasize that a *de minimis* test would only be relevant in the absence of discrimination, for the following reasons:

> The impact on access to the market of measures applicable without distinction may vary greatly, depending on the nature of the measure in issue. Where such a measure prohibits the sale of goods lawfully placed on the market in another Member State . . . it may be *presumed to have a substantial impact on access* to the market, since the goods are *either denied access altogether* or can *gain access only after being modified* in some way; the need to modify goods is itself a substantial barrier to market access. Where, on the other hand, a measure applicable without distinction simply restricts certain selling arrangements, by stipulating when, where, how, by whom or at what price goods may be sold, its impact will depend on a number of factors, such as whether it applies to certain goods . . . or to most goods . . . or to all goods (as in *Keck*), on the extent to which other selling arrangements remain available, and on whether the effect of the measure is direct or indirect, immediate or remote, or purely speculative and uncertain. Accordingly, the magnitude of the barrier to market access may vary enormously: it may range from the insignificant to a quasi-prohibition. Clearly, this is where a *de minimis* test could perform a useful function.[34]

He also cast doubt on the certainty with which *van de Haar* had been interpreted as an absolute rejection of the relevance of *de minimis* since: '[the Court] went on to rule, in the same judgment, that a price-fixing regulation is contrary to Article [34] only if prices are fixed *at such a level* as to prevent imported goods from being marketed profitably or to cancel out a competitive advantage enjoyed by the manufacturer of imported products. That is not very different, in effect, from saying that Article [34] only comes into play if there is a *substantial barrier to market access*'.[35]

Oliver has argued that the Court's approach in *Keck* is preferable to the *de minimis* test proposed by AG Jacobs for two main reasons: '(i) while a *de minimis* rule entails the evaluation of complex economic data, the Court's approach is "rule-based" and thus far easier for national courts to apply; and (ii) the *de minimis* test entails tolerating restrictions which may have harsh effects on a group of traders or consumers, just because that group is small; in contrast, the Court's approach could only very rarely, if ever, produce such an unfortunate result'.[36] The second argument is a powerful deterrent; but the first point is worth looking at in more

[31] E.g. S Weatherill, 'After Keck: Some thoughts on how to clarify the clarification' (1996) 33:5 CMLRev 885; see further, Chapter 7.

[32] AG Jacobs in *Leclerc-Siplec*, para. 42 of the Opinion.

[33] E.g. Oliver, n20, 797 ('the Advocate General did not suggest a specific yardstick for applying the test: questions such as to how the market is to be defined and the length of the period to be considered are not broached in his Opinion').

[34] AG Jacobs in *Leclerc-Siplec*, paras 44–45 of the Opinion (emphasis added).

[35] AG Jacobs in *Leclerc-Siplec*, para. 46 of the Opinion (emphasis added).

[36] Oliver, n20, 799.

detail. Raising a similar concern about the inadvisability of shifting to a system based on complex economic assessments, Davies has argued as follows:

> [I]f market effects are to be the basis of [free movement] law, and that is to be taken seriously, then empirical market investigation becomes the heart of the legal process. This would be a disaster. Competition law is largely a game played between large companies and the government, and the choice to pay for economic reports is one that they all broadly agree on... Free movement law is more often about the smaller actor and the state, litigated in lower courts, and if it is not accessible and reasonably speedy and affordable then it will become ineffective law. Market investigation as a standard part of the free movement litigation process is not a viable option.[37]

Davies asserts that the practical consequences of a pronounced shift to *de minimis* would be immense and should not be underestimated: the way in which free movement law has developed in practice is precisely part of its success and it is also a big part of why the doctrines of primacy and direct effect have a degree of real impact, notwithstanding their alien nature vis-à-vis many national (especially dualist) constitutional orders. Moreover, the way in which Oliver supports the same viewpoint has particular relevance for the idea of coherence as an element of constitutional responsibility: 'the Court's guiding principle should surely be legal certainty, without which national courts will be lost, as indeed they were in the years preceding *Keck*. To introduce economic assessment on a case by case basis, whether it be for the purpose of a *de minimis* test or for establishing discrimination or to any other end, would surely be courting disaster in terms of legal certainty'.[38] In fact, AG Jacobs made a similar point himself in a later Opinion. Discussing the relationship between Articles 34 and 110 (on discriminatory internal taxation) TFEU, and commenting specifically on *de minimis* and Article 34, the Advocate General observed that 'in defining such a threshold, it would seem impossible to meet the necessary requirements of practical applicability and legal certainty without selecting some purely arbitrary criterion'.[39]

Putting these cautions to one side for the moment, it is clear that in recent case law on rules regulating the use of goods, discussed in Chapter 7, and also in other areas of free movement law, as will be seen just below, the threshold of substantial impact *is* now part of the framework of evaluation. However, it is also clear that the Court applies a qualitative and intuitive rather than data-based and quantitative assessment of that threshold, raising a critical question: is this an adjusted application of *de minimis*, as we understand it in EU law in the competition context, or is it something else? What we seem to have ended up with is a rule-based approach to *de minimis* that is not dependent on the evaluation of complex economic data; it is, in other words, a *de minimis* framework detached in form from its competition law roots and more attuned to the Court's usual approach to free movement law.

[37] G Davies, 'The Court's jurisprudence on free movement of goods: pragmatic presumptions, not philosophical principles' (2012) *European Journal of Consumer Law* 25 at 31.

[38] Oliver, n20, 806.

[39] AG Jacobs in Case C-383/01 *De Danske Bilimportører v Skatteministeriet, Told- og Skattestyrelsen* [2003] ECR I-6065, para. 61 of the Opinion.

Whether the resulting test reflects the best or worst of both worlds will be picked up again below.

Turning for now to the second point—more oblique applications of *de minimis* in free movement case law practice—there are several clusters of free movement decisions in which the Court seems to apply an appreciability threshold: without reconciling that decision with the more generally confirmed preclusion set by *van de Haar*. First, for Article 34 TFEU (and aside from case law on rules regulating the use of goods, addressed separately in Chapter 7), the Court included the following statement in *Burmanjer*:

> [T]he information available to the Court does not enable it to establish with certainty whether the national rules on itinerant sales affect the marketing of products from Member States other than the Kingdom of Belgium to any greater degree than that of products from that State. *Nevertheless*, it seems to follow from the information in the file transmitted to the Court that, if those rules did have such an effect, it would be *too insignificant and uncertain* to be regarded as being such as *to hinder or otherwise interfere with trade* between Member States.[40]

Leaving the 'uncertainty' limb to one side for the moment, since it reflects the *de minimis*/remoteness conceptual spillage introduced in subsection (c), it is difficult to decouple the idea of 'too insignificant' from appreciability. The Court was even willing to contemplate the application of that threshold in the event of discrimination, going completely against the grain of AG Jacobs' reasoning in *Leclerc-Siplec*. The Court has never repeated or otherwise commented on this paragraph of the judgment in *Burmanjer*, even though the case has been frequently cited in other contexts.[41] It was picked up by AG Kokott in *UTECA*,[42] however, as discussed in subsection (c). It was also cited by AG Bot in *Trailers*, as evidence for, in his view, a new and distinct 'wholly insignificant effects' test.[43]

If the *Burmanjer* case provides an example of apparent *de minimis* reasoning that did not have concrete effects in the case at hand, an actual application and not just invocation of appreciability was effected in *Viacom Outdoor* in the context of restrictions on the provision of services.[44] Considering the effects of an Italian municipal tax imposed on outdoor advertising, levied here in connection with

[40] Case C-20/03 *Criminal Proceedings against Burmanjer, van der Linden and De Jong* [2005] ECR I-4133, para. 31 (emphasis added).

[41] E.g. as an authority on how to decide between the application of the Treaty provisions on goods and services (Case C-108/09 *Ker-Optika bt v ÀNTSZ Dél-dunántúli Regionális Intézete* [2010] ECR I-12213, para. 43); on the role of the national court in the application of proportionality (e.g. AG Poiares Maduro in Case C-434/04 *Criminal proceedings against Ahokainen and Leppik* [2006] ECR I-9171, para. 32 of the Opinion).

[42] Case C-222/07 *Unión de Televisiones Comerciales Asociadas (UTECA) v Administración General del Estado* [2009] ECR I-1407.

[43] AG Bot in *Commission v Italy (Trailers)*, para. 117 of the Opinion. The Advocate General distinguished this principle from hypothetical effects and also from 'totally uncertain and indirect effects' or remoteness; cf. Horsley, who also discusses 'insignificant effects' as a distinct category but argues that there is no difference in reality between its application and that of 'effects too uncertain and indirect', the test considered in Section 3 (Horsley, n2, 748–9).

[44] Case C-134/03 *Viacom Outdoor Srl v Giotto Immobilier SARL* [2005] ECR I-1167.

bill-posting carried out by Viacom on behalf of a property sales company established in France, the Court first rehearsed the general statement that Article 56 TFEU 'requires the elimination of *any restriction* of the freedom to provide services, even if it applies to national providers of services and to those of other Member States alike, when it is liable to prohibit or otherwise impede the activities of a provider of services established in another Member State where he lawfully provides similar services'.[45] Having established that the tax in question was levied without any discrimination, the Court continued:

> [S]uch a tax is applied only to outdoor advertising activities involving the use of public space administered by the municipal authorities and its amount is fixed *at a level which may be considered modest in relation to the value of the services provided* which are subject to it. *In those circumstances*, the levying of such a tax is not on any view liable to prohibit, impede or otherwise make less attractive the provision of advertising services to be carried out in the territory of the municipalities concerned, including the case in which the provision of services is of a cross-border nature on account of the place of establishment of either the provider or the recipient of the services.[46]

In her Opinion, AG Kokott had posited two options: the levy either fell outside the scope of free movement law altogether as an indistinctly applicable tax measure; or it fell within its scope, on account of its municipal rather than general nature, but was justifiable. Both outcomes would find support in existing lines of case law. But the Court's focus on the 'modest' nature of the charge seems to have come from nowhere. Like *Burmanjer*, it also seems to have *gone* nowhere in subsequent case law, apart from AG Kokott's comment in *Régie Networks*, again addressing a special tax on advertising transmitted through radio and television broadcasting, that 'the amount of the tax should not weigh so strongly in the balance as to have the effect of restricting freedom to provide services'.[47] Later, however, in *Presidente del Consiglio dei Ministri*, she reverted to her original argument that non-discriminatory taxes should fall outwith the scope of free movement law altogether.[48] That argument also fits with an established line of case law holding that 'measures, the only effect of which is to create additional costs in respect of the service in question and which affect in the same way the provision of services between Member States and that within one Member State, do not fall within the scope of Article [59] of the Treaty'.[49] More generally, *Viacom* tends to be cited as authority for a different proposition: that 'it is essential that the referring court provide at the very least some explanation of the reasons for the choice of the [Union] provisions which it requires to be interpreted and of the link it establishes between those provisions and the

[45] *Viacom*, para. 35 (emphasis added). [46] *Viacom*, para. 38 (emphasis added).

[47] AG Kokott in Case C-333/07 *Société Régie Networks v Direction de contrôle fiscal Rhône-Alpes Bourgogne* [2008] ECR I-10807, para. 119 of the Opinion.

[48] AG Kokott in Case C-169/08 *Presidente del Consiglio dei Ministri v Regione Sardegna* [2009] ECR I-10821, para. 50 (although she went on to demonstrate that the tax at issue in that case was not indistinctly applicable).

[49] Joined Cases C-544/03 and C-545/03 *Mobistar SA v Commune de Fléron; Belgacom Mobile SA v Commune de Schaerbeek* [2006] ECR I-6675, para. 31.

national legislation applicable to the dispute'.[50] Perhaps that omission, rather than the 'modesty' of the tax imposed, was the real target of the Court's decision.

Finally, a third line of case law, introduced in Chapter 4, turns on the requirement of demonstrating '*serious* inconvenience'. But the impact here goes further than either *Burmanjer* or *Viacom*, since a set of cases on one specific issue has generated a condition that is finding its way into generalized expressions of restrictions on personal free movement rights more broadly. Horsley traces the genesis of the test in free movement law back to *Konstantinidis*.[51] There, the Court held that national rules on the transcription of surnames could infringe the applicant's right to freedom of establishment 'only in so far as their application causes... *such a degree* of inconvenience as in fact to interfere with his freedom to exercise the right'.[52] Later, as shown in Chapter 4, the Court accepted that the potential *serious* inconvenience likely to be caused by national rules on the registration of surnames amounted to a restriction on the rights conferred by EU citizenship.[53] A more generic application of the serious inconvenience test was then effected in *McCarthy*[54]—also discussed in Chapter 4 and emphasized there as an unwelcome development from the perspective of free movement case law coherence.

If, recalling *Corsica Ferries*, *any* restriction of free movement, 'even minor', comes within the scope of the Treaty, then why is an appreciability threshold set—and accepted—in the 'serious inconvenience' case law? This test is not about causation: whatever inconvenience might be caused is clearly and properly linked to the national rules being challenged. What the Court demands is that a particular *level* of inconvenience must be actually or potentially suffered. But the resulting case law is openly at odds with the apparently retained exclusion of appreciability thresholds in free movement law more generally. In a recent Opinion on freedom of establishment, AG Sharpston presented the core issues as follows:

[W]hilst I can sympathise with the view that Article [49 TFEU] should not be concerned with *trifling regulatory effects*, and that it might be desirable for the Court to adopt an *explicitly coherent* approach, following its *Keck and Mithouard* line of case-law, with regard to all the fundamental freedoms guaranteed by the Treaty, I do not believe that such considerations can affect the relevance of Article [49] in the present case. As for the argument that the Court has, in certain judgments, stressed the *seriousness* of a particular interference with freedom of establishment, that fact does not mean that it has made the existence of a serious

[50] E.g. Case C-453/04 *innoventif Ltd* [2006] ECR I-4929, para. 26.

[51] Horsley, n2, 749 (though, again, he groups the relevant decisions under the umbrella of remoteness rather than appreciability); Case C-168/91*Konstantinidis v Stadt Altensteig—Standesamt and Landratsamt Calw—Ordnungsamt* [1993] ECR I-1191.

[52] *Konstantinidis*, para. 15 (emphasis added).

[53] See e.g. Case C-148/02 *Garcia Avello v Belgian State* [2003] ECR I-11613 and Case C-353/06 *Grunkin and Paul* [2008] ECR I-7639; but cf. the harder stance in Case C-208/09 *Sayn-Wittgenstein v Landeshauptmann von Wien* [2010] ECR I-13693 and Case C-391/09 *Runevič-Vardyn and Łukasz Paweł Wardyn v Vilniaus miesto savivaldybės administracija and others* [2011] ECR I-3787.

[54] Case C-434/09 *McCarthy v Secretary of State for the Home Department* [2011] ECR I-3375, paras 51 and 52.

interference *a condition* for the applicability of Article [49] EC, particularly when *it has not stressed that aspect systematically.*[55]

In contrast to the case law on establishment, however, the Court *has* rendered serious inconvenience as 'a condition for the applicability' of movement rights that stem from EU citizenship. This highlights the subjective and problematic challenge of how to determine 'serious' inconvenience in the first place, which was demonstrated in Chapter 4 through comparison of the apparently unacceptable inconvenience that might be caused in the future because of different surname formats (*Garcia Avello*) versus the acceptable inconvenience, in the eyes of the Court, of either living without your husband in your home State or uprooting your family to another State in order to live with him (*McCarthy*). This question is picked up again in Section 3. The broader point, reinforced by the parallel growth of case law on *substantial* restrictions of market access, discussed in Chapter 7, is whether we should move away from the fiction that there are no appreciability thresholds operating in free movement law and concentrate instead on how best to rationalize, define, apply, and delimit them.

(c) *De minimis*, remoteness, and conceptual spillage

The ebbs and flows of the case law led AG Jacobs to state in *PreussenElektra*—even before decisions such as *Burmanjer*—that 'it is not clear whether there is a *de minimis* rule in relation to [Article 34], excluding from [its] scope . . . all measures lacking an appreciable effect on trade'.[56] Interestingly, however, the cases that he cited to support the operation of a *de minimis* principle address questions connected to uncertainty and indirectness—questions, in other words, about the principle of remoteness.[57] Horsley has argued that '[n]o special significance should be attached to the labels "effects too uncertain and indirect". . . or "insignificant effects". It is their common function that is important'.[58] Bearing the undoubted significance of that shared or 'common function' in mind, it must be asked whether there is any retained value in distinguishing between appreciability (the province of *de minimis*) and directness (the cause-and-effect concern of remoteness) in free movement case law.

It was noted in subsection (a) that AG Fennelly emphasized the conceptual difference between *de minimis* and remoteness in *Bluhme*. He repeated the point in

[55] Case C-400/08 *Commission v Spain (Shopping centres)* [2011] ECR I-1915, paras 75–76 of the Opinion (emphasis added).

[56] AG Jacobs in Case C-379/98 *PreussenElektra AG v Schhleswag AG, in the presence of Windpark Reußenköge III GmbH and Land Schleswig-Holstein* [2001] ECR I-2099, para. 204 of the Opinion (giving several references in support of both prospects in fn124).

[57] He refers to Case C-266/96 *Corsica Ferries France SA v Gruppo Antichi Ormeggiatori del porto di Genova Coop. arl. and others* [1998] ECR I-3949, para. 31 and Case C-44/98 *BASF AG v Präsident des Deutschen Patentamts* [1999] ECR I-6269 (both of which discuss effects 'too uncertain and indirect'), and 'by implication' Case C-254/98*Schutzverband gegen unlauteren Wettbewerb v TK-Heimdienst Sass GmbH* [2000] ECR I-151, para. 30 ('too random and indirect').

[58] Horsley, n2, 736.

Imperial Tobacco, noting that '[i]t is obvious from the decision of the Court in *Bluhme* . . . that the exclusion from the scope of application of the relevant Treaty provisions . . . of *merely indirect or aleatory obstacles* to trade in goods or services relates to the remoteness of their effects on trade, rather than the scale of those effects'.[59] Supporting this split, Oliver also clarifies an important difference between factual similarity and conceptual distinctiveness. Using the circumstances in *Schmidberger*—closure of a motorway for approximately 30 hours—by way of illustration, he agrees that 'it is undisputable that in that instance, the rule of remoteness would cover the same ground as a *de minimis* rule: either test would lead the Court to exclude the measure from the scope of Article 34. Yet that is not always the case: a measure may constitute an actual and direct restriction on a very small proportion of imports, as is clearly illustrated by *Bluhme*'.[60] The fact that *de minimis* and remoteness thresholds *can* 'cover the same ground' becomes even more significant in Section 4 and also in Chapter 7; for now, however, the key point is that that is not always going to be the case.

Consider, for example, AG Kokott's statement in *UTECA* that '[t]he pre-funding obligation could be considered, at most, to have an *indirect effect* on a television broadcaster's programming because of the effects on its budget. *However*, as the pre-funding obligation, *at 5 per cent of revenue*, *only affects a comparatively small proportion* of a television broadcaster's total budget, *its effects would appear to be too insignificant and uncertain* to be regarded as *seriously prejudicing* its freedom with regard to programming and to *therefore be capable of impeding its freedom* to provide chosen television broadcasting services'.[61] The Advocate General invoked the 'too insignificant and uncertain' wording used by the Court in *Burmanjer*, which clearly merges markers of appreciability with causation or remoteness. The Court's 'too uncertain *or* too insignificant' phrasing in *Morgan and Bucher* might seem preferable: except for the fact that the Court responded to rather than ruled out the defendant Government's submission on the latter—appreciability—point in that case too.[62] This terminological looseness is not confined to free movement law. For example, in *Gysen*, addressing the Staff Regulations, AG Mengozzi referred to effects 'too indirect and marginal'.[63] The same conflation appears in case law on procurement: in *Coname*, for example, the Court stated that 'it is not apparent from the file that, because of special circumstances, *such as a very modest economic interest*

[59] AG Fennelly in *Imperial Tobacco*, fn126 of the Opinion (emphasis added).

[60] Oliver, n3, 1432; Case C-112/00 *Schmidberger, Internationale Transporte und Planzüge v Republik Österreich* [2003] ECR I-5659 (discussed in Chapter 3). Cf. AG Jacobs, at para. 65 of his Opinion in *Schmidberger*: 'the Court has accepted that some restrictions *may be so uncertain and indirect in their effects* as not to be regarded as capable of hindering trade. I would suggest that they may also be *so slight* and so ephemeral *as to fall into the same category*. It would seem for example out of the question that a brief delay to traffic on a road occasionally used for intra-Community transport could in any way fall within the scope of Article [34]. A longer interruption on a major transit route may none the less call for a different assessment' (emphasis added).

[61] AG Kokott in *UTECA*, para. 56 of the Opinion (emphasis added).

[62] Joined Cases C-11 and 12/06 *Morgan and Bucher* [2007] ECR I-9161, para. 32 (emphasis added).

[63] AG Mengozzi in Case C-449/06 *Gysen v Groupe S-Caisse d'Assurances sociales pour indépendants* [2008] ECR I-553, para. 60 of the Opinion.

at stake, it could reasonably be maintained that an undertaking located in [another] Member State . . . would have no interest in the concession at issue and that the effects on the fundamental freedoms concerned should *therefore* be regarded *as too uncertain and indirect* to warrant the conclusion that they may have been infringed'.[64]

The existence of these examples of conceptual spillage is not just an abstract point. If we take the current legal position at face value, i.e. leaving the peculiarities outlined above aside for now, the application of *de minimis* in free movement law is precluded, but the application of remoteness is *not*. It is thus problematic to conflate the materially different questions underpinning both principles, since one set of questions is not even supposed to be asked in the first place. And it would be disingenuous to do so in order to create a backdoor for the application of appreciability tests without having to deal with or overturn the case law presumption against *de minimis* more generally.

Instances of this appreciability/causation conceptual spillage have increased noticeably in recent years. In these circumstances, we can hardly blame national courts for doing the same. The growing references to appreciability alongside or even as part of causation factors may just be carelessness or it may be part of more instrumental propulsion towards curbing the scope of free movement rights, to check the momentum of restrictions based on concepts such as deterrence, discouragement, and dissuasion. These questions are revisited in Section 4.

3. Too far: the principle of remoteness

The power of the *Dassonville* definition of restrictions lies in its latitude—in the idea that a national rule or practice need only have an *indirect* or even *potential* effect on free movement rights to require that arguments about justification and proportionality must be addressed. The causation review instigated by the application of a remoteness test is about attaching some limits, at least, to its scope. In this section, different ways in which a remoteness test has been expressed in the case law will first be briefly outlined. The main counterpoint to potential restrictions, i.e. hypothetical restrictions, will then be introduced before the dominant remoteness test—effects too uncertain and indirect—is examined in more detail. A coherence-based question threads through the discussion: is the application of a remoteness test in free movement law appropriately grounded in reasoned systemic principles, or is it an under-rationalized but convenient device used to dismiss seemingly trivial cases? If the latter, however, then trivial in whose view, and why?

[64] Case C-231/03 *Consorzio Aziende Metano (Coname) v Comune di Cingia de' Botti* [2005] ECR I-7287, para. 20; see also, AG Sharpston in Case C-195/04 *Commission v Finland* [2007] ECR I-3351, paras 85–86. In *Commission v Ireland*, AG Stix-Hackl raised 'the fact that it is open to question where the limit lies as to what is "modest"' but did not challenge the application of that criterion in the context of remoteness (Case C-532/03, [2007] ECR I-11353, para. 88 of the Opinion).

(a) Is remoteness a principle or principles?

The Court does not systematically test alleged restrictions of free movement rights against the premise of causation. Cases in which a remoteness threshold was raised, and sometimes applied decisively to dismiss the challenge, will be introduced in this section; but it is important to emphasize that in the vast majority of free movement disputes, the test is neither raised nor discussed at all. It can also be noted that 'remoteness' per se rarely features in the case law. There are scattered examples of its use by Advocates General,[65] but the Court has never used the word in free movement judgments even where it *has* invoked the defining criterion of causation.[66] As developed in subsection (c), questions about remoteness are generally articulated through an 'effects too uncertain and indirect' test. But the Court is not consistent in its use of language and relevant case law provides several examples of the unchecked proliferation of concepts, principles, and tests point made in Chapter 2. The Court has considered causation questions through various expressions that include: 'no connection';[67] 'too tenuous';[68] 'too random and indirect';[69] and 'too indirect' (on its own).[70]

Although it would of course be better if the Court adopted and applied more standard wording, it is submitted that the proliferation of phrases in a literal sense is not causing significant fragmentation problems in this corner of free movement case law. To borrow the words of AG Cruz Villalón in a different context (on the meaning of 'implementing' EU law per Article 51 of the Charter), 'the different formulations used as expressions... are not qualitatively different'.[71] What the following discussion tries to find out, therefore, is whether there is consistent

[65] See AG Fennelly in *Bluhme* (para. 19 of the Opinion) and *Imperial Tobacco* (fn126 of the Opinion), and AG Sharpston in *Government of the French Community and Walloon Government* (para. 62 of the Opinion, referring to 'remoteness and uncertainty').

[66] E.g. Case C-291/09 *Francesco Guarnieri & Cie v Vandevelde Eddy VOF* [2011] ECR I-2685, para. 17 (considering whether the impact of national civil procedural rules could constitute a restriction on the sale of imported goods within the meaning of Article 34 TFEU).

[67] Case 75/81 *Blesgen v Belgian State* [1982] ECR 1211, para. 9. The Court ruled out a 'connection' to Article 34 TFEU in this case because no discrimination was present, but the case law has now moved past that threshold (see Chapter 7).

[68] Case C-159/90 *Society for the Protection of Unborn Children Ireland Ltd (SPUC) v Stephan Grogan and others* [1991] ECR I-4685, para. 24 ('the link between the activity of the students associations... and medical terminations of pregnancies carried out in clinics in another Member State is too tenuous for the prohibition on the distribution of information to be capable of being regarded as a restriction within the meaning of Article 5[6] of the Treaty'). A related amalgam of 'too tenuous and indirect' was used by AG La Pergola in *Centros* in the context of freedom of establishment (Case C-212/97 *Centros Ltd v Erhverus- og Selskabsstyrelsen* [1999] ECR I-1459, para. 222 of the Opinion) and by AG Mischo in *Bachmann* on the free movement of capital (Case C-204/90 *Bachmann v Belgian State* [1992] ECR I-249, para. 31 of the Opinion).

[69] *TK-Heimdienst*, para. 30 (free movement of goods).

[70] Case C-256/06 *Jäger v Finanzamt Kusel-Landstuhl* [2008] ECR I-123, para. 33 (free movement of capital). In *de Groot*, AG Léger used 'too uncertain' in the context of the free movement of workers (Case C-385/00 *De Groot v Staatssecretaris van Financiën* [2002] ECR I-11819, paras 46–47 of the Opinion).

[71] AG Cruz Villalón in Case C-617/10 *Åkerberg Fransson*, judgment of 26 February 2013, para. 27 of the Opinion.

application of causation through an appropriately rationalized framework, differing expressions of it aside. The nature of the remoteness principle—i.e. whether it operates in free movement law as an exclusionary principle or as part of the positive scope of restrictions—will also be addressed. More broadly, the case law on remoteness opens up critical questions about judicial reasoning and the nature of adjudication. Linking back to the discussion in Section 2 about the different methods applied in competition and free movement case law, and to the framing questions identified in Chapters 1 and 2 more generally, the resolution of free movement disputes through the application of judicial intuition materializes as a particular challenge here.

(b) Hypothetical restrictions

A point that emerged from Chapter 4 in particular is that a significant challenge facing the Court at present is how and where to draw the boundaries of Treaty-caught restrictions for situations that do not involve *actual* restrictions on free movement rights. In that respect, one established limit to the 'potential' element of *Dassonville* is that hypothetical restrictions are always *too* remote: as the Court put it in *B&Q*, the effects of national rules can be 'direct, indirect or *purely speculative*' and the last category fails a causation test.[72] As a formal rule, the position is therefore clear. But determining what amounts to a fatally hypothetical restriction is more problematic in practice. We also saw in Chapter 4 that the haziness of the space between potential and hypothetical restrictions reinforces an obligation to avoid arbitrary application of the purely internal rule in response.

The circumstances in *Moser* and *Kremzow* are the classic case law examples normally invoked to illustrate the meaning of hypothetical restrictions.[73] In *Moser*, the applicant was refused permission to complete the training necessary for him to qualify as a teacher even though he met the relevant academic entry requirements. That refusal was based on uncertainty regarding his loyalty to the Basic Law—a condition for public service employment codified in the relevant *Land* legislation—because of his membership of the German Communist Party. Responding to an argument that the *Land*'s obstruction of Mr Moser's access to the teaching profession might have the effect of depriving him from applying for teaching positions in other Member States, the Court classified the circumstances of the case as purely internal, finding that '[a] purely hypothetical prospect of employment in another Member State does not establish a sufficient connection with [Union] law to justify the application of Article [45 TFEU]'.[74]

The situation in *Kremzow* concerned the continued detention of the applicant in prison in Austria (his home State) notwithstanding a finding made by the European

[72] Case C-169/91 *Council of the City of Stoke-on-Trent and Norwich City Council v B & Q plc* [1992] ECR I-6635, para. 15 (emphasis added).

[73] Case 180/83 *Moser v Land Baden-Württemberg* [1984] ECR 2539; Case C-299/95 *Kremzow v Austria* [1997] ECR I-2629.

[74] *Moser*, para. 18.

Court of Human Rights that his right to a fair trial as protected by Article 6 ECHR had been violated. In the course of subsequent national proceedings, based on the argument that Austria had not yet rectified the relevant Convention violation, Mr Kremzow raised a series of questions about the relationship between national law, EU law, and the ECHR. Confirming that the applicant needed first to establish a connecting factor between his situation and EU law before questions about the substantive protection of his fundamental rights could be addressed, the Court of Justice, citing *Moser*, stated that '[w]hilst any deprivation of liberty may impede the person concerned from exercising his right to free movement, the Court has held that a purely hypothetical prospect of exercising that right does not establish a sufficient connection with [EU] law to justify the application of [EU] provisions'.[75] This construction acknowledges the *literal* impediment to Mr Kremzow's free movement rights at one level, supporting the idea that hypothetical restrictions operate as an exclusionary principle based on more qualitative principles or thresholds.

How do these archetypal cases fit with the case law more generally? As a preliminary point, a link can once again be drawn to the discussion in Chapter 4, where it was shown that, sometimes, the Court side-steps the purely internal appearance of disputes referred to it by emphasizing that the referring court may nonetheless be assisted if the Court provides a response on the substantive questions of EU law raised. In *Nour*, however, a decision issued soon after the judgment in *Kremzow*, the Court sent quite a different answer, rejecting the preliminary reference by Order on the grounds, inter alia, that 'the decision making the reference does not show in what respect [EU] law could apply. . . . The national tribunal merely draws the Court's attention to the fact that, in future, doctors who are nationals of other Member States might perhaps be involved in similar disputes. It is settled case-law that the Court may not rule on an alleged breach of the general principles of [EU] law in the case of a dispute which is not connected in any way with any of the situations contemplated by the Treaty provisions'.[76] The Court has confirmed on several occasions that it can refuse jurisdiction under Article 267 TFEU where 'a problem is hypothetical'.[77] However, and reflecting a finding demonstrated several times in preceding chapters, the Court does not join up these two conflicting strands of case law: sometimes it responds to but sometimes it rejects the questions sent to it by national courts, without engaging particularly convincing distinctions either way.

The concept of a hypothetical restriction has been raised several times since the decisions in *Moser*, *Kremzow*, and *Nour* but, aside from its impact at the preliminary stage of admissibility, it has not been used to decisive exclusionary effect by itself—i.e. independently of other grounds e.g. the effects too uncertain and indirect test—since then. This would seem to suggest that as a distinct concept, hypothetical

[75] *Kremzow*, para. 16.

[76] Case C-361/97 *Nour v Burgenländische Gebietskrankenkasse* [1998] ECR I-3101, paras 18–19.

[77] E.g. Case C-380/01 *Schneider v Bundesminister für Justiz* [2004] ECR I-1389, para. 22; Case C-165/03 *Längst* [2005] ECR I-5637, para. 32.

restrictions constitute a cautionary tale more than a substantive limit, as we saw similarly for abuse of rights in Chapter 3.[78] This may be just as well since, as noted above, the fuzziness of the dividing line between problematically hypothetical and acceptably potential effects makes it a difficult and subjective barrier to determine, something that is consistently demonstrated in post-*Kremzow* case law. For example, why is the serious inconvenience that might be encountered by the children in *Garcia Avello* should they decide to move to Spain, at some unspecified point in the future, a *Dassonville*-blessed potential restriction rather than a *Kremzow*-excluded hypothetical one? Is the fact that they hold dual nationality really enough here, as a substantiating factor? In *Government of the French Community and Walloon Government*, addressing Article 45 TFEU, AG Sharpston distinguished between hypothetical effects, on the one hand, and potential even if uncertain effects, on the other, reasoning that 'for a measure to constitute an obstacle, it is sufficient that it should be *reasonably likely* to have that effect on migrant workers'.[79] Taking a similar approach to Article 34 TFEU in *Trailers*, AG Bot considered that an 'obstacle does not therefore need to be actual and significant, but must be *at least possible*'.[80] In *Ruiz Zambrano*, however, AG Sharpston also articulated a synthesis of potential and hypothetical movement;[81] was that a slip of the pen or was she more consciously calling a spade a spade?

Interestingly, in his Opinion in *D'Hoop*, AG Geelhoed considered that the applicant came within the personal scope of the Treaty's citizenship provisions, which he then merged with Article 18 TFEU to find that her exclusion from entitlement to a post-university social benefit in her home State, just because she had completed her secondary education in another Member State, was contrary to EU free movement law. Reflecting on whether the same circumstances brought her within the scope of the Treaty provisions on services, however, he argued as follows:

> The effect of the [national] provision in this instance can only be indirect and marginal. From the point at which pupils opt to pursue and complete their secondary education in Belgium or in another Member State, *it will normally be some years* before they may come up against the requirements of the [relevant law] regarding eligibility for tideover allowances. The restrictive effects which the contested provision has on free provision of services are to

[78] Consideration of hypothetical effects has now become more absorbed in the notion of uncertain effects, as discussed in subsection (c); see e.g. AG Mengozzi in Case C-310/09 *Ministre du Budget, des Comptes publics et de la Fonction publique v Accor SA*, judgment of 15 September 2011, para. 42 of the Opinion.

[79] AG Sharpston in *Government of the French Community and Walloon Government*, para. 65 of the Opinion (emphasis added).

[80] AG Bot in *Trailers*, para. 117 of the Opinion (emphasis added).

[81] AG Sharpston in *Ruiz Zambrano*, para. 132 of the Opinion: 'ever since *Dassonville* potential as well as actual physical movement has been relevant to free movement of goods. Although that specific case-law does not require actual previous movement to have taken place, it is nevertheless still the idea of movement (*even if that movement is hypothetical*) that serves as the key to the rights granted by the fundamental freedoms' (emphasis added). Later in the Opinion, AG Sharpston partly rationalized her proposed extension of EU competence for the protection of fundamental rights on the grounds that 'it avoids the need to create or promote fictitious or hypothetical "links with Union law" of the kind that have, in the past, sometimes confused and possibly stretched the scope of application of Treaty . . . [i]n terms of legal certainty, the improvement would be significant' (para. 167).

my mind *so uncertain and indirect* that they cannot be considered a barrier to the freedom to provide and receive services as between Member States.[82]

It is interesting to note that AG Geelhoed was reluctant to join situations far apart in time for the purposes of finding a restriction on free movement rights—an approach that would surely have defeated the claims in *Garcia Avello* too.

A recent application of the remoteness test provides a good illustration of the difficulty in pinning down a meaningful difference between hypothetical and uncertain events. In *Commission v Spain (Hospital care)*, infringement proceedings were initiated because national legislation governing the reimbursement of medical expenses distinguished between hospital costs incurred in Spain and incurred during a temporary stay in another State: essentially, costs relating to the latter that were not borne by the institution of stay would be reimbursed in Spain only in the exceptional event of life-saving treatment. The Commission argued that 'the effect of the Spanish legislation is to restrict not only the provision of hospital care, but also the provision of tourist or educational services, the obtaining of which can be the reason for a temporary stay in another Member State'.[83] It then highlighted two potential effects in particular: first, that the legislation 'is liable to induce a person insured under the Spanish national health system, who is faced with [a deterioration in health during a temporary stay in another State] and has a choice between going to hospital in the Member State of stay and an early return to Spain to be treated there, to choose the second option whenever the level of cover applicable in the Member State of stay is less favourable than that applicable in Spain'; and, second, that the legislation 'is such as to dissuade elderly insured persons or those suffering from a chronic illness—with the attendant risk of having to be admitted to hospital—from travelling, as tourists or students, to a Member State in which the conditions governing insurance cover for hospital treatment are less advantageous than in Spain'.[84] But the Court was not convinced, finding that the situations presented by the Commission under both scenarios were 'too uncertain and indirect'[85]—not beyond the bounds of possibility, which the idea of hypothetical restrictions would imply, but still too amorphous to rationalize a finding that the legislation restricted services within the meaning of EU law. The concept of hypothetical restrictions is probably best thought of, therefore, as an extreme pole of remoteness: *far* too uncertain and indirect.

In contrast to the judgment of the Court, however, AG Mengozzi *did* consider that Article 56 TFEU was unduly restricted by the national legislation with respect to certain medical services while dismissing the Commission's arguments about restricting services more generally as 'mere supposition':[86]

[82] AG Geelhoed in Case C-224/98 *D'Hoop v Office national de l'emploi* [2002] ECR I-6191, para. 26 of the Opinion (emphasis added).

[83] Case C-211/08 *Commission v Spain (Hospital care)* [2010] ECR I-5267, para. 40.

[84] *Commission v Spain (Hospital care)*, paras 41–42.

[85] *Commission v Spain (Hospital care)*, para. 72.

[86] AG Mengozzi in *Commission v Spain (Hospital care)*, see esp. paras 80–88 of the Opinion.

> [T]he only case in which the Commission's argument might be confirmed is that of persons with chronic diseases who of necessity must undergo medical treatment (such as dialysis) during their stay abroad. In all other cases, even those involving persons at greater risk, such as elderly persons, pregnant women or persons with existing illnesses, *the purely hypothetical nature* of a medical necessity occurring, *despite the higher probability of such an eventuality*, is not, in my view, sufficient reason for supposing that the system in force in the state of affiliation for the reimbursement of medical expenses incurred abroad *has any real impact* on the decision to go to another Member State in order to receive a non-medical service there.[87]

This passage arguably confuses the threshold of hypothetical effects even further: does the 'higher probability' point not defeat the argument that the other scenarios must be treated as hypothetical too? There may well be a *remoteness* point here, which was in fact confirmed by the Court; but surely the risks are not hypothetical. Prejudging what may or may not have 'any real impact on the decision to go to another Member State' is also dangerously subjective ground, a risk inherent in the threshold tests being considered in this chapter and returned to below.

One further point about the circumstances in *Commission v Spain* should be noted here too. The rules established by the national legislation were applied in a non-discriminatory way—i.e. they applied without reference to the nationality of the insured person—but the differential treatment built into it related to services received in other Member States. If the decision to apply a remoteness test in this case does not quite pierce the general presumption against doing so in situations involving discrimination, as will be outlined in more detail in the next subsection, it is not quite in line either with the more typically 'genuinely' non-discriminatory circumstances in which the test is presumed to be relevant. It can be concluded more generally for now, however, that if the reach of potential restrictions needs to be contained in some respects, the yardstick of hypothetical restrictions provides only limited respite.

(c) The core test: too uncertain and indirect

Most discourse on the threshold of causation takes place around an assertion that the *effects* of a national rule or practice on free movement rights are *too uncertain and indirect*. Since the *Dassonville* test explicitly catches *indirect* obstacles to movement, we must assume that either (a) the test is cumulative i.e. the restriction must be too uncertain *as well as* indirect; and/or (b) we should split the test into two parts i.e. effects too uncertain *and too* indirect. However, applying either interpretation would help to delimit the dissuasion, deterrence, and prospective lines of case law on the scope of restrictions, raised as a line of case law that can go too far in Chapter 4. The circumstances of *Garcia Avello* can be used once again to illustrate: while the restriction contemplated by the Court in that case might be considered to be *uncertain*, future 'inconvenience' would at least still be *directly* connected to the Belgian surname registration rules. This example thus provides an early caution too,

[87] AG Mengozzi in *Commission v Spain (Hospital care)*, para. 82 of the Opinion (emphasis added).

about exaggerating the constraining capacity of remoteness to manage problems of overreach in free movement law.

Unsurprisingly, given the openness of the restriction test established by *Dassonville*, the origins of effects too uncertain and indirect also lie in the Court's interpretation of Article 34 TFEU. In *Krantz*, the Court stated that 'the possibility that nationals of other Member States would hesitate to sell goods on instalment terms to purchasers in the Member State concerned because such goods would be *liable to seizure* by the collector of taxes if the purchasers failed to discharge their Netherlands tax debts is *too uncertain and indirect* to warrant the conclusion that a national provision authorizing such seizure is *liable to hinder trade* between Member States'.[88] This part of the judgment followed as a 'furthermore' from the Court's statement that the contested rule applied to both domestic and imported goods without distinction, reflecting concerns about the relevance of discrimination that had intensified pre-*Keck*. The *Krantz* test was confirmed in *Motorradcenter*,[89] but its expression in *Peralta* emphasized an additional, though up to that point implicit, dimension. Considering the compatibility with Article 34 of Italian legislation that required certain ships to be equipped with expensive decontamination equipment, the Court reasoned as follows:

> [I]t is sufficient to observe that legislation like the legislation in question makes no distinction according to the origin of the substances transported, *its purpose is not to regulate trade in goods with other Member States* and the restrictive effects which it might have on the free movement of goods are too uncertain and indirect for the obligation which it lays down to be regarded as being of a nature to hinder trade between Member States . . .[90]

Writing in 1990, Gormley described the second condition—whether or not the measure was 'designed' to regulate inter-State trade—as a 'non-sequitur [which] appears to be in danger of becoming popular as an instrument of judicial reasoning'.[91] Reflecting a line of authority that can be drawn back to *Völk*, the Court would later move away from the language of 'purpose' and renew its interest in the object *or effect* of national rules.[92] The cyclical way in which judicial, and academic, debates emphasize either the scope or limits of the *Dassonville* test is

[88] Case C-69/88 *Krantz GmbH & Co. v Ontvanger der Directe Belastingen and Netherlands State* [1990] ECR I-583, para. 11 (emphasis added).

[89] Case C-93/92 *CMC Motorradcenter GmbH v Pelin Baskiciogullari* [1993] ECR I-5009, para. 12.

[90] Case C-379/92 *Criminal proceedings against Peralta* [1994] ECR I-3453, para. 24 (emphasis added); see similarly e.g. Case C-266/96 *Corsica Ferries France SA v Gruppo Antichi Ormeggiatori del porto di Genova Coop. arl. and others* [1998] ECR I-3949, para. 31.

[91] L Gormley, 'Recent case law on the free movement of goods: Some hot potatoes' (1990) 27:4 CMLRev 825 at 829. For another view, distinguishing between non-discriminatory rules intended to regulate trade and non-discriminatory rules not intended to regulate trade in respect of relative burdens of proof, see E Spaventa, 'The outer limit of the Treaty free movement provisions: Some reflections on the significance of *Keck*, Remoteness and *Deliège*' in C Barnard and O Odudu (eds.), *The Outer Limits of European Law* (Hart Publishing, 2009) 245 at 252 ff and esp. 263–4. See similarly, C Barnard, 'Fitting the remaining pieces into the goods and persons jigsaw?' (2001) 26:1 ELRev 35 at 45.

[92] See e.g. Case C-244/06 *Dynamic Medien Vertriebs GmbH v Avides Media AG* [2008] ECR I-505, para. 27: '[e]ven if a measure is not intended to regulate trade in goods between Member States, the determining factor is its effect, actual or potential, on intra-[Union] trade'.

examined in Chapters 6 and 7; for now, the genesis of the effects too uncertain and indirect test in the free movement of goods can be placed in the context of its timing—mapping the trajectory from the Sunday trading challenges to the shutters-down tone of *Keck*.[93]

The continuing relevance of the first condition expressed in *Peralta*—that remoteness should be questioned only in the context of non-discriminatory restrictions—is borne out both by the actual application of effects too uncertain and indirect in the case law, and by a broader argument that discriminatory restrictions are *never* too uncertain and indirect.[94] The judgment in *ED* seems to be an exception.[95] It concerned Article 35 TFEU and the export of goods. Addressing national rules on debt recovery procedures, the Court first acknowledged that their effect was 'to subject traders to different procedural rules according to whether they supply goods within the Member State concerned or export them to other Member States'.[96] It might have been expected that the Court would confirm that the rules constituted a restriction under Article 35 TFEU that could, however, be justified by reasons of public interest. Instead, the Court stated that 'the possibility that nationals would therefore hesitate to sell goods to purchasers established in other Member States is too uncertain and indirect for that national provision to be regarded as liable to hinder trade between Member States'.[97]

It is important to remember, however, that case law on the import and export of goods has not developed in parallel. This becomes clearer when reading the Opinion of AG Cosmas, who first drew attention to and accepted the remoteness argument submitted by two governments: 'the restrictive effects which the provision at issue could have on the free movement of goods, and exports in particular, are far too uncertain and indirect to warrant the conclusion that it is liable to hinder trade between Member States. Since the national provision *shows no perceptible effects on exports*, it is superfluous to examine either whether it favours Italian domestic trade or whether it can be justified on the basis of the exceptions provided for by Article 36 of the Treaty'.[98] If that reasoning were applied in a case concerning imports, it would provide an example of conceptual spillage between *de minimis* and remoteness. Instead, it reflects here the *Groenveld* criteria that defined measures having equivalent effect to quantitative restrictions *on exports* as measures 'which have as their specific object or effect *the restriction of patterns of exports* and thereby the establishment of a difference in treatment between the domestic trade of a Member State and its export trade *in such a way as to provide a particular advantage for national production or for the domestic market* of the State in question, at the

[93] On these historical parallels, see Spaventa, n91, 250; exploring enduring conceptual linkages between the effects too uncertain and indirect and 'certain selling arrangements' tests, see Horsley, n2, (these links are discussed further in Chapter 7).

[94] See e.g. Horsley, n2, 743–4.

[95] Case C-412/97 *ED Srl v Italo Fenocchio* [1999] ECR I-3845.

[96] *ED*, para. 11. [97] *ED*, para. 11.

[98] AG Cosmas in *ED*, para. 55 of the Opinion (emphasis added).

expense of the production or of the trade of other Member States'.[99] What the Court was saying in *ED*, through the confusing application of remoteness language, was that the national rules being challenged simply caused no such effect.[100]

In the foundational case law on remoteness, it can be also seen that the test was operating as an exclusionary principle. The existence or components of the relevant restriction were not being called into question in a technical sense. Instead, the Court was contemplating whether the effects it caused warranted the application of the Treaty: was it, as AG La Pergola put it in *BASF*, an *undue* restriction?[101] In *Bluhme*, commenting on the decisions in *Krantz*, *Motorradcenter*, and *Peralta*, AG Fennelly commented that 'the causal link between these measures and any effect on intra-Community trade was *a matter of pure chance*; in other words, it was too remote. The Court was simply not prepared to accept that national rules on discharges from ships into the sea, on planning authorisation and licensing of shops, on the seizure of goods in the possession of tax defaulters and on the provision of information in good faith when concluding contracts were liable to have a discernible effect on trade'.[102] The Advocate General's phrasing here—that the Court was *simply not prepared to accept* that certain national rules should attract the attention of the Treaty—is interesting, reviving questions about the perception of subjectivity that hangs over the application of remoteness, returned to below. It is clear, however, that the Opinion in *Bluhme* was a milestone in terms of distinguishing between appreciability and causation, and also of insisting that the former concern had no place in free movement law. AG Fennelly's later Opinion in *Graf* performed the converse function for remoteness—ensuring that the principle was embedded more definitively in free movement law, and beyond the free movement of goods in isolation.[103]

The timing of *Graf* places it just after the limits set by and early responses to the decision in *Keck*, but also after the Court confirmed in *Bosman* that Article 45 TFEU could catch genuinely non-discriminatory restrictions on the free movement of workers.[104] The facts concerned an argument that the refusal by an employer to pay compensation to an employee who had terminated his contract of employment in order to take up a position in another Member State constituted a restriction on the employee's freedom to move under Article 45 TFEU. The national law challenged created an entitlement to compensation only where the contract ended without the termination being on the initiative of or attributable to the

[99] *Groenveld*, para. 7 (emphasis added).

[100] This interpretation is supported by the Court's pointing (in para. 11 of *ED*) to authority on the scope of quantitative restrictions on exports rather than on remoteness (Case C-339/89 *Alsthom Atlantique SA v Compagnie de construction mécanique Sulzer SA* [1991] ECR I-107, para. 14). The impact of the decision in Case C-205/07 *Gysbrechts and Santurel Inter BVBA* [2008] ECR I-9947 on the scope of Article 35 TFEU is addressed in Chapter 6.

[101] AG La Pergola in *BASF*, para. 18 of the Opinion (emphasis added; see similarly, the judgment of the Court in the same case, paras 20–21).

[102] AG Fennelly in *Bluhme*, para. 19 of the Opinion (emphasis added).

[103] Case C-190/98 *Graf v Filzmoser Maschinenbau GmbH* [2000] ECR I-493.

[104] Case C-415/93 *Union royale belge des sociétés de football association ASBL v Bosman* [1995] ECR I-4921.

employee. AG Fennelly first noted that recent case law on the free movement of persons[105] was concerned with advancing the premise that non-discriminatory obstacles could hinder free movement or make its exercise less attractive, and that 'the Court did not advert expressly to any such limitation of the scope of application of the criteria it laid down in those cases'.[106] He then outlined a burden of proof argument: '[w]here an alleged obstacle to freedom of movement does not result from a formal condition of market participation but is instead alleged to arise from *some neutral material barrier or disincentive* deriving from national regulations, the prejudice to the exercise of [Union]-law rights *must be established*'.[107] Drawing a distinction between rules regulating access to an employment market and rules regulating the exercise of economic activity—returned to in Chapter 7—he then drew a direct link to the reasoning in *Krantz* and *Peralta,* arguing that '[t]he effect of the loss of *a merely potential and uncertain right* is, in my view, *far too tenuous, remote and uncertain* to constitute a restriction on free movement'.[108]

Both AG Fennelly and the Court considered that denial of compensation in cases of voluntary termination of employment fell squarely within the objectives pursued by the application of a causation threshold—but by framing the applicant's loss of employment through *involuntary* circumstances as the relevant uncertain and indirect (or 'future and hypothetical') event and ignoring the *certain* fact that the applicant had already terminated the employment at his own behest. Following the analysis of AG Fennelly, the Court emphasized that non-discriminatory obstacles must affect the *access* of workers to the labour markets of other Member States:

> Legislation of the kind at issue . . . is not such as to preclude or deter a worker from ending his contract of employment in order to take a job with another employer, because the entitlement to compensation on termination of employment is not dependent on the worker's choosing whether or not to stay with his current employer but *on a future and hypothetical event,* namely the subsequent termination of his contract without such termination being at his own initiative or attributable to him. Such an event is *too uncertain and indirect* a possibility for legislation to be capable of being regarded as liable to hinder freedom of movement for workers where it does not attach to termination of a contract of employment by the worker himself the same consequence as it attaches to termination which was not at his initiative or is not attributable to him.[109]

[105] In addition to *Bosman*, AG Fennelly cited Case C-19/92 *Kraus v Land Baden-Württemberg* [1993] ECR I-1663 and Case C-55/94 *Gebhard v Consiglio dell'Ordine degli Avvocati e Procuratori di Milano* [1995] ECR I-4165.

[106] AG Fennelly in *Graf,* para. 31 of the Opinion.

[107] AG Fennelly in *Graf,* para. 31 of the Opinion (emphasis added).

[108] AG Fennelly in *Graf,* para. 34 of the Opinion (emphasis added). The Advocate General found support for both the market access and remoteness points in the arguments of AG Jacobs in Case C-384/93 *Alpine Investments BV v Minister van Financiën* [1995] ECR I-1141, paras 57 and 58 of the Opinion.

[109] *Graf,* paras 24–25 (emphasis added; supporting AG Fennelly's interest in convergence across the freedoms, the Court also cited its decisions in *Krantz* and *BASF*). For an example of a situation in which the loss of benefits *was* argued to constitute a restriction within the meaning of Article 45, see AG Kokott in Case C-379/09 *Casteels v British Airways plc* [2011] ECR I-1379, esp. paras 45 and 57–61 of the Opinion.

Again, however, this response sidesteps the actual arguments submitted by the applicant and the actual circumstances in which he found himself at the time. It would have been more logical to deal with the case through the language and concepts of market access. The applicant had *already* left his current employment and had *already* commenced his employment in another Member State by the time of the proceedings. In those circumstances, his access to the latter State's labour market could hardly be described as having been precluded or even affected by the rules on compensation in the first State. *Graf* was therefore a powerful vehicle for the transmission of remoteness logic from goods to the free movement of persons but, ironically, it was not really needed to resolve the particular dispute at issue. More generally, the intricate links between the remoteness threshold and market access are a critical issue in the context of fixing the line between negative and positive scope, and of defining the latter in particular.[110] These questions are picked up in Section 4 and addressed more fully in Chapter 7.

Finally, before turning in Section 4 to the *nature* of the problem that remoteness is being deployed to address, two interlinked criticisms of its application per se should first be considered. Commenting on Article 34 TFEU but with wider relevance, AG Kokott cautioned in *Mickelsson and Roos* that 'the Court has attempted from time to time to exclude national measures whose effects on trade are too uncertain and too indirect . . . However, an argument against these criteria is that they are *difficult to clarify* and thus *do not contribute to legal certainty*'.[111] The second point—absence of a contribution to legal certainty—is clearly echoed in the literature.[112] Questions of causal connection seem, on the whole, to be *assumed* rather than *tested* in free movement case law. For example, was there a sufficient causal connection between Mr Carpenter's occasional provision of services in other States and his wife's permanent residence in his home State? He certainly raised one—the provision of care for his children at home in his absence—but, as noted in Chapter 4, the Court did not explicitly specify the relevance of that factor to its decision.[113]

The case law generates four types of remoteness outcome overall: (1) cases—constituting the vast majority—where remoteness is neither raised nor considered; (2) cases where remoteness is raised either by the parties involved or in State submissions, but is not then addressed by the Court (almost always, in the absence

[110] See e.g. Case C-602/10 *SC Volksbank România SA v Autoritatea Naţională pentru Protecţia Consumatorilor—Comisariatul Judeţean pentru Protecţia Consumatorilor Călăraşi (CJPC)*, judgment of 12 July 2012, paras 80–81: 'it is not evident that that national provision renders access to the Romanian market less attractive and, in the event of access thereto, genuinely reduces the ability of the undertakings concerned to compete effectively, from the outset, against undertakings traditionally established in Romania. *In those circumstances*, the effect of that national provision on trade in services is too uncertain and indirect for such a national measure to be regarded as liable to hinder intra-[Union] trade' (emphasis added).

[111] AG Kokott in Case C-142/05 *Åklagaren v Mickelsson and Roos* [2009] ECR I-4273, para. 46 of the Opinion (emphasis added).

[112] See e.g. Spaventa, n91, 270; S Enchelmaier, 'Always at your service (within limits): The ECJ's case law on Article 56 TFEU (2006/11)' (2011) 36:5 ELRev 615 at 630.

[113] Case C-60/00 *Carpenter v Secretary of State for the Home Department* [2002] ECR I-6279, esp. paras 39 and 42; also discussed in Chapters 3 and 4.

of admissibility bars, because the Court finds that there *is* a restriction of free movement rights); (3) cases where remoteness is raised and considered, but rejected; and (4) cases—still constituting the minority[114]—where remoteness is raised and considered, and applied decisively to negate the assertion of a free movement restriction.

Both the undisciplined use of similar-but-different wording and instances of conceptual spillage between causation and appreciability make it harder to understand what is really driving decisions arrived at through the application of remoteness. This, in turn, makes it harder to explain or to predict when or how remoteness will in fact be engaged. It is important to re-emphasize that the absence of coherence here is not about an abstract preference for neatness or a quasi-linguistic investigation about where/when/why/how different words are used. The critical point is that there is a line beyond which situations fail to attract the interest of the Treaty even though all of the other elements normally required are in place, and that is it extremely difficult to locate that line. However, placing a situation on either side of it has significant legal consequences—either the case goes no further, and the national rule or practice legitimately persists; or if a restriction is established, either the demanding criteria of justification and proportionality must be met or the national rule or practice must be disapplied in the case at hand: at the very least, since, in reality, formal regulatory change is probably inevitable.

AG Kokott's first point—difficult to clarify—evokes a recurring question about the extent to which tests based on criteria such as indirectness raise accusations of subjectivity: as previously expressed somewhat tongue-in-cheek but with an entirely serious undertone, that the answers might seem 'to depend on the length of the judge's foot'.[115] The distinction between the data-based and rule-based approaches to competition and free movement law respectively was outlined earlier; as was the fact that the balance of scholarship favours preserving that difference. The distinction is sometimes presented as a quantitative/*de minimis* and qualitative/remoteness dichotomy, with emphasis on the more intuitive character of the latter.[116] But qualitative methods are also a constituent of *science* i.e. both quantitative and qualitative methods produce empirical data, which will meet the benchmark of science only if they have been generated in a rigorous and robust manner. In other words, science is science on account of its adherence to rigorous method and not because the applied method is generating either quantitative or qualitative data

[114] Although Horsley (n2) stresses the increase in such cases in recent years.

[115] D Edward and N Nic Shuibhne, 'Continuity and change in the law relating to services' in A Arnull, P Eeckhout, and T Tridimas (eds.), *Continuity and Change in EU Law: Essays in Honour of Sir Francis Jacobs* (OUP, 2008) 243 at 256. See similarly, Enchelmaier, n112, 648: 'how uncertain is "too uncertain", how indirect is "too indirect"? How long is a piece of string? Pick your answer: any will do. There is simply no way of knowing, of arriving at any result that is not arbitrary and subjective'.

[116] E.g. Edward and Nic Shuibhne, n115. See similarly, J Snell, 'The notion of market access: A concept or a slogan?' (2010) 47:2 CMLRev 437 at 459; in the context of market access rather than remoteness but reflecting the same distinction: '[t]he assessment of whether a measure creates a substantial restriction on market access will either have to be based on quantitative data that will be difficult for the litigants to produce or become a highly intuitive exercise lacking in predictability'.

per se.[117] A poorly derived economic study is no more scientific than a badly conducted qualitative assessment.

Court judgments that project likely free movement scenarios are not, of course, going to meet the standards of or be considered as scientific data, but neither do they need to be. There is a broader message here, which cautions us not to fall into the trap of assuming that free movement case law is *legally* softer than competition case law, or that it does not demand the same methodological rigour and robustness from its authors. A related point is reflected in the following extract:

> [T]he question 'Is there an "obstacle" to freedom of movement?' . . . is *more economic and practical than legal*—'What is the obstacle and how does it work?' The answer will, of course, depend on judicial assessment of the facts but *that assessment need not be arbitrary and should be evidence-based.* If, as a practical matter, there is no obstacle, then the situation in question is too 'remote' to fall within the scope of Community law.[118]

Fundamentally, these questions are *more economic and practical than legal*—however, both the Court of Justice and national courts are the institutions charged by the Treaty with resolving them in the absence of legislative harmonisation. Courts normally *have* to resolve these questions because of legally channelled resistance to political decisions already taken; legally channelled demands that the spaces left by political *in*decision need to be filled; or legally channelled exposition of problems or questions that no one did or reasonably could have anticipated when framing the contested measure or practices.

The application of judicial intuition is a sharply double-edged sword; it presents methodological attractions but also significant methodological challenges and risks. A rule-based approach is broadly agreed to be more suited to free movement law and to the carving of principles that can then be applied in subsequent cases, especially by national courts. It also avoids some of the difficulties identified in Chapter 1 that stem from the merging of constitutional and first instance functions within the preliminary rulings procedure: additionally, there is something 'less bad' about the *application* of intuition being exercised not by the Court of Justice but by the national courts, to whom the relevant claimants and their disputes are more directly connected. In the interests of guiding national courts and tribunals more clearly, however, the Court has to address how questions of proof should be managed for a test based on causation. What exactly do claimants have to *show* in terms of their own actual (obviously easier) or potential (necessarily harder) free movement situations? Must they, as AG Fennelly argued in *Graf*, work harder if the restriction being challenged has no discriminatory effects? Spaventa has emphasized that acceptance of *likely* effects relieves claimants 'from the need to prove any existence of factual discrimination' but, on the other hand, that the 'assumptions' made by relying 'on purely theoretical reasoning . . . do not always stand a rigorous

[117] See e.g. W Hollway and T Jefferson, *Doing Qualitative Research Differently: Free Association, Narrative and the Interview Method* (Sage, 2000); M Denscombe, *Ground Rules for Good Research: A 10 Point Guide for Social Researchers* (Open University Press, 2002); J Mason, *Qualitative Researching*, 2nd edn (Sage, 2002).

[118] Edward and Nic Shuibhne, n115, 257 (emphasis added).

scrutiny'.[119] Mirroring the discussion developed in Chapter 4, perhaps the real problem here is the extent to which potential or prospective effects have Treaty-relevance more generally. This question, intimately bound up with the scope of market access and the deter/disadvantage/discourage lines of case law more generally, is taken up more substantively in Chapter 7.

In *Government of the French Community and Walloon Government*, the Court brought the key aspects of its post-*Graf* understanding of remoteness and *de minimis* together:

> [U]nlike the case giving rise to the judgment [in *Graf*] . . . possible entitlement to the insurance care benefits at issue depends, *not on a future and hypothetical event* for the employed or self-employed worker concerned, but on a circumstance *linked*, ex hypothesi, to the exercise of the right to freedom of movement, namely, the choice of transfer of residence. Likewise, as regards the . . . argument that that legislation could in any case have only a *marginal effect* on freedom of movement, in view of the limited nature of the amount of benefits in question and the number of persons concerned, it need merely be observed that, according to the Court's case-law, the articles of the Treaty relating to the free movement of goods, persons, services and capital are fundamental Community provisions and *any restriction, even minor*, of that freedom is prohibited . . . [120]

This extract reflects the main findings presented in this chapter: first, hypothetical restrictions are an extreme form of remoteness; second, the main objective of causation is to identify links that are too uncertain and indirect; and, third, those questions are conceptually distinct from questions of appreciability. It does not, however, address or even acknowledge the appreciability case law anomalies identified in Section 2.

4. Between negative and positive scope: renewing or reframing the boundaries of Treaty-caught restrictions on movement?

If we accept momentarily the dual case law premises examined in this chapter—that a threshold of appreciability does not apply in free movement law; but a remoteness test does, to confirm an appropriate causal connection between a contested rule or practice and the restriction on free movement rights claimed—then the nature and purpose of the remoteness test, in particular, needs to be understood in the context of the broader nature and purpose of free movement rights and how restrictions on them are defined. It would also be important to consider, then, whether a chain of causation needs to be determined more systematically in free movement rights case law. Additionally, however, it was argued in Section 2, and will be developed further in Chapter 7, that it is in fact misleading to assert that no appreciability thresholds operate in free movement law. The

[119] Spaventa, n91, 256.

[120] *Government of the French Community and Walloon Government*, paras 51 and 52 (emphasis added).

challenge there is to work out more coherently where, why, and how a limited appreciability threshold doctrine could make a positive case law contribution. In essence, the knots between market access, *de minimis*, and remoteness need to be untied more rationally and more convincingly.

Snell demonstrates that the Court has shifted its focus from whether or not obstacles are sufficiently direct—in remoteness language, *too* indirect—to whether or not they are 'significant'.[121] He then nails the resulting coherence problem caused by conflicting messages in the case law: '[c]urrently, the Court's analysis in the main seems to focus on the significance of the impact of the measure, with all the uncertainties this approach entails. *At the same time*, it denies that rules with an insignificant effect fall outside the scope of the Treaty'.[122] The Court's shift in focus seems to be simply towards different problems. The critical question here is what 'significance' actually means: is it a shift from remoteness to *de minimis* or is it a variant of remoteness?[123] In *DocMorris*, AG Stix-Hackl outlined an approach to Article 34 TFEU based on whether or not a national measure 'significantly impedes' market access—drawing support mainly from case law on services.[124] She went on to distinguish between market access and *de minimis*:

> The approach ... taken here, focusing on the impact on market access, cannot, however, be construed as meaning that the crucial factor is *the extent of the impact* of the national measure. In contrast with a *de minimis* provision, such as in competition law, *no economic data requires evaluation here*. However, an important criterion for whether market access is made *appreciably* more difficult is whether other lawful and effective forms of distribution exist.[125]

However, it is argued here that the presence or absence of economic data is not enough, on its own, to distinguish appreciability criteria from a *de minimis* test. They are one and the same in conceptual terms—as clearly demonstrated by AG Jacobs in *Leclerc-Siplec*. Rather, the need for and evaluation of economic data goes to questions of proof. The Court has never, in its *van de Haar* case law, equated its understanding of *de minimis* in free movement law with its application of *de minimis* in competition law. It has always simply stated that the Treaty must be applied 'even though the hindrance is *slight*' or that 'any restriction, *even minor*' is prohibited. It is a premise based on proscription, not a premise based inexorably on either data or degree.

However, that conclusion does not in itself explain why or how a doctrine of appreciability *does* operate in parts of the free movement case law. It does not reconcile the gap between case law statements and case law practice, recalling Snell's words above. As observed in Chapter 1, the volume of free movement case law that

[121] Snell, n116, esp. 452–5; he also shows persuasively why focusing on 'directness' is problematic.

[122] Snell, n116, 471 (emphasis added).

[123] Supporting the second claim i.e. that these tests are qualitative variants of remoteness, see Horsley, n2, 751–2.

[124] AG Stix-Hackl in Case C-322/01*Deutscher Apothekerverband eV v 0800 DocMorris NV and Jacques Waterval* [2003] ECR I-14887, esp. paras 74–80 of the Opinion.

[125] AG Stix-Hackl in *DocMorris*, paras 81–82 of the Opinion (emphasis added).

now exists makes it easier at one level to step back and identify general patterns. We can point to what seem to be case law blips i.e. instances or even phases of case law that temporarily, but not definitively, shift the current of the law. But when we overlay that task with the relative fluidity of court-made law (especially principle-driven, constitutional court-made law), the different dynamics that drive case law fragmentation (which include, for present purposes, the heterarchically expressed objectives of the primary Treaty texts), and the evidenced tendency of the Court to nurture concurrent strands of discordant case law, then how do we distinguish the blips from the authentic case law path? On the free movement of goods, for example, which phase will turn out to be the mutation: the expansive case law post-*Keck* (which fits with *Dassonville*) or *Keck* itself (which fits with *Krantz* and *Graf*)? Leaning towards the former, Spaventa remarks incisively that 'the *broader* interpretation given to [free movement] provisions, as controversial as this might be, gives rise to a jurisprudence which is more internally consistent. The applicability of the Treaty freedoms is excluded only in relation to *a handful of situations* where it is *impossible* to establish a causal effect between rule and alleged barrier'.[126] In Chapter 4, however, we saw the opposite dynamic gaining traction in current case law on the free movement of persons, underscoring the importance of stepping back from the virtues of case law convergence and assessing differences as well as similarities in global case law patterns and trends.

In the context of Article 34 TFEU but with broader resonance, Horsley argues that different types of exclusionary principles serve a common purpose i.e. to remove from the scope of the Treaty 'genuinely non-discriminatory national measures that simply outline the conditions for economic activity within individual Member State markets. In other words, the term characterises national measures that do not prevent (block) the free movement of goods between the Member States or discriminate directly or indirectly in favour of the national market in any way'; he then criticizes recent case law that focused on 'substantial' hindrances to the free movement of goods, arguing that 'the Court should consider rationalising *and reasserting* its case law on the exclusionary rules'.[127] Similarly, Spaventa has suggested that if there is no causal connection, the free movement provisions simply *cannot* apply i.e. the measure challenged cannot ever be an actual or potential restriction on free movement rights.[128] Oliver holds the opposite view, however, preferring to view remoteness as 'within the terms of the *Dassonville* test'—he argues that applying remoteness as 'a separate principle which qualifies that test' would 'add an additional and . . . unnecessary principle without giving any guidance as to how the test of "certainty and directness" is to be applied'.[129] The resolution of this quandary is innately bound up with gaining a better understanding of the contours of the positive as well as exclusionary scope of the Treaty. That is why,

126 Spaventa, n91, 270 (emphasis added).

127 Horsley, n2, 736 (emphasis added).

128 Spaventa, n91, 253.

129 Oliver, n20, 789. See similarly, AG La Pergola in *BASF*, para. 18 of the Opinion (where he describes the 'too uncertain and too indirect' test as 'laid down' in *Dassonville*) and AG Tizzano in Case C-442/02 *CaixaBank France v Ministère de l'Économie, des Finances et de l'Industrie* [2004] ECR I-8961, paras 73–75 of the Opinion.

here, the principles of *de minimis* and remoteness are located, for now, as sitting somewhere between negative and positive scope.

5. Conclusion

We have seen in this chapter that a remoteness test grounded in causation, and most commonly expressed as effects too uncertain and indirect, is both relevant and increasing in relevance in free movement case law. It remains to be established whether questions about causation could valuably be addressed even more systematically or whether such a step adds an unhelpful and overly subjective layer of analysis to already complex case law. It was also shown that the case law sometimes blurs the properly distinct nature and objectives of causation and appreciability.

More fundamentally, it is clear that exclusions from the scope of the Treaty *are* sometimes based on appreciability criteria, notwithstanding the Court's repeated rejection of a *de minimis* rule more formally. In the interests of integrity and coherence, it needs to be acknowledged that the *van de Haar* case law has been adjusted: in other words, the profile and effects of appreciability as a framework principle operating in free movement law need to be articulated. It may be that appreciability is a less loaded way to think about de facto *de minimis.* In Chapter 7, these questions will be picked up as part of broader debates about limiting the positive scope of free movement law, into which the discussion here necessarily collapses. The pliability of the objectives shaping the internal market are not much discussed in either the Opinions or judgments relating to appreciability and remoteness; but that factor is a critical linchpin in trying to work out both their existing impact and the extent to which their potential should be further tapped—or more tightly contained.

6

The Positive Scope of Free Movement Law: Discriminatory Restrictions

1. Introduction

Agreeing with Snell, '[p]erhaps the most fundamental question of internal market law is what amounts to a restriction on free movement'.[1] But also agreeing with AG Poiares Maduro in *Viking Line*, '[s]ometimes, when the questions are complicated, the answers are simple. This is not one of those occasions'.[2] Over preceding chapters, analysis of the negative scope of the Treaty revealed that a series of principles, often of unsettled nature or application, has the capacity, at least, to take situations beyond the reach of free movement law. Reflecting on the dynamics of negative scope necessarily introduced the character of restrictions on free movement rights in a positive sense too. The same words emerged consistently over a range of different contexts: breadth, reach, scale, and openness on the one hand; curtailing, refining, delimiting, and constraining on the other. A central tension framing debates about positive scope is that there is a relatively consistent *definition* of restrictions operating in the case law, but the *boundaries* of that definition demonstrably shift in various ways, at different points in time, and/or in the interests of an apparently varied range of purposes. There is coherence at the core, in other words, but persistent fragmentation at the edges.

This chapter seeks to understand how the foundational dynamics of *discrimination* shape the positive scope of free movement law in the first instance. In many respects, discrimination is the 'easy' framework principle: protectionism is anathema to the very idea of a frontier-free market. In Section 2, the Treaty framework and case law criteria applied to determine whether a national rule or practice is capable of constituting a restriction of free movement rights will first be briefly presented. The significance of discrimination in the case law will then be outlined in Section 3, looking at, first, the relevance of discrimination for delivering and achieving the objectives of the internal market and, second, the distinction between

[1] J Snell, 'And then there were two: Products and citizens in Community law' in T Tridimas and P Nebbia (eds.), *European Union Law for the Twenty-First Century: Volume II* (Hart Publishing, 2004) 49 at 50.

[2] AG Poiares Maduro in Case C-438/05 *International Transport Workers' Federation and Finnish Seamen's Union v Viking Line ABP and OÜ Viking Line Eesti* [2007] ECR I-10779, para. 1 of the Opinion.

direct and indirect discrimination in case law practice. Finally, impelling the discussion towards how and why non-discriminatory restrictions fall within the scope of the Treaty in Chapter 7, the limits of discrimination analysis will be introduced in Section 4.

2. Restrictions: the basic framework

As noted in Section 1, the shape of the Treaty's positive scope has emerged inversely to some extent already, through the conclusions drawn about the negative scope of free movement law in previous chapters. In this section, the basic elements of what *does* constitute a restriction of or obstacle to free movement rights will be summarized. First, it is clear that the Treaty does not *require* discrimination before free movement rights can be restricted within the meaning of EU law:

Citizenship: Discrimination not required (Article 21(1) TFEU: 'Every citizen of the Union shall have the right to move and reside *freely* within the territory of the Member States'; see also Article 20(2)(a) TFEU)

Goods: Discrimination not required (Article 30 TFEU: 'Customs duties on imports and exports *and charges having equivalent effect shall be prohibited* between Member States'; Article 34 TFEU: 'Quantitative restrictions on imports and *all measures having equivalent effect* shall be prohibited between Member States')

Workers: Discrimination relevant—(Article 45(2) TFEU: 'Such freedom of movement *shall entail the abolition of any discrimination based on nationality* between workers of the Member States as regards employment, remuneration and other conditions of work and employment'; Article 45(3) TFEU: '(c) to stay in a Member State for the purpose of employment *in accordance with the provisions governing the employment of nationals of that State*')—**but not required** (Article 45(3) TFEU: '[Such freedom of movement] shall entail the right... (a) to accept offers of employment actually made; (b) *to move freely* within the territory of Member States for this purpose;... (d) to remain in the territory of a Member State after having been employed in that State')

Establishment: Discrimination relevant—(Article 49 TFEU: 'Freedom of establishment shall include the right to take up and pursue activities as self-employed persons and to set up and manage undertakings... *under the conditions laid down for its own nationals by the law of the country where such establishment is effected*')—**but not required** (Article 49 TFEU: '*restrictions on the freedom of establishment* of nationals of a Member State in the territory of another Member State *shall be prohibited*')

Services: Discrimination relevant—(Article 57 TFEU: 'the person providing a service may, in order to do so, temporarily pursue his activity in the Member State where the service is provided, *under the same conditions as are imposed by that State on its own nationals*')—**but not required** (Article 56 TFEU: '*restrictions on freedom to provide services within the Union shall be prohibited* in respect of nationals of Member States who are established in a Member State other than that of the person for whom the services are intended')

Capital: Discrimination not required (Article 63(1): '*all restrictions on the movement of capital* between Member States and between Member States and third countries *shall be prohibited*')

This overview shows that discrimination on the grounds of nationality is mentioned expressly in certain Treaty provisions, but it also demonstrates that the scope of free movement rights is not confined to discriminatory restrictions for any of the freedoms either. It is thus important to emphasize that it is not (just) *the Court* that is pushing for an understanding of restrictions beyond discrimination—it is (also) *the Treaty*. It follows that the definition of a restriction developed in *Dassonville* for Article 34 TFEU, introduced in Chapter 5, was Treaty-compliant.[3] That the Treaty was concerned with but not confined to eradicating discriminatory restrictions was confirmed in *van Binsbergen*:

> The restrictions to be abolished pursuant to Articles [56 and 57 TFEU] *include* all requirements imposed on the person providing the service by reason in particular of his nationality or of the fact that he does not habitually reside in the State where the service is provided, which do not apply to persons established within the national territory *or which may prevent or otherwise obstruct the activities of the person providing the service. In particular*, a requirement that the person providing the service must be habitually resident within the territory of the State where the service is to be provided may, according to the circumstances, have the result of depriving Article [56] of all useful effect, in view of the fact that the *precise object of that Article is to abolish restrictions on freedom to provide services* imposed on persons who are not established in the State where the service is to be provided.[4]

The implications of this approach emerged more definitively in later case law. For example, in its judgment in *Säger*, the Court stated that 'Article [56] requires *not only the elimination of all discrimination* against a person providing services on the ground of his nationality but *also the abolition of any restriction, even if it applies without distinction to national providers of services and to those of other Member States*, when it is *liable to prohibit or otherwise impede* the activities of a provider of services established in another Member State where he lawfully provides similar services'.[5] Therefore, assuming that the preconditions outlined in Chapters 3 and 4 are satisfied—i.e. Treaty-relevant personal and material scope, including questions of horizontality; no abuse of EU rights; cross-border connection (unless narrowly defined citizenship exceptions apply)—and building on the analysis in Chapter 5 on *de minimis* and remoteness, Figures 6.1 and 6.2 offer a provisional template to represent how a restriction is defined in free movement case law at present.

Three points can be emphasized at this stage. First, because the *Dassonville* definition is the test cited most consistently across all sectors of free movement law, its main elements are used to frame the definition of a restriction here irrespective of the Treaty provision at issue. Second, we have seen in previous chapters that, by reinforcing and building on the openness of the *Dassonville* language, the Court has steadily amplified the potential for contested rules to amount to restrictions of free

[3] Case 8/74 *Procureur du Roi v Dassonville* [1974] ECR 837, para. 5: '[a]ll trading rules enacted by Member States which are capable of hindering, directly or indirectly, actually or potentially, intra-Community trade are to be considered as measures having an effect equivalent to quantitative restrictions'.

[4] Case 33/74 *Van Binsbergen v Bestuur van de Bedrijfsvereniging voor de Metaalnijverheid* [1974] ECR 1299, paras 10–11 (emphasis added).

[5] Case C-76/90 *Säger v Dennemeyer & Co. Ltd* [1991] ECR I-4221, para. 12 (emphasis added).

Direct or indirect (i.e. discriminatory object or effect)	
Actual or potential (incl. deter, disadvantage, discourage, dissuade, etc.)	
→ *Presumptions:*	*Object or effect prevents or hinders movement*
⇒ *Thresholds met:*	- Effects are certain and direct (or not *too* indirect)
	- Effects are sufficiently significant or substantial

Fig. 6.1 Discriminatory restrictions

Direct or indirect (i.e. restrictive object or effect)	
Actual or potential (incl. deter, disadvantage, discourage, dissuade, etc.)	
→ *Conditions to be established:*	*Object or effect might prevent or hinder movement*
	- Sufficient causal link
	- Sufficiently appreciable impact
⇒ *Exclusions from scope:*	*Too uncertain and indirect*
	Insignificant impact

Fig. 6.2 Non-discriminatory restrictions

movement rights. National measures or practices can constitute Treaty-relevant barriers, obstacles, or restrictions if they do *or are liable to* deter,[6] disadvantage,[7] dissuade,[8] hinder,[9] impede,[10] make less attractive,[11] or seriously inconvenience[12] the exercise of free movement rights; or if they prevent,[13] or are liable to hinder or

[6] E.g. Case C-370/90 *R v Immigration Appeal Tribunal and Singh, ex parte Secretary of State for the Home Department* [1992] ECR I-4265, para. 19, Articles 45 and 49 TFEU.

[7] E.g. Case C-224/98 *D'Hoop v Office national de l'emploi* [2002] ECR I-6191, para. 34, Article 21 TFEU.

[8] E.g. Joined Cases C-578/10 to C-580/10 *Staatssecretaris van Financiën v Van Putten, Mook and Frank*, judgment of 26 April 2012, para. 40, Article 63 TFEU.

[9] E.g. *Dassonville*, para. 5, Article 34 TFEU.

[10] E.g. Case C-42/07 *Liga Portuguesa de Futebol Profissional and Bwin International Ltd v Departamento de Jogos da Santa Casa da Misericórdia de Lisboa* [2009] ECR I-7633, para. 51, Article 56 TFEU.

[11] E.g. Case C-19/92 *Kraus v Land Baden-Württemberg* [1993] ECR I-1663, para. 32, Articles 45 and 49 TFEU.

[12] E.g. Case C-148/02 *Garcia Avello v Belgian State* [2003] ECR I-11613, para. 36, Article 20 TFEU.

[13] E.g. Case C-415/93 *Union royale belge des sociétés de football association ASBL v Bosman* [1995] ECR I-4921, para. 99, Article 45 TFEU.

impede[14] or affect[15] access to (the markets of) other States. Speaking about the free movement of persons but with broader resonance, AG Sharpston depicted the essence of a restriction as follows: 'does [the national rule] potentially have a "chilling effect" on any EU citizen contemplating exercising free movement rights within the EU as a worker, a self-employed person or simply as a citizen'?[16] However, problems caused by the *resulting* and/or *varying* reach of both actual and prospective effects have been mapped in Chapters 4 and 5 too. Third, we saw in Chapter 5 that limits based on the concepts of remoteness and *de minimis* are increasingly being applied to constrict the scope of the Treaty, normally in respect of non-discriminatory restrictions. But we also saw that the underpinning principles and tests are not properly defined, worked out, or distinguished in conceptual terms; they are not consistently applied; their application creates particular risks for subjective or arbitrary decision-making; and the impact of appreciability thresholds, in particular, has not been reconciled with apparently contradictory lines of authority that reject the relevance of *de minimis* concerns in free movement law. These points will be addressed again in Chapter 7, as will the *desirability* as well as the completeness of the framework suggested by Figure 6.2 for non-discriminatory restrictions. The remainder of the discussion in this chapter is concerned with the principles, and limits, relevant to discriminatory restrictions, as summarized in Figure 6.1.

3. Discriminatory restrictions

The prohibition of discrimination is one of the fundamental driving forces of free movement law. As argued in Chapter 4, equal treatment is a general principle of EU law with multiple facets and considerable dormant potential.[17] However, the Treaty, in what is now Article 18 TFEU, has always expressly stipulated a directly effective prohibition of *nationality* discrimination. We should not forget that the EU internal market is an artificially engineered space. A sustained commitment to the breaking down of national frontiers and protectionist instincts is critical for its realization. In this section, the basic principles of non-discrimination as it relates to nationality will first be briefly outlined, and the implications of the distinction between direct and indirect discrimination will then be considered. As noted in Section 1, the limits of discrimination analysis will be introduced in Section 4,

[14] E.g. Case C-142/05 *Åklagaren v Mickelsson and Roos* [2009] ECR I-4273, para. 28, Article 34 TFEU.

[15] E.g. Case C-171/08 *Commission v Portugal (Golden shares)* [2010] ECR I-6817, para. 67, Articles 49 and 63 TFEU; the qualifier of 'directly' affecting access had appeared in earlier case law e.g. Case C-384/93 *Alpine Investments BV v Minister van Financiën* [1995] ECR I-1141, para. 38, Article 56 TFEU.

[16] AG Sharpston in Joined Cases C-523/11 and C-585/11 *Prinz v Region Hannover; Seeberger v Studentenwerk Heidelberg*, pending; para. 38 of the Opinion.

[17] See generally, M Bell, *Anti-Discrimination Law and the European Union* (OUP, 2002). The significance of non-discrimination beyond free movement law was exemplified by, for example, its application to former Third Pillar instruments even before the ratification of the Lisbon Treaty; see Case C-123/08 *Wolzenburg* [2009] ECR I-9621.

paving the way for discussion in Chapter 7 of the dominant concern, in both case law and academic discourse, with the prohibition of *non*-discriminatory obstacles to movement.

(a) The significance of discrimination

In his Opinion in *Marks & Spencer*, AG Poiares Maduro outlined the significance of discrimination in free movement law in the broader context of an internal market regulated through the exercise of shared competence, accentuating the significance of requiring a cross-border connection and the principle of remoteness:

> In an internal market 'characterised by the abolition, *as between Member States*, of obstacles to the free movement of goods, persons, services and capital', the Member States are no longer at liberty to ignore the constraints imposed by those matters on the definition and application of their national policies. In that context the task of the Court is *not to engage in challenging every rule of State origin having an indirect or wholly uncertain effect* on the *exercise of the freedoms of movement.* It is not for it to review the political choices made by the Member States. Judicial review of measures likely to prohibit, impede or render less attractive the exercise of the freedoms of movement rather seeks to ensure *that those choices take account of the impact which they may have on transnational situations.* The policies adopted *must not result in less favourable treatment* being accorded to transnational situations than to purely national situations . . . Only that interpretation is such as to reconcile the principle of *respect for State competences* and the *safeguarding of the objective of establishing an internal market* in which the rights of European citizens are protected.[18]

Whatever else internal market law can and should achieve, the dissolution of discriminatory barriers to transnational movement is perhaps its most vital foundational task. The abolition of discrimination can also be easily defended as a defining normative objective for realizing a frontier-free economic space.[19]

Directly discriminatory restrictions on free movement rights openly apply *different* rules or procedures through the condition of nationality, conveying deliberate protectionist intent.[20] As might be expected, condemning directly discriminatory measures for incompatibility with the developing common market was an important element of early free movement case law, but it would be a mistake to think that the task is complete or that overtly protectionist national measures are by now extinct.[21] In Chapter 5, it was shown that the Court had also embedded in

[18] AG Poiares Maduro in Case C-446/03 *Marks & Spencer plc v Halsey (Her Majesty's Inspector of Taxes)* [2005] ECR I-10837, para. 37 of the Opinion (emphasis added).

[19] On the normative foundations of discrimination as the basic principle of EU free movement law, see N Bernard, 'Discrimination and free movement in EC Law' (1996) 45:1 ICLQ 82.

[20] E.g. Case C-85/96 *Martínez Sala v Freistaat Bayern* [1998] ECR I-2691 (Article 20 TFEU); Case 249/81 *Commission v Ireland (Buy Irish)* [1982] ECR 4005 (Article 34 TFEU); Case 167/73 *Commission v France* [1974] ECR 359 (Article 45 TFEU); Case 2/74 *Reyners v Belgian State* [1974] ECR 631 (Article 56 TFEU); Case 186/87 *Cowan v Trésor public* [1989] ECR 195 (Article 59 TFEU); Case C-302/97 *Konle v Republik Österreich* [1999] ECR I-3099 (Article 63 TFEU).

[21] At the time of writing, for example, the city of Antwerp had introduced differential—i.e. for Belgians compared to non-Belgians—fees for residents registering with its local authorities, charging €17 and €267 respectively; see <http://euobserver.com/justice/119230>.

foundational case law the idea that national measures having the *effect*—and not just the object—of restricting free movement rights are caught by the Treaty too.[22] This idea is given general expression across free movement law through the principle that instances of both direct *and indirect* nationality discrimination are prohibited. Bringing indirectly discriminatory measures within the scope of the Treaty was a critical step in terms of ensuring meaningful impact. It also had softening political implications in a positive sense, dissociating possible breaches of EU law from a discourse of blame and intent.

It was also noted in Section 2 that the scope of free movement law was never confined to correcting discriminatory effects. The foundational judgments in *Dassonville* and *van Binsbergen* pitched the scope of free movement rights broadly, articulating the idea of restrictions or hindrances rather than discrimination. In reality, however, most of the national measures initially reviewed by the Court *did* involve discriminatory restrictions—and mostly directly discriminatory restrictions. The concerns of the case law changed over time, but it is important to remember that the Court continues to apply discrimination reasoning exclusively for some aspects of free movement law. First, as mentioned in Chapter 5, the scope of Article 35 TFEU, on the export of goods and measures having equivalent effect, did not develop along the same trajectory as the more expansive case law on Article 34. In *Groenveld*, the Court defined measures having equivalent effect to quantitative restrictions on exports as measures 'which have as their specific object or effect the restriction of patterns of exports and *thereby the establishment of a difference in treatment* between the domestic trade of a Member State and its export trade in such a way as to provide a *particular advantage for national production* or for the domestic market of the State in question, at the expense of the production or of the trade of other Member States'.[23] The Court revised that position to some extent in *Gysbrechts*, aligning the scope of Articles 34 and 35 more closely.[24] AG Trstenjak outlined three arguments in favour of moving on from the *Groenveld* test. First, if a product is made solely for the export market, national rules restricting its export, even severely, could never come within the scope of Article 35 since no comparative advantage for the domestic market could possibly be shown. Second, she emphasized that Articles 34 and 35 TFEU 'are based on the same principle, namely the elimination of barriers to trade flows in intra-[Union] trade'. Third, she supported convergence within free movement law more generally, since '[t]he definition of measures having an equivalent effect to quantitative restrictions on exports remains the only one of the fundamental freedoms in which the Court has persisted in requiring the existence of different treatment in order to find a restriction on that freedom'.[25]

[22] Case 15/79 *PB Groenveld BV v Produktschap voor Vee en Vlees* [1979] ECR 3409, para. 7 (Article 35 TFEU); confirmed in e.g. Case C-108/09 *Ker-Optika bt v ÀNTSZ Dél-dunántúli Regionális Intézete* [2010] ECR I-12213, para. 49 (Article 34 TFEU).

[23] *Groenveld*, para. 7 (emphasis added).

[24] Case C-205/07 *Gysbrechts and Santurel Inter BVBA* [2008] ECR I-9947.

[25] AG Trstenjak in *Gysbrechts*, paras 42–48 of the Opinion.

The solution applied by the Court was more modest. It accepted that the contested national measure fell within the scope of Article 35 even though it applied 'to all traders active in the national territory'; but it also emphasized that 'its actual effect is none the less greater on goods leaving the market of the exporting Member State than on the marketing of goods in the domestic market of that Member State'.[26] What the decision in *Gysbrechts* emphasizes is discrimination through *effect* rather than *object*—and both elements were present in *Groenveld* already. Claims that the Court revolutionized the scope of Article 35 beyond discrimination in *Gysbrechts* are thus overstated, betraying a terminological confusion between indirect discrimination and 'genuinely' non-discriminatory obstacles.[27] That is not to say, of course, that the Court might not take a bigger step in the future.[28]

Second, the Court generally reasons case law on restrictions caused by the application of tax rules through a requirement of discriminatory treatment. In the context of service provision, for example, the Court held in *Mobistar* that the application of tax rules will not contravene Article 59 TFEU if they 'apply without distinction to all [relevant service providers] and... foreign operators are not, either in fact or in law, more adversely affected by those measures than national operators'.[29] It was noted in Chapter 5 that the reasoning in *Mobistar* hinges on the premise that 'measures, *the only effect of which is to create additional costs* in respect of the service in question and which affect in the same way the provision of services between Member States and that within one Member State, do not fall within the scope of Article [59]'.[30] This exclusion patently qualifies the scope of the open-ended definition of a restriction on free movement rights more generally. Additional costs make the exercise of free movement 'less attractive' in a literal sense and that may well hinder or deter natural or legal persons from undertaking transnational activity. But it is not a factor that will suffice to generate a Treaty-concerned restriction. The decision in *Mobistar* thus exemplifies a limited but distinct impetus reinforcing the necessity of discrimination in certain regulatory circumstances. As AG Geelhoed emphasized in *Thin Cap*, 'the concept of indistinctly applicable "restrictions" of freedom of movement used in the Court's general free movement case-law cannot meaningfully be transposed per se to the direct tax sphere. Rather, due to the fact that criteria for asserting tax jurisdiction

[26] *Gysbrechts*, para. 43.

[27] See similarly, P Wenneras and KB Moen, 'Selling arrangements, keeping *Keck*' (2010) 35:3 ELRev 387 at 393. On the scope of Article 35 TFEU more generally, see M Szydło, 'Export restrictions within the structure of free movement of goods: Reconsideration of an old pardigm' (2010) 47:2 CMLRev 753, and A Dawes, 'A freedom reborn? The new yet unclear scope of Article 29 EC' (2009) 34:4 ELRev 639.

[28] A Tryfonidou, 'Further steps on the road to convergence among the market freedoms' (2010) 35:1 ELRev 36 at 54–5.

[29] Joined Cases C-544/03 and C-545/03 *Mobistar SA v Commune de Fléron; Belgacom Mobile SA v Commune de Schaerbeek* [2006] ECR I-6675, para. 32.

[30] *Mobistar*, para. 31 (emphasis added).

are generally nationality- or residence-based, the question is whether the national direct tax measure is indirectly or directly discriminatory'.[31]

Another constraint informing the extent to which discrimination is relevant in tax cases, even in clearly transnational scenarios—e.g. where workers reside in a State other than their place of employment—was expressed in *Gschwind*:

> As far as direct taxes are concerned, the situations of residents and of non-residents in a given State *are not generally comparable*, since income received in the territory of a State by a non-resident is in most cases only a part of his total income, which is concentrated at his place of residence, and a non-resident's personal ability to pay tax, determined by reference to his aggregate income and his personal and family circumstances, is more easy to assess at the place where his personal and financial interests are centred, which in general is the place where he has his usual abode.[32]

Additionally, picking up on case law noted in Chapter 4, the Court emphasized in *Schempp* that '[w]hile in the present state of [Union] law direct taxation falls within the competence of the Member States, the latter must none the less exercise that competence in accordance with [Union] law, in particular the provisions of the Treaty concerning the right of every citizen of the Union to move and reside freely within the territory of the Member States, and therefore *avoid any overt or covert discrimination on the basis of nationality*'.[33] Two related points can be made about the Court's focus on citizenship in *Schempp*. First, its entrenchment of discrimination was not citizenship-specific; the underlying principles were already well established in case law on economic activity.[34] Second, conversely, citizenship has not had a significant effect on the substance of that economic framework one way or the other: the obligation on States to respect equal treatment principles in the application of their taxation rules pre-dated the status of citizenship, but citizenship has not extended State obligations beyond discrimination in that context.[35] Rather, the Court has confirmed that 'the Treaty offers no guarantee to a citizen of the Union that transferring his activities to a Member State other than that in which he previously resided will be neutral as regards taxation. Given the relevant disparities in the tax legislation of the Member States, such a transfer may be to the citizen's advantage or not, according to circumstances'.[36] However,

[31] AG Geelhoed in Case C-524/04 *Test Claimants in the Thin Cap Group Litigation v Commissioners of Inland Revenue* [2007] ECR I-2107, para. 48 of the Opinion.

[32] Case C-391/97 *Gschwind v Finanzamt Aachen-Außenstadt* [1999] ECR I-5451, para. 22 (emphasis added).

[33] Case C-403/03 *Schempp v Finanzamt München V* [2005] ECR I-6421, para. 19 (emphasis added).

[34] E.g. Case C-279/93 *Finanzamt Köln-Altstadt v Schumacker* [1995] ECR I-225.

[35] In *Schumacker*, the Court applied reasoning that goes back to Joined Cases 6 and 11/69 *Commission v French Republic* [1969] ECR 523 to derive the obligation of non-discrimination with respect to Article 45 TFEU and the application of national taxation rules.

[36] Case C-240/10 *Schulz-Delzers and Schulz v Finanzamt Stuttgart III*, judgment of 15 September 2011, para. 42; on the same point for Article 45 TFEU, see Case C-387/01 *Weigel v Finanzlandesdirektion für Vorarlberg* [2004] ECR I-4981, para. 55.

the Court's prevailing emphasis on discrimination in the field of taxation presents particular challenges in the sphere of double taxation.[37]

(b) Direct and indirect discrimination

The Court frequently refers to measures as 'non-discriminatory' but, in substance, it is actually considering *indirectly* discriminatory effects.[38] In *Sotgiu*, addressing Article 45 TFEU, the Court held that '[t]he rules regarding equality of treatment... forbid not only overt discrimination by reason of nationality but also *all covert forms of discrimination* which, by the application of other criteria of differentiation, lead in fact to the same result'.[39] As outlined in subsection (a), *directly* discriminatory measures are discriminatory both in law and in effect i.e. they are *distinctly* applicable to *host* State nationals, products, services etc. only and so, in *Dassonville* language, they convey both discriminatory *object* and discriminatory *effect*. Conversely, *indirectly* discriminatory measures are discriminatory in their effects only i.e. they apply *indistinctly* in law to both host *and* home State nationals, products, services etc. but their effects impact *more* on the former. The judgment in *O'Flynn* is the classic exposition of indirect discrimination in free movement law:

> [C]onditions imposed by national law must be regarded as indirectly discriminatory where, although applicable irrespective of nationality, they *affect essentially* migrant workers... or the *great majority of those affected* are migrant workers,... where they are indistinctly applicable but can *more easily be satisfied* by national workers than by migrant workers... or where there is a risk that they may *operate to the particular detriment* of migrant workers...[40]

Residence conditions constitute one of the most common examples of indirect discrimination in free movement case law.[41] Mapping the reasoning summarized in *O'Flynn*, the Court has explained that 'a measure under which a distinction is drawn on the basis of residence or ordinary residence... is liable to operate mainly to the detriment of nationals of other Member States, since non-residents are in the

[37] See generally, J Snell, 'Non-discriminatory tax obstacles in Community law' (2007) 56:2 ICLQ 339; Snell also discusses underlying policy concerns to rationalize the Court's cautious approach to review of national tax rules.

[38] See e.g. Case 120/78 *Rewe-Zentrale AG v Bundesmonopolverwaltung für Branntwein (Cassis de Dijon)* [1979] ECR 649. This point is discussed further in Chapter 7.

[39] E.g. Case 152/73 *Sotgiu v Deutsche Bundespost* [1974] ECR 153, para. 11 (emphasis added).

[40] Case C-237/94 *O'Flynn v Adjudication Officer* [1996] ECR I-2617, para. 18 (emphasis added); see recently e.g. Case C-172/11 *Erny v Daimler AG—Werk Wörth*, judgment of 28 June 2012, para. 41: '[u]nless it is objectively justified and proportionate to its aim, a provision of national law or a clause in an agreement must be regarded as indirectly discriminatory if it is *intrinsically liable to affect migrant workers more than national workers* and if there is a consequent risk that it will place the former *at a particular disadvantage*' (emphasis added).

[41] E.g. Case C-388/01 *Commission v Italy (Admission to museums)* [2003] ECR I-721 (Article 56 TFEU); conditions connected to residence can also be imposed on legal persons, see e.g. Case C-254/98 *Schutzverband gegen unlauteren Wettbewerb v TK-Heimdienst Sass GmbH* [2000] ECR I-151 (Article 34 TFEU; cf. the Opinion of AG La Pergola, who considered the restrictions to be non-discriminatory selling arrangements and thus, as discussed in Chapter 7, outside the scope of Article 34).

majority of cases foreigners'.[42] Other common examples of indirectly discriminatory measures include language rules,[43] conditions attached to the recognitions of qualifications,[44] and product composition or packaging rules.[45] Two further points can be noted about the Court's methodology in cases involving indirect discrimination. First, it was observed in Chapter 4 that the Court's level of engagement with the existence and situation of a comparator in this context—a classic feature of discrimination analysis—is essentially light-touch. Second, linked to the capacity of the *Dassonville* definition to catch potential restrictions and reflecting the broader discussion in Chapter 5, the Court confirms indirect discrimination by the application of intuitive reasoning rather than through systematic evaluation of empirical evidence.[46]

As a final point, another innovation in *Cassis* i.e. the relevance of mutual recognition for internal market law should be noted. In its judgment, the Court stated that '[t]here is . . . no valid reason why, provided that they have been lawfully produced and marketed in one of the Member States, alcoholic beverages should not be introduced into any other Member State'.[47] The idea of mutual recognition had been considered in the context of recognizing professional qualifications (e.g. in *Reyners* and *van Binsbergen*), pending the adoption of Treaty-mandated legislation to implement that objective. But the reasoning in *Cassis* introduced mutual recognition as a subliminal framework principle that was intended to work quietly alongside the prohibition of direct and indirect discrimination in free movement law. Perhaps it has done so too quietly, since the potentially significant tolerance ethos of mutual recognition—which allows national regulators to shape market rules for public interest reasons, but equally allows products or services reflecting diverse standards to participate seamlessly in the same market—never established deep roots in the free movement case law outwith consideration of specific legislative frameworks, a point returned to in Chapter 7. Contemporary discourse on mutual recognition has focused instead on its shaping of EU criminal law.[48]

(c) Questions at the edge

Two connected issues will be considered in this subsection. First, even if it seems that the prohibition of nationality discrimination is completely and securely

[42] Case C-103/08 *Gottwald v Bezirkshauptmannschaft Bregenz* [2009] ECR I-9117, para. 28.

[43] E.g. Case 379/87 *Groener v Minister for Education and the City of Dublin Vocational Educational Committee* [1989] ECR 3967 (Article 45 TFEU); Case C-193/05 *Commission v Luxembourg* [2006] ECR I-8673 (Article 49 TFEU).

[44] E.g. *D'Hoop* (Article 21 TFEU).

[45] E.g. Case C-368/95 *Vereinigte Familiapress Zeitungsverlags- und vertriebs GmbH v Heinrich Bauer Verlag* [1997] ECR I-3689 (Article 34 TFEU).

[46] See further, D Wilsher, 'Does *Keck* discrimination make any sense? An assessment of the non-discrimination principle within the European single market' (2008) 33:1 ELRev 3. The same point applies to establishing 'substantial' impediments to market access, discussed in Chapter 7.

[47] *Cassis de Dijon*, para. 14.

[48] E.g. G Taupiac-Nouvel, 'The principle of mutual recognition in criminal matters: A new model of judicial cooperation within the European Union' (2012) 2:3 EuCLR 236; I Bantekas, 'The principle of mutual recognition in EU criminal law' (2007) 32:3 ELRev 365; V Mitsilegas 'The constitutional implications of mutual recognition in criminal matters in the EU' (2006) 43:5 CMLRev 1277.

entrenched as a framework principle of free movement law, does the decision in *Bressol* caution that we should not take that for granted?[49] Second, linking back to the overview of the justification stage outlined in Chapter 1, does the increasingly fragile distinction between the Treaty-based derogation and Court-created justification frameworks mean that the formally persisting requirement to classify a measure as either directly or indirectly discriminatory has dissolved in reality?

Beginning with the decision in *Bressol*, the circumstances of the case related to restrictions placed on access to certain university courses in Belgium. More generally, the case raises the fact of uneven migration flows within the EU. In case law concerning access to universities specifically, the underlying issue is that States seeking to operate a policy of free or low-threshold access to their university programmes inevitably attract high numbers of migrant university students: primarily, because of lower programme entry requirements relative to the students' home States, but also influenced by the language(s) through which instruction is provided. In landmark proceedings against Austria, the Court had found that differential university entry requirements for students who gained their entrance-level qualifications in Austria compared to students who did so in other Member States amounted to a classic instance of indirect discrimination: the system in place was 'liable to have a greater effect on nationals of other Member States than on Austrian nationals'.[50] The Court also concluded that Austria had failed to demonstrate that the rules were based on objective considerations independent of the nationality of the persons concerned. The decision sparked significant public criticism of the Court, from within Austria but also from other Member States.[51]

Subsequently, in *Bressol*, rules put in place in Belgium to restrict access to nine medical or paramedical university programmes—driven by concerns about teaching quality and the sustainability of the affected region's health infrastructure owing to a significant increase in student numbers from other States (especially France)[52]—were challenged by a coalition of French students and Belgian university teachers. Students who met the codified residence criteria had open access to the relevant programmes. All other students were subject to a 30 per cent threshold rule, the places for which were assigned through the drawing of lots. In her Opinion, aligning with the decision in *Commission v Austria*, AG Sharpston found that the contested Belgian rules contravened Articles 18 and 21 TFEU, and could not be justified by objective reasons in the public interest. While not ignoring the acknowledged challenges faced by the national regulator, she emphasized the fundamental nature of non-discrimination on grounds of nationality:

[49] Case C-73/08 *Bressol and Others and Céline Chaverot and Others v Gouvernement de la Communauté française* [2010] ECR I-2735.

[50] Cases C-147/03 *Commission v Austria* [2005] ECR I-5969, para. 47. The Court had previously found against Belgium for the imposition of similar rules; no justification arguments had been raised in the earlier case (Case C-65/03 *Commission v Belgium* [2004] ECR I-6427).

[51] See S Garben, case comment, (2010) 47:5 CMLRev 1493 at 1496–7.

[52] For the relevant statistics, see AG Sharpston in *Bressol*, para. 20 of the Opinion.

The prohibition on discrimination should . . . be seen as *the cornerstone of the Treaty* precisely because it leaves Member States' regulatory autonomy intact—provided that their laws apply equally to nationals and non-nationals. The key underlying principle is that all citizens of the Union must be treated as individuals, without regard to their nationality. 'Free and equal access to education for all' therefore means exactly what it says. It may not mean 'free and equal access to education for all my nationals'. I accept that the problems faced by the French Community are not insignificant. However, they must be resolved in a way that is not a variant of 'equality for those inside the magic circle' (in this case Belgian nationals), but that respects the 'fundamental status' of EU citizenship by ensuring equal access to education for all EU citizens regardless of nationality.[53]

The Advocate General considered that more appropriate solutions lay in either a politically negotiated but Treaty-compliant outcome agreed between Belgium and France, or harmonisation measures having a wider territorial scope.[54]

Surprisingly, the Grand Chamber took a softer stance in its judgment. First, referring to Articles 165 and 166 TFEU and reflecting the approach of the Court to review of national tax rules outlined in subsection (a) above, the Court first stated that '[t]he Member States are . . . free to opt for an education system based on free access—without restriction on the number of students who may register—or for a system based on controlled access in which the students are selected. However, where they opt for one of those systems or for a combination of them, the rules of the chosen system must comply with European Union law and, in particular, the principle of non-discrimination on grounds of nationality'.[55] Second, the Court restated the fundamentals of its reasoning on indirect discrimination: '[u]nless objectively justified and proportionate to the aim pursued, a provision of national law must be regarded as indirectly discriminatory if it is *intrinsically liable to affect nationals of other Member States more than nationals of the host State* and there is a consequent risk that it will place the former *at a particular disadvantage*'.[56] It then found that the contested national rules constituted such a restriction. In a distinctly hands-off final stage, however, the Court left the determination of justification and proportionality to the referring court—providing detailed guiding principles, but reflecting nothing like the prescriptive condemnation expressed in *Commission v Austria* (or in AG Sharpston's Opinion) since the Court was satisfied that

[53] AG Sharpston in *Bressol*, paras 142–143 of the Opinion (emphasis added); see also, para. 133: '[t]o accept the restrictions put in place by the French Community would amount to allowing Member States to compartmentalise their higher education systems. The Court should therefore be very slow to accept that access to higher education may be restricted even by indirectly discriminatory measures that satisfy the proportionality test (which, so far as appears from the material before the Court, the Belgian measures do not)'.

[54] AG Sharpston in *Bressol*, paras 151–154 of the Opinion. See similarly, D Damjanovic, '"Reserved area" of the Member States and the ECJ: The case of higher education' in H Micklitz and B de Witte (eds.), *The European Court of Justice and the Autonomy of the Member States* (Intersentia, 2012) 149 at 166: 'EU-wide cross-border access can only work to its fullest extent under the conditions of some sort of an EU wide compensation mechanism for the financing of cross-border higher education'.

[55] *Bressol*, para. 29. [56] *Bressol*, para. 41 (emphasis added).

arguments submitted about safeguarding public health might establish a legitimate justification in principle.[57]

The Court's respect for the function of the referring court in determining justification and proportionality is a positive element of the decision in *Bressol.* But the overall change in tone from *Commission v Austria* in a case reviewing the deployment of residence conditions and quotas—archetypal discrimination techniques—was striking, especially since the Court had expressly acknowledged that access to higher education in other Member States is 'an opportunity which constitutes *the very essence* of the principle of freedom of movement for students'.[58] Significantly, links have been drawn between the timing of the judgment in *Bressol* and political decisions by the Commission to suspend a second set of infringement proceedings against both Austria and Belgium with respect to their university admission rules—not because of positive changes in national practice, but because of broader political pressure to secure the ratification of the Lisbon Treaty, 'ignor[ing] the fact that the political truce did not stand in the way of matters ending up in the Court of Justice through the preliminary reference procedure'.[59]

At one level, the case law on access to universities demonstrates the difference in law between *permissible* and *impermissible* discrimination, and reminds us that the former is something that any system allowing for objective justification has to recognize too. But it also exemplifies the dynamics of oscillation that modulate the line between protection of free movement rights and the uneven pursuit of other objectives: by both the Member States *and* the EU institutions. It has to be asked whether the Court's recognition of potentially permissible discrimination in *Bressol* was warranted by what else the decision achieved: notably, respect for national regulatory autonomy, by acknowledging the goals of open access education while simultaneously managing significant resulting pressures on the higher education system caused by clustered migration flows; but also, a more general polity contribution to securing safe passage for the Lisbon Treaty. In other words, was the Court properly cooperating with the change in tack agreed within (and/or imposed upon) the Commission, or improperly shifting the coordinates of free movement law to accommodate short-term political interest? It is important to remember the proviso contained in Article 18 TFEU: discrimination on the grounds of nationality is prohibited '[w]ithin the scope of application of the Treaties' but 'without prejudice to any special provisions contained therein'. Article 165(1) TFEU requires that EU action in the field of education 'fully respect[s] the responsibility of the Member States for . . . the organisation of education systems'—is this a 'special provision' that can legitimately clip the force of discrimination law? The fact that there is no obvious answer to this question links back to the Lisbon-intensified constitutional gap described in Chapter 2 and demonstrated through examples throughout preceding chapters i.e. different parts of the Treaty do not

[57] For further discussion of the contrasting reasoning and outcomes in both cases from the angle of standard of proof, see further, N Nic Shuibhne and M Maci, 'Proving public interest: The growing impact of evidence in free movement case law' (2013) 50:4 CMLRev, forthcoming.

[58] *Bressol*, para. 79 (emphasis added).

[59] Garben, n51, 1497–8.

include appropriate guidance about their relative internal or systemic weight—compounding the problems then generated by the potential legal relevance of different perceptions of the Treaty's unsettled objectives and purposes.

In her Opinion in *Bressol*, AG Sharpston also drew attention to a different problem i.e. it is not always easy to establish whether a national rule or practice is generating direct or indirect discrimination.[60] The relevance of that question is critically linked to another convention, summarized in Chapter 1: if the derogations from free movement rights specified in the Treaty provide the only public interest defences that can be considered in cases involving direct discrimination, then it remains essential to classify free movement restrictions according to their directly or indirectly discriminatory effects. However, in a limited but growing line of authority, mainly on protection of the environment, the Court has applied the broader public interest justification framework, which is supposedly confined to indirectly (and non-) discriminatory measures, in situations where the contested rule in question was *directly* discriminatory. We can also see a distinct change over time in the relevant case law. Initially, the Court at least attempted, albeit not very convincingly, to site the measure in the sphere of direct discrimination.[61] Now, it remains silent about the nature of the measure, thereby avoiding the language of discrimination and related questions about the proper scope of justification arguments altogether.[62]

For example, in *Commission v Austria (Air quality)*, the Court was called upon to review a ban that precluded certain vehicles weighing over 7.5 tonnes from carrying certain goods, affecting a motorway route with significant implications for trans-alpine traffic. Even though the Commission had argued that the measure was discriminatory, the judgment of the Grand Chamber devoted 53 paragraphs to outlining the submissions of the parties but just two paragraphs to its finding that the contested national rule was a measure having equivalent effect to a quantitative restriction that was precluded by Article 34 TFEU—with no comment on the *nature* of the restriction at all. The exclusion of local and regional traffic from the scope of the ban underpinned the Commission's classification of the measure as discriminatory; and, furthermore, rendered the more justification-friendly solution of *indirect* discrimination less compelling.

60 AG Sharpston in *Bressol*, paras 43–76. On the collapsing of the boundaries between *indirect* discrimination and other forms of restriction, see AG Mengozzi in Case C-341/05 *Laval un Partneri Ltd v Svenska Byggnadsarbetareförbundet, Svenska Byggnadsarbetareförbundets avdelning 1, Byggettan and Svenska Elektrikerförbundet* [2007] ECR I-11767, para. 228 of the Opinion.

61 E.g. Case C-2/90 *Commission v Belgium (Walloon waste)* [1992] ECR I-4431; Case C-379/98 *PreussenElektra AG v Schhleswag AG, in the presence of Windpark Reußenköge III GmbH and Land Schleswig-Holstein* [2001] ECR I-2099 (cf. the Opinion of AG Jacobs). In Case C-28/09 *Commission v Austria (Air quality)*, judgment of 21 December 2011, AG Trstenjak described the Court's approach in *Walloon Waste* as 'work[ing] around' the rule on discriminatory restrictions and Treaty-based derogations (see fn34 of the Opinion).

62 Weatherill has described the Court as 'appear[ing] to go out of its way to insist on the continuing salience of presence or absence of discrimination on the basis of origin in determining the available scope of justification' (S Weatherill, 'Free movement of goods' (2012) 61:2 ICLQ 541 at 544, citing Case C-153/08 *Commission v Spain* [2009] ECR I-9735, para. 37 and Case C-400/08 *Commission v Spain (Shopping centres)* [2011] ECR I-1915, para. 73).

In her Opinion on the case, AG Trstenjak referred to jurisprudence confining the justification of discriminatory measures to Treaty-set public interest grounds as 'traditional case-law'—but she cited authority from as recently as 2009 to support the point.[63] The continued renewal of that 'traditional' case law is what reinforces the problem: the Court is, again, neither explaining nor reconciling two contradictory lines of case law that provide different answers to the same legal question. In his Opinion in *PreussenElektra*, AG Jacobs called direct attention to this point: 'the Court has not formally abandoned the rule that imperative requirements cannot be invoked in connection with directly discriminatory measures. In view of the fundamental importance for the analysis of Article [36] of the Treaty of the question whether directly discriminatory measures can be justified by imperative requirements, the Court should, in my view, clarify its position in order to provide the necessary legal certainty'.[64] His call remains unheeded.

Weatherill has argued that '[t]here is strong normative appeal to a model whereby all types of justification are in principle available, but according to which the presence of discrimination would make the job of the regulator in showing that the chosen scheme is lawful particularly onerous'.[65] In *Commission v Austria,* AG Trstenjak proposed a framework through which such concerns could be accommodated at a practical level. She supported 'in principle' the premise that protection of the environment should be available as an overriding reason in the public interest to justify discriminatory measures 'under any circumstances'.[66] But she then suggested that 'justification necessarily has to be examined in identical fashion in relation to discriminatory and non-discriminatory measures. Instead, it must be assumed that the discriminatory character of a measure restricting the free movement of trade can be taken into account in a proportionality test in which the necessity and reasonableness of such measures in particular can be examined more closely'.[67] If the Court were to reverse the convention that justification of directly discriminatory measures is confined to the grounds spelled out in the Treaty, it would enable the more seamless understanding of restrictions on free movement that we can trace in the case law to take explicit effect, also obviating the need for the Court to resolve the questions about how to distinguish between *types* of discrimination raised by AG Sharpston in *Bressol.* It cannot be ignored, however, that to collapse the distinction between derogation and justification so definitively would revoke the significance of having a limited pool of public interest grounds actually stipulated in the Treaty in the first place in many respects. It would also, as observed in Chapter 1, aggravate the propulsion forward of many of the complexities that we encounter in free movement law to the third stage of analysis i.e. the

[63] AG Trstenjak in *Commission v Austria*, fn32 of the Opinion (emphasis added), citing *Commission v Spain* (C-153/08), para. 36; Case C-451/03 *Servizi Ausiliari Dottori Commercialisti Srl v Giuseppe Calafiori* [2006] ECR I-2941, paras 36–37; and Case C-388/01 *Commission v Italy (Admission to museums)*[2003] ECR I-721, para. 19.

[64] AG Jacobs in *PreussenElektra*, paras 228–229 of the Opinion.

[65] Weatherill, n62, 544.

[66] AG Trstenjak in *Commission v Austria*, paras 83 and 89 of the Opinion respectively.

[67] AG Trstenjak in *Commission v Austria*, para. 90 of the Opinion.

determination of proportionality, a stage of review already more than burdened with its own share of interpretative problems.

4. The limits of discrimination

The prohibition of differential treatment is universally accepted as an appropriate baseline objective for the creation and regulation of the EU internal market—irrespective of the freedom in question. An argument can thus be made that discrimination should be the *primary* (at least) guiding paradigm for free movement law.[68] Moreover, discrimination can be made to work harder if decoupled from the criterion of nationality: in Chapter 4, for example, the added value of conceptualizing home State migration penalty case law as 'migration discrimination' was outlined. But it is essential to acknowledge too that while discrimination is critically *relevant* to the definition of free movement restrictions, the scope of Treaty-caught restrictions on free movement rights exceeds a threshold requirement of differential treatment. In Chapter 7, the framework principle 'competing' with discrimination—market access—will be examined in detail, but the main rationales for taking free movement law beyond discrimination will first be summarized here.

First, the legal framework of free movement law does not require discrimination. Beginning with the Treaty, it was shown in Section 2 that Articles 20, 21, and 45 TFEU place emphasis on moving *freely*; for goods, the *effect* of the restriction is paramount (Articles 34 and 35); and the provisions on establishment, services, and capital (Articles 56, 59, and 63 TFEU) refer to *restrictions* without qualification by discrimination. Furthermore, it was also stated above, and shown in more detail in Chapter 5, that the foundational case law was framed neutrally with respect to a requirement or otherwise of discrimination. That beyond-discrimination potential has since been confirmed for all of the relevant Treaty provisions (with the exception of Article 35 TFEU, discussed above).[69] Second, more practically, patent

[68] See e.g. G Davies, 'The Court's jurisprudence on free movement of goods: Pragmatic presumptions, not philosophical principles' (2012) 2 *European Journal of Consumer Law* 25; T Horsley, 'Subsidiarity and the Court of Justice: Missing pieces in the subsidiarity jigsaw?' (2012) 37:6 ELRev 734; AP van der Mei, 'The outer limits of the prohibition of discrimination on grounds of nationality: A look through the lens of Union citizenship' (2011) 18:1–2 MJ 62; and Bernard, n19.

[69] E.g. Case C-353/06 *Grunkin and Paul* [2008] ECR I-7639, paras 19–23 (Article 21 TFEU); *Mickelsson and Roos*, para. 26 ('[e]ven if the national regulations at issue do not have the aim or effect of treating goods coming from other Member States less favourably, which is for the national court to ascertain, the restriction which they impose on the use of a product in the territory of a Member State may, depending on its scope, have a considerable influence on the behaviour of consumers, which may, in turn, affect the access of that product to the market of that Member State'); Case C-464/02 *Commission v Denmark* [2005] ECR I-7929, para. 45 ('[Article 45 TFEU] prohibits not only all discrimination, direct or indirect, based on nationality, but also national rules which are applicable irrespective of the nationality of the workers concerned but impede their freedom of movement'); Case C-442/02 *CaixaBank France v Ministère de l'Économie, des Finances et de l'Industrie* [2004] ECR I-8961, para. 11 ('[Article 56] requires the elimination of restrictions on the freedom of establishment. All measures which prohibit, impede or render less attractive the exercise of that freedom must be regarded as such restrictions'); *Säger*, para. 12 ('Article 59 of the Treaty requires not only the elimination of all discrimination against a person providing services on the ground of his nationality

obstacles to free movement are not necessarily discriminatory. For example, an indistinctly applicable product ban or a precondition on the taking up of employment that is completely dissociated from any form of discrimination (including discrimination in effect) can block or prevent free movement *completely*. In other words, just because an obstacle is not discriminatory, it does not make it any less of a barrier to the exercise of free movement rights in real terms. On what basis could the Treaty ignore such restrictions, given that its wording clearly does not *require* that it should?

Third, while the Court does not engage in systematic analysis of either the existence or situation of comparators in its discrimination case law, that does not cancel out both conceptual and pragmatic difficulties associated with the need to *identify* a comparator nonetheless.[70] Fourth, if the internal market space is intended to be genuinely frontier-free, undue emphasis on discrimination actually serves to harden the continuing relevance of State frontiers. Fifth, and relatedly, it was seen in Chapters 3 and 5 that market partitioning rules can also impact at the sub-national level; protectionist instincts are not, in other words realized only at national frontiers. Finally, it will be shown in Chapter 7 that commentators have identified several problems with the Court's conceptualization and application of market access; but that is not a sufficient reason to fall back on discrimination, it is instead a mandate for the Court (and the rest of us) to work harder to understand, refine, and demarcate the shape of the 'other' principle.

More generally, discrimination and market access are sometimes presented as two distinctly relevant and distinctly applied devices, each with their own purpose and functions. But it is also considered that the concept of discrimination is just descriptive of one *type* of free movement restriction i.e. that discrimination is one (significant) part of a broader conception of restrictions driven predominantly by the dynamic of access. In *UTECA*, for example, AG Kokott—addressing services, establishment, and capital—first considered that all three freedoms 'encompass *both* a prohibition on discrimination and a prohibition on restriction'.[71] She then observed that '[t]here is a fluid borderline between indirect discrimination and restrictions. As it is, indirect discrimination is sometimes considered to be *just a special instance of restriction* of a fundamental freedom'.[72] If we extend that logic to

but also the abolition of any restriction, even if it applies without distinction to national providers of services and to those of other Member States, when it is liable to prohibit or otherwise impede the activities of a provider of services established in another Member State where he lawfully provides similar services'); Case C-367/98 *Commission v Portugal (Golden shares)* [2002] ECR I-4731, para. 44 ('[Article 63] lays down a general prohibition on restrictions on the movement of capital between Member States. That prohibition goes beyond the mere elimination of unequal treatment, on grounds of nationality, as between operators on the financial markets').

70 See C Barnard, *The Substantive Law of the EU: The Four Freedoms*, 3rd edn (OUP, 2010) 19–21.

71 AG Kokott in Case C-222/07 *Unión de Televisiones Comerciales Asociadas (UTECA) v Administración General del Estado* [2009] ECR I-1407, para. 77 of the Opinion (emphasis added).

72 AG Kokott in *UTECA*, para. 77 of the Opinion (emphasis added), citing Case C-411/03 *SEVIC Systems AG* [2005] ECR I-10805, para. 23, Case C-170/05 *Denkavit Internationaal and Denkavit France SARL v Ministre de l'Économie, des Finances et de l'Industrie* [2006] ECR I-11949, paras 29 and 30, and Case C-231/05 *Oy AA* [2007] ECR I-6373, para. 39, 'in which the "difference in treatment" is considered to be a restriction on [establishment]' (fn57). She also observes that in Case C-318/05

direct discrimination too—as an extra-special instance of restriction of a fundamental freedom—the main free movement frameworks can thus be merged together, which in turn positions the discrimination/market access debate as one about the nature and scope of a core singularity: *restrictions* on free movement rights, whether they impact differentially on free movement actors or not.[73]

Such an approach has clear appeal for the perspective of coherence, but it comes at a broader price. For example, Davies has depicted the compulsion beyond discrimination in free movement law in a very striking way, arguing that it 'can only be understood as a call for positive action—some kind of requirement that governments actively prefer out-of-state economic actors over native ones'.[74] It is an undoubted challenge to discount that impression when reflecting on some aspects of the free movement case law, especially in recent years since the breadth largely latent in the foundational cases has now come more strongly to fruition. Davies goes on to observe that any *express* call in the regulatory direction he outlined would be 'immediately dismissed, lacking any normative, political or economic basis and indeed directly conflicting with the foundational legal, political and economic principles of the internal market. That such a standpoint is nevertheless maintained by many is therefore odd and can best be explained by the absence in free movement law of any *clear, consistent and substantial definitions of the central terms*—of discrimination, of market access, or of a restriction on free movement. That absence allows incoherence in the law and academic doctrine to thrive'.[75] Davies has identified precisely the right challenge, since restrictions beyond discrimination are coded into the Treaty and the implications of that have been progressively realized through case law right across the span of free movement rights. Writing on the scope of Article 34 TFEU, Spaventa put it as follows: 'the case law is here, and probably here to stay, and it would be hypocritical to try to hide its true significance. It is therefore essential at least to attempt to provide a strong constitutional foundation for those developments and to acknowledge that the needs and aims of the internal market naturally develop with time, also as a result of progress already made in dismantling barriers to movement'.[76] She equally acknowledges the inherent constitutional risks.

The basic tension—from constitutional, economic, political, and practical perspectives—is that discrimination does not go far enough but a principle of access can go much too far. If access has always been/is now the foundational principle of free movement law, then the distinctions between discriminatory and

Commission v Germany [2007] ECR I-6957, para. 117, 'the Court similarly talks of difference in treatment likely to "make it more difficult" for the party concerned to exercise its rights, which corresponds to the normal definition of a restriction'.

73 See generally, Barnard, n70, 253–61.

74 G Davies, 'Discrimination and beyond in European economic and social law' (2011) 18:1–2 MJ 7 at 9.

75 Davies, n74, 9 (emphasis added).

76 E Spaventa, 'Leaving *Keck* behind? The free movement of goods after the rulings in *Commission v Italy* and *Mickelsson and Roos*' (2009) 35:6 ELRev 914 at 929.

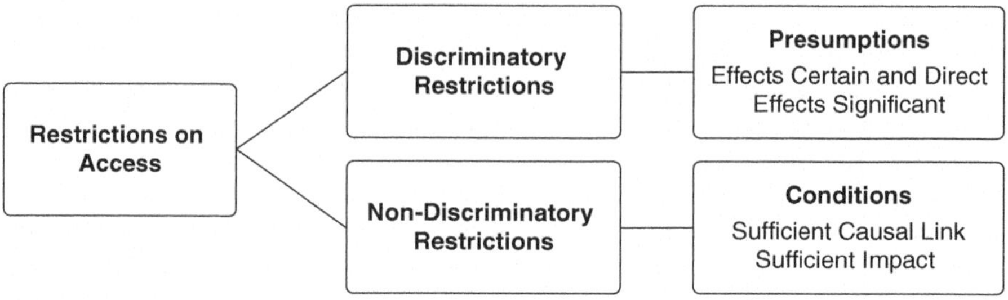

Fig. 6.3 Restrictions on access

non-discriminatory restrictions summarized in Section 2 still remain significant but should perhaps be reconfigured as shown in Figure 6.3.

The fact that discriminatory obstacles are accompanied by presumptions whereas non-discriminatory restrictions have to meet specified conditions can be used to demonstrate both a sliding scale of regulatory capture and a conceptual distinction between both forms of restriction. Access would, in other words, be affected in a *particular* way by discriminatory restrictions and the legal framework can reflect this. But that does not mean that non-discriminatory restrictions *cannot* affect access in a Treaty-relevant way too. If that configuration is to be persuasive, however, two questions have to be engaged with, addressing the challenges set by Davies and Spaventa. First, can a 'clear, consistent and substantial' definition, built upon adequate conceptual groundings, be established in order to defend the *concept* of access as a sufficiently convincing *principle* of free movement law? And second, what *limits* can and/or should be strapped onto it? These questions set the basic objectives and challenges for the discussion in Chapter 7.

7

The Positive Scope of Free Movement Law: Non-Discriminatory Restrictions

1. Introduction

The extent to which the Treaty should be concerned with non-discriminatory restrictions has materialized as a focal point around which several critical questions coalesce. The issue is particularly tied to one of the drivers identified in Chapter 2: how multiple objectives shape but also fragment the basic constructs of internal market law. An argument that measures not producing discrimination in either their object or their effects should nevertheless come within the scope of the Treaty does not discount the eradication of protectionism as a critical internal market objective. Rather, it is premised on a conviction that other objectives have to be seen as relevant too. In free movement law, the principal other objective—presented variably as rivalling, complementing, or subsuming discrimination—is expressed through the language of market access.

As seen in Chapter 6, neither the Treaty nor its framing case law expressly establishes access as the regulatory paradigm of free movement law. But the open way in which restrictions have been conceived—again, in both the Treaty and case law—clearly positions access as a credible market philosophy. Judgments from all sectors of free movement law now include non-discriminatory restrictions as part of the applicable framework for determining positive scope. The following characteristics of access as a framework principle might be suggested by the discussion thus far:

(1) *Access as a principle can be applied in all sectors of free movement law*—i.e. the dynamic of access is not confined to economic/trade situations. Case law on the free movement of persons also reflects concerns about accessing other States and associated rights and benefits. In Chapter 2, that point was distinguished from a convergence-driven perspective that advocates overlaying economic freedoms with citizenship-trade rights—the internal market is understood here in simpler spatial terms i.e. the space in which free movement rights are realized.

(2) *Access requires that conditions* (e.g. the limits of horizontal scope; establishing a cross-border connection) *and definitions* (e.g. who is a worker; what is a service) *relating to the personal and material scope of the Treaties must be satisfied*—generally, the right-

holder's motivation for exercising free movement rights should not be taken into account but access can be legitimately denied when a defined threshold of abuse of rights is reached (Chapters 3 and 4). However, acknowledging that potential effects on free movement rights can establish a sufficient cross-border connection depresses the force of the purely internal rule in the majority of cases (Chapter 4).

(3) *Discrimination i.e. differential treatment in law or in effect meets presumptions that access has been or might be restricted* (Chapters 5 and 6).

But that summary does not uncover the *core* features and objectives of access as a framework principle of free movement law. We know that access transcends discrimination and inter-State protectionism; but what does it stand for or seek to achieve instead? Additionally, if non-discriminatory restrictions can legitimately come within the scope of the Treaty, what limits to the principle of access should be applied?

The purpose of this chapter is to consider how access can be credibly defended, defined, and applied as a framework principle of free movement law. It is about locating appropriate boundaries to the Treaty's positive scope, considering the constitutional, economic, and regulatory implications of that task. The argument developed is that conceiving of access as a principle concerned with *access to the exercise of free movement rights* could address some of the criticism that *market* access is a contested and/or ineffectual principle more generally. But it will also be emphasized that questions about the limits that need to be placed on access—i.e. refining the parameters of potential effects; managing the gradation of restrictions that prevent, impede, or affect access; and working out the relevance of remoteness and appreciability thresholds—have to be confronted and resolved more coherently. In Section 2, the emergence and entrenchment of access in the case law will first be illustrated, mainly through the presentation of case law on the scope of Article 34 TFEU. Defining and limiting access as a principle will then be addressed in Section 3. It will be suggested that the Court has important choices to make in order to restore greater coherence to the system of free movement law overall.

2. Non-discriminatory restrictions and market access: emergence and entrenchment

In Chapter 6, a series of judgments was cited to demonstrate that non-discriminatory restrictions come within the scope of all of the Treaty's free movement provisions with the exception of Article 35 TFEU. Looking at the same examples again, it can also be seen that the Court has developed an extensive vocabulary to communicate the nature of these restrictions. For Article 21, the Court referred in *Grunkin and Paul* to '[n]ational legislation which places certain of the nationals of the Member State concerned at a disadvantage simply because they have exercised their freedom to move and to reside in another Member State'.[1] In *Mickelsson and Roos*, on Article 34 TFEU, the expression used was that 'the restriction . . . impose[d] on the use of a product in the territory of a Member State may, depending on its scope, have a considerable influence on the behaviour of consumers, which may, in turn, affect the access of that product to the market of that Member State'.[2] For workers, it was 'national rules which are applicable irrespective of the nationality of the workers concerned but impede their freedom of movement'.[3] In *CaixaBank*, the Court articulated a comparably broad test for restrictions on establishment i.e. '[a]ll measures which prohibit, impede or render less attractive the exercise of that freedom must be regarded as such restrictions'.[4] Very similar language has been used for restrictions on the provision of services: 'the abolition of any restriction, even if it applies without distinction to national providers of services and to those of other Member States, when it is liable to prohibit or otherwise impede the activities of a provider of services established in another Member State where he lawfully provides similar services'.[5] Finally, for restrictions on capital movements, it has been established that the prohibition in Article 63 TFEU 'goes beyond the mere elimination of unequal treatment, on grounds of nationality, as between operators on the financial markets'.[6]

These tests all reflect the breadth of the direct/indirect/actual/potential template established by *Dassonville* and validated in *van Binsbergen*.[7] They also set up the key challenges that will be taken up in Section 3: first, attempting to unite the impulses powering the different expressions used more coherently under a framework of access; and, second, facing up to the virtually limitless reach of the Treaty that results if the tests are taken at pure face value. The purpose of this section is to provide the backdrop for that analysis, by outlining the narrative shift beyond discrimination and the corollary elaboration of access in free movement case law practice. The discussion is broadly divided into two phases, first considering the *emergence and evolution* of concepts that later enabled the *entrenchment* of access to guide the positive scope of free movement law.

(a) Emergence and evolution: market access and non-discriminatory restrictions

The case law milestones that shape how restrictions are defined can be grouped under four main stages. First, there is the *framing case law*. It has already been established that the definitions developed initially by the Court did not make

[1] Case C-353/06 *Grunkin and Paul* [2008] ECR I-7639, para. 21.
[2] Case C-142/05 *Åklagaren v Mickelsson and Roos* [2009] ECR I-4273, para. 26.
[3] Case C-464/02 *Commission v Denmark* [2005] ECR I-7929, para. 45.
[4] Case C-442/02 *CaixaBank France v Ministère de l'Économie, des Finances et de l'Industrie* [2004] ECR I-8961, para. 11.
[5] Case C-76/90 *Säger v Dennemeyer & Co. Ltd* [1991] ECR I-4221, para. 12.
[6] Case C-367/98 *Commission v Portugal (Golden shares)* [2002] ECR I-4731, para. 44.
[7] Case 8/74 *Procureur du Roi v Dassonville* [1974] ECR 837, para. 5; Case 33/74 *Van Binsbergen v Bestuur van de Bedrijfsvereniging voor de Metaalnijverheid* [1974] ECR 1299, paras 10–11.

discrimination a precondition for the activation of Treaty rights. But it is also important to remember that the restrictions reviewed by the Court in this formative phase were actually discriminatory—whether directly discriminatory, as in *Dassonville* itself, or discriminatory in effect (for example, in *Säger*, national legislation required specific professional qualifications before patent renewal services could be provided in the territory). Thus the framing case law went beyond the *language* of discrimination, but the scope of the free movement provisions did not actually (have to) go beyond discrimination in substantive terms. Even where the Court described restrictions as 'non-discriminatory'—as it did in *Cassis*, for example[8]—the scope of Article 34 TFEU was being considered in the light of national rules prescribing e.g. the composition or packaging of products. The Court considers such rules to be a restriction on trade because of 'the obligation to make adjustments to goods coming from other Member States in order to comply with the conditions laid down by the Member State in which they are marketed. By requiring repackaging or modification of a product's composition, for example, such rules give rise to *additional difficulties and costs for importers*'.[9] 'Additional difficulties and costs' are classic benchmarks of discrimination in effect.

The second stage of the case law could be described as *Article 34 TFEU: confusion*. That characterization refers to a stream of conflicting judgments in the 1980s and early 1990s, which, taken together, projected a confused picture of the scope of the *Dassonville* test. The fact that the test could effectively snare *any* national rule as a possible restriction of free movement rights was becoming more and more apparent—not just to the Court and to academic commentators, but also to lawyers who increasingly raised arguments about indirect or potential restrictions of inter State trade in what were essentially internal regulatory disputes. The basic question was: did Article 34 catch genuinely non-discriminatory national measures—regulating *how* goods were to be sold, in particular—that could nonetheless be argued to have an impact or a potential impact on imported goods?[10] Arguments supporting a positive answer were often based on a technical claim that rules restricting the *practice* of trade necessarily led to a reduction in the *volume* of imports—a line of reasoning made entirely possible by the fact that the Court chose, as seen in Chapter 5, to construct the *Dassonville* formula in free movement

[8] Case 120/78 *Rewe-Zentrale AG v Bundesmonopolverwaltung für Branntwein (Cassis de Dijon)* [1979] ECR 649.

[9] AG Bot in Case C-110/05 *Commission v Italy (Trailers)* [2009] ECR I-519, para. 66 (emphasis added).

[10] Consider the broad approach taken in e.g. Case 286/81 *Criminal proceedings against Oosthoek's Uitgeversmaatschappij BV* [1982] ECR 4575 (prohibition on offering of free gifts for sales promotion purposes, restriction of Article 34 but justified) and Case 382/87 *Buet and Educational Business Services (EBS) v Ministère public* [1989] ECR 1235 (prohibition on canvassing for the selling of educational material, restriction of Article 34 but justified); but cf. Case 155/80 *Oebel* [1981] ECR 1993 (prohibition on night work (production, transport, and delivery) in bakeries, no restriction of Article 34), Case 75/81 *Blesgen v Belgian State* [1982] ECR 1211 (restrictions on the consumption, sale, or offering without charge of drinks exceeding a specified alcoholic strength, no restriction of Article 34), and Case C-23/89 *Quietlynn Ltd and Richards v Southend Borough Council* [1990] ECR I-3059 (prohibition on the sale of lawful sex articles from unlicensed sex establishments, no restriction of Article 34).

law without the *de minimis* rule applied in competition law. The second case law phase culminated in a series of references about whether national rules restricting Sunday trading hours should come within the scope of Article 34, and thus require States to establish justification and proportionality defences, or not. Different degrees of engagement with the substance, and more particularly with the proportionality, of the contested national rules were also clearly evident.[11]

Throughout this period, the Court swayed between imposing a requirement of differential treatment and pushing Article 34 beyond discrimination. The incoherence of the resulting case law was sharply depicted by AG Tesauro in *Hünermund.*[12] A vibrant but often divided body of commentary had also developed, identifying the critical systemic questions that had been multiplying under the surface of individual challenges and calling attention, in particular, to the level of regulatory competence retained by the EU and by the Member States respectively: not just in the field of trade but also at the junctures of trade and political, social, cultural, and even moral issues.[13] The structural purpose of free movement law and of the internal market more broadly was a dominant discussion point, and a basic division began to emerge: some were concerned with setting limits to what was perceived as the unchecked spread of negative integration; others advocated the desirability of a more penetrating and deregulatory market model. The third and fourth case law phases—*Article 34: retreat* and *market access: resurgence*—will now be outlined in more detail in this chapter.

The third/retreat phase was dominated by the decision in *Keck*,[14] which reinforced the relevance of differential treatment for infringement of Article 34. But it will also be seen that the Court was reluctant to transplant that reasoning to other areas of free movement law, with the result that the doctrines of non-discriminatory restrictions and market access thrived elsewhere. In subsection (b), discussion of the fourth phase/resurgence will demonstrate that explicit references to market access *are* now built into the case law on Article 34 too: but alongside the fragmenting reverberations of the fact that *Keck* remains good law. The *Keck* case exemplified how EU law was being used by the mid 1990s i.e. arguments developed by home State nationals or traders to challenge indistinctly applicable national rules by

[11] See esp. Case C-145/88 *Torfaen Borough Council v B & Q plc* [1989] ECR I-3851, Case C-312/89 *Union départementale des syndicats CGT de l'Aisne v SIDEF Conforama, Société Arts et Meubles and Société Jima* [1991] ECR I-997, Case C-332/89 *Criminal proceedings against Marchandise, Chapuis and SA Trafitex* [1991] ECR I-1027, and Case C-169/91 *Council of the City of Stoke-on-Trent and Norwich City Council v B&Q plc* [1992] ECR I-6635.

[12] AG Tesauro in Case C-292/92 *Hünermund and others v Landesapothekerkammer Baden-Württemberg* [1993] ECR I-6787; at para. 11 of the Opinion, the Advocate General stated that the relevant 'case-law . . . —why conceal it?—is certainly not amenable to systematic interpretation'.

[13] See e.g. A Arnull, 'What shall we do on Sunday?' (1991) 16:1 ELRev 112; K Mortelmans, 'Article 30 of the EEC Treaty and legislation relating to market circumstances: Time to consider a new definition' (1990) 28:1 CMLRev 115; J Steiner, 'Drawing the line: Uses and abuses of Art 30 EEC' (1992) 29:3 CMLRev 749; WPJ Wils, 'The search for the rule in Article 30 EEC: Much ado about nothing?' (1993) 18:6 ELRev 475; and E White, 'In search of limits to Article 30 of the EEC Treaty' (1989) 26:2 CMLRev 235.

[14] Joined Cases C-267/91 and C268/91 *Criminal Proceedings against Keck and Mithouard* [1993] ECR I-6097.

asserting a potential restriction of free movement rights—here, that French legislation precluding the resale of products at a loss was a measure having equivalent effect to a quantitative restriction and therefore merited being caught by Article 34 TFEU. The contested legislation distinguished between the manufacturers of a product, to whom the measure did not apply, and retailers. Criminal proceedings for breaching the restrictions placed on retailers were initiated against the applicants in their capacity as supermarket managers.

In his first Opinion on the case, AG van Gerven, reflecting on recent case law that had edged the boundaries of Article 34 outwards, drew an analogy between rules on resale at a loss and restrictions on advertising and other sales promotion methods.[15] On that basis, he concluded that the French legislation was, in principle, a restriction within the meaning of Article 34. He then examined whether the rule could be justified as a proportionate mandatory requirement, arguing that it could not. However, in a move presaging steps seen later in *Trailers*, the Court transferred the case from the Second Chamber to the Full Court and asked for a second opinion (from the same Advocate General). AG van Gerven was asked to consider whether a prohibition of resale at a loss really did proscribe a sales promotion method or was instead part of a generally applicable price control system; and, if the latter, whether such rules have direct, indirect, or just purely speculative effects on transnational trade.[16]

In the second Opinion, AG van Gerven focused on game-changing observations that had been submitted at the oral hearing by the French Government:

> French experience in detecting and penalizing sales at a loss shows that this type of sale is primarily used as an offensive technique by the big distribution networks which are highly concentrated in France. Furthermore, most of the infringements committed against the prohibition of resale at a loss *do not in practice involve newly-launched products* but well-known consumer products . . . the usual price of which is known by consumers. It would therefore follow that the rules on resale at a loss, unlike the rules in question in the *Oosthoek* case . . . or in the *Buet* case . . . are *general rules for regulating the market* which *do not have as their purpose the regulation of trade flows between the Member States* but are the result of a choice of economic policy, which is to achieve a certain level of transparency and fairness in conditions of competition.[17]

He emphasized, however, that those observations were specific to market conditions in France and 'do not alter the fact that resale at a loss is a sales technique which may, *in certain specific circumstances*, make it impossible or more difficult to sell imported products'.[18] Here are the seeds of the Court's decision—an emphasis on either *differential treatment* with respect to the selling of imported products, whether in law or in effect, or otherwise the *impossibility* of selling them at all.

[15] AG van Gerven in *Keck and Mithouard*, paras 4–5 of the first Opinion.

[16] AG van Gerven delivered his Opinions in *Keck and Mithouard* on 18 November 1992 and 28 April 1993. See further, the judgment in *Stoke- on-Trent v B&Q*, which was delivered in the interim period; it was addressed by AG van Gerven in paras 10–11 of the second Opinion.

[17] AG van Gerven in *Keck and Mithouard*, para. 3 of the second Opinion (emphasis added).

[18] AG van Gerven in *Keck and Mithouard*, para. 4 of the second Opinion (emphasis in original).

Addressing the proportionality test developed by the Court in *Stoke-on-Trent v B&Q* in the interim, AG van Gerven considered that the rules could be justified, arguing that 'a statutory prohibition of resale at a loss is not incompatible with Article [34] since it appears that the events at issue in the main proceedings occurred at the retail level, that is to say at a level in respect of which a recognized ground of justification may be invoked for the rules in question and that at that level there is *no more than a purely hypothetical effect on trade between Member States* and certainly *no more than an hypothetical hindering of trade flows*'.[19] However, the emphasis placed here on 'purely speculative effects' arguably fits more with exclusion from the scope of Article 34 altogether than with justification, a distinction that came to pass in the judgment.

The Court made no attempt to disguise the impetus driving its decision: its highly atypical framing of the outcome as 'contrary to what has previously been decided' was contextualized around 'the increasing tendency of traders to invoke Article [34] of the Treaty as a means of challenging *any rules* whose effect is to limit their commercial freedom even where such rules are not *aimed at* products from other Member States'.[20] The Court then continued:

> [T]he application to products from other Member States of national provisions restricting or prohibiting *certain selling arrangements* is not such as to hinder directly or indirectly, actually or potentially, trade between Member States within the meaning of the *Dassonville* judgment . . . so long as those provisions *apply to all relevant traders* operating within the national territory and so long as they *affect in the same manner, in law and in fact, the marketing of domestic products and of those from other Member States.* Provided that those conditions are fulfilled, the application of such rules to the sale of products from another Member State meeting the requirements laid down by that State is *not by nature* such as to *prevent their access to the market* or *to impede access any more than it impedes the access of domestic products.* Such rules therefore fall outside the scope of Article [34].[21]

For the first time, although arriving at the same outcome in effect as AG van Gerven,[22] the Court built a restriction rule directly around the *form* of a national measure—certain selling arrangements—and established a related presumption

[19] AG van Gerven in *Keck and Mithouard*, para. 13 of the second Opinion (emphasis added).

[20] *Keck and Mithouard*, paras 16 and 14 respectively (emphasis added). In Joined Cases C-94/04 and C-202/04 *Cipolla v Fazari; Macrino and Capoparte v Meloni* [2006] ECR-11421, AG Poiares Maduro cast a softer light on the Court's phrasing, suggesting (in fn17 of the Opinion) that 'the Court took into consideration the consequences of its earlier case-law in the social context of the relevant rules and the legal systems responsible for applying them'.

[21] *Keck and Mithouard*, paras 16–18 (emphasis added).

[22] AG van Gerven had also admitted some discomfort with the breadth of scope being accorded to Article 34 in the case law; but he then observed that since, on balance, 'the broad *Dassonville* formula still remains the cornerstone of the Court's case-law concerning the sphere of application of Article [34] . . . it cannot be excluded that a statutory prohibition of resale at a loss, such as that existing in France, might hinder "directly or indirectly, actually or potentially" intra-[Union] trade' (paras 8–9 of the second Opinion). He went on to distinguish between methods applied to the sale of products established in the market 'either as a means of eliminating a competitor or in order to attract customers' (para. 13) and the specific challenges faced by those seeking to break into a new market: an early statement of the approach subsequently applied to advertising restrictions post-*Keck and Mithouard*, discussed below.

about innocuous *effects*. The language of market access was used, but it was fused with a requirement of differential treatment unless access was *prevented*. By pulling back to preventing—i.e. not impeding, hindering, or affecting—the Court was also correcting the scope of *potential* effects. As discussed further below, however, this constriction was not repeated in other sectors of free movement law.

It was noted in Chapter 5 that the decision in *Keck* provoked a divided response, causing sharp critique from AG Jacobs in *Leclerc-Siplec* (returned to in Section 3) and reservations in the academic literature.[23] In *Tankstation*, AG van Gerven outlined an insightful list of questions and ambiguities raised by *Keck*, including: did the Court intend to assess the effects on the marketing of domestic and imported products in individual situations or more generally with regard to a measure's overall effect; to what *degree* did the Court intend to constrict the *Dassonville* test; what were the implications of the renewal of discrimination for the application of justification arguments not codified in the Treaty; and had the Court intended to reverse the burden of proof for national measures regulating issues other than product requirements.[24] That analysis clearly showed that the definitive tone in which the judgment had been expressed did not equate to material clarity. For example, in *Commission v Greece*, the Court assessed national rules restricting the sale of infant milk products to pharmacies in this way:

> [The contested] legislation, the effect of which is to limit the commercial freedom of traders irrespective of the actual characteristics of the product referred to, concerns the selling arrangements of certain goods, inasmuch as it . . . generally determines the points of sale where they may be distributed. Moreover, the legislation objected to by the Commission, which applies, without distinction according to the origin of the products in question, to all of the traders operating within the national territory, does not affect the sale of products originating in other Member States any differently from that of domestic products. *The fact, invoked by the Commission, that the Hellenic Republic does not itself produce processed milk for infants does not undermine those findings.* The applicability of Article [34] of the Treaty to a national measure for the general regulation of commerce, which concerns all the products concerned without distinction according to their origin, cannot depend on *such a purely fortuitous factual circumstance, which may, moreover, change with the passage of time.* If it did, this would have the illogical consequence that the same legislation would fall under Article [34] in certain Member States but fall outside the scope of that provision in other Member States. The situation would be different only if it was apparent that the legislation at issue protected domestic products which were similar to processed milk for infants from other Member States or which were in competition with milk of that type. In this instance, the Commission has not shown that that was the case. It follows . . . that the Greek legislation . . . is confined to limiting the places where the product concerned may be distributed by regulating the marketing of that product, without thereby preventing access

[23] See e.g. N Reich, 'The November revolution of the European Court of Justice: *Keck, Meng* and *Audi* Revisited' (1994) 31:3 CMLRev 459; S Weatherill, 'After *Keck*: Some thoughts on how to clarify the clarification' (1996) 33:5 CMLRev 885; C Barnard, 'Fitting the remaining pieces into the goods and persons jigsaw' (2001) 26:1 ELRev 35.

[24] AG van Gerven in in Joined Cases C-401/92 and C-402/92 *Criminal proceedings against Tankstation't Heukske vof and Boermans* [1994] ECR I-2199, paras 23–24 of the Opinion.

to the market of products from other Member States or specifically placing them at a disadvantage.[25]

In his Opinion, however, AG Lenz approached the absence of domestic comparator products very differently:

In Greece no domestic production of infant formulae takes place . . . There are apparently fourteen competing products on the market, coming from other Member States of the Community. *Consequently, it is not possible to make a genuine comparison of the restriction of access to the market for domestic and imported products.* Accordingly, *any increased difficulty* resulting from the measure at issue as regards marketing possibilities *specifically affects imported products.* Whilst in the judgment in *Keck and Mithouard* there is a criterion for excluding 'certain' selling arrangements from the scope of Article [34] . . . ' provided that [the sales arrangements] affect in the same manner, in law and in fact, the marketing of domestic products and of those from other Member States', the converse conclusion can be inferred in this case that since in fact *only the marketing of products from other Member States is affected*, the measure must be categorized as a measure having equivalent effect [to a quantitative restriction].[26]

The different approaches taken and outcomes reached demonstrate the complexity of both the conceptualization of discriminatory restrictions and the determination of appropriate comparators, points raised in Chapter 6. But they also reflect a powerful instinct that is central to defending any Treaty-relevance for non-discriminatory restrictions: even in the absence of additional burdens, measures *affecting* market access—and not just *preventing* it—can also lead to outcomes that should at least be *tested* against the requirements of justification and proportionality.

The Court continues to apply *Keck* in current case law.[27] However, three issues cast serious doubt on its potency as authority for the longer term. First, the emphasis in *Keck* on the *form* of the contested rule, creating presumptions relevant to selling arrangements only, simply does not fit with the emphasis placed on the *effects* of national measures in Article 34 case law and in free movement case law more generally. AG Jacobs argued as follows in *Leclerc-Siplec*:

[25] Case C-391/92 *Commission v Greece* [1995] ECR I-1621, paras 15–20 (emphasis added); see further, AG Kokott in *Mickelsson and Roos*, paras 61–62 of the Opinion.

[26] AG Lenz in *Commission v Greece*, paras 23–24 of the Opinion (emphasis added); he continued in para. 25 that 'there is, to my mind, *no doubt* that the monopoly arrangement should be assessed as being a measure having equivalent effect within the meaning of Article [34]' (emphasis added).

[27] E.g. Case C-108/09 *Ker-Optika bt v ÀNTSZ Dél-dunántúli Regionális Intézete* [2010] ECR I-12213, paras 51–56; Case C-531/07 *Fachverband der Buch- und Medienwirtschaft v LIBRO Handelsgesellschaft mbH* [2009] ECR I-3717, paras 20–29; and Case C-141/07 *Commission v Germany (Pharmacies)* [2008] ECR I-6935, paras 29–36. In all three cases, the contested selling arrangements were not found to affect all traders in the same manner i.e. they had to be justified and evaluated against a proportionality test. In Case C-441/04 *A-Punkt Schmuckhandels GmbH v Schmidt* [2006] ECR I-2093, the Court left the determination of the selling arrangement question to the referring court, on the basis that the information available to it did not allow it to decide 'beyond doubt' (para. 25). For a recent discussion and application of *Keck and Mithouard* by the EFTA Court, see Case E-16/10 *Philip Morris Norway AS v Norwegian State, represented by the Ministry of Health and Care Services* [2011] EFTA Court Report 330, available at <http://www.eftacourt.int/cases/detail/?tx_nvcases_pi1%5Bcase_id%5D=134&cHash=b2da5d67f0333033e95f786573522f5e>.

[I]t is inappropriate to make rigid distinctions between different categories of rules, and to apply different tests depending on the category to which particular rules belong. The severity of the restriction imposed by different rules is *merely one of degree*. Measures affecting selling arrangements may create extremely serious obstacles to imports. For example, a rule permitting certain products to be sold only in a handful of small shops in a Member State would be almost as restrictive as an outright ban on importation and marketing.[28]

Reflecting AG van Gerven's instinctive classification of rules on resale at a loss as valuable sales promotion devices in *Keck* itself, commentators have agreed that, leaving the merits of the reasoning of the Court to one side, there is a strong argument that the rule challenged in *Keck* should not have fallen on its own sword.[29]

There are clear instances of straightforward application of *Keck* in subsequent case law i.e. with the Court finding that challenged national selling arrangements did not prevent access to the market for imported products or did not impede their access any more than for domestic products.[30] But the scope of the selling arrangement definition was also quickly limited. For example, where a national rule might be considered to exhibit characteristics of both product rules and selling arrangements, the Court tended to settle on classification as the former, bringing the measure within the scope of Article 34 and provoking an assessment of justification and proportionality.[31] Even more significantly, and despite the application of *Keck* in *Hünermund* just three weeks later to exclude restrictions on the advertising of pharmaceutical products from the scope of Article 34,[32] the

[28] AG Jacobs in Case C-412/93 *Société d'Importation Edouard Leclerc-Siplec v TF1 Publicité SA and M6 Publicité SA* [1995] ECR I-179, para. 38 of the Opinion (emphasis added).

[29] See e.g. G Davies, 'The Court's jurisprudence on free movement of goods: Pragmatic presumptions, not philosophical principles' (2012) *European Journal of Consumer Law* 25 at 33, who argues that 'selling at a loss is an archetypal way to break into a new market'. This argument is underscored by the Court's application of *Keck and Mithouard* to legislation prohibiting sales at very low profit margins in Case C-63/94 *Groupement National des Négociants en Pommes de Terre de Belgique (Belgapom) v ITM Belgium SA and Vocarex SA* [1995] ECR I-2467. See similarly, L Woods, 'Consistency in the chambers of the ECJ: A case study on the free movement of goods' (2012) 31:3 *Civil Justice Quarterly* 340 at 349.

[30] In addition to *Commission v Greece* and *Tankstation*, see e.g. Joined Cases C-69/93 and C-258/93 *Punto Casa SpA v Sindaco del Comune di Capena* [1994] ECR I-2355.

[31] E.g. Case C-470/93 *Verein gegen Unwesen in Handel und Gewerbe Köln eV v Mars GmbH* [1995] ECR I-1923, para. 13 (since the rule at issue would 'compel the importer to adjust the presentation of his products according to the place where they are to be marketed and consequently to incur additional packaging and advertising costs'); Case C-368/95 *Vereinigte Familiapress Zeitungsverlags- und vertriebs GmbH v Heinrich Bauer Verlag* [1997] ECR I-3689, para. 11 ('even though the relevant national legislation is directed against a method of sales promotion, in this case it bears on the actual content of the products, in so far as the competitions in question form an integral part of the magazine in which they appear'); Joined Cases C-158/04 and C-159/04 *Alfa Vita Vassilopoulos AE and Carrefour Marinopoulos AE v Elliniko Dimosio and Nomarchiaki Aftodioikisi Ioanninon* [2006] ECR I-8135, para. 19 (condemning in principle a national rule 'requiring vendors of "bake-off" products to comply with all of the requirements imposed on traditional bakeries, including, in particular, the requirement of having a flour store, an area for kneading equipment and a solid-fuel store, does not take the specific nature of those products into account and entails additional costs, thereby making the marketing of those products more difficult'). See also, Case C-244/06 *Dynamic Medien Vertriebs GmbH v Avides Media AG* [2008] ECR I-505, paras 31–35 (contra the Opinion of AG Mengozzi).

[32] See similarly, the decision in *Leclerc-Siplec*, on restrictions placed on televised advertising for certain sectors of economic activity. The judgments in *Keck and Mithouard* and *Hünermund* were both delivered by the Full Court, sharing an identical composition.

considerable potential impact of the *Keck* limitation was undercut by the evolution of the Court's approach to restrictions on advertising. The Court engages with the discriminatory effects of such rules by outlining the particular difficulties faced by traders trying to break into a new product market relative to home traders manufacturing, selling, or marketing products in the State already.[33] In *DocMorris*, the strands of the case law on advertising restrictions were sewn together as follows:

In order to ascertain whether a particular measure affects in the same manner the marketing of both domestic products and those from other Member States, the scope of the restrictive measure concerned must be ascertained. Thus, the Court has found that a prohibition on pharmacists from advertising quasi-pharmaceutical products outside the pharmacy, which they were authorised to offer for sale, did not affect the ability of traders other than pharmacists to advertise those products [*Hünermund*, paragraph 19]. Similarly, the prohibition on broadcasting the advertising at issue in *Leclerc-Siplec* was not extensive, since it covered only one particular form of promotion (television advertising) of one particular method of marketing products (distribution)... By contrast, the Court has accepted the relevance of the argument that a prohibition on television advertising deprived a trader of the only effective form of promotion which would have enabled it to penetrate a national market [*De Agostini*, paragraph 43]. Furthermore, the Court has found that in the case of products such as alcoholic beverages, the consumption of which is linked to traditional social practices and to local habits and customs, prohibiting all advertising directed at consumers in the form of advertisements in the press, on the radio and on television, the direct mailing of unsolicited material or the placing of posters on the public highway is liable to impede access to the market for products from other Member States more than it impedes access for domestic products, with which consumers are instantly more familiar [*Gourmet International Products*, paragraphs 21 and 24].[34]

It can be seen in this extract that the Court clearly considers the scope or scale of the contested restriction on advertising, something described by AG Stix-Hackl as 'an important criterion for whether market access is made *appreciably more difficult* is whether other lawful and effective forms of distribution exist'.[35] As noted in Chapter 5, she expressly rejected the argument that this was a *de minimis* test since 'no economic data requires evaluation here'.[36] But it was countered that data sets up a question about proof rather than dismissing a *de minimis* threshold in substance. The Court's focus on the *scale* of advertising restrictions thus reopens

[33] See e.g. Joined Cases C-34/95, C-35/95, and C-36/95 *Konsumentombudsmannen (KO) v De Agostini (Svenska) Förlag AB and TV-Shop i Sverige AB* [1997] ECR I-3843; Case C-405/98 *Konsumentombudsmannen (KO) v Gourmet International Products AB (GIP)* [2001] ECR I-1795; and Case C-239/02 *Douwe Egberts NV v Westrom Pharma NV; Souranis and Douwe Egberts NV v FICS-World BVBA* [2004] ECR I-7007. Advertising restrictions that apply to imported products only had always been easily distinguished from 'certain' i.e. straightforwardly permitted selling arrangements see e.g. Case C-320/93 *Ortscheit GmbH v Eurim-Pharm Arzneimittel GmbH* [1994] ECR I-5243.

[34] Case C-322/01 *Deutscher Apothekerverband eV v 0800 DocMorris NV and Jacques Waterval* [2003] ECR I-14887, paras 71–72. AG Bot later remarked that '[f]reedom to advertise thus appears to be an essential corollary to the fundamental freedoms laid down in the Treaty' (Case C-500/06 *Corporación Dermoestética SA v To Me Group Advertising Media* [2008] ECR I-5785, para. 84 of the Opinion).

[35] AG Stix-Hackl in *DocMorris*, para. 82 of the Opinion (emphasis added).

[36] AG Stix-Hackl in *DocMorris*, para. 81 of the Opinion.

the difficult question of pinning down the appreciability concerns that are having an effect in free movement law.[37] This question is returned to in Section 3, especially for the complex province of almost-bans.

The case law on advertising illustrates how the Court's interpretation of free movement law changes over time. For example, its reasoning on the particular challenges faced by new market entrants has spread outwards from advertising restrictions to the regulation of online sales. In *DocMorris*, the Court held that 'it is not disputed that the [contested national] provision contains both a requirement that certain medicines be sold only in pharmacies and a prohibition on mail-order sales of medicines. It is true that such a prohibition on mail-order sales may be regarded as merely the consequence of the requirement for sales to be made exclusively in pharmacies. However, the emergence of the internet as a method of cross-border sales means that the scope and, by the same token, the effect of the prohibition must be looked at on a broader scale'.[38] The Court concluded that the national rule was a selling arrangement that did *not* fulfil the *Keck* criteria for exclusion from the scope of Article 34 TFEU, since 'for pharmacies not established in Germany, the internet provides *a more significant way to gain direct access* to the German market. A prohibition which has *a greater impact on pharmacies established outside German territory* could impede access to the market for products from other Member States more than it impedes access for domestic products'.[39] The Court's overriding concern is that Article 34 TFEU should catch national measures that impede access by having 'the effect of depriving an economic operator of an effective way of competing in order to penetrate a market'.[40] The same theme can be seen in case law on other sectors of free movement too, where working out the differential burden likely to befall the incoming market actor feels creative, to say the least. In *Attanasio*, for example, addressing freedom of establishment, the Court held that 'a rule such as that at issue . . . which makes the opening of new roadside service stations subject to the compliance with minimum distances between service stations, constitutes a restriction within the meaning of Article [49 TFEU]. Such a rule, which applies only to new service stations and not to service stations already in existence before the entry into force of the rule, makes access to the activity of fuel distribution subject to conditions and, by being more advantageous to operators who are already present on the Italian market, is liable to deter, or even prevent, access to the Italian market by operators from other Member States'.[41] At this stage of the analysis, however, it must be emphasized that the case law developments outlined here can be treated conceptually as instances of

[37] E.g. *Gourmet International Products*, para. 20: 'a prohibition on advertising such as that at issue in the main proceedings not only prohibits a form of marketing a product but in reality prohibits producers and importers from directing any advertising messages at consumers, with a few *insignificant* exceptions' (emphasis added).

[38] *DocMorris*, para. 73.

[39] *DocMorris*, para. 74 (emphasis added); see similarly, *Ker-Optika*, paras 54–55. In *DocMorris,* the Court went on to accept elements of a justification argument on the protection of public health.

[40] AG Bot in *Trailers*, para. 122 of the Opinion.

[41] Case C-384/08 *Attanasio Group Srl v Comune di Carbognano* [2010] ECR I-2055, para. 45.

discrimination in effect. This first set of challenges to the continuing authority of *Keck* is therefore about its diminution in practical effect, and not (yet) a definitive conceptual shift beyond discrimination altogether.

The second set of challenges stems from that fact that, in contrast to the dynamic of cross-fertilization seen for other principles of free movement law, the form-based proviso of *Keck* has never found equivalent expression in case law on other free movement rights. It is not that the logic or potential application of *Keck* outwith the field of goods has been expressly rejected.[42] Instead, in cases where a *Keck* analogy is drawn in the submissions, the Court usually observes that the contested measure has effects beyond the national territory, in contrast to the selling arrangement in *Keck*.[43] However, the Court's resistance on this point has arguably become more tenuous. In one of the *Golden shares* decisions, for example, the Court observed that the non-discriminatory national rules being challenged—effecting a system of prior administrative approval for, inter alia, the acquisition of shares in commercial undertakings in which States hold a significant proportion of the share capital—'affect the position of a person acquiring a shareholding as such and *are thus liable to deter investors from other Member States* from making such investments *and, consequently, affect access to the market*'.[44] This interpretation may fit with the understanding of market access in free movement law generally—a point returned to immediately below—but that is not the same thing as rejecting a *Keck* analogy for the internal effects reason noted above. As pointed out above, selling arrangements may impede access to a domestic product market very significantly; for example, depriving a trader of an effective market-penetrating sales method. This means that two levels of inconsistency are apparent here i.e. inconsistency *within* and *across* the freedoms. It should again be emphasized that the comparative point is made here in terms of the coherent application of principles unless otherwise rationalized, and not to advocate a more organic spread of convergence per se; but the Court has never articulated a convincing reason to defend the form-based oddity that persists through the application of *Keck*.

Another point of distinction between case law on goods and other free movement rights is that the threshold of market access *prevention* set by *Keck* for

[42] In *Schindler*, for example, AG Gulmann drew from the then recent ruling in *Keck and Mithouard* to support the analogous view that 'some, *but not necessarily all*, other measures that restrict the activities of foreign providers of services in the host country may be caught by Article [56]' (Case C-275/92 *Her Majesty's Customs and Excise v Schindler* [1994] ECR I-1039, para. 57 of the Opinion, emphasis added).

[43] See e.g. Case C-415/93 *Union Royale Belge des Sociétés de Football Association ASBL v Bosman* [1995] ECR I-4921, paras 102–104 (Article 45 TFEU); Case C-384/93 *Alpine Investments BV v Minister van Financiën* [1995] ECR I-1141, paras 33–38 (Article 56 TFEU); Case C-463/00 *Commission v Spain (Golden shares)* [2003] ECR I-4581, paras 59–61 (Article 63 TFEU).

[44] *Commission v Spain (Golden shares)*, para. 61 (emphasis added); see similarly, Case C-98/01 *Commission v United Kingdom* [2003] ECR I-4641, para. 47 (restrictions on voting rights); Case C-171/08 *Commission v Portugal* [2010] ECR I-6817, para. 67 (restrictions on the acquisition of holdings and participation in the management of a privatized company); Case C-543/08 *Commission v Portugal* [2010] ECR I-11241, para. 68 (restrictions on the acquisition of holdings and participation in the management of a privatized company); Case C-212/09 *Commission v Portugal*, judgment of 10 November 2011, para. 65 (participation in the management of a privatized company).

non-discriminatory restrictions of Article 34 was not replicated for the other Treaty freedoms either. The judgment in *Alpine Investments*, for example, was delivered just 18 months after *Keck*. For restrictions on service provision, the test—with the Court having just cited the test for goods in *Keck*—was reformulated as '*directly affect[ing] access* to the market in services in . . . other Member States'.[45] That wording is notably less stringent than the prevention standard in *Keck*. Instead, it reflects the pre-*Keck* decision on the scope of Article 56 TFEU in *Säger*, in which the prevention of market access was just one element of a twin-pronged test: 'the abolition of any restriction, even if it applies without distinction to national providers of services and to those of other Member States, when it is liable to prohibit *or otherwise impede* the activities of a provider of services established in another Member State where he lawfully provides similar services'.[46]

The inter-freedom dynamics of market access are not straightforward. Somewhat ironically, the judgment in *Keck* has been cited as the cradle of the market access principle that was transposed to workers in *Bosman* in order not to restrict but to open up the scope of Article 45 TFEU.[47] More pointedly than this, however, the strongest challenge to the continued relevance of the *Keck* framework has come from case law on Article 34 itself, examined in subsection (b). Judgments on national rules that regulate the use of goods now mirror the '(liable to) impede' as well as 'prevent' reasoning applied to the other Treaty freedoms, as outlined just above for services and more extensively for the other free movement provisions in Chapters 4 and 6.

Finally, a third reason to question the longevity of *Keck* lies in the suggestion that the real objective of the decision was to locate a threshold of appreciability, not to pronounce on the relative merits of discrimination and market access as the guiding principle of free movement law.[48] Consider again paragraph 13 of the judgment: '[s]uch legislation may, admittedly, restrict the volume of sales, and hence the volume of sales of products from other Member States, in so far as it deprives traders of a method of sales promotion. But the question remains *whether such a possibility is sufficient* to characterize the legislation in question as a measure having equivalent effect to a quantitative restriction on imports' (emphasis added). The Court did then articulate a role for access in the case law on Article 34, but only in a literal sense i.e. at the level of access *prevention*. In his Opinion in *Graf*, AG Fennelly considered that the case law on goods 'including *Keck*, furnishes useful guidance on the application of [Article 45 TFEU]' but, on the convergence question discussed above, he was cautious:

[A]nalogies between the two fields are rarely perfect and . . . in particular, the reasoning in *Keck* can only be extended to the field of freedom of movement of workers if it is *reduced to*

45 *Alpine Investments*, para. 38 (emphasis added). 46 *Säger*, para. 12 (emphasis added).

47 E.g. AG Léger in Case C-232/01 *Criminal proceedings against van Lent* [2003] ECR I-11525, fn14 of the Opinion.

48 See e.g. T Horsley, 'Unearthing Buried Treasure: Art 34 TFEU and the Exclusionary Rules' (2012) 37:6 ELRev 734.

its essential elements, shorn of the more rigid and formalist distinctions—between product rules and certain selling arrangements—which are specific to the process of production and distribution of goods. Persons are not products and the process of migration for the purposes of employment or establishment abroad, including preparation therefor, cannot be so neatly divided into (mass) production and marketing stages. Furthermore, *the dichotomy between product and selling rules is not exhaustive of the range of possible restrictions even in the field of trade in goods.*[49]

The final point in this extract foreshadows precisely the dilemma faced in case law on rules regulating the use of goods, addressed in the next subsection. More importantly for present purposes, AG Fennelly went on to point out that pre-*Keck* case law had (erroneously) captured 'national rules which were neither discriminatory *nor particularly restrictive* of trade' in contrast to e.g. product rules 'which by the very fact of disparities in national regulation imposed *serious impediments* on the free movement of goods'.[50] Implicitly picking up on the distinction between *de minimis* as a rule based on complex data and analysis, on the one hand, and as an expression of judicial intuition on the other, he continued as follows:

It was reasonable for the Court to respond by developing *presumptions*, in the light of *experience and of its knowledge of market behaviour*, regarding the *likely effects* of different types of regulation on the achievement of the ultimate objective of Article [34]: the establishment of an internal market to which products from the different Member States have both equal and, subject to qualifications in the public interest, free access. Such presumptions should not, however, be conclusive. It is legitimate for the Court to develop presumptions about the market effects of different broadly defined categories of rules, provided that, in concrete cases, the validity of the presumption may be tested against the underlying criterion of market access, *rather than automatically being taken as being sufficient in itself to dispose of the case.* Such an approach would temper and refine the application of a broad uniform definition of restrictions such as that in *Dassonville* through a concrete assessment of the market effects of what are perceived to be more marginal types of regulation, while providing guidance both to national regulators and to economic actors as to the likely judicial response to such regulations.[51]

This argument sites the *Keck* milestone in its context, but it also makes a persuasive case against form-based rules on balance. The reasoning is rooted in *Dassonville* but AG Fennelly also perceives the need for appropriate limits, supporting the more rule- than data-based analysis of market effects advocated in Chapter 5. The Advocate General did not expand further on how 'market effects' or 'more marginal types of regulation' should actually be defined, but appreciability is at least

[49] AG Fennelly in Case C-190/98 *Graf v Filzmoser Maschinenbau GmbH* [2000] ECR I-493, para. 18 of the Opinion (emphasis added).

[50] AG Fennelly in *Graf*, para. 19 of the Opinion (emphasis added).

[51] AG Fennelly in *Graf*, para. 19 of the Opinion (emphasis added). See similarly, AG Tesauro in *Hünermund*, especially at para. 9 of the Opinion, where he observed, in the context of causation and appreciability, that the Court had not always 'mechanically applied the *Dassonville* principle' in cases concerning measures of various kinds but all sharing the common feature of displaying no connection, other than indirectly and vaguely, with imports and of affecting domestic and imported goods in the same way' (citing the decision in e.g. Case C-69/88 *Krantz GmbH & Co. v Ontvanger der Directe Belastingen and Netherlands State* [1990] ECR I-583, discussed in Chapter 5, to illustrate).

implicitly pertinent. His reasoning thus exposes the weaknesses of *Keck* at one level, and encourages us to hone a more systematic understanding of both the application and limits of market access.

(b) Entrenchment: the use of goods case law

The case law on rules regulating the use of goods is presented chronologically here not because of an absence of astute commentary,[52] but because unpeeling the layers of the narrative illuminates the profound impact of process as much as the evolution of substance. Over a series of judgments within a short space of time, critical tests are both expressed and applied in different ways that may seem minor in some respects but, in fact, indicate quite different parameters for the positive scope of Article 34 in reality. The use of goods narrative also puts the Chapter 4 critique of the citizenship test conceived in *Ruiz Zambrano*[53] into broader perspective. The Court's shaping of that test was flawed but recent, whereas the issues examined here go right back to *Dassonville*—again. Three distinct case law phases are distinguished below: up to the first Opinion in *Trailers*; from the second Opinion in *Trailers* to the decision in *Mickelsson and Roos*; and tracing the initial imprint of *Trailers* and *Mickelsson and Roos* in subsequent case law.

We saw in subsection (a) that after the decision in *Keck*, Advocates General signalled that national rules that might fall to be considered against the scope of Article 34 TFEU were not necessarily neatly divisible into the two (primarily[54]) categories used by the Court: product rules—i.e. 'rules concerning the conditions (such as those relating to designation, form, size, weight, composition etc.) to which goods coming from other Member States, where they are lawfully manufactured and marketed, must conform'[55]—and selling arrangements. In *Alfa Vita*, AG Poiares Maduro highlighted the flexibility applied by the Court in practice, challenging the seemingly rigid nature of the two formal categories.[56] Initially, he observed that '[s]uch solutions demonstrate the pragmatism that the Court has

[52] See e.g. S Enchelmaier, '*Moped Trailers*, *Mickelson & Roos*, and *Gysbrechts*: The ECJ's case law on goods keeps on moving' (2010) 29 YEL 190; M Fallon and D Gerard, 'Trailing the *Trailers* in search for a typology of barriers: Sketching a scale of relative gravity and exploring its implications' 2012/6 *Cahiers du CeDie Working Papers*, available at <http://www.uclouvain.be/cps/ucl/doc/ssh-cdie/documents/2012-6-M_Fallon-D_Gerard_(5_June_2012).pdf>; LW Gormley, 'Free movement of goods and their use: What is the use of it?' (2009–2010) 33 Fordham Int'l L.J. 1589; T Horsley 'Anyone for *Keck*?' (2009) 46:4 CMLRev 2001; P Oliver, 'Of trailers and jet skis: Is the case law on Article 34 TFEU hurtling in a new direction?' (2009) 33 Fordham Int'l L.J. 1423; L Prete, 'Of motorcycle trailers and personal watercrafts: The battle over *Keck*' (2008) 35:2 LIEI 133; E Spaventa, 'Leaving *Keck* behind? The free movement of goods after the rulings in *Commission v Italy* and *Mickelsson and Roos*' (2009) 35:6 ELRev 914; and P Wenneras and K Bøe Moen, 'Selling arrangements, keeping *Keck*' (2010) 35:3 ELRev 387.

[53] Case C-34/09 *Ruiz Zambrano v Office national de l'emploi (ONEm)* [2011] ECR I-1177.

[54] A third category implicit in *Keck and Mithouard* concerned rules 'designed to regulate trade in goods between Member States' (see e.g. Case C-185/94 *Commission v Italy* [1997] ECR I-5789, para. 31), discussed in Chapter 5.

[55] AG Cosmas in Joined Cases C-418etc/93 *Semeraro Casa Uno and others v Sindaco del Comune di Erbusco and others* [1996] ECR I-2975, paras 8–10 of the Opinion.

[56] AG Poiares Maduro in *Alfa Vita*, paras 26–29 of the Opinion.

displayed in this field. The case-law has been able to adapt to the circumstances of each case and to the economic realities encountered'.[57] But he then suggested that this flexibility also demonstrated 'three major disadvantages' of the *Keck* framework: first, uncertainty for economic operators; second, case law complexity, which 'results, in particular, in a tendency on the part of the Court to refer back to the national court the responsibility of ascertaining the character and scope of the rule in question'; and, third, case law inconsistency, especially having regard to case law on the other economic freedoms where, as shown in subsection (a), the idea of a restriction on free movement rights captures 'all measures which prohibit, impede or render less attractive the exercise of that freedom'.[58] In his view, the explicitly stated desire in *Keck* to limit actions engaging Article 34 had led to the opposite result in reality. He then asked: 'is there cause to abandon this case-law? I do not think so. However, it is important to clarify it, in particular by reference to the case-law developed in the other fields of free movement'.[59]

The opportunity to do precisely that soon followed. Initially, questions addressing rules regulating the use of goods snuck through the case law undetected. In *Toolex Alpha*, concerning a general prohibition on the use of trichloroethylene in industrial processes that could be overridden only by the granting of individual exemptions, the Court spent little time deciding that the national rule fell within the scope of Article 34, on the basis that 'the obligation imposed upon economic operators to apply for exemption or a dispensation from a national measure itself amounts to a quantitative restriction or measure having equivalent effect'.[60] Six years later, in October 2006, AG Léger took a similar approach in the first Opinion in *Trailers*. The contested Italian rules essentially prohibited mopeds from towing trailers. The Commission explained its pursuit of infringement proceedings by arguing that 'the measure at issue *precludes the use* of trailers legally produced and marketed in the other Member States, *thereby impeding imports and sales of such trailers* in Italy. [S]uch a measure, constituting an obstacle to imports within the meaning of Article [34], could only be considered compatible with the Treaty if it were justified by one of the public-interest grounds set out in Article [36] or by one of the imperative requirements recognised by the case-law of the Court'.[61] Recalling the fundamental premises of *Dassonville* and *Cassis*, AG Léger agreed that the Italian rules were caught by the Treaty: 'by imposing *a general and absolute prohibition* on the towing of trailers by mopeds throughout Italian territory, the national rules at issue *impede* the free movement of goods and, in particular, that of trailers'.[62] The 'general and absolute' nature of the national rule was clearly important for the Advocate General, since he continued:

[57] AG Poiares Maduro in *Alfa Vita*, para. 30 of the Opinion.
[58] AG Poiares Maduro in *Alfa Vita*, paras 31–33 of the Opinion.
[59] AG Poiares Maduro in *Alfa Vita*, para. 35 of the Opinion.
[60] Case C-473/98 *Kemikalieinspektionen v Toolex Alpha* [2000] ECR I-5681, para. 37; however, the Court considered that the measure was both justified and proportionate.
[61] AG Léger in *Trailers*, para. 22 of the Opinion (emphasis added).
[62] AG Léger in *Trailers*, para. 39 of the Opinion (emphasis added).

Although that prohibition *relates only to mopeds*, it seems to me that the coupling of a trailer to a vehicle of that kind constitutes a normal and frequently used means of transport, particularly in rural areas. However, those rules, although not prohibiting imports of trailers and their marketing in Italy, have the effect of *limiting their use throughout Italian territory*. I am therefore of the opinion that such a prohibition is *liable to limit opportunities for trade between the Italian Republic and the other Member States* and *to hamper imports and the marketing in Italy of trailers from those States*, even though they are lawfully manufactured and marketed there.[63]

AG Léger's reasoning is suggestive of a possible defence on grounds of appreciability, reinforced by his statement in the next paragraph that the Italian rules were in principle precluded by Article 34 'in those circumstances'.[64] While accepting justification arguments grounded in road safety in principle, the Advocate General disputed the proportionality of the national rules, mainly because they applied only to mopeds that had been registered in Italy.[65]

Tracking the case law chronologically, the next development came just a few weeks afterwards, with AG Kokott's Opinion in December 2006 in *Mickelsson and Roos*, a case examining the compatibility with EU law of Swedish rules providing that 'the use of personal watercraft other than on general navigable waterways and on waters on which the county administrative board has permitted the use of personal watercraft is prohibited and punishable by a fine'.[66] Here, the Commission's submission characterized the national rules as 'restrictions on use', something picked up on by AG Kokott as potentially raising a new category of rule with respect to the scope of Article 34.[67] Recalling the 'excesses' (per AG Poiares Maduro in *Alfa Vita*) to which too broad an interpretation of Article 34 can give rise, as well as the Court's response to that risk in *Keck*, AG Kokott suggested that rules regulating the use of goods should similarly fall outside the scope of Article 34 in principle, unless the same conditions established in *Keck*—*prevention* of access to the market, making considerations of discriminatory effects redundant for restrictions of that *degree* of impact;[68] or *impeding* market access for imported products *more than for domestic products*—could be satisfied.[69] This correlation was prudent, in her view, as '[i]n the context of arrangements for use, ultimately individuals may even invoke Article [34] as a means of challenging national rules whose effect is *merely to limit their general freedom of action*'.[70] At first glance, AG Kokott's proposal for rules regulating the use of goods was more cautious than AG Léger's

[63] AG Léger in *Trailers*, para. 40 of the Opinion (emphasis added).

[64] AG Léger in *Trailers*, para. 41 of the Opinion.

[65] AG Léger in *Trailers*, para. 58 of the Opinion, mirroring the submission of the Commission as summarized in para. 23; see also, para. 60: 'it is incumbent upon the Italian authorities to consider carefully, before adopting a measure *as radical as a general and absolute prohibition*, whether it might be possible to resort to measures less restrictive of freedom of movement and to rule them out only if their unsuitability for attainment of the aim pursued is clearly established' (emphasis added).

[66] AG Kokott in *Mickelsson and Roos*, para. 2 of the Opinion.

[67] AG Kokott in *Mickelsson and Roos*, para. 39 of the Opinion.

[68] AG Kokott in *Mickelsson and Roos*, para. 67 of the Opinion.

[69] AG Kokott in *Mickelsson and Roos*, esp. paras 47–48 and 52–55 of the Opinion.

[70] AG Kokott in *Mickelsson and Roos*, para. 48 of the Opinion (emphasis in original).

blunter *Dassonville* reasoning in *Trailers*. But the end result was the same, given AG Kokott's tough analysis of the disproportionate character of the national rules—it was just arrived at here through a different, *Keck*-framed route.[71] In another respect, however, she went further: suggesting that 'it is *not only rules which result in complete exclusion*, such as a general prohibition on using a certain product, that are to be regarded as *preventing* access to the market. A situation *where only a marginal possibility for using a product remains* because of a particularly restrictive rule on use is *to be regarded as preventing access* to the market'.[72]

The final steps in the first case law phase—which is distinguished by the basic presence of coincidental cases rather than an explicitly joined-up narrative—came one year later. In December 2007, AG Trstenjak delivered her Opinion in *Commission v Portugal*,[73] assessing the lawfulness of national rules prohibiting the fixing of tinted film to the windows of passenger or goods vehicles. With no discussion of the 2006 Opinions beyond a brief reference to *Trailers* to acknowledge road safety as a legitimate public interest argument,[74] AG Trstenjak was of the view that 'there can be no doubt' that the national rules fell within the scope of Article 34, focusing on the impact on the marketing of the relevant product: '[e]ven if such a prohibition is applicable without distinction and is thus not discriminatory in nature, it is essentially aimed towards and capable of hindering or even making impossible the marketing in Portugal of tinted film lawfully manufactured and/or marketed in another Member State'.[75] On 10 April 2008, the Third Chamber confirmed her approach in a judgment that dealt very briefly with confirming a restriction within the meaning of Article 34, just noting that '*potential customers, traders or individuals have practically no interest in buying* [the relevant product] in the knowledge that affixing such film to the windscreen and windows alongside passenger seats in motor vehicles is prohibited'.[76]

The way in which that judgment placed emphasis not just on the impact of the rules on marketing but also on the needs of consumers as well as traders became even more important in the second phase. Here, the Court considered overtly whether rules regulating the use of goods constituted a new category of restrictions within the meaning of Article 34, as proposed by AG Kokott in *Mickelsson and Roos*; or were merely a no-fuss offshoot of the *Dassonville* test, following *Toolex Alpha*, *Commission v Portugal*, and the first Opinion in *Trailers*. The Court picked up on the building momentum in this area in March 2007 in the middle of the proceedings for *Trailers*. It reopened the oral proceedings, reassigned the case from a five-judge chamber to the Grand Chamber, and requested a second Opinion

[71] AG Kokott in *Mickelsson and Roos*, paras 85–87 of the Opinion; although she accepted that the rules were justified in principle, on the grounds of environmental protection, her conclusions on proportionality relied in particular on the open-ended nature of county administrative board powers with respect to taking a decision to designate relevant waterways appropriately.

[72] AG Kokott in *Mickelsson and Roos*, para. 67 of the Opinion (emphasis added).

[73] Case C-265/06 *Commission v Portugal (Tinted film)* [2008] ECR I-2245.

[74] AG Trstenjak in *Commission v Portugal*, para. 54 of the Opinion.

[75] AG Trstenjak in *Commission v Portugal*, para. 54 of the Opinion; she also considered that the rules were, while justifiable in principle, disproportionate in effect.

[76] *Commission v Portugal*, para. 33 (emphasis added).

(delivered by AG Bot in July 2008) explicitly to address 'the extent to which and the conditions under which national provisions which govern not the characteristics of goods but their use, and which apply without distinction to domestic and imported goods, are to be regarded as measures having equivalent effect to quantitative restrictions on imports'.[77] As well as the Commission and Italy, eight Member States submitted observations—with seven of those States supporting AG Kokott's position in *Mickelsson and Roos* i.e. transposition of the *Keck* approach beyond selling arrangements to encompass rules regulating use. Following those submissions, the rules would not come within the scope of Article 34 in principle but, interestingly, it was conceded that '*an exception may be made* to that principle if it is shown that the measures in question purely and simply prohibit the use of a product *or authorise only marginal use*, thereby *limiting* the product's access to the market'.[78] That phrasing clearly etches a new Article 34 index beyond the benchmark of access prevention. Leaving *Keck* out of it altogether, the Commission simply argued that use rules constituted restrictions on the free movement of goods, citing *Toolex Alpha*.[79]

AG Bot pointed to examples submitted by the Commission to illustrate the different ways in which rules could affect the use of products i.e. '[c]ases in which it is necessary to possess an administrative authorisation (for example, permission to bear arms), or to have attained a particular age before acquiring or using certain products, or cases in which use of the product is prohibited in certain places or at certain times of day (for example, the prohibition of using mobile telephones in hospitals)'.[80] These examples suggest a spectrum of use rules that could be refined, in terms of their potential for capture by Article 34, through causation and appreciability tests—a framework returned to in Section 3. More importantly for present purposes, AG Bot argued against distinguishing between different *types* of rules at all, bringing the reach of Article 34 squarely back to the *Dassonville* focus on effect and emphasizing that both the Court and national courts should assess each case in the context of its individual circumstances—echoing AG Fennelly in *Graf*. AG Bot acknowledged the legitimacy of developing 'presumptions regarding the effects of various categories of measures on the market'. But he too considered that type-based distinctions may be 'artificial and the demarcation line between those different categories of measures may be uncertain' and therefore 'may be a source of confusion for national courts'.[81] He pointed to several examples of case law incoherence that had resulted when the Court either ostensibly categorizes rules by type or 'abandons that distinction and makes an analysis based only on the effects of the rules'.[82] He conceded that the judgment in *Keck* had neither clarified the scope of Article 34 nor 'facilitated [its] implementation'; however, he did 'not

[77] AG Bot in *Trailers*, para. 6 of the Opinion.
[78] AG Bot in *Trailers*, para. 38 of the Opinion (emphasis added).
[79] AG Bot in *Trailers*, paras 32–33 of the Opinion.
[80] AG Bot in *Trailers*, fn13 of the Opinion.
[81] AG Bot in *Trailers*, paras 80, 81, and 90 of the Opinion.
[82] AG Bot in *Trailers*, para. 81 of the Opinion.

think that at the present time it is appropriate to depart from that case-law'.[83] It is far from clear how that mixed message confronts acknowledged case law incoherence.

Ultimately, AG Bot considered that the principle of access to the market should guide the analysis of restrictions on the free movement of goods, which would also fit with case law on free movement more generally.[84] He placed particular importance on the principle of proportionality as a crucial mechanism that enables a balance to be struck between the need 'to ensure that the national courts are not prompted to exclude too many measures from the prohibition laid down by [Article 34]' and the fact that, at the same time, 'the Court's role is not systematically to challenge policing measures adopted by the Member States'.[85] For the restriction in this case, he argued that complete product bans—'*in contrast to the rules* at issue in *Mickelsson and Roos* [which] *just limit* the use of a product'[86]—were caught by Article 34 since they 'prohibit the use of a product outright'.[87] AG Bot thus stuck to the prevention threshold set by *Keck* in practical effect. To establish that level of restriction in this case, he used familiar reasoning on the implications for traders seeking to break into a new market:

> The prohibition in question makes it *practically impossible* to penetrate the Italian market. The extent of the prohibition is such that it leaves no scope for anything other than *purely marginal use* of trailers. They are rendered *entirely useless* because they cannot be used for the normal purpose for which they are intended, namely to increase the luggage-carrying capacity of a motorcycle. The prohibition therefore dissuades distributors from importing them. It is rather pointless to import them if the retailer knows that they will not be sold or rented. The prohibition will therefore have the effect of *significantly reducing imports*. Consequently, I consider that the rules at issue, which *prohibit outright the use of a product* throughout national territory, give rise to a *substantial, direct and immediate* obstacle to intra-[Union] trade.[88]

Again reflecting the arguments of AG Fennelly in *Graf*, AG Bot considered that the Court should 'examine [the] specific impact on patterns of trade' (but not in a way that would 'involve any complex economic assessment') and that, apart from 'purely *hypothetical* effects or *totally uncertain and indirect* effects or again *wholly insignificant* effects', an obstacle to trade within the meaning of Article 34 'does not therefore need to be actual and significant, but must be at least possible'.[89] Following the general line taken by the other Advocates General in related case

[83] AG Bot in *Trailers*, paras 84–85 of the Opinion.

[84] AG Bot in *Trailers*, paras 82–83 and 119 of the Opinion.

[85] AG Bot in *Trailers*, paras 99–101 of the Opinion, noting that '[i]t is thus the review of proportionality which enables the Court to weigh the interests associated with attainment of the internal market against those relating to the legitimate interests of the Member States'.

[86] AG Bot in *Trailers*, para. 153 of the Opinion (emphasis added).

[87] AG Bot in *Trailers*, para. 104 of the Opinion, noting that '[e]ven if those rules apply in the same way to domestic and imported products, they prevent the latter from gaining access to the market'.

[88] AG Bot in *Trailers*, paras 157–159 of the Opinion (emphasis added).

[89] AG Bot in *Trailers*, paras 116–117 of the Opinion (emphasis added).

law, AG Bot also concluded that the Italian rules were justifiable in principle, for the purpose of ensuring road safety, but disproportionate in effect.

In February 2009, the Grand Chamber delivered its judgment. Citing *Dassonville*, it combined discrimination and access reasoning, but in a way that distinctly extended the prevention standard in *Keck*: 'measures adopted by a Member State the object or effect of which is to treat products coming from other Member States less favourably are to be regarded as measures having equivalent effect to quantitative restrictions on imports within the meaning of Article [34]. *Any other measure which hinders access of products* originating in other Member States to the market of a Member State *is also covered* by that concept'.[90] The Court then confined its analysis in the present case to the market for 'trailers which are specifically designed to be towed by motorcycles'.[91] On that basis, it found that:

> [T]he possibilities for their use other than with motorcycles are very limited. [A]lthough it is not inconceivable that they could, in certain circumstances, be towed by other vehicles... such use is inappropriate and remains at least insignificant, if not hypothetical. [A] prohibition on the use of a product in the territory of a Member State has a considerable influence on the behaviour of consumers, which, in its turn, affects the access of that product to the market of that Member State. Consumers, knowing that they are not permitted to use their motorcycle with a trailer specially designed for it, have practically no interest in buying such a trailer... Thus [the national rule] *prevents a demand from existing in the market at issue* for such trailers and *therefore hinders their importation*. It follows that the prohibition laid down... to the extent that its effect is to hinder access to the Italian market for trailers which are specially designed for motorcycles and are lawfully produced and marketed in Member States other than the Italian Republic, constitutes a measure having equivalent effect to quantitative restrictions on imports within the meaning of Article [34], unless it can be justified objectively.[92]

It is critical to note that the Court established a more open test than it actually applied in the extract above: as AG Bot had, the Court substantiated the relevant restriction here at the level of de facto *prevention*. That open test/narrower application approach also reflects the concession made by the Member States in their submissions, noted above. Moreover, situating the reasoning in consumer needs once again arguably aimed to shift the foundations of market access away from the right to trade debate of the 1990s.[93]

[90] *Trailers*, para. 37 (emphasis added). [91] *Trailers*, para. 54.

[92] *Trailers*, paras 55–58 (emphasis added).

[93] Somewhat reversing the same theme in a case about advertising restrictions, however, see AG Geelhoed in *Douwe Egberts*, para. 70 of the Opinion: 'the Court recognises the function which advertising performs in the economic sphere and, more generally, in the integration of the market. [T]his function is not simply limited to providing the consumer with information and attracting his custom. It is also a means for manufacturers in the Member States to penetrate other markets, to confront consumers with products with which they may not be familiar or, on the other hand, to offer them an alternative to products with which they are familiar. Advertising is the means which may help to increase the transparency of the market, to stimulate market forces and to counteract market rigidity. A general prohibition of advertising, a prohibition of the advertising of certain products or a prohibition of the advertising of the distinctive characteristics of a product are bound, by their nature, to have implications for trade in the products to which they relate. It cannot be said, therefore, that such arrangements are a fortiori neutral with respect to intra-[Union] trade'. See also, the discussion in

As a result of the decision in *Trailers*, Member States are likely to have to account under EU law for more national regulatory choices than they might have anticipated, but their public interest arguments also seem to be registering greater force. Significantly, the Court—contrary to both Opinions submitted on this case—considered that the national measure was both justifiable *and* proportionate. Recalling AG Bot's presentation of proportionality as a balancing mechanism, it could be said that the Court recalibrated the constitutional balance mindful of its responsibilities in the scheme of judicial review: widening the scope of review but softening its implications. However, Spaventa perceives the judgments in both *Trailers* and *Mickelsson and Roos,* returned to below, as evidence of a trend 'from abstract to concrete proportionality assessment', which means that the Treaty provisions become 'a tool to impose a [Union] view of good governance, so that the way in which legislation is adopted or implemented, the finer details, will become increasingly important in determining the compatibility of national rules of the Treaty... This might not be a bad thing, leading as it can to increased economic efficiency; and yet it is also problematic, in that *it further directs (and constrains) the discretion of the national regulator*'.[94] Reflecting that view also for restrictions on establishment and capital, AG Ruiz-Jarabo Colomer considered that 'the principle of proportionality presupposes the promotion of market integration', observing too that the Court was distinctly 'stricter' in its review of national measures compared to measures adopted by the EU institutions.[95]

It is too soon to know whether the trend in the use of goods case law that seems to countenance wider State discretion for justification and proportionality will continue to inform case law on non-discriminatory restrictions of Article 34 and/ or spread across free movement law more generally. But when this embryonic shift is coupled with the stricter approach taken for potential impediments to the free movement of persons in citizenship case law, discussed in Chapter 4, it puts the perception that the Court has been radically expanding the scope of free movement law unchecked in a more tempered perspective at least.

The last step in the second case law phase was the Second Chamber's decision in *Mickelsson and Roos* in June 2009. Citing the test articulated in *Trailers*—and recalling from Chapter 2 that no Advocate General or judge had been involved in all three use of goods cases—the Court focused here on the fact that no waters had as yet been designated as open to navigation by the national authorities, meaning that personal watercraft could be used on general navigable waterways only. On that basis, the Court observed that '[t]he actual possibilities for the use of personal watercraft in Sweden are, therefore, *merely marginal*'.[96] Drawing then from the 'limited interest' that consumers would have in buying such products, also

Spaventa, n52, 922; and see generally, J Snell, 'The notion of market access: A concept or a slogan?' (2010) 47:2 CMLRev 437.

[94] Spaventa, n52, 926 (emphasis added).

[95] Case C-326/07 *Commission v Italy (Statutes of privatised undertakings)* [2009] ECR I-2291, para. 61 of the Opinion.

[96] *Mickelsson and Roos*, para. 25 (emphasis added).

discussed in *Trailers*, the Court concluded that 'where the national regulations for the designation of navigable waters and waterways have the effect of *preventing users of personal watercraft from using them for the specific and inherent purposes* for which they were intended *or of greatly restricting their use*, which is for the national court to ascertain, such regulations have the effect of hindering the access to the domestic market in question for those goods'[97]—although, as noted above, the restriction was considered by the Court to be justifiable and proportionate, subject to verification of certain conditions by the national court. Nevertheless, the judgment takes a significant step beyond *Trailers*. What the Court described in *Mickelsson and Roos* as rules 'greatly restricting use', AG Bot had considered—and distinguished—as 'just limiting' use. But the Second Chamber did not confine the scope of Article 34 to a threshold of de facto prevention. It accommodated an *additional level* of breach clearly beneath the bar of prevention.

Turning finally to the third phase, i.e. post-*Mickelsson and Roos* case law on Article 34, there is an expected degree of case law consolidation and, additionally, continuing devolution of decisions on Article 34 away from the Grand Chamber. For example, Belgian legislation prohibiting the manufacture, marketing, and use of equipment designed to increase the engine power or speed of mopeds was found to contravene Article 34 in *Lahousse and Lavinchy* unless it could be justified. The First Chamber (five judges, with an Opinion) noted that it had 'no information' on whether or not 'there is a measure that is less restrictive than a general prohibition but that is as effective in ensuring road safety', and it left that determination to the national court.[98] In *Elenca*, citing *Trailers* and *Ker-Optika*, the Fifth Chamber (three judges, no Opinion) added reference to the principle of mutual recognition alongside non-discrimination and access to national markets.[99] Finally, lending weight to the argument that free movement law definitions are converging, the Court has also cited *Trailers* to define a restriction on market access in other sectors of free movement law.[100]

But other strands of post-*Trailers* case law are more troubling, and seem to be nudging the scope of Article 34 wider still. In *Bonnarde*, the contested national legislation required a registration document for all demonstration motor vehicles, irrespective of their origin, in order to qualify for an ecological subsidy—it was not a discriminatory restriction, it was not an innate burden in the manner of a product

[97] *Mickelsson and Roos*, para. 28 (emphasis added).

[98] Case C-142/09 *Criminal proceedings against Lahousse and Lavichy BVBA* [2010] ECR I-11685, paras 44–47.

[99] Case C-385/10 *Elenca Srl v Ministero dell'Interno*, judgment of 18 October 2012: 'Article 34 TFEU reflects the obligation to comply with the principles of non-discrimination and of mutual recognition of products lawfully manufactured and marketed in other Member States, as well as the principle of ensuring free access of EU products to national markets' (para. 23). See similarly, AG Mazák in Case C-333/08 *Commission v France* [2010] ECR I-757, para. 60 of the Opinion.

[100] Case C-400/08 *Commission v Spain (Shopping centres)* [2011] ECR I-1915, para. 64 (freedom of establishment): 'the concept of "restriction" for the purposes of Article [49 TFEU] covers measures taken by a Member State which, although applicable without distinction, affect access to the market for undertakings from other Member States and thereby hinder intra-[Union] trade' (also citing e.g. *CaixaBank*, para. 11).

rule, and it was not a rule prohibiting or even greatly restricting use. Nevertheless, the Court—sitting as a three-judge chamber, with no Opinion and citing *Trailers*—held that, since not all Member States provided for such a requirement, the Belgian measure 'may influence the behaviour of consumers and, consequently, affect the access of those vehicles to the market of that Member State'.[101] This case exemplifies the Court's longstanding focus on the effects of the national rule at one level. The judgment resonates with the method established for restrictions on services or establishment, but it marks a seismic jump from the way in which the more permissive test now shaping Article 34 was applied in *Trailers* itself. Also, as we saw in Chapter 6 in another context, there was no discussion of what *type* of rule (product rule, selling arrangement, or use rule) this actually was—a discussion that cannot be rendered obsolete since the Court has not overruled *Keck*—and no discussion of any impact on marketing or the particular challenges faced by new market entrants. The Court also, itself, decided that the measure was disproportionate.

Similarly, in *ANETT*, the Court—Third Chamber, five judges, no Opinion—considered that national legislation requiring tobacco retailers to procure their supplies from authorized wholesalers constituted a restriction within the meaning of Article 34 with no discussion of whether the rule *might* constitute a selling arrangement. The reasoning of the Court merits extracting in full, since it demonstrates the breadth of an exclusively access-based analysis very graphically:

> [T]he retailers in question can only *sell* a tobacco product coming from another Member State if such a product is included in the range of products offered by the authorised wholesalers in Spain and if those wholesalers have the product in stock. Hence, where the range of products offered by those wholesalers does not include a specific product, the tobacco retailers have no direct, flexible and quick means of *meeting the demands of their own customers* who are interested in this product. This finding is not called into question by the importers' obligation to guarantee the availability of tobacco products throughout the national territory, where demand for these products exists, as the national legislation provides. The importers may choose to avoid importing certain products where demand is judged to be insufficient, or to delay the importation of such products. On the other hand, any tobacco retailer would undoubtedly be able to react, in the place of the importers, more flexibly and quickly to the demands of its customers with whom it is in direct and frequent contact. Moreover, the tobacco retailers are prevented from procuring supplies in other Member States, even if the manufacturers and wholesalers located there could offer more advantageous procurement conditions, particularly in border areas, either because of their geographic proximity or because of the specific delivery methods they offer. All of these elements are capable of having *a negative effect on the choice of products that the tobacco retailers include in their range of products* and, ultimately, on the access of various products coming from other Member States to the Spanish market.[102]

[101] Case C-443/10 *Bonnarde v Agence de Services et de Paiement*, judgment of 6 October 2011, para. 30.

[102] Case C-456/10 *Asociación Nacional de Expendedores de Tabaco y Timbre (ANETT) v Administración del Estado*, judgment of 26 April 2012, paras 38–43 (emphasis added).

As in *Bonnarde*, the absence of any consideration of the relevance of *Keck* as well as the extension of the consumer demand rationale well beyond even the 'greatly restricting use' benchmark in *Mickelsson and Roos* is deeply concerning. Even the *title* of a first response to the judgment in the literature—'What about Sunday trading...? The rise of market access as *an independent criterion* under Article 34 TFEU'—exposes the fundamental question and the fundamental conceptual challenge that should have engaged the Court.[103]

Finally, in *Sandström*, which follows on directly from the proceedings in *Mickelsson and Roos*, the Court—Third Chamber, five judges, no Opinion—was asked to review the subsequently adopted national regulations that now authorized the use of jet skis on certain waterways.[104] While the Court did concede that the decision was ultimately one for the national court, since it entailed facts-based analysis, it nevertheless provided 'in a spirit of cooperation' its own guidance on the extent to which the conditions set by the earlier judgment had, in its view, been met. This is an extraordinary section of the judgment: the Court is, in effect, indicating a view on the extent to which criteria established in an earlier judgment have been *met*, which involves a review of substantive local decisions: but without highlighting any connection to any degree of access to any particular market at all. It is fair to conclude that despite the efforts of the Grand Chamber in *Trailers* to contain the reach of its test,[105] the case law aftermath is already showing quite a different uptake of the potential embedded there in reality.

3. From concept to principle: access to what, and when?

The use of goods case law narrative is sharply revealing in several respects, raising questions about both the substance of free movement law and the process of free movement *case* law. Two overriding thematic questions will be examined here: first, if market access can be conceptualized as a framework principle of free movement law, what is it actually trying to achieve; and, second, assuming that the first question can be resolved, where should the considerable radius of that principle properly *stop*? Again, the case law on goods provides a focal point, but the analysis will also draw links to discussions in the preceding chapters, especially on the consequences of potential effects and the location of appropriate limits.

(a) Defining access as a principle: what is it trying to achieve?

The central premise of access as articulated by the Court is that even national measures that apply irrespective of nationality with neither the aim nor effect

103 M Jesse, (2012) 3:3 *European Journal of Risk Regulation* 437 (emphasis added).

104 Case C-433/05 *Criminal proceedings against Sandström* [2010] ECR I-2885.

105 A point also picked up in the academic commentary at the time; see e.g. Wenneras and Bøe Moen, n52, 396: 'the qualified nature of the market hindrance test suggests, therefore, that it will have limited complementary value next to the prohibition on discriminatory restrictions of market access'.

of producing differential treatment on that basis—i.e. that do not treat people, companies, products, services, or capital payments *from other States* less favourably—can still constitute Treaty-caught restrictions if they affect access to the market of the State, also expressed as hindering or impeding or being liable to prohibit or otherwise inhibit freedom of movement. This is because the achievement of an internal market requires, in theory, not only the elimination of all discrimination but also the abolition of any restriction on inter-State economic activity. We saw in Section 2 (and in Chapter 6) that the wording of the Treaty provisions that confer free movement rights does, taken literally, support that basic assertion. Re-engaging with the objectives of the internal market and the EU polity more generally, however, is the inexorable breadth of the positive scope of the Treaty that then results defensible in a wider sense too?

In Chapter 5, the Opinion of AG Jacobs in *Leclerc-Siplec* was flagged for its proposing of a *de minimis* test to delimit the scope of Article 34 TFEU. Just before that section of the Opinion, responding to the limitations set by *Keck* for selling arrangements at least (i.e. either differential treatment, or the prevention of access to a national market altogether), he had considered more generally why the scope of Article 34 should be shaped by a test based on access in the first place. In a critical passage, he stated, first, that a test based on discrimination was 'inappropriate' and then continued:

> The *central concern* of the Treaty provisions on the free movement of goods is *to prevent unjustified obstacles to trade between Member States.* If an obstacle to inter-State trade exists, it cannot cease to exist simply because an identical obstacle affects domestic trade . . . Equally, from the point of view of *the Treaty's concern to establish a single market*, discrimination is not a helpful criterion: from that point of view, the fact that a Member State imposes similar restrictions on the marketing of domestic goods is simply irrelevant. The *adverse effect on the [Union] market is in no way alleviated*; nor is the adverse effect on the economies of the other Member States, and so on the [Union] economy . . . Restrictions on trade should not be tested against local conditions which happen to prevail in each Member State, but against the aim of *access to the entire [Union] market.* A discrimination test is therefore *inconsistent as a matter of principle with the aims of the Treaty* . . . There is one guiding principle which seems to provide an appropriate test: that principle is that *all undertakings which engage in a legitimate economic activity in a Member State should have unfettered access to the whole of the [Union] market, unless there is a valid reason for denying them full access to a part of that market.* In spite of occasional inconsistencies in the reasoning of certain judgments, that seems to be the *underlying principle which has inspired the Court's approach* from *Dassonville* through '*Cassis de Dijon*' to *Keck.* Virtually all of the cases are, *in their result, consistent with the principle*, even though some of them appear to be based on different reasoning.[106]

By drawing interpretative lines back to *Dassonville* and also reflecting the wording of relevant Treaty provisions, AG Jacobs presents a compelling case in favour of access as the central framework principle of free movement law. Moreover, his arguments have resonance not only for Article 34 but across the span of the Treaty freedoms. For example, AG Trstenjak has stated more recently that judgments such

[106] AG Jacobs in *Leclerc-Siplec*, paras 39–41 of the Opinion (emphasis added).

as *Alpine Investments* and the *Golden shares* case law show that 'the Court understands the fundamental freedoms *primarily as instruments for opening up markets* and therefore, in examining whether a restriction on fundamental freedoms exists in an individual case, assesses national provisions according to whether or not they impede market access'.[107] These rationales provide conceptual—as well as constitutional, economic, and political—underpinning for the direction that the Court's case law has clearly already taken. But two powerful and interlinked objections to the application of an access-based framework that persist must also be addressed: definitional ambiguity and questions of overreach.

(i) Definitional ambiguity

One of the main attractions of a framework based on discrimination is that it is an established principle with both credible and feasible legal attributes. It is an expression of the fundamental—and recognized—principle of equal treatment and, in neutral legal terms, it prohibits the making of a distinction that cannot be defended within a pre-defined framework of justification.[108] The idea of access has, in contrast, been criticized as an elastic formula of more indeterminate nature. It is, on this view, an economic model or a policy value preference, but it is neither a suitably nor a sufficiently law-like or *law-useful* criterion. It is not therefore eligible to be a *principle*. For example, Spaventa has suggested that 'market access is a rather deceiving term that masks the evolution to a "freedom to trade" interpretation of the free movement provisions'.[109] Similarly, Snell argues that 'when pressed, the notion of market access collapses into economic freedom or anti-protectionism, and obscures the need to choose between the two competing paradigms of free movement law... The very ambiguity of the term may explain its use by and usefulness for the Court'.[110] Davies criticizes the fact that '[l]itigants who challenge non-protectionist regulation are not in fact claiming that they are denied market access. They are claiming that a different market should exist'.[111] He is particularly dismissive of arguments based purely on a reduction in the volume of imports for claims connected to Article 34—returned to below—but he argues more generally as follows:

> Quite apart from the fact that Article 34 is not written as a prohibition on disproportionate regulation of economic activity, there is absolutely no economic consensus that it would be desirable to use Article 34 to address over-regulation. The extent to which over-riding local preferences is efficient is still hotly contested, while alongside the issue of the substantive rule

[107] AG Trstenjak in Case C-81/09 *Idryma Typou AE v Ypourgos Typou kai Meson Mazikis Enimerosis* [2010] ECR I-10161, para. 75 of the Opinion (emphasis added).

[108] D Edward, 'Non-discrimination as a legal concept' in R Schulze (ed.), *Non-Discrimination in European Private Law* (Mohr Siebeck, 2011) 3 at 5; similarly, he notes (at 7) that '[discrimination] is useful as a legal principle because it offers a *practical* way of approaching the problem of giving legal effect to the principle of equal treatment' (emphasis added).

[109] Spaventa, n52, 929, which, she also notes, is 'far from being unproblematic'.

[110] Snell, n93, 468. [111] Davies, n29, 29.

in question one must always consider the economics and politics of federalism: the desirability of allocating power to a particular level, irrespective of the 'good sense' of what they may do with it... A deregulatory use of Article 34 is not a bending of the rules in the pursuit of an uncontested good, but a setting aside of the text of the law in favour of a particular political agenda. It is an attempted coup d'état.[112]

Picking up on the discussion in Chapter 1, this line of commentary essentially exposes the fact that the Court makes internal market policy in a way that subdues the appearance—and distinct responsibilities—of policy-making. Addressing the absence of mutual recognition as a principle that has had *material* effects in the case law, Snell also notes that the kinds of challenges currently being supported by the Court 'contradict the basic starting point of *Cassis de Dijon* that in the absence of common rules *it is for the Member States to regulate* all matters relating to the production on their own territory, but such products must be mutually recognised by other countries'.[113] That argument raises a further, recurring, question about the relationship between different lines of live case law authority that are not reconciled.

Part of the criticisms articulated by Davies, Snell, and Spaventa concerns questions about the objectives of the internal market, picked up below in the context of overreach. But Snell also demonstrates the elasticity of market access at the level of basic definition, contrasting AG Jacobs' use of the concept to *undermine* a free movement framework confined to discrimination with AG Poiares Maduro's discussion of access in *Alfa Vita* in a way that is actually *intertwined* with it.[114] These points can be further explained by addressing a related question connected to access/discrimination definitional ambiguity i.e. the point at which access *alone* actually applies. Rationalizing why the Treaty should catch national measures that effect complete bans or prohibitions exposes the issues here. As a first step, it was shown in Chapter 6 that differential treatment occurring *in effect* amounts to indirect nationality discrimination, something that is perhaps not looked for or sufficiently recognized in cases that are managed and discussed through the language of access. Bans are more obviously discriminatory where the alleged completeness of the prohibition turns out to be 'complete' by reference to activities involving *other* States only—where there are, in other words, no comparable restrictions on home State market actors.[115] More subtly, however, and very *Keck*-resonantly, the Court reasoned as follows in *Gourmet International Products*:

[I]n the case of products like alcoholic beverages, the consumption of which is linked to traditional social practices and to local habits and customs, a prohibition of all advertising

[112] Davies, n29, 29. [113] Snell, n93, 460 (emphasis added).

[114] AG Poiares Maduro in *Alfa Vita*, esp. paras 38–39, 41 and 45–46 of the Opinion. That reasoning is similar to the ideas the same Advocate General expressed subsequently in Case C-446/03 *Marks & Spencer plc v Halsey (Her Majesty's Inspector of Taxes)* [2005] ECR I-10837, outlined in Chapter 6; it also reflects the approach of the Court in *Keck and Mithouard*.

[115] E.g. on Article 34 TFEU, cf. the circumstances of and decision in Case 121/85 *Conegate Limited v HM Customs & Excise* [1986] ECR 1007 with the earlier case of Case 34/79 *R v Henn and Darby* [1979] ECR 3795, returned to below.

directed at consumers in the form of advertisements in the press, on the radio and on television, the direct mailing of unsolicited material or the placing of posters on the public highway is liable to impede access to the market by products from other Member States *more than it impedes access by domestic products*, with which consumers are instantly more familiar [and] must therefore be regarded as affecting the marketing of products from other Member States *more heavily* than the marketing of domestic products and as therefore constituting an obstacle to trade between Member States caught by Article [34] of the Treaty.[116]

This passage shows that market access is not necessarily irrelevant as soon as discrimination *is* relevant. Rather, the principle of equal treatment also provides conceptual foundations for restrictions on access in such circumstances.

Genuinely non-discriminatory bans and prohibitions cannot be rationalized in the same way. However, though not based on a universally accepted logic,[117] commentators do not tend to take issue, at least, with the *Keck* baseline in this respect i.e. it is generally accepted that the Treaty should catch non-discriminatory national rules that *completely prevent or block access* to the markets of other States, whether that marks a right of market entry or a right of market exit. For workers, the situation in *Bosman* illustrates this degree of restriction at the point of entry-access. If the UEFA-mandated transfer fee rules remained in place, it would be (literally) impossible for the applicant to take up his offer of employment in another Member State—or in his own State, but the absence of a cross-border connection removes that version of events from the interest of the Treaty. A generally applicable product ban—i.e. however expressed, a de facto ban on manufacture, sale, and import—provides another example of an entry-access restriction that will have to meet justification and proportionality requirements if it is to be allowed to remain in place. For example, long before *Trailers*, the Court reasoned in *Henn and Darby* that Article 34 'includes a prohibition on imports inasmuch as this is *the most extreme form of restriction*. The expression used in Article [34] must therefore be understood as being the equivalent of the expression "prohibitions or restrictions on imports" occurring in Article 36'.[118]

The Court has also confirmed that non-discriminatory exit-access measures are caught by the Treaty, with the exception of quantitative restrictions on the export of goods (Article 35 TFEU) as discussed in Chapter 6. For example, a prohibition on leaving the national territory because of unresolved tax liability was considered to be a restriction of the rights conferred by Article 21 TFEU since '[t]he right of freedom of movement includes both the right for citizens of the European Union to enter a Member State other than the one of origin and the corresponding right to leave the State of origin. [T]he fundamental freedoms guaranteed by the Treaty

[116] *Gourmet International Products*, paras 21 and 25 (emphasis added).

[117] See e.g. AG Gulmann in *Schindler*, para. 61 of the Opinion: 'strong grounds can be put forward for holding that national rules which contain a general prohibition of a specified activity and which are neither overtly nor covertly discriminatory are not incompatible with Article [56] of the Treaty. Such rules are equally burdensome for national and foreign providers of services and it is not immediately clear why foreign providers of services should be able to exercise an activity which is prohibited for nationals merely because those foreign providers lawfully exercise that activity in their own State'.

[118] *Henn and Darby*, para. 12 (emphasis added).

would be rendered meaningless if the Member State of origin could, *without valid justification*, prohibit its own nationals from leaving its territory in order to enter the territory of another Member State'.[119] That principle originated in case law on the economic freedoms.[120] An exit-block rationale was applied in *Alpine Investments*, for example, addressing national rules that prohibited financial intermediaries from cold calling i.e. contacting potential customers either by telephone or in person without their prior written consent, covering the Netherlands and other Member States in its geographical reach. Having observed that the rule 'deprives the operators concerned of a rapid and direct technique for marketing and for contacting potential clients in other Member States', the Court continued that '[a] prohibition such as that at issue is imposed by the Member State in which the provider of services is established and affects not only offers made by him to addressees who are established in that State or move there in order to receive services but also offers made to potential recipients *in another Member State*. It therefore *directly affects access to the market in services* in the other Member States and is thus capable of hindering intra-[Union] trade in services'.[121]

Situations involving complete bans or prohibitions, whether at the point of entry or exit, are clearly not discriminatory with respect to nationality. For completeness, it should be remembered that exit restrictions are addressed through discrimination *only* for goods.[122] But it should also be recalled that, after *Trailers*, restrictions on exports and case law on national tax rules mark the last outposts of reasoning through discrimination *only* in the free movement case law—making those case law currents the exception, not the rule. Seeking to defend the place of bans within the scope of the Treaty, even in the absence of discrimination, Davies argues that 'prohibitions have distinctive consequences':

> [B]y contrast with mere restrictions, they are more likely to have the effect of diverting customers to competing products, and that raises the question whether this diversion is *of a protectionist nature*. Secondly, such bans will be politically hard to adopt if there is significant local production, making it plausible that bans will tend to be imposed *where it is imports that are primarily hurt*. Thirdly, even if domestic industry is initially affected, it will typically either adapt to make permitted competing products or withdraw from the now non-existent market, so that as with a product rule, the measure *will then affect only would-be importers*. There are good reasons to think that where a prohibition on use of a product is imposed, a

[119] Case C-434/10 *Aladzhov v Zamestnik director na Stolichna direktsia na vatreshnite raboti kam Ministerstvo na vatreshnite raboti*, judgment of 17 November 2011, para. 25 (emphasis added).

[120] See e.g. Case C-379/92 *Criminal proceedings against Peralta* [1994] ECR I-3453, para. 31 ('the rights guaranteed by Article [56] *et seq*. would be rendered meaningless if the Member State of origin could prohibit undertakings from leaving in order to establish themselves in another Member State'); and *Bosman*, para. 97 (where the Court held that 'the same considerations apply' viz. Article 45 TFEU).

[121] *Alpine Investments*, paras 28 and 38 (emphasis added).

[122] See e.g. the discussion in J Snell, 'And then there were two: Products and citizens in Community law' in T Tridimas and P Nebbia (eds.), *European Union Law for the Twenty-First Century: Volume II* (Hart Publishing, 2004) 49 at 52–3.

protectionist effect may not be far away, and that a state should be asked to explain and justify its regulatory choice.[123]

But if any protectionist effect can be shown, the analysis falls within the sphere of discrimination in effect.[124]

Genuinely non-discriminatory bans do not produce protectionist effects, and they do not fit with the idea of migration discrimination developed in Chapter 4 either. That concept was grounded in the principle of equal treatment; the ability to locate complete bans on access in the same framework would add conceptual weight to the idea of access as a principle. It was shown in Chapter 4 that restrictions on free movement rights conferred by Article 21 TFEU are often caused by what was termed migration (as distinct from nationality) discrimination i.e. differential treatment caused by the fact that someone has moved, intends to move, or is likely to move in the future. But in cases such as *Bosman* and *Alpine Investments,* there is no *differential* treatment. In Chapter 4, the common factor in the cases outlined was that a migration *penalty* of some sort was applied (or was likely to be relevant in the future) to the applicant. However, reflecting the nature of the non-discriminatory prohibitions discussed here, AG Elmer argued as follows in *Franzén*:

An interpretation of Article [34] to the effect that the prohibition it lays down covers measures which are capable of barring or impeding access to the market by goods manufactured in another Member State is also necessary to prevent lacunae in the protection of the free movement of goods where there is no domestic production of the goods in question. In such cases *there cannot by definition be discrimination against products coming from other Member States in comparison with domestic products* and a Member State might therefore be encouraged to impose charges on such products, since it can do so without having to impose comparable charges on domestic products. There would be nothing to preclude such obstacles to trade if Article [34] were understood as only containing a prohibition of discrimination against products of other Member States in comparison with domestic products.[125]

Similarly, it was observed just above that in *Bosman*, the restriction imposed by the transfer fee system applied equally to someone precluded from accessing a contract of employment in their home State i.e. no differential treatment results from the added dimension of transnational migration, as distinct to nationality—in contrast to the circumstances in cases like *D'Hoop* and *Garcia Avello*, where invoking the

[123] Davies, n29, 35 (emphasis added).

[124] The Court also reaffirms consistently that, for restrictions applied within part of the territory of a Member State only, 'for a national measure to be categorised as discriminatory or protective for the purposes of the rules on the free movement of goods, it is not necessary for it to have the effect of favouring national products as a whole or of placing only imported products at a disadvantage and not national products' (Joined Cases C-1/90 and C-176/90 *Aragonesa de Publicidad Exterior and Publivía v Departamento de Sanidad y Seguridad Social de la Generalitat de Cataluña* [1991] ECR I-4151, para. 24; confirmed in e.g. Case C-254/98 *Schutzverband gegen unlauteren Wettbewerb v TK-Heimdienst Sass GmbH* [2000] ECR I-151, para. 27).

[125] AG Elmer in Case C-189/95 *Criminal proceedings against Franzén* [1997] ECR I-5909, para. 65 of the Opinion (emphasis added).

situation of a non-migrant or static comparator *did* reveal differential treatment linked to past, current, or future cross-border movement.[126] In such cases, however, we also saw that the Court tends to frame the issue in this way:

> [A]ll of the Treaty provisions relating to the freedom of movement for persons are intended *to facilitate the pursuit by [Union] nationals of occupational activities of all kinds throughout the [Union]*, and preclude measures which might place [Union] nationals *at a disadvantage* when they wish to pursue an economic activity *in the territory of another Member State*... In that regard, provisions which *prevent or deter* a national of a Member State from leaving his State of origin to exercise his right to freedom of movement *constitute an obstacle to that freedom even if they apply without regard to the nationality* of the workers concerned.[127]

This extract revives questions about the conceptual thinness of a framework based on concepts such as deterrence or disadvantage, which was the very reason for developing the migration discrimination argument in Chapter 4. Access cannot draw from equal treatment foundations in the same way, but what non-discriminatory restrictions on access do reflect is the common thread of *migration*. It was emphasized in Chapter 4 that cross-border connections should not be elevated to the status or meaningfulness of a 'principle' per se. But their realization is an undoubted Treaty objective—a core constitutional signal—that can be folded into the shaping of a principle *of access*.

It is submitted here that a principle based on access should not, therefore, be tied exclusively to the market, but could be expressed as protecting *access to the exercise of free movement rights*. This interpretation reflects the emphasis placed on the market as a defined space in Chapter 2 rather than slipping into problematic policy questions about the Court shaping access to achieve a *particular kind of market* in substantive regulatory terms, recalling the strong criticisms of the latter approach in the literature summarized above and, indeed, also by the Court itself in *Keck*. Thus, adapting Spaventa's description of free movement restrictions post *Trailers* and *Mickelsson and Roos*,[128] the market access dynamic that conveys 'barriers to economic freedom [as barriers] to the freedom to trade' would be changed to: barriers to economic freedom *if access to* the freedom to trade *transnationally* is restricted. Discriminatory barriers, whether they relate to nationality or migration discrimination, clearly satisfy that definition; but the crucial point for the present discussion is that non-discriminatory restrictions can meet it too.

The proposal has three distinct advantages. First, conceptualizing the substance of the principle as concerning access to the exercise of free movement rights, rather than access to the market, responds to criticisms about the ambiguity and even deceptiveness of the *content* of access, summarized above. Second, it addresses the scepticism noted in Chapter 2 that *market* access 'introduces an inappropriate

[126] Case C-224/98 *D'Hoop v Office national de l'emploi* [2002] ECR I-6191; Case C-148/02 *Garcia Avello v Belgian State* [2003] ECR I-11613.

[127] Case C-209/01 *Schilling and Fleck-Schilling v Finanzamt Nürnberg-Süd* [2003] ECR I-13389 paras 24–25 (emphasis added); confirmed for e.g. establishment in Case C-345/05 *Commission v Portugal* [2006] ECR I-10633, para. 18.

[128] Spaventa, n52, 929.

distinction into the field of persons, as it cannot be utilised in the context of non-economic free movers relying on Article [21 TFEU], who are not seeking access to any market'.[129] It was shown in Chapter 4 that all of the Treaty provisions that affect persons *except for* Articles 20 and 21 TFEU require a cross-border connection, affirming the fact that transnational activity must, in general, form the nucleus of an access principle shaping the scope of the other Treaty provisions that confer free movement rights. It was also shown that cases involving static EU citizens under Articles 20 and 21 could, at something of an admitted stretch, be conceptualized through the premise of migration discrimination. Such situations—which are, to date, about loss of Member State nationality or forced departure from the territory of the Union—could alternatively be rationalized on the basis of consequential loss of access to the exercise of free movement rights for the future, even if the citizens involved were static up to the relevant point in time. AG Sharpston drew attention to this way of interpreting things in her Opinion in *Ruiz Zambrano*, but she also commented on the problematic movement fiction that would be perpetuated under that approach.[130] It is better, therefore, to focus on the fact that cases involving static EU citizens do not have to be rationalized through an access principle anyway: because it was also shown in Chapter 4 that the wording of Articles 20 and 21 has the capacity to take citizenship situations out of the scope of free movement law altogether. In other words, the Court's case law on the role of EU rights, exceptionally, in purely internal citizenship situations is conceptually and constitutionally something *else*.

Third, it was noted above that conceiving of access as being about free movement rights rather than markets shifts the focus away from problematic regulatory value judgments. It also dilutes the need to consider engaging complex economic models and data-based reasoning in free movement cases, as discussed in Chapter 5. It fits, in other words, with the conception of access *as a principle of free movement law* at the level of definition, translating a problematic 'slogan' (drawing from Snell) into a fit-for-purpose principle that can be explained to and applied by national courts and tribunals without a fundamental change in either the underpinning pivot of transnational activity or how rule-based tests are applied in free movement case law practice.

There are questions that the construction of access outlined above does not address, however: especially arguments about EU regulatory overreach and the incoherent case law on delimiting thresholds discussed in Chapter 5. The latter point, which concerns the placing of firmer limits on access as a principle, will be returned to in subsection (b), following discussion first of the issue of overreach.

(ii) Questions of overreach

It was noted in Chapter 4 that, as a general rule, natural and legal persons who exercise or wish to exercise free movement rights must, broadly speaking, take

[129] Snell, n93, 471.

[130] AG Sharpston in *Ruiz Zambrano*, esp. paras 75–88 of the Opinion.

different trading conditions in the different States as they find them. That rule marks an outer boundary of the reach of the access principle. For example, addressing the lawfulness of Italian rules on maximum fee tariffs for lawyers, the Court held that '[t]he existence of a restriction within the meaning of the Treaty cannot... be inferred from the mere fact that lawyers established in Member States other than the Italian Republic must become accustomed to the rules applicable in that latter Member State for the calculation of their fees for services provided in Italy. *By contrast*, such a restriction exists, in particular, if those lawyers *are deprived of the opportunity of gaining access* to the market of the host Member State *under conditions of normal and effective competition*'.[131] But where and how is that line properly drawn?

Much of the criticism directed at a principle of *market* access suggests that the line is drawn inappropriately at present. For example, in a case about Italian legislation imposing an obligation to contract on insurance undertakings operating in the field of third-party liability motor insurance, finding that the measure constituted a restriction on freedom of establishment and the freedom to provide services, the Court reasoned that '[i]f they wish to enter the Italian market under conditions which comply with Italian legislation... undertakings will be required *to re-think their business policy and strategy*, inter alia, by considerably expanding the range of insurance services offered... Inasmuch as it involves changes and costs on such a scale for those undertakings, the obligation to contract renders access to the Italian market less attractive and, if they obtain access to that market, reduces the ability of the undertakings concerned to compete effectively, from the outset, against undertakings traditionally established in Italy'.[132] In line with the use of goods case law, the Court did find that the rules were justified and proportionate. But the judgment also evokes the general market-conditions reasoning seen in *Bonnarde* and *ANETT*. Even taking the particular plight of new market entrants into account, is the obligation to 'rethink business policy and strategy' really that objectionable a burden to place on an economic operator seeking—choosing—to exploit a new market? Or, put another way, why is it so objectionable a burden that the EU should intervene and assess it?

In *Alfa Vita*, reflecting the concerns summarized in part (i), AG Poiares Maduro argued that '[Union] nationals cannot draw from [Article 34] an *absolute right to economic or commercial freedom*. Indeed, the Treaty provisions relating to the free movement of goods aim to guarantee the opening-up of national markets, offering producers and consumers the possibility of fully enjoying the benefits of a [Union] internal market, and *not to encourage a general deregulation of national economies*'.[133] But it has become difficult to perceive a sufficiently material distinction between an obligation to ensure that trader Y and consumer Z can access product X unless there are good reasons otherwise (unless the policy strategies deployed by the State are non-discriminatory selling arrangements, which do not have to be justified under

131 Case C-565/08 *Commission v Italy* [2011] ECR I-2101, paras 50–51 (emphasis added).
132 Case C-518/06 *Commission v Italy* [2009] ECR I-3491, paras 69–70 (emphasis added).
133 AG Poiares Maduro in *Alfa Vita*, para. 37 of the Opinion (emphasis added).

EU law at all, irrespective of their effects); and an obligation on States positively to *ensure* a market for product X. Framing the principle of access as access to the exercise of free movement rights at the level of definition does not, by itself, respond to that concern beyond reinforcing the basic threshold requirement of a cross-border dimension, which is already coded into the relevant Treaty provisions anyway.

It was argued in previous chapters that the ability to create a sufficient link with EU law through the *potential* and/or *indirect* as well as actual and/or direct impact of a national measure on free movement rights is a critical factor in the opening up of the Treaty's scope. But Spaventa suggests that the Court is now, in effect, reviewing what Mortelmans called market circumstances rules—defined by Horsley as 'genuinely non-discriminatory national measures that simply *outline the conditions for economic activity within individual Member State markets*. In other words, the term characterises national measures that do not prevent (block) the free movement of goods between the Member States or discriminate directly or indirectly in favour of the national market in any way'.[134] Spaventa considers whether the case law trajectory can be justified by what she calls the 'changing telos' of free movement law towards the 'aim of ensuring the competitiveness of the internal market as a whole'—after all, being categorized as a Treaty-relevant restriction does not mean that a national measure *must* be disapplied; it triggers a requirement that standards of justification and proportionality (now defined by the Court more than by the Treaty) must be met.[135] She notes that the widening scope of restrictions seems to have been accompanied by a mitigating stance on justification and proportionality. But she also identifies a broader shift in the circumstances of the case law from concern about actual to potential restrictions—describing, as noted above, what is now precluded as 'barriers to economic freedom, to the freedom to trade'.

In Section 2, the case law narrative on use of goods rules revealed a classic slippery slope: from the complete ban in *Henn and Darby*, to a prohibition on use in *Trailers*, to rules 'greatly restricting use' in *Mickelsson and Roos*. Following AG Jacobs in *Leclerc-Siplec*, the Treaty objective of creating a genuinely frontier-free market would not suggest a distinction between national rules because of their form, but would measure the impact on access on a case-by-case basis. In *Alpine Investments*, the same Advocate General referred to the Court's long-held view that 'the concept of the common market involves the elimination of all obstacles to intra-[Union] trade "in order *to merge the national markets into a single market* bringing about conditions as close as possible to those of a genuine internal market"'.[136] But he did emphasize the centrality of the transnational dimension in distinguishing national and supranational regulatory jurisdiction: while a

[134] Mortelmans, n13; Horsley, n48, 736 (emphasis added).

[135] Spaventa, n52, esp. 925–9.

[136] AG Jacobs in *Alpine Investments*, para. 48 of the Opinion (emphasis added), citing Case 15/81 *Schul v Inspecteur der Invoerrechten en Accijnzen* [1982] ECR 1409, para. 33 and Case C-381/93 *Commission v France* [1994] ECR I-5145, para. 17.

Member State 'is free to regulate the marketing in its territory of services provided by persons established in that State . . . it does not have unlimited freedom to regulate the marketing of such services in the territory of other Member States'—in the latter case i.e. a non-discriminatory exit-block, the national measures will have to be tested against the justification and proportionality standards set by EU law.[137] However, following AG Poiares Maduro in *Marks & Spencer*, in a passage extracted in full in Chapter 5, this could amount to reviewing 'the political choices made by the Member States' to an inappropriate degree, since the objective of creating the market must be balanced against 'the principle of respect for State competences'.[138]

The profoundly divisive tension exposed by the contrasting positions outlined above permeates the case law on free movement and the discourse built around it. Dougan presents the more general significance of that tension as follows:

> EU lawyers might be accused of fetishizing the case law on the scope of the Treaty rules on the free movement of goods. But some fetishes are there to be wallowed in . . . [C]hoices about the interpretation of Article 34 TFEU are decisive for defining *both the fundamental ambitions and the institutional dynamics of the internal market bargain*. If the Court adopts a restrictive understanding of Article 34 . . . it signals that the judicial role is limited to scrutinizing national measures that have a direct and specific impact on cross-border trade; the pursuit of any deeper form of economic integration lies (if at all) with the political institutions. By contrast, when the Court expands the potential reach of Article 34 . . . it risks beginning to ensnare domestic rules which tend simply to restrict the market freedom of economic undertakings, *even in the absence of any distinctly cross-border obstacle to trade*. In the latter situation, Article 34 . . . morphs *from a guarantee of cross-border trade into an instrument for promoting free trade*: the deregulatory power of the primary Treaty provisions is certainly enhanced; the harmonizing competence of the Union institutions is potentially expanded.[139]

This critique has implications well beyond Article 34, but recent case law on the scope of that provision has revived the acuteness of the debate since Article 34 had essentially withstood 'pure' access analysis up to that point, notwithstanding the latent potential of the *Dassonville* test.

Resolving the question of overreach is strongly connected to several of the pressure points discussed in Chapter 2—the unsettled objectives of the Treaty; their accommodation within an atypical constitutional hierarchy; the proliferation of concepts, definitions, and conflicting strands of case law; and the impact on all of this caused by the absence of a more distinctly empowered, or at least consistently constituted, apex court or chamber. But resolving the question is also an impossible ask: as was also pointed out in Chapter 2, the Treaty is ultimately agnostic about the balance between the positions and choices identified by Dougan. The openness

[137] AG Jacobs in *Alpine Investments*, para. 51 of the Opinion.

[138] AG Poiares Maduro in *Marks & Spencer*, para. 37 of the Opinion.

[139] M Dougan, 'Legal developments' (2010) 48:4 Annual Review JCMS 163 at 165 (emphasis added); see generally, J Snell, 'Who's for the power? Free movement and allocation of competences in EC law' (2003) 22 YEL 323.

of the free movement provisions inclines toward a liberalizing view; principles such as conferred powers and subsidiarity incline away from it. In steering the course of that debate through disputes grounded in free movement law, the institutional power of the Court is immense. In *varying* its approach in different phases and/or pockets of case law, the consequences for coherence become clear. Essentially, we still do not know how to answer the question asked by AG Tesauro in *Hünermund*, generating the most famous opening line of any Opinion: '[i]s Article [34 TFEU] a provision *intended to liberalize intra-[Union] trade* or is it intended *more generally to encourage the unhindered pursuit of commerce* in individual Member States?'.[140]

Importantly, however, having unpicked the fragmenting case law on Article 34 that existed at that time (outlined in Section 2), AG Tesauro referred to restrictions that 'make access to the market more difficult and/or less profitable for traders'.[141] Commentary on *Trailers* and *Mickelsson and Roos* rekindled unease about the latter dimension, querying whether the Court's primary concern was merely, and improperly, the *expansion* of the market for the products, and thus the traders, affected.[142] But the distinction drawn in AG Tesauro's statement is crucial: a principle shaped around access to the exercise of free movement rights would retain the relevance of 'more difficult' but it does not follow that the principle must connect to 'less profitable'. The Advocate General's analysis also reflected that position, asserting that 'the purpose of Article [34] is to ensure the free movement of goods in order to establish a single integrated market, eliminating therefore those national measures which in any way create an obstacle to *or even mere difficulties for the movement* of goods; its purpose is not to strike down the most widely differing measures in order, essentially, to ensure the *greatest possible expansion of trade*'.[143] In *Carbonati Apuani*, AG Poiares Maduro articulated a similar position, citing *Keck* to support his impression of 'a more general desire on the part of the Court not to interpret the rules on free movement of goods in the light of a principle of freedom to engage in commercial activity. One of the essential reasons for *restricting the scope of the rules on free movement to transnational situations* is that they should be used only with a view to liberalising trade'.[144]

The Court has signalled general agreement with this philosophy too in some of its case law. For example, in *A-Punkt Schmuckhandels*, it reasoned as follows:

> [T]he fact that a marketing method *is apparently more efficient and profitable is not a sufficient reason* to assert that the national provision prohibiting it is caught by the prohibition laid down in Article [34]. Such a provision constitutes a measure having equivalent effect only if the exclusion of the relevant marketing method affects products from other Member States more than it affects domestic products. In this respect, it is common ground that the prohibition at issue in the main proceedings does not concern all the ways of marketing the

[140] AG Tesauro in *Hünermund*, para. 1 of the Opinion (emphasis added).

[141] AG Tesauro in *Hünermund*, para. 16 of the Opinion (emphasis removed).

[142] See e.g. Spaventa, n52, 924, referring to 'not only . . . a right to access the market [but] the right to assess as wide (and cheap) a market as possible'.

[143] AG Tesauro in *Hünermund*, para. 28 of the Opinion (emphasis added).

[144] AG Poiares Maduro in Case C-72/03 *Carbonati Apuani Srl v Comune di Carrara* [2004] ECR I-8027, para. 49 of the Opinion (emphasis added).

goods in question, but only one of them, and therefore does not exclude the possibility of selling those goods in Austria by other methods.[145]

The advantage of that model, which expresses the limitations established by *Keck* (i.e. either differential effect or *prevention* of access), is that it sets very *clear* and *definitive* limits. But the fundamental problem is that, with the exception of selling arrangements, free movement case law is nowhere else confined to it. This empirical fact makes the refining of *limits* to access as a principle all the more critically important, reviving the relevance of causation and appreciability tests as either presumptions or conditions.

Just over ten years after *Hünermund*, AG Tizzano took the opportunity in *CaixaBank* to reflect on the overall shape of the free movement case law against the purpose and objectives of the internal market. From the starting point of freedom of establishment, he proposed the following market framework:

> I find it difficult to describe national measures that regulate the pursuit of an economic activity *without directly affecting access to that activity* and *without discriminating* either in law or in fact between national and foreign operators as restrictions contrary to the Treaty *for the sole reason that they reduce* the economic *attractiveness* of pursuing that activity. Such an interpretation... would end up firstly contradicting the system of powers set out in the Treaty. It is acknowledged that the provisions on establishment did not grant the [Union] general powers to regulate economic activities as a self-employed person. On the contrary, they left in place the State powers in that regard, merely prohibiting discrimination and obstacles to establishment and creating defined Community powers to harmonise national legislation. Secondly, that interpretation would permit economic operators—both national and foreign—*to abuse* [emphasis added] Article [49 TFEU] in order to oppose any national measure that, solely because it regulated the conditions for pursuing an economic activity, could in the final analysis narrow profit margins and hence reduce the attractiveness of pursuing that particular economic activity. However, that would be tantamount to bending the Treaty to a purpose for which it was not intended: that is to say, not in order to create an internal market in which conditions are similar to those of a single market and where operators can move freely, but in order to establish a market without rules. Or rather, a market in which rules are prohibited as a matter of principle, except for those necessary and proportionate to meeting imperative requirements in the public interest.[146]

The principle of access proposed in this chapter resonates strongly with AG Tizzano's understanding of the Treaty's internal market philosophy—the gravity of which seems somehow sharpened rather than tempered by knowing that the Court went on to find a restriction in its subsequent judgment. AG Tizzano did not undercut the empirical weight of case law on non-discriminatory restrictions, but he did argue that such national measures that hinder or make the exercise of free movement law more difficult should be caught 'only when certain conditions apply, even though in abstract terms they are likely to affect the freedom of movement'.[147] By focusing on the dynamics of transnational market movement,

[145] *A-Punkt Schmuckhandels*, paras 23–24 (emphasis added).
[146] AG Tizzano in *CaixaBank*, paras 58–63 of the Opinion (emphasis in original).
[147] AG Tizzano in *CaixaBank*, para. 65 of the Opinion.

the Advocate General took seriously the most basic steer coded into the Treaty in his framing of the parameters of the market. In essence, the Court is *not* free to apply market access as a political philosophy or an economic model *unless* it can be linked to that most basic of constitutional instructions.[148] AG Tizzano stressed that this 'interpretational approach ... makes it possible *to reconcile the objective* of merging the different national markets into a single common market with the continuation of Member States' general powers to regulate economic activities'.[149]

Conceiving of access as access to the exercise of free movement rights secures the Treaty significance of cross-border connections for all of the economic freedoms. Judicial exploitation of market access as an economic or political template that suggests (or can be bended to suggest) a broader sweep of purely internal and/or deregulatory intention is then more starkly exposed as a step too far. Moreover, the lack of clarity in the relevant constitutional instructions is *precisely* why the Court should avoid making such fundamental choices. The objectives underpinning the market are so unsettled and malleable, and the connections between them raise so many problematic asymmetries, that questions about reach and overreach are inevitably subjectively felt. In *CaixaBank*, AG Tizzano argued that a non-discriminatory national measure should constitute a Treaty-relevant restriction on free movement only where it 'directly affects market access'.[150] To substantiate that test, he considered that 'pointers' offered by *Alpine Investments*—i.e. complete prevention of access, which he rationalized by citing *Keck*—but also, critically, by the judgment in *Graf*—a hub of the logic of remoteness—should mark the limits of the Treaty's positive scope.[151] AG Tizzano reinforced these connections by noting that '[t]he tightening-up ... proposed ... is aimed solely at ensuring that too vague a formulation of that concept [of a restriction] does not give rise to distorted readings ... that lead to measures being classified as restrictions whose effects on the exercise of that freedom are merely hypothetical or entirely uncertain and indirect'.[152] Adding to that framework, it is submitted here that the other threshold test discussed in Chapter 5—appreciability—must also be considered in the context of limits, given the examples of its manifestation that are clearly increasing in recent case law. In Chapter 6, the scope of the free movement provisions was represented graphically as shown again here in Figure 7.1.

But to reflect and accommodate the development of the discussion in this chapter too, the model should be extended as shown in Figure 7.2.

[148] Reaching a similar conclusion but through different reasoning, using economic categorization of 'market-regulating measures' to develop a more, not less, 'market-centric' model that has synergies with competition law, see G Davies, 'Understanding market access: Exploring the economic rationality of different conceptions of free movement law' (2010) 11 *German Law Journal* 671, available at <http://www.germanlawjournal.com/index.php?pageID=11&artID=1264>.

[149] AG Tizzano in *CaixaBank*, para. 68 of the Opinion (emphasis added); see similarly, AG Poiares Maduro in *Marks & Spencer*, para. 40 of the Opinion: 'not every restriction on economic or commercial freedom is a restriction on the exercise of the freedoms of movement'.

[150] AG Tizzano in *CaixaBank*, para. 66 of the Opinion.

[151] AG Tizzano in *CaixaBank*, paras 72–73 of the Opinion.

[152] AG Tizzano in *CaixaBank*, para. 75 of the Opinion.

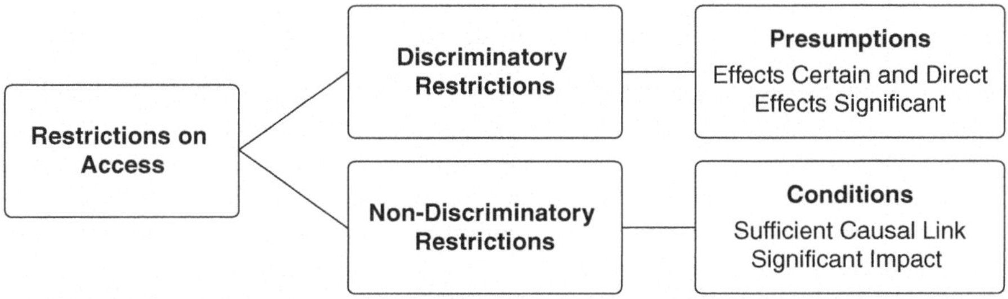

Fig. 7.1 Restrictions on access

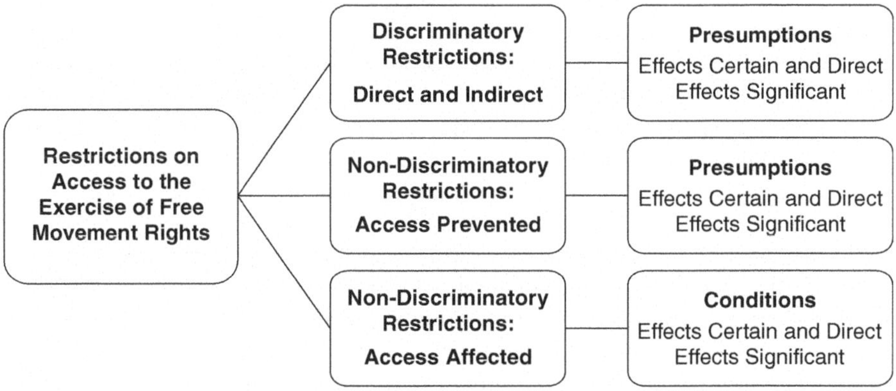

Fig. 7.2 Restrictions on access to the exercise of free movement rights

Reflecting the condition-construction proposed in Figure 7.2 for non-discriminatory restrictions, AG Fennelly articulated a valuable understanding of the relevant burden of proof in *Graf*: '[w]here an alleged obstacle to freedom of movement does not result from a formal condition of market participation but is instead alleged to arise from *some neutral material barrier or disincentive* deriving from national regulations, the prejudice to the exercise of [Union]-law rights *must be established*'.[153] In the expanded access model presented in Figure 7.2, causation and appreciability are conceptualized as *presumptions* for discriminatory restrictions and restrictions preventing access; but for non-discriminatory restrictions that affect access, they instead set *conditions* that 'must be established'. This distinction underscores the need for tighter guidance from the Court: not only on differential burdens of proof,[154] but on the substance of these threshold tests too.

[153] AG Fennelly in *Graf*, para. 31 of the Opinion (emphasis added).

[154] Also discussing a presumption/condition burden of proof angle, but from the perspective of arguments about partitioning the market, see C Barnard, 'Restricting restrictions: Lessons for the EU from the US?' (2009) 68:3 CLJ 575 at 603–5.

(b) Access as a principle: refining the limits

Writing before the use of goods case law, Spaventa argued that the 'rigid system of presumptions which characterised the *Keck* ruling [had evolved] into a flexible system of presumptions which is still useful but not conclusive'.[155] The application of judicial intuition is inherently imperfect, as discussed in Chapter 5. Nonetheless, a more rule-based approach was still argued to be preferable to a more rigid and complex data-based approach. Even for practical reasons alone, the Court is not going to introduce complex economic modelling to free movement law—mainly because it is not going to impose the associated burdens of analysis on national lawyers and national courts, since most practitioners and courts will encounter free movement cases far too rarely on the whole to develop sustained expertise. But intuition must be overlaid with structure and coherence in order to deliver principles: in that vein, more *systematic* consideration of the limits of free movement law would help the Court (and national courts) to develop and articulate 'intuitively *convincing* thresholds'.[156] Otherwise, the Court will remain susceptible to the damaging charges outlined above, exemplified by Snell's stark caution: '[as market access] lacks a clear content, the Court may use it freely either to approve or to condemn measures that it happens to like or . . . [it] may simply provide a sophisticated-sounding garb that conceals decisions based on intuition'.[157]

Some adjustments that could be made in the case law are relatively straightforward, reflecting steps that the Court should be practising anyway. For example, it has been emphasized repeatedly that the Court should delegate concrete decision-making to national courts in preliminary ruling proceedings more systematically than it does, to tighten the connection between the decision-maker and the policymaker as well as to the parties actually affected by the outcome. It should avoid expressing its reasoning as it did in *Gourmet*, for example, where it found that '[e]ven *without its being necessary to carry out a precise analysis of the facts* characteristic of the Swedish situation, which it is for the national court to do, *the Court is able to conclude* that, in the case of products like alcoholic beverages, the consumption of which is linked to traditional social practices and to local habits and customs, a prohibition of all advertising directed at consumers . . . is liable to impede access to the market by products from other Member States more than it impedes access by domestic products, with which consumers are instantly more familiar'.[158] But other refinements of free movement law will require more transformative case law shifts. In particular, as outlined in Chapter 5, the tests of causation and appreciability play an erratic role in delimiting the scope of free movement law at present.

[155] E Spaventa, 'The outer limit of the Treaty free movement provisions: Some reflections on the significance of *Keck*, Remoteness and *Deliège*' in C Barnard and O Odudu (eds.), *The Outer Limits of European Law* (Hart Publishing, 2009) 245 at 247–8.

[156] R Craufurd Smith and D Tambini, 'Measuring media plurality in the United Kingdom: Policy choices and regulatory challenges' (2012) 4:1 *The Journal of Media Law* 35 at 59 (emphasis added).

[157] Snell, n93, 469.

[158] *Gourmet International Products*, para. 21 (emphasis added); see similarly, Fallon and Gerard, n52, 10–11.

Looking first at the threshold of causation, the main point of concern in the case law at present was shown to be inconsistency: sometimes a test of remoteness is applied,[159] but more typically it is not. It was argued in Chapter 5 that a presumption of causation is met in cross-border situations involving discrimination. Situations involving the prevention of access to free movement altogether also constitute an obviously direct restriction for the rights-holder. In his Opinion in *Alpine Investments*, AG Jacobs expressed it as follows: '[w]hether a rule of the Member State of origin constitutes a restriction on the freedom to provide services should be determined by reference to a *functional criterion*, that is to say, whether it *substantially impedes the ability of persons established in its territory to provide intra-Community services*. It seems to me that that criterion is consonant with the notion of an internal market and more appropriate than the criterion of discrimination'.[160] A complete prevention 'substantially impedes' the transnational actor in the way outlined by AG Jacobs, which is why it is treated as a presumption rather than a condition in the model presented in Figure 7.2.

Beyond the complete ban, however, things become fuzzier. Also addressing causation from the perspective of the directness of the restriction at issue, Weatherill draws an interesting parallel between the judgments in *Carpenter* and *Keck*:

> [I]t is striking how easy the Court finds it to establish a connection [in *Carpenter*] between the threatened deportation and the perceived impediment to trade . . . The Court's practice makes plain that a *wider* scope for EU free movement law means a correspondingly *wider* scope for affording individuals the protection of fundamental rights recognised by the EU legal order. It widens the scope of its own adjudicative function too. But it also means a correspondingly *narrower* scope for national rule-making which is sheltered from the need to show compliance with standards demanded by EU free movement law. In this sense a connection may usefully be made with discussion . . . about the legitimate limits of EU law's review of national regulatory choices. The issues raised by the Court's shaping of the scope of [Art 56 TFEU] in *Carpenter* are thematically linked to those relevant to Article 34 TFEU addressed in *Keck and Mithouard*. . . But *Carpenter* has none of the feel of caution about over-extension of EU trade law which is so conspicuous in *Keck and Mithouard*.[161]

Arguably, the situation in *Carpenter* would fail a test based on impediments to access to the exercise of free movement rights on the marker of causation, unless the

[159] See e.g. on Article 34, Case C-291/09 *Francesco Guarnieri & Cie v Vandevelde Eddy VOF* [2011] ECR I-2685, para. 17 ('[t]he causal link between the possible distortion of intra-Community trade and the difference in treatment at issue is . . . not established'); and on Article 56, Case C-602/10 *SC Volksbank România SA v Autoritatea Națională pentru Protecția Consumatorilor—Comisariatul Județean pentru Protecția Consumatorilor Călărași (CJPC)*, judgment of 12 July 2012, paras 80–81: 'it is not evident that that national provision renders access to the Romanian market less attractive and, in the event of access thereto, genuinely reduces the ability of the undertakings concerned to compete effectively, from the outset, against undertakings traditionally established in Romania. In those circumstances, the effect of that national provision on trade in services is *too uncertain and indirect* for such a national measure to be regarded as liable to hinder intra-Community trade' (emphasis added).

[160] AG Jacobs in *Alpine Investments*, para. 47 of the Opinion (emphasis added).

[161] S Weatherill, *Cases and Materials on EU Law*, 10th edn (OUP, 2012) 415–16 (emphasis in original).

child-minding functions of Mrs Carpenter were emphasized more than they actually were in the Court's decision or, along the lines traced by Weatherill, the Court reverts more explicitly to the concealed fundamental rights impulse really impelling the judgment in *Carpenter*—but that is something that the Court has pulled away from in cases like *McCarthy* and *Dereci*, as demonstrated in Chapter 4. For non-discriminatory obstacles that are argued to impede access, it is submitted that a causation threshold, expressed primarily in the case law at present as a test about effects '*too* uncertain and indirect'—and rightly reminding us that the indirectness of a restriction is not per se a problem qua *Dassonville*—should be applied more systematically as a *condition* and not largely ignored as a presumption. In preliminary ruling proceedings, the Court should leave determination of whether the condition is satisfied or not to the referring court.

Refining a test of appreciability is more difficult, since even agreeing that it exists in free movement case law is a controversial position. Again drawing from Article 34 discourse, a reduction or projected reduction in the volume of goods imported could excuse the review of almost any trade-depressing national measure if Article 34 is taken literally, since there will then be a measure indirectly restricting the *quantity* of goods imported. But such a simplistic conclusion is precisely what produces an aversion to a framework based on access without the tempering effect of differential treatment or the patent extremity of a complete ban.[162] The undesirability of leaving access unchecked is what forces us to confront the extent to which free movement rights should be subject to a *de minimis* threshold. Davies has argued as follows:

> The clear intention of the text of Article 34 is *to capture measures which specifically affect cross-border movement*, that is to say which have some effect on imports over and above any domestic effect. This is what a quantitative restriction does—a protectionist measure par excellence—and so, logically, should be what a measure of equivalent effect should do. Moreover, the internal market is consistently understood throughout the Treaty in terms of an area of equal and undistorted competition—a level playing field for competitors and consumers... It is fair and open competition between domestic producers and importers which is the point, not maximizing total sales as such... [I]f a mere impact on sales of imports is sufficient to engage Article 34 then the article is almost unbounded, since everything from income tax rules to reform of housing markets and environmental rules protecting natural parks may have this effect. It is manifestly the case that this was not the intention behind Article 34, nor does its text suggest such a broad application, and nor would it be politically sustainable in the context of the EU.[163]

The Court's longstanding concern with depriving traders of effective methods of market penetration rests on a similarly shaky footing since, as seen above, that line of reasoning can be perceived as not being just about access to the exercise of free

[162] See Davies, n148, 687: '[i]t is clearly unacceptable to subject the entire body of socio-economic regulation of a state to free movement proportionality review merely on the grounds that it affects the economy and therefore influences the volume of cross-border trade. This does not correspond to the Treaty text or policy, nor would it be constitutionally acceptable to the Member States, and it would be staggeringly inefficient and uncertain'.

[163] Davies, n29, 28 (emphasis added).

movement rights, but about *optimal* access to markets. In *Karner*, AG Alber argued that the latter impulse was 'fundamentally changed' by *Keck*.[164] The challenge now is to understand how an access approach that condemns, in principle, the inability of traders to break into the Italian market for moped trailers or the Swedish market for jet skis is *sufficiently* conceptually distinct from an approach that seeks merely to maximize their sales.

Davies argues that arguments based in the reduction of sales 'only [have] persuasive force if [it can be shown] that there is some illegitimacy in the way the market is defined'. He favours discrimination as the criterion that distinguishes legitimacy from illegitimacy in that regard: '[i]f they can show protectionism in the market definition, then both Article 34 and the Treaty ban on discrimination provide clear support for a claim that national markets should not be defined in this way'; in other words, '[i]nstead of all sales being reduced, importers are protected while domestic producers continue to suffer the burden'.[165] However, as Weatherill points out, the rule at issue in *Mickelsson and Roos* 'did not make life especially difficult for imported goods compared with local products. Nor did it demand that the product be adapted as a pre-condition for access to the target market—the "*Cassis de Dijon*" problem. The product could be freely sold in Sweden. But it could not be used in the circumstances outlawed by the national measure'.[166] That summary unseats the recent case law turn on Article 34 at one level, since an accusation of what Davies depicts as 'positive action'—i.e. the proactive market-opening approach of the Court—is difficult to ignore. In subsection (a), however, it was argued that AG Tesauro's distinguishing between *more difficult* and *less profitable* is the essential distinguishing criterion in this context too, emphasizing the fact that the access we should be concerned with is to the exercise of free movement rights—and not just access to a sympathetic market space. As Judge Joliet, a member of the Court when *Keck* was decided, has written, 'Article [34] is an instrument for the liberalization of trade among Member States, and nothing else. It is not an instrument of economic deregulation'.[167]

The more intractable challenge raised by the use of goods narrative is therefore the Court's continuing staunch insistence that there is no *de minimis* threshold in free movement law,[168] a finding that sits imperviously alongside decisions clearly assessing the *extent* of the impact of non-discriminatory national rules. Reading *Trailers* and *Mickelsson and Roos* together, an absolute prohibition on use or one *very close to it* is what seems to be intended before Article 34 will be engaged. Such a test adds an extra layer of review in order to determine whether a national rule

164 AG Alber in Case C-71/02 *Karner Industrie-Auktionen GmbH v Troostwijk GmbH* [2004] ECR I-3025, para. 47 of the Opinion.

165 Davies, n29, 29.

166 S Weatherill, 'Free movement of goods' (2012) 61:2 ICLQ 541 at 542.

167 R Joliet, 'The free circulation of goods: The *Keck and Mithouard* decision and the new directions in the case law' (1996) 1 Colum. J. Eur. Law 436 at 450.

168 See e.g. *Commission v Germany (Pharmacies)*, para. 43: '[s]ince the contested provisions are liable to hinder intra-Community trade, they must be considered as a measure having equivalent effect to a quantitative restriction on imports within the meaning of Article 28 EC, without it being necessary to prove that they have had an appreciable effect on such trade'.

impedes access. As Davies argues, '[a]ll substantive economic rules must have a *de minimis* rule and exclude marginal effects, whether judges choose to admit this or not'.[169]

It was argued in Chapter 5 that a *de minimis* rule is a condition about *scale*, whether it is data-based or rule-based. However, it may simply be that the language of *de minimis* is too loaded, given its prior embeddedness in EU law as a quantitative test in competition law. Straetmans describes the appropriate benchmark for free movement law as a 'non-quantitative appreciability test',[170] which does reflect the language in recent judgments to some extent but does not capture the full range of language, or concerns, in the case law presented in Chapter 5. The appropriate test may therefore be best phrased more simply as an unqualified test of appreciability, with Janus-like quantitative dimensions expressed more qualitatively through rule-based premises.

It was shown in Chapter 5 that the method calcifying in case law on the use of goods at present can also be detected in other sectors of free movement law e.g. the 'serious inconvenience' test seen in case law on the scope of EU citizenship. It is also significant that the Court frequently applies an *inverse* appreciability test i.e. it specifically points out that obstacles do amount to 'substantial' hindrances to or interferences with access.[171] But commenting on *Mickelsson and Roos*, Weatherill argues:

> The Court's *cautious but imprecise* insertion of the adjective 'considerable' into its definition of the reach of Article 34 aims to capture the notion that just because national laws vary does not of itself trigger the application of Article 34. The threshold at which divergence becomes a matter of concern for the EU is higher. But, as a general observation, that was the ambition underpinning *Keck and Mithouard* 20 years ago. The problem is pinning down with precision where Article 34 TFEU stops and where national regulatory autonomy begins. The adjective 'considerable' carries precisely that *heavy constitutional weight*, but it is hard to grasp how one can sensibly measure whether an influence on consumer behaviour is considerable or not. *The threshold is crucial, but alarmingly elusive*, and seems inevitably to point to *messy case-by-case application*. The lurking fear is that if the Court delves into a review of national measures which do not affect the construction of an internal market it is intruding into national regulatory autonomy without adequate justification and thereby damaging the legitimacy of EU law.[172]

Weatherill also noted that the judgment in *Bonnarde* 'drops the qualification that the influence on consumer behaviour must be "considerable", and therefore seems to throw the doors of Article 34 TFEU wide open . . . *Bonnarde* is a decision of the Fifth Chamber. It seems implausible that it really should be taken at face value, so it

[169] Davies, n148, 676.

[170] G Straetmans, 'Market access, the outer limits of free movement of goods and . . . the law?' in M Bulterman, L Hancher, A McDonnell, and HG Sevenster (eds.) *Views of European Law from the Mountain: Liber Amicorum for Piet Jan Slot* (Kluwer Law, 2009) 91 at 104.

[171] See e.g. Case C-518/06 *Commission v Italy* [2009] ECR I-3491, para. 66 (establishment and services); Case C-28/09 *Commission v Austria (Air quality)*, judgment of 21 December 2011, para. 116 (goods).

[172] Weatherill, n166, 542–3 (emphasis added).

is probably simply not a reliable decision. In an area where so much has been established—adjusted, adapted—by the case law of the Court over the years, such lack of attention to detail is frankly a source of dismay'.[173] Weatherill's concern mirrors many of the arguments made here, but it is difficult to take formal solace from the fact that the judgment in *Bonnarde* was a Fifth Chamber decision. As pointed out in Chapters 1 and 2, national courts must somehow understand and apply the *edifice* of the Court's case law: irrespective of who, in chamber terms, actually made it. It was also shown in Section 2 that the expansive decision in *Bonnarde* is not an isolated glitch. Neither is the Court's reluctance to involve the Grand Chamber or to ask for an Advocate General's Opinion.

It is thus argued that the Court needs to modify the trajectory of its recent case law and here it faces a choice: either to exclude the vocabulary of appreciability from the case law altogether, or to admit that a rule-based assessment of *de minimis* actually *is* operating, rightly, in parts of free movement law. The former solution is preferable for its clarity—in terms of the balance of existing authority rejecting *de minimis* and also to address the judicial practice concerns highlighted by Weatherill. But it is highly unlikely that the Court will revert to the differential treatment and access prevention thresholds set by *Keck* at a more general level, even for the free movement of goods in isolation.

A rule-based appreciability test would at least check the reach of access as a principle in cases involving non-discriminatory restrictions beneath the benchmark of access prevention. The model sketched in Figure 7.2 proposes a condition of appreciability alongside a test of causation in such cases. That choice was guided empirically by the Court's own case law. Conversely, sufficiently significant effects on free movement can be presumed in cases involving discriminatory restrictions and non-discriminatory restrictions that prevent or block access to the exercise of free movement rights altogether.

Articulating the meaning of *sufficiently significant* as a condition rather than a presumption for non-discriminatory restrictions affecting access is part of the responsibility of the Court. As seen in Chapter 5, there is a pool of relevant tests or expressions—around the ideas of marginal, serious, significant, substantial, and so on—that the Court can draw from across the span of free movement law to explain in a more systematic way what it—and thus national courts—are actually looking for. Since systematic coherence rather than convergence is the overall aim, the Court could adapt one of those tests or an amalgam of them across free movement law generally, or it could defend the application of different tests for different sectors. As a baseline, it is worth noting that the benchmark of *substantial effects* proposed by AG Jacobs has long been supported in the literature too.[174]

A rule-based application of appreciability—remembering that this condition would only require to be established, as distinct from being presumed, in the limited circumstances of non-discriminatory restrictions *affecting* access—is necessarily susceptible to the risks outlined by Weatherill. But it is better than the

[173] Weatherill, n166, 543.

[174] See e.g. Barnard, n23, 44–7 and Weatherill, n23, 897.

unchecked spread of access altogether. Davies observes that '[j]udges can draw lines, if not perfectly, at least well enough to keep the legal system going'.[175] That may be all we can ask for, with coherence achieved at the level of confirming an appreciability test in the first place and a more settled communication of its definition through more systematic and settled use of whatever 'adjective' is settled on by the Court. This imperfect solution also suits the sheer massiveness—geographical and regulatory—of the EU internal market, questioning the naivety of thinking that the Court can (or indeed should) micro-manage the application of free movement law in national legal contexts.

4. Conclusion

The model developed in this chapter pushes the cross-border dimension of free movement law to the fore by focusing on access as a principle concerned with the exercise of free movement rights and not just access to the market. It recognizes the effects-based reasoning that characterizes free movement case law and acknowledges that access to free movement rights can be affected in situations other than the points of entry to or exit from the market. But it demands more *systematic* application of causation and appreciability thresholds, and develops a sliding scale based on the nature of restrictions so that relevant limits are also properly effected. In rule-based judicial interpretation, which constitutional case law exemplifies, we have to accept a certain degree of messiness in the resulting case law resource. Thinking about access as a principle that has strong Treaty-based foundations as well as both defined and appropriately nuanced content helps to shape a more organized constitutional framework, and a more organized judicial culture.

The expansive dynamic inherent in a system that recognizes potential as well as actual effects on free movement rights as a legitimate trigger of Treaty-relevance is a challenging one to contain. But it is too deeply engrained in the case law as a whole to reverse. The decision in *Keck* offers an attractive free movement paradigm in a normative sense, but it is simply outweighed in empirical case law terms. As a discordant case law anomaly, it should therefore be reversed—not because of a convergence argument vis-à-vis the other Treaty freedoms, but because it is even out of sync with the standard Article 34 case law premise of *effects*.

It may be that the more restrictive emphasis on the here and now seen in recent case law on the free movement of persons, discussed in Chapter 4 (though argued there to be problematic in some respects too), will spread to other sectors of free movement law also. More recent case law on Article 34 indicates, however, that it will not. Migration discrimination adds conceptual weight to the free movement framework where differential treatment that is not about nationality can be established. Access to the exercise of free movement rights fixes a complementary compass point for genuinely non-discriminatory restrictions.

[175] Davies, n148, 676.

Conclusion

What does or does not come 'within the scope of EU law' has become one of the most important but also difficult questions to resolve in any individual case; it might be thought that the answer is more obvious in free movement law than in many other spheres of EU legal practice, but we have seen that this is simply not the case.

The analysis presented in previous chapters does not establish that there is a major breakdown or crisis affecting the coherence of EU free movement law to the extent that the very legitimacy of the Court of Justice should be called into question. But there are distinct pockets of damaging case law fragmentation—in conceptual, substantive, and structural senses—generating a systemic problem that is greater than the sum of its parts. Furthermore, legitimacy was considered at the outset as a point further along the same spectrum as incoherence, meaning that we cannot afford to be complacent about the state of the case law at present either. The impact of the drivers of fragmentation outlined in Chapters 1 and 2—protection of fundamental rights; proliferation of principles; unsettled purpose(s) of the internal market and free movement; and structure of the Court and its decision-making processes—was shown to affect different areas of free movement law in different ways: raising sector-specific problems in distinct parts of the case law but also causing more pervasive problems that recur across different sectors of free movement.

A series of broader themes and conclusions can also be extracted. First, looking at the substance of free movement law, framework principles are necessarily fluid constructs. That does not mean that they have to be unhelpfully blunt constructs. However, when articulating the content and scope of the principles shaping free movement law, the Court tends to create tests that are so open, they cause all sorts of problems downstream—either in the immediate case law aftermath (e.g. looking at recent case law on the internal effects of EU citizenship rights) or over decades of protracted yet unresolved debate (e.g. defining a measure having equivalent effect to a quantitative restriction on imports). To balance the need to carve principles that are sufficiently flexible for application across a free movement space of this sheer size but also sufficiently clear and robust for that same purpose, it was argued that some framework principles should be reset in order to reflect and embody a more appropriate degree of free movement specificity and nuance (for example, recasting 'access to the market' as a principle concerned with 'access to the exercise of free movement rights'). Relatedly, it was emphasized that the Court needs to decide on and apply the *limits* of framework principles more carefully and consistently too. Loading all of the problems onto the justification and proportionality stages of free movement law because of an overstretched conception of the Treaty's scope is not an effective or constitutionally useful solution.

Second, the Court must revise elements of its own case law practice. It is an unusual constitutional court but in preliminary rulings proceedings—the main sphere of case law for free movement issues—the Court should avoid falling into overly individualized framings of its decisions or making concrete determinations of the outcome. Those responsibilities are and must be the province of national courts and tribunals: to ensure that the relevant facts and evidence-bases are properly considered, but also to render meaningful and support the ambition that national courts are substantively functional EU courts too. Neither the internal market nor its legal framework can work otherwise. Lines of conflicting case law on the same questions have also been exposed. As stressed at several points, we cannot demand case law to be perfect, but we can expect it to be coherent. Appropriate engagement with existing authority—since citing existing authority is the Court's self-chosen legal method—means either consistently following previous decisions on comparable legal questions, or explaining and rationalizing new legal choices that are being made.

These conclusions have been framed by an argument that the institutional responsibilities attaching to constitutional courts are relevant to the Court of Justice too. In other words, the Court can—and should—take greater responsibility for the coherence of its own case law. Increasingly, however, the Court transmits an impression of an institution that has either forgotten how or feels unable to tell a constitutional *story* anymore, which raises a whole series of questions about how well—politically—the Court is itself being supported. Its foundational constitutional judgments were about the most mundane issues in many respects but that Court was not afraid to challenge us, and to use language that signalled an explicit and profound change in the premises and impact of transnational law or law beyond the State. The construct of dialogue, whether inter-institutional (broadly speaking: judicial, legislative, executive) at the horizontal i.e. EU level or vertical i.e. EU/Member State level, undoubtedly progresses constitutional law beyond more traditional understandings of a hierarchical template. What it loses, however, is a measure of the extent to which the Court is there not just to dialogue with political actors but sometimes to remind them of the constitutional constraints under which they, too, must act as bound constitutional subjects.

When constitutional standards are entrenched by case law and not changed by Treaty amendment, the role of the Court is still politically charged but perhaps clearer from the perspective of constitutional authority. When the Treaty *is* amended, what happens to the constitutional standards that were already entrenched? The practice of amendment has been more about strapping additional concerns onto existing Treaty tasks than providing an overt complementary steer about the relationship between the different objectives now codified. In that context, it was argued that the legal status conferred on the Charter of Fundamental Rights sends particularly mixed signals to the Court. At the same time, however, its initial case law responses seem to retract linchpins of fundamental rights protection further than is strictly required. Who, then, is minding the constitution?

At the practical level, it has been argued that the current structure of the Court makes coherent deliberation and reflection on the multiple trajectories of the case law exceptionally difficult. If the idea(l) of a formally supreme EU court is too much, politically, to contemplate, the function and structures of the Grand Chamber of the existing Court should at least be constitutionally hardened.

The Court of Justice should demonstrate greater awareness of and confidence in its constitutional purpose and of the responsibilities that come with that purpose. And it should shape its own judicial behaviour accordingly. But the Member States need urgently to take greater responsibility for the very idea of the European Union and to take greater care of its sustainability; to articulate a stronger sense of their ownership of and commitment to this contested but enduring transnational experiment. Regrettably, this is unlikely to happen in the foreseeable future, and so we have to be mindful of these broader constraints when evaluating the work of the Court of Justice. The current state of the Court's case law is, in other words, no single actor's fault. The responsibility to do better is similarly shared.

Index

The manufacturer's authorised representative in the EU for product safety is Oxford University Press España S.A. of El Parque Empresarial San Fernando de Henares, Avenida de Castilla, 2 - 28830 Madrid (www.oup.es/en or product.safety@oup.com). OUP España S.A. also acts as importer into Spain of products made by the manufacturer.
Printed and bound by CPI Group (UK) Ltd, Croydon, CR0 4YY
14/09/2026
02216304-0007